The Irish Economy
since 1922

1. MAP OF IRELAND

Showing counties, provinces, political boundaries, and some principal physical features.

The Irish Economy since 1922

JAMES MEENAN

Professor of Political Economy and the National Economics
of Ireland, University College, Dublin

LIVERPOOL UNIVERSITY PRESS 1970

Published by
LIVERPOOL UNIVERSITY PRESS
123 Grove Street, Liverpool L7 7AF

ISBN 0 85323 210 5

First published 1970

Printed and bound in Great Britain by Hazell Watson & Viney Ltd
Aylesbury, Bucks

Preface

THIS BOOK IS DERIVED FROM LECTURES DELIVERED AT University College, Dublin, in the course known as the National Economics of Ireland, introduced in 1909. Some measure of Home Rule was then expected from the Liberal government which held office at Westminster and it was thought that a course of lectures which would analyse the economy and define its problems would be a useful provision for the future.

There may have been some difficulty in filling out the course in its early days. Individual problems had been exhaustively examined by a long and varied series of Royal Commissions and parliamentary committees. Some statistics were available. The decennial census provided a wealth of depressing information on the trends of population and emigration. Agricultural and banking returns had been collected since the 1840s. The Statistical and Social Inquiry Society of Ireland which did much (as happily it continues to do) to interpret the information thus provided was already over fifty years old in 1909. Many important activities, however, were not measured at all. Estimates of external trade had been initiated only lately: there were no returns for internal trade. Industrial production and employment were almost unexamined.

These deficiencies have now been remedied. The sustained work of the Central Statistics Office under a succession of exceptionally gifted and energetic directors, the reports of Commissions, of State companies, and the Programmes for Economic Expansion have combined with commentaries such as the reports of the Central Bank, of the National Industrial Economic Council and, more lately, of the Economic and Social Research Institute to provide an abundance of information and analysis.

The original problem has been solved but others have been

created. Apart from Professor O'Mahony's pioneering work on the Irish economy, there is no place where the information and the analysis have been brought together. In order to appreciate the course of events, students have been obliged to consult a variety of reports and other publications not all of which are now readily available. This has been a great inconvenience and the present book is primarily an attempt to bring things together.

Its first part is intended to deal with facts, statistics, and dates, and to describe the policies followed since the Anglo-Irish Treaty of 1921. Some limitation of treatment has been necessary. It therefore does not cover several aspects of the economy that are of very great importance; for example, the social services, internal trade, local government finance, nor (a particularly regrettable omission) the voluntary bodies that have been and still are of such importance in agriculture.

The second part discusses the issues that are suggested in the first. Party politics and the conflict of values and traditions which underlie them cannot be excluded from the discussion. I hope that I have succeeded in stating my own opinions clearly and in quoting fairly and accurately the opinions of others. Here again, it cannot be claimed that the discussion is comprehensive. For example, the implications of the very important NIEC report on full employment demand a full examination; while the Third Programme for Economic Expansion has only recently been published. In several other sectors the pace of change has threatened to out-run the commentary in the text. But no discussion of the Irish economy can presume to be final. This is a continuing debate.

In several places in both parts of the book, I have trespassed on the domain of the historians. This has been inevitable. Irish history and Irish economics have been mixed up together for centuries. On the other hand I have not attempted to use the methods of statistical and econometric analysis which have been so thoroughly developed in recent years. This is not to underrate the very great assistance that they can provide in many forms of economic studies. It is because this particular study is concerned with more than strictly economic elements. Its aim is to describe the political economy of Ireland.

I do not believe that political economy is a science in which the causes and course of development can be fully ascertained by quantification alone. Economic actions are ultimately dependent on decisions which, consciously or unconsciously, have been prompted by a variety of instincts which may have nothing to do with economic considerations. The actions of any society largely depend on the values by which it lives, or claims to live; and economic considerations may play only a small part in the formation of those values. The pages that follow will note several occasions when decisions of economic policy have been taken on non-economic grounds. Both the Irish people and the course of their history would be very different if their loyalties had been formed by economic calculations alone. It has been a great virtue in the tradition of economic teaching in University College that its inspiration has been humanistic and that it has never forgotten that in the last resort political economy is about people and the passions and prejudices by which their actions are swayed. It would be a bold man who would hope to enrich a tradition derived from Thomas Finlay, Thomas Kettle, and George O'Brien; but there is a plain obligation on their successor to preserve and transmit it.

I must acknowledge my deep indebtedness to the College. Those who had the good fortune to attend George O'Brien's lectures will share my admiration for his clarity of thought and expression and my gratitude for his kindness to younger people. I owe an equal debt to those who have been my students, in Arts and Commerce, in day and evening classes, for their constant kindness and patience. To write in such terms may seem less than contemporary, but I have always found University College to be a happy and often an inspiring place in which to work. I wish I had the art to express fully how much I owe to its academic generations.

JAMES MEENAN

University College, Dublin

Acknowledgements

IN WRITING THIS WORK I HAVE RECEIVED ASSISTANCE from a wide range of sources, and encouragement from many colleagues, authors, and others who have been as concerned as myself to ensure that this work should be as accurate and comprehensive as possible. Permission to make quotations has been given generously by the editors of *Administration, Annual Register, Economist, Financial Times, Irish Banking Review, Irish Press, Irish Times, Round Table*, and *Studies* and by many publishers including Messrs. Allen and Unwin, Arnold, Benn, Blackwell, Blond, Browne and Nolan, Cahill, Cambridge University Press, Cass, Cassell, Chatto and Windus, Clarendon Press, Cork University Press, Dolman Press, Duffy, Eason, Eyre and Spottiswoode, Faber and Faber, Fallon, An Foran Talúntais, Gill, Golden Eagle Press, Hamish Hamilton, Harvard University Press, Heinemann, Hodges and Figgis, Hutchinson, King, Lawrence and Wishart, Longmans Green, Macmillan, Manchester University Press, Methuen, Mount Salus, Muller, Murray, Nelson, Oxford University Press, Pall Mall Press, Parkside Press, Putnam, Routledge and Kegan Paul, and the Talbot Press.

Many institutions and organizations have been most helpful in allowing me to consult published and unpublished reports and other documents. In particular I wish to thank the executive officers of Bord na Móna, Bord Fáilte, the British Association for the Advancement of Science, Economic and Social Research Institute, Economist Intelligence Unit, Dublin and London, Electricity Supply Board, Dublin and Belfast, Ministry of Commerce, Belfast, Industrial Credit Corporation, Industrial Development Authority, Institute of Bankers in Ireland, Institute of Public Administration, Institution of Mining and Metallurgy, London, Organization for Economic Co-operation and Development, Paris, Royal Dublin Society, and the Statistical and Social

Enquiry Society of Ireland. Without their help at various stages it would have been very difficult indeed to document this book.

I am especially indebted, in this respect, to the staff of the Central Statistics Office, where most of the tables were checked, and to my colleague Mr. Gerard Quinn who read the text and made many useful suggestions. At an early stage in the writing, when I was considering the plan that the book should follow, I was greatly helped by the most thoughtful suggestions put to me by Professor Nicholas Mansergh, Master of St. John's College, Cambridge. These suggestions grew in value as the book progressed and I should like to acknowledge this influence upon the shape which the book has finally assumed.

Again, in the matter of the illustrations which the book contains I am especially grateful to Mr. T. W. Freeman, Reader in Economic Geography in the University of Manchester, author of *Ireland: A General and Regional Geography*, and Miss Janice Price of Methuens, his publishers, for the readiness with which they allowed material from this title to be redrawn, adapted, and used to illustrate in cartographic form, many of the economic, geographical, historical, and other factors with which I was concerned in Part One of the text.

The charts which illustrate Part Two have been specially designed and drawn for this work. Their visualization, and in many respects their content, is the original work of Mr. Kenneth Kirton, Senior Lecturer in Economics in the City University, London. His skill in this field combined with that of Mr. John O'Kane and Mr. Bernard Crossland, who are responsible for the graphic design of this book, has effectively illustrated many of the economic facts and themes of this section. No doubt many readers will be as grateful as I am for these visual aids. The excellent index was compiled by Mr. J. A. Kewell.

Lastly, I must fully acknowledge my debt to Mr. John O'Kane, Secretary and Publisher of the Liverpool University Press, to whom the writing of this book is very largely due. His grandfather was a political and publishing associate of John Morley so it was in the best of traditions that his involvement in the purpose of this book should become as deep as my own and he has personally seen it through the press.

The growth of modern communications and administrative and governmental structures combine to cause us to think of economic development in terms of high policy. Yet the structure and growth of any economy is ultimately determined by the attitudes and efforts of society as a whole. My hope is that all those who have contributed at home or abroad to the developments these pages describe, will see in them a social acknowledgement of their efforts.

Contents

CHARTS

APPENDICES

List of Illustrations

MAPS AND DIAGRAMS

CHARTS ILLUSTRATING THE TRENDS AND THE CHANGING PATTERN OF THE IRISH ECONOMY

List of Tables

Abbreviations

AR	Annual Register	EPC	Emigration and Population Commission
BC	Banking Commission (of 1926 or 1934–8 as indicated by date)	ERI	Economic Research Institute
BCR	Banking Commission Report (also indicated by date)	ESB	Electricity Supply Board
		FAO	Food and Agriculture Organization
C, Cd, Cmd	Command Paper	GATT	General Agreement on Tariffs and Trade
CBR	Central Bank Report	GR	General Report (of the Census of Population)
CBQB	Central Bank Quarterly Statistical Bulletin	HMSO	Her Majesty's Stationery Office
CC	Childers Commission (on Financial Relations of Great Britain and Ireland, 1896)	IAOS	Irish Agricultural Organization Society
		IBR	Irish Banking Review
CIO	Committee on Industrial Organization	ICTU	Irish Congress of Trades Unions
CIP	Census of Industrial Production	*ISB*	Irish Statistical Bulletin
DNB	Dictionary of National Biography	*ITJ*	Irish Trade Journal (until 1963)
EBNI	Electricity Board Northern Ireland	ITUC	Irish Trades Union Congress
EEC	European Economic Community	*JDATI*	Journal of the Department of Agriculture and Technical Instruction
EFTA	European Free Trade Association	*JIBI*	Journal of the Institute of Bankers in Ireland

JSSISI *Journal of the Statistical and Social Inquiry Society of Ireland*

MEBC *Minutes of Evidence to the Banking Commission* (of 1934–8)

NIEC National Industrial Economic Council

OECD Organization for Economic Co-operation and Development

P, Pr Presentation (Irish official publication)

PAYE Pay as you earn

PDDE *Parliamentary Debates: Dáil Éireann*

PDSE *Parliamentary Debates: Seanad Éireann*

POSB Post Office Savings Bank

PP Parliamentary Paper

RT *Round Table*

SA *Statistical Abstract*

SO Stationery Office, Dublin

T Table

NOTE ON STATISTICAL TABLES

A number of statistics, especially those relating to national income and production, may be subject to revision as revised figures and new estimates become available.

Introduction

SPEAKING TO THE HOUSE OF COMMONS JUST A CENTURY
ago, Disraeli described clearly the connection between political and
economic history in Ireland.[1]

Irish policy is Irish history and I have no faith in any statesman who attempts
to remedy the evils of Ireland who is either ignorant of the past or who will
not deign to learn from it.

The influence of Irish history upon the formulation and application of
economic policy has become even stronger in the decades since these
words were spoken. Irish economics have been deeply influenced by the
manner in which the Irish people have reacted to, and against, their
history. That manner has varied greatly. At times they have tried to
obliterate their past or to expunge part of what survives from it; at
other times, they have attempted to maintain, sometimes even to
invent, a continuity. They have not done any of these things consistently.

Many economic problems have been created or complicated by
political or social issues that are a legacy from the past. Thus the reaction
to a given set of economic circumstances or to a specific economic problem is not necessarily the same as it might be in countries whose development has been more directly influenced by natural resources. In
Ireland, as Sir Horace Plunkett remarked, political economy is spelt
with a large 'P' and a small 'e'.[2]

These complications are aggravated by the circumstances of the
country. It is generally agreed that the economy is not fully developed.

1. 16 March 1868. See W. F. Monypenny, *Life of Benjamin Disraeli*, Murray,
London: 1912, vol. ii, p. 175.
2. Some of the consequences are discussed later, in Chapter Nine.

But the degree, even the nature, of the under-development is still debated; whether it lies, for example, in manufacturing industry or in the fertility of the soil or in the quality of livestock breeding. Since the economy has been comparatively sheltered in some respects, the best line of advance may be debated interminably. Elsewhere, peoples have been overtaken by the march of events: they have been forced to adjust themselves to new ways of working and of living. There was no debate because there was no choice. Nothing comparable has yet occurred in modern Ireland. Our last social revolution was the reform of land tenure more than two generations ago, our last political revolution was nationalistic, a successful 1848; until very recently, technical changes in agriculture and industry have been all too few.[3]

The Irish people have been able therefore to preserve a belief that they have some freedom of choice between the various social and economic policies that may be adopted. They may decide in favour of achieving the greatest possible measure of self-sufficiency, thereby withdrawing from a world from which those who support such a policy expect little good and much possible harm. They may devote themselves to providing as much employment as possible in the hope that the persistent emigration may be checked. They may turn to the pursuit of prosperity by greater productive efficiency as other small countries have managed to do. As often happens, they may end by pursuing all three at the same time. The point is that all choices appear to be still open for discussion.

These choices, again, have had political implications. A student of economics may try to assess the relative economic values of self-sufficiency or of the maximization of production. The attempt cannot be pursued far because choices of this nature soon cross the border of economics into the realms of politics wherein the economist has no special authority.

Nevertheless there is a great deal that he can do, and should do. He should attempt to clarify the issues, to indicate the economic loss and gain that is involved in any choice, to point out, for example, that greater self-sufficiency may mean a lower standard of living while an increased foreign trade may expose the community to wider fluctuations between prosperity and depression. He should protest against the confusion of thought that leads to the simultaneous pursuit of contradictory policies or to results being claimed for policies which are the clean opposite of their purpose. He should point out, to take another example, that industrialization does not mean greater self-sufficiency in Irish conditions; it means less.

3. It is an arguable proposition that Ireland has changed more rapidly, socially and economically, in the last ten years than in the preceding sixty. But the results have not yet become fully apparent in public thought.

He should also perceive when conditions have so changed that policies must be revised. Writers should declare interest; and the present writer must confess his belief that the aims of economic policy have never since been so clearly defined, nor its methods so exactly adapted to those aims, as in the first ten years of the State when priority was given to the encouragement of agriculture and agricultural policy was directed by Patrick Hogan. Nevertheless he must concede that Hogan framed his policy in days when the British market was still free and British farmers were not protected by their government. Hogan's successors face a different situation and it is not necessarily a fault if they adopt different methods to achieve different aims. One can only hope that they will achieve that shining clarity of thought and consistency in action which, a generation after his death, inspires a deep pride that he was our countryman.

In a country such as Ireland, where there is so much lost time to be made good, it is the business of the economist to remind peoples and governments of what they would often prefer to forget, that choices may be negative as well as positive, and that what a government does not do may well be as beneficial as what it does do. Resources are always scarce in relation to the number of ways in which they may be used; and it is only common sense to use them so that ultimately there will be more for all. To borrow a phrase from *The Economist*, to be restrictive is not to be a Scrooge, it is rather to insist that every day in the year might be Christmas Day if peoples and governments would look beyond their noses and not expect to reap next month the crop that they sowed last week.

The economist must insist that things will go better and be more quickly and cheaply achieved if regard is paid to priorities, if the State does not take back with one hand what it gives with the other, if it does not repress production in one sector by ill-judged encouragement in another. This may appear to ignore opportunities of increasing production. But priorities mean choice; and choice may mean not doing B now so that A can be done properly. If A is done properly now, there may be the more resources available later to do not only B but also C and D. Perhaps the best of the all too many investigations of the Irish economy was the Recess Committee which reported in 1896. Having distinguished between 'the resources of today' and 'the resources of tomorrow', it pointed out that if the first were developed thoroughly there would ultimately be more of the second. Since then there have been too many attempts to enjoy today the fruits of the resources of tomorrow. It is little wonder that several of the recommendations made by the Recess Committee remain unimplemented nor that Irish agriculture, far from enjoying the potential appropriate to the 1960s, has only lately begun to progress from the level of the 1890s.

The economist has another duty: to remember that economic activity is only a means to an end. The ultimate justification of economic policy is not the creation of wealth for its own sake. The purpose of creating wealth is to improve the conditions in which people live, to free them from poverty and squalor, from disease and hunger. It has been taken for granted too often that public policy should be directed towards some specific aim such as the ending of emigration. The more immediate aim of policy should be to ensure that those who live in Ireland, be their numbers rising or falling, can expect a standard of decent comfort, an opportunity to improve their position in life and the power to give their children a better start than they enjoyed themselves. People do not spend their lives at work in order to restore the balance of payments or to swell the national income but to give themselves and their families a better life. The first Professor of National Economics defined the State, in days when no Irish state yet existed, as 'the great human conspiracy against hunger and cold, against loneliness and ignorance'.[4] The immediate purpose of economic progress is to carry that conspiracy to success.

These are material aims. There are also immaterial aims which are ultimately much more important. An improvement in the standard of living will not necessarily lead to the realization of the higher qualities inherent in the human character. But it is always right to strive so that these qualities will not be frustrated by the innumerable limitations that poverty and ignorance impose on the growth of character and talent. The ultimate objective of economic progress is to sweep away these obstacles and clear the path for the development of the creative faculties of human nature, so as to secure (returning to the trend of Kettle's thought) 'not merely physical existence, but that rich human existence which can be had only in community, that sort of life which Edmund Burke had in mind when he described the State as a "partnership in all science, a partnership in all art, a partnership in every virtue and in all perfection" '.[5] In the Irish context, that means to enlarge and inspire the qualities of mind and character that have been restricted and debased by our history.

Lastly, there are some things which a student of economics who respects his art must not do. He must not suggest that an economy that has been distorted for generations can be set right in a decade. He must never forget that it is people who make an economy and that no economy can be better than the people who make it. He will not underrate the social and psychological obstacles to policies of expansion nor the time-lag between sacrifices and rewards. He must recognize the possibilities of greater wealth but he must not ignore the deficiencies in

4. T. M. Kettle, *The Day's Burden*, Maunsel, Dublin: 1910, p. 22.
5. Ibid., p. 8.

natural resources, social organization, and national character which stand in the path of their realization.

These responsibilities must not be evaded but their discharge should always be inspired by hope. There must be confidence that our economic problems are soluble, if not necessarily in the manner which the nationalist tradition has taken for granted. This will involve a succession of value judgements which may not be accepted within Ireland, still less outside it. But that risk must be accepted. An Irish writer must believe that his people have something to contribute to the affairs of the world, that it would be good if their numbers should increase rather than decrease and that it would be even better if the number of Irish people living in Ireland should increase. To be sure, numbers do not matter greatly: the Irish would still be a very small people even if the population of the island were to be trebled in the next hundred years. What does matter is the quality of life. The business of the economist, therefore, is to suggest how material prosperity can be achieved so that in some future time the Irish people will not only be richer and more numerous than they are today but that they may be able to fashion for themselves a society that will justify all the tenacity and sacrifice that have filled their history. It may be true, and it will often be so argued in the pages that follow, that many past hopes have been dupes. But present fears may be liars; and with that reflection, which is as far removed from a dispassionate economic analysis as can well be imagined, we may turn to a closer examination of Irish economic problems and policies.

Part One

Part One

CHAPTER ONE

The Historical Background

IRISH ECONOMIC PROBLEMS AND POLICIES, AS WILL BE SEEN only too often, cannot be fully understood without reference to Irish history. The following pages do not presume to provide a history of modern Ireland: they have the more modest aim of noting some of the developments that have shaped the present economy. They may also suggest that economic and social changes have been as important in that shaping as the familiar sequence of political events. A well-known saying claimed that Irish history is a subject for Englishmen to remember and for Irishmen to forget. It has been amended to read that 'Irish history is a subject for Englishmen to learn and for Irishmen to learn properly'.[1]

The English engagement in Ireland commenced with the Norman invasion as far back as 1169. An energetic policy of conquest and subjection to the English crown was begun by Henry VIII. Two generations of warfare ended with the total defeat of the last of the Irish princes at Kinsale in 1601 and two further struggles, between 1641 and 1653 and between 1689 and 1691, confirmed the English conquest as far as it could be procured by force of arms.

This was not a simple transfer of political power, as it might have been had it occurred two or three centuries earlier. The successors of Henry VIII inevitably proscribed the practice of the Catholic faith. They also confiscated the most fertile areas of Irish land and provided for their plantation by settlers from England and Scotland. Thus the Anglo-Irish struggle acquired a peculiar intensity, in which racial feeling,

1. The emendation is by George O'Brien, in *The Four Green Fields*, Talbot Press, Dublin: 1936, p. 1. The original aphorism will be found in Sir Horace Plunkett's *Ireland in the New Century*, Murray, London: 1904, p. 26. A modern survey of Anglo-Irish relations is provided by Nicholas Mansergh, *The Irish Question, 1840–1910*, Allen & Unwin, London: 1965.

religious belief, and the ownership of land were all involved and reacted on each other. There was no acquiescence in the English connection as occurred in Scotland where neither religion nor land was involved. Equally, there could be no possibility of compromise because the issues were fundamental. This mixture of national and racial feeling, of religion and land ownership, made Anglo-Irish relations virtually insoluble by peaceful means. Moreover, these issues fell to be fought out between two peoples who, however unequally they might be matched otherwise, were each possessed of exceptional pride and unusual tenacity.

The Revolution of 1688 and the triumph of the Protestant and parliamentarian cause had enduring consequences for Ireland. The code known as the Penal Laws was added to the existing legislation against the practice of the Catholic religion. These laws debarred Catholics from the franchise and membership of parliament, from the professions and education, and restricted their ownership of land.[2] It has been suggested that the laws against religious worship were not rigorously enforced except in the early decades of the eighteenth century; and that the laws restricting Catholic ownership of land were frequently evaded with the help of Protestant neighbours. Instances, significantly, are still remembered. The Penal Laws, however, had the most pernicious effects on Irish society. They fostered the worst vices of ascendancy on one side and of slavery on the other; and they exacerbated divisions which sprang from differences of religious faith.[3]

It must not be thought that the legislation which followed the victory of the English Parliament was directed only against Catholics and Dissenters. Measures were also introduced which were designed to limit the prosperity of Ireland even at the cost of injuring what was then the Protestant and English interest in Ireland. Restraints on Irish exports and shipping were reinforced and extended. The right of the Parliament of Great Britain to legislate for Ireland was formally declared by statute.

The plantations—that is the dispossession of the Irish and the older Norman families by settlers from England and Scotland—were designed for the defence of the English interest in Ireland.[4] During the eighteenth century, however, the colonists themselves developed a local

2. The Dissenters were also excluded from parliament and public offices.

3. The part played by sectarian feelings in the opposition to Home Rule will be noted later. As late as 1922, the adoption of proportional representation in the electoral system of the Irish Free State had to be defended not simply on its merits but also because it would provide some protection to the southern Unionist, and mainly Protestant, minority. Special care was taken by Mr. Cosgrave's government to give that minority a large representation in the first Senate. Mr. de Valera's hostility to the exploitation of religious differences during his long period of power is one of his major contributions to the development of the State.

4. Which is to say the Protestant interest, though the first plantation was made in the reign of the Catholic monarch, Mary I. In very many cases, the 'planters' became assimilated; the great exception being in the case of the plantation of Ulster under James I.

patriotism, expressed in the claim that Ireland should be governed by the Crown and Parliament of Ireland rather than by the Crown and Parliament of Great Britain. At the crisis of the war with the American colonies the British government was obliged to concede that claim and the years between 1782 and 1800 are enshrined in Irish memory as the period of 'Grattan's Parliament'—a parliament that was acknowledged by Great Britain to possess full legislative independence.

'Grattan's Parliament' was known by this name because the struggle to assert its sovereignty was led by Henry Grattan. The best commentary on its composition and the extent of its independence is that Grattan never held office in it, and that it would have been quite inconceivable that he should have done so. The executive was appointed not by it, but by the British government. Catholics were debarred from its membership and from the parliamentary franchise.[5]

Even when its title-deeds were most fully recognized, therefore, the Irish parliament was in a hopelessly weak position. Irish Catholics claimed the franchise, to which they were admitted in a limited degree in 1793. The fact that even this measure was largely due to the insistence of the British government strengthened a feeling that they could more reasonably hope for equality from a union with Great Britain than from the persistence of the colonial parliament. The crisis was sharpened by the outbreak of the long war with the French republic and the growth of revolutionary sentiment in Ireland. The colonists were reminded that their position depended on, to quote a telling phrase used in the debate on the Union, 'the powerful and commanding protection of Great Britain'. A majority of the Irish parliament was eventually persuaded, either by argument or by inducement, to consent to the extinction of their parliament and to a legislative union with Great Britain.[6] The Union came into operation on 1 January 1801. In the course of the following century, the weaknesses and prejudices of the Irish parliament faded from popular memory and the years of 'legislative independence' were looked back to as a golden age.

The phrase 'legislative union' should be noted because it illustrates the peculiar relationship between Ireland and Great Britain thereafter. The Act provided for the union of the kingdoms of Great Britain and Ireland and for their representation by one and the same parliament. It provided for the union of the Established Churches of England and Ireland into one 'Protestant Episcopal Church' whose continuance as 'the Established Church of England and Ireland' was to be 'deemed and

5. Which was, of course, equally the case in Great Britain; but the religious divisions were very differently balanced in the larger island.

6. On their side, the Catholic leaders were persuaded that Emancipation would soon follow the passage of the Union. That did not happen. The effects of the delay upon Anglo-Irish relations have been penetratingly discussed by Professor George O'Brien in his work *The Four Green Fields*.

taken as an essential and fundamental part of the Union'. It also provided for the eventual union of the systems of customs and excise, which
was not completed until 1825. It further provided for circumstances in
which the exchequers of the two countries might be united, which was
accomplished in 1817.

But Ireland did not become a geographical expression. A separate
executive and judiciary was retained throughout the period of legislative
union. The executive was headed by the Lord Lieutenant, representing
the monarch, and the Chief Secretary, who handled the parliamentary
business. Usually, though not invariably, the Chief Secretary
was a member of the Cabinet and was therefore a person of much
greater political importance than his titular superior. Both offices were
political appointments and their holders were changed with the government. The contrast between the provision made for the government of
Ireland and that made for the government of Scotland, which did not
receive even an Under-Secretary until the 1880s, is suggestive. It
should be remembered also that during the greater part of the period
of union, Ireland was governed by coercive legislation which was un-
paralleled in any other part of the United Kingdom or in the colonies or
even in the Indian Empire.[7]

The political history of the nineteenth century consisted largely of a
recurrent struggle by the majority of the Irish people to regain their civil
and religious liberties. Daniel O'Connell's achievement of Catholic
Emancipation in 1829 set the pattern for much of what was to follow.
It provided an example of a popular movement which was ignored by
British governments until the choice of policy had narrowed to concession or civil war. What might have been given freely was seen to have
been yielded unwillingly to force. No gratitude could be claimed: none
was felt. History was to repeat itself all too often. As Trevelyan has
noted, 'England was always a generation too late'.[8]

But it is only just to make the further and most important point that the
validity of the claim to Emancipation was admitted and supported by an
influential section of British opinion. This also was to be repeated. The
reform of land tenure owed a great deal to the advocacy of John Bright
and John Stuart Mill. In the very last days of the Union, the use of the

7. In 1889 James Bryce, later Chief Secretary for Ireland and Ambassador in
Washington, visited India. He wrote:
'One receives an extraordinary impression of our power when, standing here in the
artillery platform of Jumrood at the mouth of the Khyber and watching the Union
Jack, one thinks that from here to Cape Cormorin and the furthest corner of Assam
not a dog wags its tail against us among these two hundred and sixty millions of
people. Yet we can't govern four millions of Irishmen with the aid of the loyal
garrison of one million!'
H. A. L. Fisher, *James Bryce*, Macmillan, London: 1927, Vol. 1, p. 270.
8. G. M. Trevelyan, *British History in the Nineteenth Century*, Longmans Green,
London: 1922, p. 288.

Black and Tans was denounced by many sections of the British people. In these and other cases the Irish people were aided (provided they proved the genuineness of their claims by persistence) by the British sense of justice and self-respect.

The later alliance of O'Connell with the Whig governments of the 1830s produced further measures of alleviation such as the reform of the municipalities, the limitation of the tithes paid by an overwhelmingly Catholic people to the Established Church, and a more sympathetic administration of the law.[9] By the early 1840s O'Connell had proceeded to a campaign for the repeal of the Union which collapsed when the government stood firm. In the next few years the Great Famine imposed a new pattern of society and of politics. The economic position of the country had deteriorated since the end of the high prices during the Napoleonic war. A huge and growing proportion of an increasing population[10] lived on the land or, more specifically, on the potato crops which they raised from their plots of ground. Agriculture in the true sense was almost unknown: industries (with the exception of the linen trade) had been in decline since the removal of the support given by the Irish parliament and the introduction of machinery. The repeated failure of the potato crop after 1845 entailed the starvation of thousands and the emigration of even more. The population of (all) Ireland was returned as 8,175,000 by the census of 1841: ten years later it had fallen to 6,552,000.[11]

This was so great a catastrophe that the Great Famine (the expression by which it is distinguished from the many others which preceded it but were less prolonged) has been regarded ever since as a landmark in Irish history. The memory of the years after 1845 has not yet faded; and their political and social consequences are still with us. In the economic sphere, however, many processes have been attributed to the Great Famine which were already active before it began. The introduction of steamship services across the Irish Sea facilitated not only emigration to the industrial cities of Great Britain but also the export of livestock to satisfy their growing demand for foodstuffs. The consolidation of holdings, whereby (often by wholesale evictions) the landlords threw small holdings together into larger units which would be more suitable for grazing, was well enough advanced to be noted by the Devon Commission which examined Irish land tenures between 1843

9. e.g., the Irish Executive of the late 1830s consisting of Lord Mulgrave as Lord Lieutenant, Lord Morpeth (later Lord Carlisle) as Chief Secretary, and Thomas Drummond as Permanent Under-Secretary was the first administration to recognize that Emancipation was on the statute book.

10. There was heavy emigration before the Famine but it did not offset the natural increase of population.

11. Comparable figures for the area now forming the Republic were 6,529,000 and 5,112,000.

and 1845. More generally, in some (though by no means all) parts of the country a transition from a subsistence to a mercantile economy could be discerned before then. The Great Famine certainly accelerated these developments but it did not initiate them.[12]

Emigration and the consequent loss of population continued for many years after the Famine. The last total failure of the potato crop occurred in 1848, but it was not until 1855 that the annual recorded emigration from all Irish ports fell below 100,000. It went over that level again in some of the middle 1860s. It was not until later still that emigration slackened so much as to approach the natural increase: 1877 was the first year for over three decades in which an increase of population was estimated, but the pause was short. The bad harvests of the last years of that decade combined with the falling prices and land struggle of the next to produce a new outburst of emigration which was never again equalled until, unhappily, the 1950s. It was not until the last decade of the century that emigration and population loss returned to levels that might, eventually, be tolerable.

The history of the second half of the century, therefore, was made against a background of a population decline which appeared to be uncontrollable. No remedy could be seen in the years that immediately followed the Famine. Subsequent writers have noted the conviction which then gripped so many that they must get out of Ireland at all costs and leave a country that offered nothing more than famine and disease or, at the best, inescapable poverty.[13] The justice of pessimism seemed to be confirmed by the failure of rebellion by the Young Irelanders in 1848 and of a new constitutional movement in the early 1850s. A celebrated phrase of the time described Ireland as 'a corpse on the dissecting-table'. It cannot have appeared to be an exaggeration.

The contrast between what appeared to be inevitable, and what actually did happen, is remarkable. Those who remained in Ireland made a profound adjustment of their way of life. Before the Famine, novelists depicted a carefree and irresponsible society, poor in everything except humour and song. The society of twenty years later is obviously much more dour (as it might well be, considering its experiences) and much more concerned with its survival. Even the basic institution of society was transformed. Pre-Famine Ireland was a land of early, if improvident, marriage: by the 1860s, when records became available, post-Famine Ireland already showed the lowest marriage rate in Europe. It is not easily explicable how those who grew up during the 1840s, escaping death during the Famine and emigration after it,

12. Cf. P. Lynch and J. Vaizey, *Guinness's Brewery in the Irish Economy, 1759–1876*, Cambridge University Press, London: 1960, pp. 25–36 and 161–76.
13. Cf. R. D. Edwards and T. D. Williams (eds.), *The Great Famine*, Browne & Nolan, Dublin: 1956, particularly the contribution by Dr. Oliver MacDonagh, pp. 319–90.

could have adapted themselves to a totally different set of values and code of behaviour. The middle decades of the century provide the social historian, and indeed the novelist, with a remarkable theme.

There was even more to the change. The importance of livestock to Irish farmers had been apparent before the Famine. It was increased by growing prosperity in England and a consequent demand for meat and dairy produce. The post-Famine generation took full advantage of its opportunity, and by 1870 there were already so many livestock in the country that the levels then reached have been surpassed only in very recent years.[14] This was achieved in spite of a still unreformed land system which exposed the tenant to insecurity of tenure, rack-renting, and the confiscation of his improvements. Life in Ireland during the third quarter of the nineteenth century may have been unimaginative and devoid of grace. Nevertheless, that generation has high claims on the gratitude of its successors. In the nineteenth century there were three great achievements. The first was the attainment of Catholic Emancipation, which owed almost everything to O'Connell: it is not for nothing that he is still known as the Liberator. The second was the repossession of the land; and here the credit was shared between the leadership of Davitt and Parnell and the courage of tenants who faced the risk of eviction during the Land War. The third was the acquisition of capital by careful saving. This, the people did themselves. It is deeply misleading to regard the history of modern Ireland as nothing more than the story of its leaders.

The national revival

It is not to be understood that the principal developments in the Irish nineteenth century were all constitutional nor, indeed, that they all occurred within Ireland. Throughout the century and later there were two wings of nationalism: those who trusted to constitutional action, beginning with O'Connell and ending with Redmond, and those who believed in, or were driven to, the use of force: Emmet in 1803, the Young Irelanders in 1848, and the Fenians in 1867. These two wings were often in direct opposition, but their action, however contradictory, reacted on each other. The Fenian movement, for example, was something new in Irish nationalism because it was based on the growing numbers of Irish in the United States. Its achievement appeared to be negligible: but Gladstone testified to its influence on British public opinion.[15] Thus nationalism had two forms of expression: constitutional

14. See T. Barrington, 'A Review of Irish Agricultural Prices', *JSSISI*, 1925–6, p. 249 and H. Staehle, 'Statistical Notes on the Economic History of Irish Agriculture, 1847–1913', *JSSISI*, 1950–1, p. 444.

15. John Morley, *Life of Gladstone*. For the period under discussion see Book v, chapter xv. For Gladstone's later Irish policies, see J. L. Hammond, *Gladstone and the Irish Nation*, republished by Cass, London: 1964.

and agrarian reform at home and militant separatism abroad. The peculiar strength of Parnell lay in his ability to make the two wings work together.

A new cycle of reform began in 1868 under Gladstone's first administration which disestablished the Church of Ireland in the following year. This was a violation of the Act of Union which was now seen to be no longer immutable. In 1870 a Land Act attempted, not very successfully, to restrain the absolute dominion of the landlords. A reform of land tenure had been recommended by the Devon Commission as long before as 1845: nothing had been done and the delay meant that what was done at last was not enough. Finally, in 1870 a Home Rule Association was established under the chairmanship of Isaac Butt. Within ten years it had become an organized party under the leadership of Parnell.

The political events of these years have been described so often that economic forces may be overlooked. The period between 1873 and 1896 was for long remembered, until it was patently out-classed in more recent years, as the time of the Great Depression. The world-wide fall in prices was experienced by Irish agriculture. Barrington shows[16] that in 1896 all agricultural products, with the exception of barley and eggs, sold at lower prices than in 1873. Cattle prices showed no great fall; but those of beef, mutton, and butter were down in proportions ranging from one-quarter to one-third. The price of wheat fell by almost one-half: it had become unprofitable in the face of imports from North America. Comparisons of one year with another may be influenced by temporary factors; but a reader of Barrington's paper will not fail to note the long decline of prices throughout almost a quarter of a century. The political events of the 1880s must therefore be set against a background of agricultural distress.

George Moore has remarked somewhere that 'Ireland was still feudal until the 1870s'. The land was still the principal, almost the only, source of livelihood: modern industries, such as shipbuilding, were still in process of development. What John Mitchel had written in *The United Irishman* a generation before was still true:

Land in Ireland is life. Just in the proportion that our people contrive to keep or to gain some foothold on the soil, in that proportion exactly they will live and not die.

The dominion of the landlords was still unlimited, apart from the ineffectual restraints attempted by the Land Act of 1870, although the stream of events ate at its foundations. A measure such as the Ballot Act of 1872, for example, limited the political power of the landlords over their tenants by providing for secret voting. The stream was now to

16. Op. cit.

become more violent and more destructive: the last decades of the century witnessed decisive changes in social organization.

The later 1870s saw a succession of bad seasons, culminating in the partial famine of 1879. Demands for rent which could not be met produced a new series of evictions. They were answered by Davitt's foundation of the Land League in September 1879. This was followed, twelve months later, by Parnell's celebrated injunction to the tenants to keep a firm grip of their homesteads and to boycott any tenant bidding for a farm from which there had been an eviction. The organized use of the boycott by what had appeared previously to be 'an impulsive and undisciplined peasantry'[17] showed not only that the struggle over land tenure had entered a new phase but also that it would be more sternly fought.

The general election of 1880 produced a resounding triumph for the Liberal party. In Ireland, the Home Rule party increased its numbers from fifty-one to sixty-two. Gladstone, the incoming Prime Minister, acknowledged the need for a thoroughgoing measure of reform, which was provided by the Land Act of 1881. This measure went far towards meeting the tenants' claims: it provided fixity of tenure by the institution of statutory tenancies, a fair rent by a process of judicial review, and acknowledged a right to free sale of the unexpired portion of a lease. It conceded at last to the rest of Ireland the tenant-right on which much of the prosperity of Ulster had been built. Thus it contemplated a system of dual ownership, in which the landlord retained ownership while his power to abuse his rights was severely curtailed.

In happier circumstances the Act of 1881 might have provided an acceptable solution, and in that case the social organization of modern Ireland would have been very different. But everything conspired against success. The experiment did not receive a fair start. Heavy arrears of rent were carried over from the bad years and Gladstone's attempt to carry an Arrears Act was thrown out in the House of Lords. This was bad enough; worse still, the continuing fall in prices meant that even the new judicially fixed rents could be paid only with difficulty. There was nothing, therefore, to assuage the hostility of landlord and tenant towards each other: the Gladstonian experiment was soon seen to have failed and expectations now turned to the prospect that the next Conservative government would introduce a measure of Land Purchase which would assist the tenant to full ownership of his land.

These were the years in which Parnell rose to his full parliamentary stature. As the leader of an organized party which might soon hold the balance of power at Westminster, he was in touch not only with members of the cabinet but also with leaders, such as Lord Randolph

17. Winston Churchill, *Life of Lord Randolph Churchill*, Macmillan, London: 1906, vol. i, p. 184.

Churchill, on the Conservative benches. Reviewing the parliament of 1880–5, *The Economist* remarked that it

had been signalized by the advance of the Irish Nationalist Party from a derided and despised faction to a position from which they have been more than once able to exercise a controlling and decisive influence over the course of policy and the fortunes of Ministers.[18]

In the early hours of 9 June 1885 Mr. Gladstone's second administration fell, the Liberals being out-voted by a combination of Conservatives and Irish nationalists. In the early hours of 8 June 1886 his third administration fell. On this occasion Liberals and Irish nationalists were out-voted by Conservatives and Liberal Unionists. The events of this exactly bounded period of time have exercised a profound influence on the evolution of modern Ireland. It is hardly too much to say that the form of society and state in which we live was determined during that crowded twelve months.

Gladstone's second government was succeeded by a Conservative government under Lord Salisbury. There was no overt alliance between the new administration and the Irish party, but certainly there were discussions. In August the Ashbourne Act was passed, which provided a scheme of land purchase whereby all the purchase money was advanced to the tenant-purchaser on easy terms. This went much further than any previous experiment, and it was unlikely that subsequent legislation would be less generous. The Ashbourne Act began the transfer of Irish land from the landlord to the tenant, a transfer which could not fail to produce consequences of the greatest social, economic and political importance.

The general election of November 1885, following the extension of the franchise and a redistribution of seats, made far-reaching changes in the parliamentary representation of Ireland. In the new parliament, the Nationalists held 85 of the 103 Irish seats. They had taken all the seats outside Ulster except Dublin University and even in Ulster they now held eighteen seats against seventeen Conservatives. It could no longer be argued that Parnell and his party did not represent the great majority of the people of Ireland. The Liberals won 333 seats, the Conservatives 251, so that Parnell held the balance of power at Westminster.

In December it became known that Gladstone had accepted the result of the election as a sign that some form of Home Rule must be considered. He was willing that it should be put through by the Conservatives, who could command the necessary majority in the House of Lords. The Conservatives, however, were not willing to consider tampering with the Union.[19] In January 1886, therefore, they were put out

18. 15 August 1885.
19. ' . . . thus idly drifted away what was perhaps the best hope of the settlement of Ireland which that generation was to see.' Churchill, op. cit., vol. ii, p. 31.

of office by a combination of the Liberals and the Nationalists. Gladstone, again Prime Minister, introduced the first Home Rule Bill in April. It was defeated in June by 343 votes to 313.

This was a decisive defeat, the more so because the general election in July returned 316 Conservatives and 78 dissident Liberals (thereafter known as Liberal Unionists) to 191 Liberals and 85 Nationalists; but not even the most decisive defeat could restore the situation of only twelve months before—the fact that one of the major parties had committed itself to Home Rule could never be forgotten. This was a far cry from the unrelenting opposition with which the older Whigs and Tories had combined against O'Connell's campaign for Repeal more than forty years before.

Equally, the ultimate source of opposition to Home Rule, more unyielding and less susceptible to argument than the British electorate, was now revealed. After some consideration of assisting Parnell, Lord Randolph Churchill had decided that 'the Orange card is the one to play'.[20] In a letter published while the debate on the Home Rule Bill was in progress, he used words that were only too easy to remember later:

. . . Ulster at the proper moment will resort to the supreme arbitrament of force; Ulster will fight, Ulster will be right, Ulster will emerge from the struggle victorious, because all that Ulster represents to us Britons will command the sympathy and support of an enormous section of our British community . . .[21]

In the event there was no need to play the Orange card; but a dispassionate observer (if such a person could have been found in these islands in 1886) might well have concluded that if Ireland ever got Home Rule it would almost certainly be Home Rule without Ulster, as long as the British people persevered in its determination to enforce its superior strength and retained its Protestant instinct.

The change of government in 1886 brought in a period of Conservative rule which lasted almost without interruption until 1905. An incipient revival of the Home Rule cause was destroyed by the O'Shea divorce case in 1890, the ensuing rejection of Parnell's leadership by a majority of the Irish party and his death in 1891. The general election of 1892 returned an unworkably small Liberal-Nationalist majority of forty. In 1893 Gladstone introduced the second Home Rule bill which passed the Commons to be rejected in the Lords by 419 votes to 41. In 1895 the Conservatives returned to power.

The Marquess of Salisbury held the premiership from 1886 to 1892 and again from 1895 until his retirement in 1902. While the first Home

20. 'Pray God' he added 'it turns out to be the ace of trumps and not the two.' Churchill, op. cit., vol. ii, p. 59.
21. Ibid., vol. ii, p. 65.

Rule bill was still in the Commons, he delivered a speech on the Irish question that was long remembered. To quote the summary given in the *Annual Register* for that year:

He maintained that Ireland was not a nation, but two nations; held that there were races, like the Hottentots and even the Hindoos, who were incapable of self-government; and refused to place confidence in a people who had 'acquired the habit of using knives and slugs' . . . 'My alternative policy is that Parliament should enable the Government of England to govern Ireland. Apply that recipe honestly, consistently and resolutely for twenty years, and at the end of that time you will find that Ireland will be fit to accept any gifts in the way of local government or repeal of coercion laws that you may wish to give her.'

For good measure, Lord Salisbury went on to say that he would rather employ British wealth in aiding the emigration of a million Irishmen than in buying out landlords.[22]

The government of Ireland in this period lay in the hands of Arthur Balfour, who was Chief Secretary from 1887–91, his brother Gerald (1895–1900) and George Wyndham (1900–5). The policy of resolute government was vigorously applied by Arthur Balfour, Lord Salisbury's nephew. Another element in his approach might not have engaged the sympathy of his uncle: in his judgement the demand for Home Rule might disappear if Ireland were given not only resolute but also good government, and a sincere attempt were made to solve her economic and social problems. In this view, the claim for Home Rule was invented by Irish politicians for their own purposes. If Ireland became prosperous, its people would realize the boundless opportunities which were offered to them by partnership in the United Kingdom.[23]

In this period, therefore, a succession of remedial measures was devoted to the aim of 'killing Home Rule with kindness'.[24] Land Purchase was continued, the Congested Districts Board was established for the distressed areas of the west and the Department of Agriculture and Technical Instruction was set up. Even more important, politically rather than economically, was the extension of local government to Ireland by the Act of 1898. This measure transferred local power (and patronage) from the landlords to elected bodies which, except in some counties of Ulster and a few areas elsewhere, would certainly be controlled by nationalists. In its own way, this was as far-reaching a transfer of power as the Treaty was to bring; and indeed the adherence of county

22. *AR*, 1886, pp. 181–2.
23. L. P. Curtis, *Coercion and Conciliation in Ireland, 1880–1892*, Oxford University Press, London: 1963.
24. The phrase was adopted from a speech made by Gerald Balfour in Leeds on 16 October 1895 when he said that 'they (the government) would be glad enough to kill Home Rule with kindness if they could ...', *AR*, 1895, p. 185. The phrase was too useful to be spoiled in quotation by the conditional clause.

councils and corporations to the Republican cause was to do a great deal
to make the Treaty attainable. Last, towards the end of the Conservative supremacy, the great Wyndham Act of 1903 made tenant ownership effective throughout the country. That year is one of the pivotal
dates in Irish history, and the Land Act marked the highest point of the
Conservative government of Ireland. Arthur Balfour was largely
justified when, thirty years later, he asked, 'What was the Ireland the
Free State took over? It was the Ireland that we made.'[25]

There might have been more to claim. If there had been, Balfour
would not have had occasion to talk of a Free State. The success of the
Wyndham Act, and of the conferences between landlords and nationalist leaders which had ensured that success, encouraged Wyndham's
Under-Secretary, Sir Antony MacDonnell, to consider plans of devolving
some form of local government on Ireland. The Ulster Unionists, then
as so often instinctively hostile to any Anglo-Irish settlement, protested
furiously. Balfour bowed to them, Wyndham retired from office and
Conservative policy continued to maintain the Union.

In the history of Ireland, there is only too often occasion to linger
on what might have been; the temptation is irresistible in the present
case. If the Conservative Party had sponsored some measure of self-
government at that conjuncture of good feeling and growing prosperity,
the stream of events might have flowed more peaceably. The land
question, which would have presented an insoluble problem to any
Irish government, was now out of the way. The Conservatives could
have put their proposals through the Lords, Anglo-Irish relations would
have been very different and the constitutional changes of the Parliament Act might never have been made. The two peoples were not
granted so merciful and honourable an end to their conflict.

A growing prosperity has been mentioned. By 1905 the country was
well advanced in a long cycle of rising world prices and expanding
trade. All agricultural products, except the now neglected wheat, were
selling better than in 1896: cattle prices in particular were buoyant.
Dairy products lagged behind in the advance; even here, however, the
Irish trade was changing out of recognition. These were the golden
years of the co-operative movement which still worked harmoniously
with the new Department of Agriculture and Technical Instruction.
The introduction and maintenance of higher standards of butter and
egg production, improved grading and better marketing gave an impetus to the export trade.

The traditional Irish industries profited also from world-wide
prosperity. The linen trade continued to expand its markets, not yet
restricted by multiplying tariffs. The shipyards, which had produced an
annual tonnage of about 40,000 in the later 1880s, fell below 100,000

25. B. Dugdale, *Arthur James Balfour*, Hutchinson, London: 1936, vol. i, p. 181.

tons a year only once between the beginning of the new century and the outbreak of war. In 1914 it reached a new peak of 256,000 tons. In these years the Queen's Island sent out the ill-fated *Titanic* and its sister-ship, then the largest in the world, the *Olympic*. The industrial and commercial prosperity of Belfast inspired a self-assurance which was to influence the constitutional struggle of 1912. Other industries shared in the general advance. Brewing and distilling prospered: whiskey, mineral waters, and biscuits enjoyed a seemingly secure prestige. The movement in support of Irish industries, which began about the beginning of the century, helped other forms of production, notably woollens and hosiery, which had been depressed.

The results of legislation should not be overlooked. The Land Act of 1903 increased spending-power throughout the country: the poorer areas benefited out of all expectation from the social legislation introduced after 1906. The sum involved may appear small to the reader;[26] but the pounds were gold pounds and the general price level, although moving upwards, did not move so quickly as to destroy the real gain. Admittedly, improvement began from a very low level. Nevertheless, no such sustained prosperity had been known in Ireland since the French wars a century before, and this was far more securely based. It had social effects, which were to develop political implications. Much of the money was saved or spent on the education of children: bank deposits rose and schools prospered. Ireland might have been feudal in the 1870s: thirty years later something resembling a middle class had emerged.

This was the brighter part of the picture. Some areas and some occupations were untouched by the growing prosperity. Since 1891 the Congested Districts Board, 'the best Board that ever operated in Ireland', had wrestled with the poverty of the western counties.[27] The magnitude of its task is apparent from the review of its work made by the Royal Commission on Congestion. The Commission's first report noted the preponderance in the congested districts of family budgets which might vary from £15 to nearly £80 a year. These sums included not only the value of farm produce but also all earnings and receipts from other sources.[28] Two years later, the final report noted that:

still in a 'good year' some of them are little more than free from the dread of hunger, whilst a bad year, arising from complete or partial failure of the produce of their holdings, results in a condition of semi-starvation.[29]

26. The total received in Old Age Pensions was estimated at £2.8m. in 1911–12. Cf. *Report of the Committee on Irish Finance* (the Primrose Committee), Cd 6153, 1912, p. 6.

27. Cf. W. L. Micks, *The History of the Congested Districts Board*, Eason, Dublin: 1925.

28. *First Report of the Royal Commission on Congestion*, Cd 3266, HMSO, London: 1906, pp. 32–7.

29. *Final Report of the Royal Commission on Congestion*, Cd 4097, HMSO, London: 1908, p. 5.

The position in the cities was worse still. An unskilled and irregularly employed population lived in houses which were in decay. Large parts of the urban populations not only lived in conditions of casual and lowly paid employment but were exposed to the most extreme risks of all the diseases caused by malnutrition, over-crowding, and dirt. Edwardian Dublin has been immortalized by Joyce's *Ulysses* which describes the day of 16 June 1904. In that year the death rate of children under one year of age per thousand registered births was 171 in the Dublin Registration Area against 166 in the seventy-five largest English towns and cities excluding London; 146 in London and 146 also in England and Wales. Death rates were selective as well as high at that time. The report of the City Medical Officer of Health for 1904, from which the foregoing statistics are taken, noted that the death rate among families of the 'professional and independent' class was 18.4, compared with 16.6 among the 'middle' class, 19.1 among 'artisans and petty shop-keepers', and 33.7 among 'general service and inmates of workhouses'. It would be interesting to ascertain the rate in Night-town.

The turn of the century saw the growth of new interests and the foundation of new associations. These differed very widely in their purposes and in the sources of their support. All of them, however, were aimed at changing the pattern of life in Ireland. Politically, in one case, by replacing rule from Westminster by some form of self-government; socially, in others, by establishing a socialist system on one hand or a co-operative community on the other. Culturally, in yet another, by restoring Ireland to its half-forgotten Gaelic past. In the event, only the first and most limited of these aims was attained, largely at the expense of the others and even then not completely. In their beginnings, how-ever, each of these movements, again in very different ways, increased national self-consciousness and self-reliance and thereby released forces which, whatever their immediate intent might be, strengthened the separatist tradition.[30]

The foundation of the Gaelic Athletic Association in 1884 provides an instructive example. It was designed to arrest the decline of speci-fically Irish sports, such as hurling, and to revive athletics. It was, in outward appearances, a sporting organization; but it deliberately en-couraged codes of sport that were thought to be Irish and set itself against other codes which were thought to be English in their spirit and associations.[31] This had inescapable political implications.

30. Cf. P.S. O'Hegarty, *A History of Ireland under the Union*, Methuen, London: 1952, pp. 610–49. A more general picture is given by *The Shaping of Modern Ireland*, Cruise O'Brien (ed.), Routledge & Kegan Paul, London: 1960.

31. The 'ban', which is still in force, applied to cricket, hockey, rugby, and associa-tion football, which were then held to be games played by the British garrison in Ireland and their friends. Golf was not widely known in Ireland in the 1880s (Arthur Balfour helped in its introduction during his tenure of office) and it escaped prohibition.

Even more avowedly apolitical in its intentions, even more revolutionary in its effects, was the Gaelic League which was founded in 1893 with the primary intention of assuring 'the preservation of Irish as the National Language of Ireland and the extension of its use as a spoken tongue'. Its founders were Douglas Hyde, a Protestant landowner in the west, John MacNeill, then a civil servant, and Father Eugene O'Growney, Professor of Irish at Maynooth College. Their intentions are made clear in the following extract from a lecture by Douglas Hyde in 1892:

When we speak of the 'The Necessity for de-Anglicising the Irish Nation', we mean it, not as a protest against imitating what is *best* in the English people, for that would be absurd, but rather to show the folly of neglecting what is Irish, and hastening to adopt, pell-mell and indiscriminately, everything that is English, simply because it *is* English. . . . In a word, we must strive to cultivate everything that is most racial, most smacking of the soil, most Gaelic, most Irish because in spite of the little admixture of Saxon blood in the north-east corner, this island *is* and will *ever* remain Celtic at the core. . . . We must create a strong feeling against West-Britonism, for it—if we give it the least chance, or show it the smallest quarter—will overwhelm us like a flood and we shall find ourselves toiling painfully behind the English at each step, following the same fashions, only six months behind the English one. . . .[32]

Thus the Gaelic League was not intended as a negative anti-British movement. It was positive, directed towards the rediscovery of Irish ways of life, of thought, and of expression. It attracted support from people of all politics and of none: among all of them it necessarily inspired a realization that they possessed a heritage from the Irish past. Although sincerely apolitical, such lines of thought had political implications. That was to become clear twenty years later. The political implications concerned not only the implicit insistence on the separate nationality of Ireland. They also suggested a new concept of how that nationality might be expressed. Up to that time the nationalist movement had drawn its inspiration largely from the eighteenth century, from the writings and speeches of Molyneux, Swift, and Grattan. A return to the Gaelic past necessarily followed a quite different line of thought. The task of Irish nationalism in this century has been to reconcile the Gaelic with the Anglo-Irish heritage and both with the particularism of north-east Ulster; but in its buoyant beginnings, the Gaelic League offered new worlds to all Irish people.

The last years of the century also witnessed a notable surge of creative energy in literature and the theatre. Yeats published his first collection of poems in 1889. In 1899 the Irish Literary Theatre was established; it was followed by the opening of the Abbey Theatre in 1904. Here again an overflowing into political thought and action may be seen. In 1902, *Cathleen ni Houlihan*, whose curtain line brought to-

32. Douglas Hyde, *The Revival of Irish Literature*, Fisher & Unwin, London: 1894, pp. 117 f.

gether and fused all the emotions of the time, was produced for the first time.[33] Recalling his nine years' tenure of the Chief Secretaryship, which was brought to an end by the Rising, Augustine Birrell noted that:

Irish literature and the drama, Messrs. Maunsell's list of new Irish publications, and the programme of the Abbey Theatre became to me of far more real significance than the monthly reports of the Royal Irish Constabulary.[34]

The co-operative movement produced similar results in a rather different sphere of action. Having studied the working of agricultural co-operation in the United States, Sir Horace Plunkett launched his lifework by the establishment of a co-operative creamery at Drumcollogher in 1889. His appeal to farmers to break the lines of division in politics and religion and work together in the task of improving production and exchange was greatly strengthened by the support of Father T. A. Finlay S.J. and Lord Monteagle.[35] The co-operative associations spread and were brought together in the Irish Agricultural Organisation Society in 1894. In the following year Plunkett called on his fellow Members of Parliament[36] to discuss together 'Irish business of extreme importance which is not controversial in its nature'.[37] He had such problems in mind as agricultural instruction and research, technical education, and the encouragement of fisheries and afforestation. These may appear non-controversial indeed: but to invite all Irish M.P.s to discuss them in company was a portent in a country where Parnellites would not meet anti-Parnellites nor Unionists meet either sect of Nationalist. Nevertheless, the 'Recess' Committee did meet and produced a report whose usefulness has not been exhausted seventy years later. Its principal recommendation was carried into effect by the establishment in 1899 of the Department of Agriculture and Technical Instruction. It is important to note how this body worked. Its effective head[38] was the Vice-President, not the Chief Secretary. Its Council, which was preponderantly appointed by all the county councils of Ireland, worked with increasing harmony as the years went on. Thus Ireland was afforded the example of co-operation between farmers of Unionist Antrim and Nationalist Cork in the societies and at the

33. 'Did you see an old woman going down the path? I did not, but I saw a young girl and she had the walk of a queen.'
34. *Things Past Redress*, Faber, London: 1937, p. 214. It was natural that the first class of reading should appeal to Birrell as a man of letters: as a politician he should perhaps have realized that it made the reading of the second all the more imperative.
35. Cf. Margaret Digby, *Sir Horace Plunkett*, Blackwell, Oxford: 1949.
36. Plunkett was Unionist member for South Dublin from 1892 to 1900. This aroused suspicions among the Irish Parliamentary Party that co-operation was part of the plan for killing Home Rule with kindness. Many Unionists, on the other hand, regarded Plunkett's association with Nationalists with equal suspicion.
37. *Report of the Recess Committee*, Browne & Nolan, Dublin: 1896, p. 118.
38. Plunkett was Vice-President from 1899 until his resignation, in 1907, in circumstances which are set out in Miss Digby's book, pp. 106–16.

highest level in a department of government. This was an example of all interests in Ireland coming together to work for Irish prosperity. Plunkett, as he said himself, was no Home Ruler at this time; but his work hastened the day when Home Rule might be operated successfully.

Twenty years of resolute government, therefore, ended with an Ireland more self-conscious and self-reliant than ever before. Killing Home Rule with kindness had not removed the Nationalist demand for an Irish parliament and executive. What it had done was to ensure that whatever Irish parliament was established would be a conservative body because its constituents had now something to preserve.

The politics of Home Rule

The strengthening of national feeling was accompanied by a new approach to political affairs. The Irish parliamentary party was still the largest party in the country. It had retained the gains made in 1885, with the exception of a very few marginal seats in Ulster. Parnellites and anti-Parnellites had come together in 1900 under the chairmanship of John Redmond. It seemed to stand on the threshold of final success when, at the general election of 1906, its Liberal allies obtained a sweeping majority in Great Britain.

There were other forces at work, apparently less powerful, which were to prove themselves more enduring. The Sinn Féin movement may be said to have grown from the foundation of the *United Irishman*, edited by Arthur Griffith, in 1899. In the next year, a number of societies were brought together in a loose union known as *Cumann na nGaedheal*. These societies were apparently literary but their members were predominantly separatist in politics. What came to be known as 'the Hungarian policy' was set out in a series of articles in the *United Irishman* by Griffith during 1904, which were republished towards the end of that year under the title of *The Resurrection of Hungary*. They discussed the constitutional relations of Austria and Hungary, then and since 1867 governed separately with separate parliaments but united by a common monarch. Griffith's thesis was that the Hungarians had resisted Austrian attempts to dominate them by adopting the device of a Dual Monarchy to preserve their autonomy and maintain an equality of status.

Whether Griffith set out the constitution of Austria–Hungary accurately is beside the point. His aim was to argue that the same relationship could exist, and indeed had existed between Great Britain and Ireland.[39]

39. Curiously enough Mill had discussed the same issues in 1868, reaching the conclusion that no relationship would be less suitable for the two countries than the settlement reached in Austria-Hungary. J. S. Mill, *England and Ireland*, Longmans Green, London: 1868, p. 34.

He claimed that the Act of Union was illegal and that Ireland should be governed by the constitution of 1782, that the sole body capable of legislating for Ireland was the King, Lords, and Commons of Ireland. This led him to the conclusion, which is summarized by O'Hegarty:

that we should proceed on the basis that the Constitution of 1782 and the Renunciation Act of 1783 were the only parliamentarian institutions which were legal, the only institutions which the Irish People ought to recognize, and that they ought to say so, to withdraw altogether from the British Parliament, but to use the representatives elected to that Parliament as the nucleus of an Irish national assembly which should, on the model of O'Connell's Council of Three Hundred, meet at home, be recognized by Ireland as a voluntary *de jure* National Council authorized to speak and act for the people, and use every power of the Local Boards, Corporations and County Councils to forward the main interest of the restoration of full legislative independence.[40]

To Griffith, the merit of the Hungarian policy was that it gave the widest possible basis of union between Irish people and it offered a superior constitutional status than Home Rule. A Home Rule parliament would clearly receive its powers from the Imperial parliament: it would be a subordinate body in its origin, whatever it might later become. The Parliament of 1782, on the other hand, was a sovereign parliament, whatever its shortcomings may have been.

It should be remembered that Sinn Féin was a great deal more than a political movement. To quote O'Hegarty again:

The Sinn Féin Movement was educational, practical and political. It sought to educate the people in the knowledge of their land, its history, traditions, and resources. It taught them that speeches and resolutions and patriotism were not enough, that of themselves they would not save the Nation, that the Nation could be saved only by effort, only by the slow rebuilding of the national life in Ireland itself, a rebuilding of individual and group effort until such time as power over our own affairs could be resumed.[41]

There were also many members of Sinn Féin (as the movement was formally entitled after 1908) who were prepared to progress from constitutional agitation to the use of force and regarded the constitution of 1782 as a minimum. Many of them were members of the Irish Republican Brotherhood, a secret organization dating from the late 1850s which was dedicated to complete separation from Great Britain and believed that this was unattainable without the use of force.

An Irish Socialist Republican party was founded by James Connolly in 1896 with the objects of

the public ownership by the people of Ireland of the land and instruments of production, distribution, and exchange. Agriculture to be administered as

40. P. S. O'Hegarty, *History of Ireland under the Union*, Methuen, London: 1952, p. 647.
41. Ibid, p. 653. *Sinn Féin* means 'We ourselves', *not* 'Ourselves alone'.

a public function, under boards of management elected by the agricultural population and responsible to them and to the public at large. All other forms of labour necessary to the well-being of the community to be conducted on the same principles.[42]

In 1903 Connolly emigrated to the United States. Returning in 1910 he found that the organization of workers had progressed under the leadership of Jim Larkin. Larkin had organized strikes of unskilled workers in Belfast in 1907, and in 1908 the Irish Transport and General Workers Union, now much the largest and most powerful trade union, was founded. There was a succession of strikes in the industrial cities of Belfast, Dublin, and Cork to improve conditions of employment and wages. The clash between employers and labour in Dublin came in 1913, and lasted for eight months. It ended indecisively but it brought a much greater solidarity to the workers. It also led to the establishment of the Irish Citizen Army. Constitutional methods had become unfashionable in 1913.

On the other side, the Irish Unionists had stood for generations in unrelenting opposition to anything that any section of nationalist opinion, moderate or extremist, violent or constitutional, might demand. They were unshakeably attached to the British connection and to their share in the prosperity and prestige of the United Kingdom. Here again, elements of dissolution were at work. The Unionists of the north, centred in Belfast, held firm in their opposition to any form of Home Rule. In the south and west, however, Unionists began to reconsider their position. They had already lost much, and were clearly destined to lose all, of their privileged position. Many of them began to consider what place they might fill in a country that had achieved Home Rule. The role of Lord Dunraven and his colleagues in the discussions before the 1903 Land Act and in the devolution scheme showed that not all Unionists in Ireland shared the intransigence of those in the north.

The continued strength of the demand for Home Rule was soon shown. In 1907 the Liberal government introduced an Irish Council Bill which contemplated that the administration of services such as education and local government should be given to an Irish representative body. It was rejected by a convention of the Irish party and was then withdrawn. This may have been another lost opportunity. The Council would have been an inadequate substitute for a parliament but it could not have been opposed so bitterly as the Home Rule Bill of 1912 was to be, and its operation would have given further opportunities for Irishmen to work together. Nevertheless, the project was abandoned; and

42. Cf. C. D. Greaves, *Life and Times of James Connolly*, Lawrence & Wishart, London: 1961, p. 61. Cf. also *James Larkin* by Emmet Larkin, Routledge & Kegan Paul, London: 1965. See especially Connolly's own book. *Labour in Irish History*, Maunsel, Dublin: 1910.

the government turned its attention to the better provision of university education by the Irish Universities Act of 1908.[43]

The following years were occupied by the dispute between the Commons and the Lords over the budget of 1909, the two general elections of 1910 and the limitation of the powers of the Upper House by the Parliament Act of 1911. It was very well understood on all sides that the abolition of the veto of the Lords removed the major parliamentary obstacle to the passage of Home Rule. In 1911 Redmond might be excused for thinking that Home Rule was indeed just around the corner. But the apparent strength of his position was deceptive. In appearance, he held the balance of power at Westminster after the general elections of 1910.[44] In fact, the Irish party had been committed to the Liberal alliance ever since 1886. They had no freedom of choice between the two British parties. Moreover, the time now approached when parliamentary majorities would not be accepted without question; in Great Britain, as in Ireland, an appeal to arms would soon receive a response which would have been almost unimaginable even ten years before.

The third Home Rule Bill was introduced in April 1912. The measure of autonomy that it proposed appears in retrospect to have been extraordinarily limited. It has been described by Sir Keith Hancock as

a scheme of provincial autonomy so circumscribed that an Australian colony, even sixty or seventy years earlier, would have rejected it with indignation. It contained 'limitations' excluding from the competence of the Irish parliament trade regulation in all its forms, navigation, postal services and trade-marks. In addition it specified certain 'reserved' matters—not counting truly imperial matters such as foreign policy and defence—which might pass to Irish

43. The demand for adequate university education for Catholics had been one of the themes of the nineteenth century. For a variety of reasons, Trinity College, Dublin (which had been founded by Elizabeth I in 1592), was unacceptable. The foundation of the Queen's University with colleges in Belfast, Cork, and Galway between 1845 and 1850 was also unsatisfactory. The Catholic University, of which Newman was the first Rector, was opened in 1854 but its work was greatly restricted by the fact that its degrees were not legally recognized. Nevertheless its medical school, which was able to circumvent this difficulty, was most successful. Its faculties of arts and science were entrusted in 1883 to the Society of Jesus which reorganized them as University College, Dublin. Students could proceed to a degree in the Royal University which replaced the Queen's University in 1879 but was only an examining body. The Act of 1908 established the college at Belfast as the Queen's University, Belfast, and grouped its sister colleges in Cork and Galway with University College, Dublin, into the National University of Ireland.

The secular importance of this long controversy was that (generally speaking and with obvious exceptions on both sides) the students of Trinity College could be said to be as Unionist as students of University College might be taken to be Nationalists. When the administration of the Irish Free State came to be organized in 1922, it was of no small importance that a graduate body of Nationalist sympathies had been created.

44. The general election of January 1910 returned 275 Liberals, 273 Conservatives, 82 Home Rulers, and 40 Labour. The election of the following December returned 272 Liberals, 272 Conservatives, 84 Home Rulers, and 42 Labour. But not all Home Rulers were under Redmond's control.

control only at a later date. Among these 'reserved' matters were police, savings banks, friendly societies, and public loans raised before the passing of the Act. Ireland, to all intents and purposes, remained within the British financial system: at the head of six limitations on her fiscal autonomy, customs and excise were listed.[45]

A reader who has grown to maturity in a sovereign Irish state may read this summary with astonishment. It seems incredible that the prospect of a parliament that could not even give orders to the police outside its gates in College Green should have brought these islands to the verge of civil war. The welcome given to the Bill in Ireland sprang from an instinct sharpened by the vicissitudes of history rather than from any confidence in freedom slowly broadening down from precedent to precedent. A parliament sitting in Dublin would be a visible symbol of Irish individuality. It would be a sign that Ireland was not simply a western extension of Great Britain. Its mere existence would encourage national self-confidence and give further impetus to the consciousness of cultural and social individuality which had grown up in recent years. Many, therefore, whose aims ranged far beyond any possible instalment of Home Rule, were willing to give the Bill a chance.

On 31 March 1912 a monster demonstration in favour of the Home Rule Bill was held in Dublin. One of the speakers was Pearse, who said:

We have no wish to destroy the British, we only want our freedom. We differ among ourselves on some small points, but we agree that we want freedom in some shape or other. . . . But I should think myself a traitor to my country if I did not answer the summons to this gathering, for it is clear to me that the Bill which we support to-day will be for the good of Ireland and that we shall be stronger with it than without it. . . . Let us unite and win a good Act from the British; I think it can be done. But if we are tricked this time, there is a party in Ireland, and I am one of them, that will advise the Gael to have no counsel with the Gall for ever again, but to answer them henceforward with the strong hand and the sword's edge.[46]

The reasons why Nationalists accepted the Bill were, of course, precisely the reasons why Unionists fought it through both Houses of Parliament and were prepared at the end to challenge the rule of law. North-eastern Ireland was the centre of resistance. In September 1912 the loyalists of Ulster were invited to sign a solemn League and Covenant against Home Rule. Thousands did so with impressive ceremony. The deliberate return to the spirit and language of the Scottish League and Covenant of 1638 revived the racial and religious bitterness that had never been far removed from life in the north of Ireland. The next step was decisive. The Ulster Volunteers were formed; their avowed

45. *Survey of British Commonwealth Affairs: Problems of Nationality, 1918–1936*, vol. i, Oxford University Press, London: 1937, pp. 94–5.
46. Quoted, in translation from the Irish, by Stephen Gwynn, *John Redmond's Last Years*, Arnold, London: 1919, pp. 63–4.

object was to oppose the implementation of Home Rule, by arms if necessary. They were encouraged by a succession of speeches by the leaders of the Conservative party which were not inaptly described as constituting 'a grammar of anarchy'. Comparisons were freely made with the situation existing before the revolution of 1688; for some, the German Emperor was to play the part of a new Prince of Orange. The Volunteers received active assistance not only from politicians but also from distinguished officers and ex-officers in the Army. They proved their efficiency by a successful running of guns into Larne in April 1914.

The avowed aim of the Ulster Volunteers and their supporters was to resist the inclusion of Ulster in Home Rule. This masked the paramount intention to make Home Rule impossible for any part of Ireland. Subsequent events have shown that an Irish state can exist, however maimed spiritually and economically, without the city and environs of Belfast. No one thought so fifty years ago. What was clear then was the commercial and industrial prosperity of the north. Speaking in Belfast in April 1912 Bonar Law (the leader of the Conservative party) claimed that the Irish Unionists constituted one-quarter of the population of Ireland but paid one-half of its taxation and carried on more than one-half of its trade.[47] These proportions may well have been roughly true at that time. It was not unreasonable, therefore, to assume that a parliament in Dublin which did not rule in Belfast could not rule at all and that Home Rule could be killed by procuring the exclusion of Ulster.[48]

The Irish party appear to have advised Asquith's government that the northern movement was a bluff which would be seen as such when it was called at the appropriate moment. Whether they were right cannot now be known because the bluff, if it was one, was never called. The surprising point was that arming in the north seems to have taken the Nationalist leaders by surprise. As lately as 1893, when the second Home Rule Bill was in the Commons, armed resistance was organized by the then leader of the Ulster Unionists, Colonel Saunderson.[49]

The Home Rule Bill followed the procedure laid down by the Parliament Act. It would become law, over the veto of the Lords, at the end of the parliamentary session of 1914; that is to say, at the end of July or the beginning of August 1914. But the appeal to arms revived ancestral forces. What could be done in one part of Ireland could be done in another. In November 1913 the Irish Volunteers were founded. The organizing committee was composed of constitutional Nationalists.

47. *AR*, 1912, p. 71.
48. Cf. the biography of Bonar Law by R. Blake, *The Unknown Prime Minister*, Eyre & Spottiswoode, London: 1955, p. 150. See also Gollin, *Proconsul in Politics* (a life of Lord Milner), Blond, London: 1964; and A. P. Ryan, *Mutiny at the Curragh*, Macmillan, London: 1956.
49. Cf. R. Lucas, *Colonel Saunderson M.P.*, Murray, London: 1908.

This was a decisive step. Never since the end of the seventeenth century had it been possible for all Irishmen openly and legally to drill and bear arms.[50] Now it was being done. The Irish Republican Brotherhood calculated that if Irishmen had arms, sooner or later they would use them.[51]

The Irish Volunteers were not welcomed by Redmond, a sincere parliamentarian who believed that a majority at Westminster was the only guarantee of success that was needed. In June 1914 he forced them to allow his nominees to form a majority of the organizing committee. In July, arms were run into Howth; the Ulster Volunteers had done as much and on a larger scale earlier in the year. Both organizations were now armed, if in an unequal degree.

At the outbreak of war in August Redmond declared that all British troops might be withdrawn from Ireland which could then be defended by the Irish and Ulster Volunteers. He acquiesced in the suspension of Home Rule; the Act was put on the Statute book but its operation was postponed for a year or until the end of the war which, it was then thought, might well be within twelve months. These decisions have been severely criticized ever since. It seems plain that Redmond believed that Great Britain was bound in honour to implement Home Rule and that, if the two bodies of Volunteers worked together, a sense of union would be fostered. Certainly, this calculation was soon proved to be wrong: but no later generation has yet had any greater success than Redmond in achieving the combination of self-government and unity.

In September 1914 Redmond went far beyond his attitude at the outbreak of war. Speaking at Woodenbridge, he advised the Volunteers to

go on drilling and make yourselves efficient for the work, and then account for yourselves as men, not only in Ireland itself, but wherever the fighting line extends, in defence of right, and freedom, and religion in this war.[52]

This speech had far-reaching results. The original committee of the Volunteers expelled Redmond's nominees and regained control. Redmond formed a new body, the National Volunteers, which was numerically stronger than the Irish Volunteers but was much less active. There was now the nucleus of an armed force which was outside the control of the parliamentary party. A second result was a wave of volunteering for the British forces. In it were caught up not only those who were impelled by their loyalty to the Crown but also an astonishingly large number of Irish Nationalists who felt no such sentiment but believed that their country, now (as they thought in the first years of the war), on the verge of self-government, was bound in honour to defend

50. The Arms Act, which prohibited the import of arms into Ireland, had been allowed to lapse in 1907.
51. Cf. P. S. O'Hegarty, op. cit., pp. 674–702.
52. Stephen Gwynn, *John Redmond's Last Years*, pp. 154–5.

the liberty of small nations.[53] Even today, Gallipoli and the Somme are remembered more vividly in many Irish homes than any battle of the Second World War.

Volunteering was certainly wasteful of Irish lives. But it might have provided circumstances in which Anglo-Irish relations could have progressed to a peaceful and honourable solution. Such hopes were frustrated by the shift of political power in Great Britain. The war strengthened the position of the Army and correspondingly weakened the position of ministers. Nationalist volunteers were coldly received: no concessions were made to Irish sentiment. Further, in May 1915 the Liberals were forced to admit the Conservatives into a coalition government. This brought into power Unionists such as Bonar Law and Carson, who had been prominent in the Ulster threat of civil war. It became increasingly doubtful if Home Rule would be given to even the south and west of Ireland: it was certain that the resistance of the Unionists had been successful and that Ireland would be divided in some way or another. Thus the constitutional movement suffered shipwreck within sight of harbour. An appeal to arms remained. It was made in Easter Week 1916 by a section of the Irish Volunteers and the Citizen Army under the inspiration of the Irish Republican Brotherhood.[54]

The Anglo-Irish conflict

There is a sense in which the Rising was a very old-fashioned affair; certainly the contrast between what was done in 1916 and what was to be done by Collins in 1920–1 is instructive. No attempt was made at guerilla warfare; the insurgents came into the open, or rather into buildings which could be surrounded and shelled. They relied, as the proclamation of the Republic set out, on 'gallant allies in Europe', the Germans now cast in the role once occupied by the Spaniards and the French.[55] And, again according to the canon, the leaders were executed after the rising had failed.

It is clear that popular feeling, at first hostile to the rebels, swung around after the executions. Pearse had counted on that, regarding

53. The exemplar must be Tom Kettle, who had been a Nationalist Member of Parliament and became the first Professor of the National Economics of Ireland in University College, Dublin. He was killed in France in 1916, leaving the still vivid memory of a deeply attractive personality.

54. See Desmond Ryan, *The Rising*, Golden Eagle Press, Dublin: 1949. Also F. X. Martin, *The Irish Volunteers*, Duffy, Dublin: 1963; M. Caulfield, *The Easter Rebellion*, Muller, London: 1964; T. D. Williams (ed.), *The Irish Struggle*, Routledge & Kegan Paul, London: 1966; and E. Holt, *Protest in Arms*, Putnam, London: 1960.

55. And playing it, it might be added, with no greater degree of usefulness. The reference to 'gallant allies' will not be found in the condensed text of the Proclamation which occupies the plinth of the memorial statue in the General Post Office. The memorial was unveiled in 1935.

the rising not so much as a military operation as an affirmation of nationality. This was dangerous doctrine and in later years Ireland was to be plagued by ideas of a blood sacrifice. But Pearse and his fellow-leaders were prepared to pay the price, and it was successful in 1916.

The following two years saw the failure of renewed attempts to reach a settlement within the constitutional framework. These attempts ended with the failure of the Irish Convention which sat in 1917 and 1918 under the chairmanship of Sir Horace Plunkett. The stumbling block was then as ever the claim of a part of Ulster to exclusion. In the meantime, the Parliamentary party gradually lost support. The Sinn Féin candidates won a series of by-elections during 1917. As a party it had had nothing to do with the Rising: but its name had been associated with Easter Week, inaccurately but not altogether unjustly. It was joined by those who had been interned for some time after Easter Week and by those who despaired of the constitutional movement. At its convention in October 1917 it abandoned the Hungarian policy for a new aim, both wider and more narrow. It declared its aim to be:

securing the international recognition of Ireland as an independent Irish Republic. Having achieved that status, the Irish people may by referendum freely choose their own form of government.[56]

The older Sinn Féin policy had aimed at independence without laying down what constitutional form it should take. The country was now committed to a republic both by the proclamation of Easter Week and by the Sinn Féin resolution. Many took the claim at less than its face-value, believing that something less, though much more than Home Rule, would be achieved. Others took it literally, in 1917 and again in 1922. There was a further change: Arthur Griffith stood down from the leadership in favour of Eamon de Valera, who had been one of the commandants in Easter Week.

It was not long before Sinn Féin became the dominant force throughout the country outside the north-east. It gained further prestige by its part in the successful resistance to an attempt to impose conscription on Ireland in the spring of 1918. Its position was confirmed, if the matter may be put paradoxically, by its suppression by the British government in the following July. It had now supplanted the parliamentary party whose leader, John Redmond, died in March 1918. The end of the First World War brought the dissolution of the parliament which had been elected in such different circumstances in December 1910. The general election of 1918 brought as decisive a change as that of 1885—Sinn Féin won seventy-three seats and Unionists twenty-six. The parliamentary party was reduced to six seats, four of which were held by agreement with Sinn Féin.

56. Cf. P. S. O'Hegarty, op. cit., p. 715.

In January 1919 the Sinn Féin members of parliament met in Dublin and adopted three declarations.[57] The first was a declaration of independence, which ratified the declaration of the Republic. The second was a message to free nations, asking for recognition of the Republic and of Ireland's right to be represented at the Peace Conference at Versailles. The third was a democratic programme, which will be noted later. A skeleton government was set up later, as a *de jure* government which gradually assumed the functions of a government *de facto*, controlling many of the local authorities, instituting courts, and successfully floating a loan. This went on until *Dáil Éireann*, the title which had been adopted for the legislative body, was suppressed as a 'dangerous association' in September 1919.

From 1919 until the Truce in July 1921 a guerilla warfare gradually developed. The British intelligence system in Ireland was destroyed and the armed police force attacked with growing frequency. The number of regular troops in Ireland was greatly increased. Eventually, in 1920, the British government introduced bodies of irregular troops, known since as the Black and Tans. From then onwards, the fighting became more savage.

It has been argued that this last Anglo-Irish struggle was unnecessary and that as much might have been obtained without fighting. Griffith's policy, indeed, had been in favour of passive resistance. But that had been framed ten years before, in the very different circumstances of a long peace. In 1919 physical force and republics were in the air: it could not be expected that the most prudent courses would be followed when barely known nationalities were emerging into independence all over Europe. There was also, above all, the plain fact that no promise of a British government would have been trusted after the fate of the Home Rule Act. Coldly viewed, it certainly did not seem prudent to challenge Great Britain at the hour of victory when the Kaiser had gone the way of Napoleon, and British arms appeared to be invincible. Subsequent decades have shown that victory had been so dearly bought that the British will to rule had been desperately weakened. But no one anywhere—least of all in Ireland—could have foreseen so clearly in 1919.

The events of 1919–21 took place within a strictly political framework. The third declaration adopted by the Dáil in January 1919 envisaged far-reaching social programmes. It began with a reference to Pearse and proceeded:

We declare that the Nation's sovereignty extends not only to all men and women of the Nation, but to all its material possessions, the Nation's soil and

57. All members elected for Irish constituencies were invited. The Unionists and parliamentarians abstained; and half of the Sinn Féin members were in prison. Cf. P. S. O'Hegarty, op. cit., pp. 724–34.

all its resources, all the wealth and all the wealth-producing processes within the Nation, and with him we reaffirm that all right to private property must be subordinated to the public right and welfare.[58]

It may be, as O'Hegarty suggests,[59] that this declaration was taken seriously only by its authors. In any case a government and Dáil that was 'on the run' had more immediate problems to solve. Even when the British administration had broken down over large areas of the country, all attempts to seize and divide large estates were severely repressed by the Irish Republican Army. Similarly, labour in the cities suffered heavily from the growing cost of living; but social and economic issues were put aside for the duration of the political struggle.

These, it should be remembered, were years of rising prices and booming trade. The war sealed the prosperity of Irish farmers who benefited further from the encouragement given to tillage; and the traditional products doubled or trebled in price. The trade returns compiled by the Department of Agriculture show a succession of export surpluses. The boom came to an abrupt end when prices fell heavily in 1920, and the consequences were to provide the new Irish state with one of its worst problems. Nevertheless, Ireland had never traded more heavily or more profitably with Great Britain than during the years of armed conflict between the two countries.

Fighting was ended by a truce in July 1921, and negotiations proceeded until the Anglo-Irish treaty was signed in the following December. This gave the Irish state, now designated as the Irish Free State, the constitutional status of Canada. This implied full autonomy, partly qualified by vestiges of imperial supremacy which Irish, Canadian, and South African ministers joined in removing at subsequent Imperial Conferences.

To Nationalists, the great defects were that Northern Ireland was entitled to opt out of the Free State, subject to a review (which proved abortive) of its boundaries[60] and that an oath to the Crown was prescribed for the members of future Irish parliaments. These were grave defects indeed, and subsequent politics have largely revolved around them. It may be worth while to remember that the Treaty was

---

58. *Minutes of Proceedings of Dáil Éireann*, p. 22.

59. Op. cit., pp. 726–7. He personally, as is obvious from his account, was interested only in the political issue.

60. The Government of Ireland Act in 1920 provided for the establishment of parliaments with limited powers in Dublin and Belfast. These powers were to be, and have been, exercised by the government and parliament of Northern Ireland in the six counties of Antrim, Down, Armagh, Derry, Fermanagh, and Tyrone—the largest area in which an over-all Unionist majority could be assured. The Act was ignored by the Dáil on the ground that Great Britain could no longer legislate for any part of Ireland. But it was obviously of immense importance to northern Unionists that their government and parliament should be in existence before negotiations began.

no more palatable to Great Britain. The unsuccessful attempt to deny Irish self-government had occupied her energies for forty years. It had demanded the sacrifice of time-honoured parliamentary procedure, the destruction of bicameral government and the loss of years in which 'the state of England' might have received attention. These were not all— at the end, Ireland provided an example of triumphant nationalism which was to prove fatal to the British Empire. Many of these things (which were not necessarily welcome to all Irish Nationalists) would no doubt have happened if the Irish question had never existed; but they might not have happened in quite the same way, nor in so short a time.

After a prolonged discussion the Dáil ratified the Treaty in January 1922. By that time, the Sinn Féin movement was visibly divided. The split was primarily a split in the Dáil and in the Irish Republican Army. Those who spoke and voted for the Treaty did not do so because they favoured a Free State as such but because it provided, in Collins's phrase, a stepping-stone to freedom. Many members of the Dáil eventually made their decision through sympathy with Griffith and Collins, the leaders of the delegation that had signed it, or with Mr. de Valera who opposed it.[61] Equally there were some who felt themselves bound by their oath to the Republic. Others cast their vote on lower and less impersonal grounds, such as the deputy of whom Collins predicted 'dishonourably for, or dishonourably against'.[62] It was a true division on a political issue, unaffected by social or economic factors. No doubt the propertied interests favoured acceptance of the Treaty: so did the Labour party.

An interregnum followed in which a provisional government attempted to construct the machinery of administration. It had also to provide itself, more urgently, with an army and police force. The basis of society appeared to be crumbling. Life in Ireland had now been in turmoil for nearly ten years: the ultimate arbiter appeared to be the gun. Later in 1922 Kevin O'Higgins remarked that:

It would perhaps be a generous estimate to say that 20 per cent of the militant opposition to the Government is idealism. I know that there is a percentage, whatever that percentage is. It would be, perhaps, a generous estimate also to say that only 20 per cent of it is crime. And between these two 20 per

61. Mr. Eamon de Valera's scheme of 'external association' closely resembled the position to which he brought Anglo-Irish relations fifteen years later. The British attitude was much more co-operative then than it was in 1921-2. An interesting survey of the change will be found in N. Mansergh, *Survey of British Commonwealth Affairs, Problems of External Policy*, Oxford University Press, London: 1952, pp. 283-7. In an earlier work, *The Irish Free State*, Allen & Unwin, London: 1934, pp. 268-9, the same writer traces the controversy over the oath to a difference of political thought between the two countries rather than to an issue of sovereignty, though that too was involved.

62. Cf. the biography of Collins by Frank O'Connor entitled *The Big Fellow*, Nelson, London: 1937, p. 241.

cents, there flows 60 per cent of sheer futility that is neither one thing nor the other but that will go on until some very definite reason is put up to it why it should not go on.[63]

The fact that, forty years later, the civil war has not yet received a dispassionate examination is easily understood—it is not a subject on which Irish people wish to dwell—but, when that examination is made, it will be clear that a great deal of what happened in 1922 and 1923 had nothing to do with either Free State or Republic.

That indeed soon ceased to be the issue. It became increasingly clear that the ratification of the Treaty by the Dáil would not be accepted by some of the IRA. The position of Griffith, Collins and their supporters was that the Treaty had been accepted by the Dáil; and that it could be rejected by the people at an election, but not by defiance of the parliamentary decision. Once again, O'Higgins summed up the matter. Speaking in May, he said:

But if civil war occurs in Ireland it will not be for the Treaty. It will not be for a Free State versus anything else. It will be for a vital, fundamental, democratic principle—for the right of the people of Ireland to decide any issue, great or small, that arises in the politics of this country.[64]

Unfortunately, a general election was delayed until June. When it was held, the anti-Treaty party received less than one-quarter of the total vote. The long interval between ratification and the election was surely one of the contributory causes of the civil war.

The civil war was fought with great bitterness. Many of the 'irregulars' believed that the republic had been betrayed; many government supporters felt that it must be shown at all costs that an Irish government could govern and that Lord Salisbury's taunt was not justified. Griffith died in August 1922 and Collins was killed in an ambush ten days later; thus the principal figures on the pro-Treaty side vanished from the scene. Mr. Cosgrave took over a government whose prospects of survival looked small indeed. It adopted, in the long run, stern methods of repression, which were successful in so far as armed resistance ceased in the spring of 1923. These methods, it might be added, were endorsed by the electorate, who retained Mr. Cosgrave's government in office through three general elections after the civil war until 1932. This again was not to say that the electorate had a decided preference to a Free State rather than a Republic: first and last, it wanted an end of the rule of gunmen.

All this had consequences which have influenced Irish politics ever since. The Treatyites, as has been said, did not regard the Treaty as an ultimate settlement; they were prepared to defend it in the circum-

63. *PDDE*, 1, 859–60. Quoted by T. de Vere White in his book, *Kevin O'Higgins*, Methuen, London: 1948, p. 123.

64. Official Reports, Dáil Éireann, p. 464, in report of sitting on 19 May 1922.

stances of 1922. In the last resort, Mr. Cosgrave's government rested on the opposition to the rule of violence. After the immediate threat of violence had been removed, his support began to crumble. His government worked out an economic policy which in general served well during the rest of the 1920s; but Mr. de Valera, once he had accepted defeat, had much greater freedom to choose his course.

The second consequence is of still greater importance. The split over the Treaty has governed political life to the present day, even if a great part of the original bitterness has disappeared. It was a vertical, not a horizontal, split; and it has remained so. Thus political life is not organized along the lines of social or economic interest, except in a very general way. Although they spring originally from Westminster, Irish politics are organized on American rather than English lines. Each party contains many diverse interests; the result is that sections, such as the farmers or the trade unions, have never obtained the direct parliamentary representation that their numbers might appear to justify.

Some other influences may be mentioned here. It was provided in 1922 that elections to the Dáil should be conducted by proportional representation. Originally this was intended as a reassurance to the Unionist minority, but that reason has happily been long irrelevant. Its adoption has not prevented the emergence of governments with a clear majority in the Dáil during eighteen of the forty years which have elapsed since the membership of the Dáil became complete in 1927. Strong government, likewise, has been possible even without such a majority, but there have been periods in which an administration has depended on the votes of parties, even of individuals, with no great support in the country as a whole.

The more dangerous possibilities of such a situation have very largely been avoided, because the division created by the civil war has remained dominant in our politics; the stability of governments has therefore been remarkable. In the forty-five years following the establishment of the Irish Free State in December 1922, there have been five changes of government against eight in the United Kingdom.[65]

The evils of that division, however, were notable in that so much political activity revolved for so long around the issues that were disputed in 1922—the oath of allegiance, the sovereignty of the Dáil, and such-like matters. What Bagehot described as 'the educative function' of Parliament has therefore been in eclipse for long periods. This may have been partly owing to the remarkable fact that several leaders, who might have been expected at the time of the Treaty to be prominent for years, were soon removed by death. In 1959 Mr. de Valera retired from active politics in his seventy-seventh year. In 1922, Arthur Griffith

65. In the same period, there have been five heads of Government in Ireland, compared with nine in the United Kingdom.

was aged fifty, Michael Collins thirty-two, and Kevin O'Higgins thirty. One can only guess what course Irish politics would have taken if three men of such strongly marked personality had survived, but one can be reasonably certain that it would have been different from what we know.

Perhaps the deepest consequence of the civil war was the least tangible: the disillusionment that disfigured Irish life for many years. Those who influenced thought before 1914, such as Griffith and Pearse, Plunkett and George Russell, differed widely in their political aims but they all looked forward to a country that would not only possess some form of self-government but would also, and much more importantly, create a new kind of Irish society that would not be merely derivative. Such hopes were brutally disappointed. After the civil war the people of the new State were moved not only by what was then the pervading cynicism which followed the first war but also by what amounted to a loathing of their own recent aspirations. The new government was on the defensive from the start. It had enough to do to create a new State: a new Ireland was beyond its reach. Whatever its wishes might have been it could not go against the sour disillusionment of the time.

This mood was most marked amongst those who had joined the Sinn Féin movement at one time or another before 1921, and it lasted a long time because they were then very young. Many others (it has never suited commentators to consider how many there were) had their own reasons for bitterness: those who mourned the overthrow of the Irish Party, those who had returned from the war to find themselves rejected by all sides and those who had remained loyal to the Union. The last word may be left with George Russell, who belonged to none of these camps.

The champions of physical force have, I am sure, without intent, poisoned the soul of Ireland. All that was exquisite and lovable is dying. They have squandered a spirit created by poets, scholars, and patriots of a different order, spending the treasure lavishly as militarists in all lands do, thinking little of what they squander save that it gives a transitory gilding to their propaganda. With what terrible images have they not populated the Irish soul as substitutes for that lovable life? The very children in the streets play at assassination, ambush, and robbery . . .[66]

Introduction to independence

The new State therefore began its career under the most unfavourable circumstances that could well be imagined. The buoyant optimism of the pre-war years had disappeared. The voluntary bodies that had played such a part in the early years of the century were almost irretrievably weakened; their membership had been divided as deeply as

66. 'Lessons of Revolution', *Studies*, 1923, p. 4.

the rest of the country by the civil war, and their sense of purpose was now almost lost. The first government received no aid from circumstances when it began the framing of policy.

Matters were made worse by the fall in prices after 1920, which affected agriculture with special severity. In the easy years of the wartime boom, many farmers had contracted debts to the banks which proved almost impossible to service, and agricultural credit was almost destroyed. The co-operative movement had suffered most of all, from the erosion of co-operative principles when money was easy to make, from the widespread destruction of creameries by the Black and Tans and from the personal antagonisms created by the civil war. Much ground also had been lost in the export market. Irish agriculture had been a highly important source of supply to Great Britain during the war: it had abused its opportunities in the quality of produce supplied; and now that Denmark was back in the market and New Zealand entering it, the Irish farmer found himself handicapped by his record.

The then fashionable principles of public finance were also highly unfavourable to growth. The 1920s was a period of deflation, of balanced budgets, and of the return to the gold standard. This made things difficult for a new state which had to establish its credit. It did not prevent the implementation of the Shannon Scheme, but it did mean that public finance was ruled by the accepted necessity for economy.[67]

Economic policies since 1922 are the subject of the pages that follow; it is therefore not necessary to do more than sketch the succession of events. The Cosgrave government's policy was founded on giving priority to the improvement of agricultural production for export, on a modified and cautious policy of tariff protection for industry and on the re-establishment of the public finances and the reduction of taxation. The thorough manner in which they worked out a system of priorities between the various sectors of the economy will be commented on favourably in this book. It is fair to remember that they obtained some advantage from the sequence of events. Following its defeat in the civil war, the major opposition party went through a period of difficulties and dissensions. In 1926 Mr. de Valera founded the Fianna Fáil party, and in the following year he took the oath and entered the Dáil.[68]

67. e.g. at the very end of its period of office, immediately before the general election of 1932, the government announced its intention of reducing the pay of national teachers and of the police.

68. This decision was forced on him by the enactment of the Electoral Amendment Bill in August 1927. This measure provided that every candidate for election to either Dáil or Senate should swear an affidavit that, if elected, he would take the oath prescribed by the constitution. Failure to do so would involve disqualification and the vacation of the seat. The aim of the government was to end abstention. That the result would be not only to complete the active membership of the Oireachtas but also to provide an alternative government was foreseen. Cf. Mr. Cosgrave's speech on the Bill, *PDDE*, 20, 1051.

Between 1923 and 1927, therefore, the government had a secure parliamentary majority, balanced only by the Labour Party, whose opposition, under the leadership of Mr. Thomas Johnson, was highly constructive—as its support of the disputed Shannon Scheme proved. By 1927, the main lines of policy had been laid down and the revival of agriculture, under the vigorous direction of Patrick Hogan, was well advanced.

That policy was overwhelmed at the beginning of the 1930s by the great depression. The prices of some Irish products were better maintained than those of other primary producers: cattle prices held up relatively well as late as 1931. The depression, however, brought a temporary ending to emigration and the return of many who had gone to the United States in recent years. This provided an obvious argument for more energetic State policies. Hogan believed that the depression would pass and that his policies of efficiency in production and marketing would bear fruit eventually, but his was an increasingly lonely voice. To many in Ireland, as elsewhere, it seemed as if the depression would go on for ever and that the long reign of the exchange economy had ended, to be replaced by self-sufficiency. This feeling was immensely strengthened by the weight of nationalist tradition which was heavily protectionist. The devaluation of sterling by abandoning the gold standard in September 1931 and the decision of the new British government to reverse the traditional policy of free trade conveyed a deep symbolism.

Other emotions were involved. As an Australian observer noted:

These were the ends which the Cosgrave government pursued with a proud resolution. It was not enough for this government to create out of chaos an Irish state; the new state must prove itself under every head to be a model state ... The Irish Free State under Mr Cosgrave was the objective, the unemotional, scientific, intellectual state. Throughout Europe, and not least in Ireland, people were beginning to tire of this kind of state. They wanted more emotion and more drama. The political artists were pushing aside the political scientists. The party state was challenging the neutral state. In Ireland people were getting tired of their government's very virtues. They were tired of hearing Mr Cosgrave called the just. It did Mr Hogan no good to be labelled the best Minister of Agriculture in Europe ...[69]

The general election of 1932, therefore, brought a change of government. This transfer of power should be carefully examined. It was a change of government from those who had won a civil war ten years

69. Hancock, op. cit., pp. 323–4. But all of this brilliant passage, which might again become relevant to our affairs, should be read. Events between 1921 and 1939 are described, from different stand-points, by Macardle, *The Irish Republic*, The Irish Press, Dublin; O'Sullivan, *The Irish Free State and its Senate*, Faber, London: 1940. T. P. Coogan, *Ireland since the Rising*, Pall Mall Press, London, 1966 and T. Gray, *The Irish Answer*, Hienemann, London, 1966, give a general picture of the whole period since the Treaty.

before to those who had lost it. It took place without incident; the decision of the electorate was accepted by outgoing ministers, the civil service, and the army. Equally, the incoming ministers made no changes in the personnel or structure of the administration which their adversaries had created. It is difficult, it is perhaps impossible, to think of a parallel in modern Europe.

Mr. de Valera's first period of office, from 1932 to 1948, was almost equally divided between peace and war. In his earlier years when an Irish government had some freedom of action, his economic policy was based on high protection for industry and agriculture, dictated by a desire for self-sufficiency. Politically, he felt his way towards a position of external association with the British Commonwealth. Both these policies received added strength from the dispute with the United Kingdom over the land annuities which dragged on from 1932 to 1938. Before this was composed by the Anglo-Irish agreements of 1938 he had achieved his aim of framing a new constitution to replace the original instrument which dated from 1922. The agreements might have initiated a new turn of policy; but in the event, the country was forced into a more stringent self-sufficiency by the outbreak of war in 1939.

A coalition, or 'inter-party' government headed by Mr. J. A. Costello came into office in 1948. It abandoned Mr. de Valera's policy of external association by leaving the Commonwealth. In economic affairs it attached emphatic importance to agriculture but it did not disturb the protective tariffs for industry which it inherited.

Between 1948 and 1957 governments were dependent on small and shifting majorities. Mr. de Valera returned to office in 1951 and was replaced by Mr. Costello's second inter-party government in 1954. In 1957 he secured an over-all majority and formed his last administration. He was elected to the Presidency of the Republic in 1959 when he was succeeded as head of the government by Mr Lemass. In 1966 Mr. Lemass retired and was succeeded by Mr. J. Lynch.

It seems unsatisfactory (though it would certainly be more prudent) to conclude with the foregoing recital of ministerial changes. Something should be said, however selective and subjective it must be, about the altered tone of life in Ireland. It cannot be denied that there are changes: their permanence and their extent are still uncertain. Some of these changes have been caused by the policies of economic development which are described in the pages that follow. Others, which are a great deal more important in an ultimate sense, reflect the slowly developing views of the Irish people on the kind of society they wish to create in their country and what place in the world they envisage for it.

There is a sense in which the Irish people were never sure of their place in the world for years after 1922. Until then, the Irish question had convulsed British politics: governments had been unmade, ministerial careers had been wrecked by it. All this happened on the stage of the world because so much of the world's affairs was settled at Westminster. In 1922 Ireland stepped out of the limelight, no longer with any power to make or break the government of an Empire which itself was not quite what it had been in the confident days of Gladstone and Disraeli. For a time, Irish nationalism became arid, introspective, and unsure of itself.[70]

The first solvent of that aridity might, with some paradox, be traced to a policy which was criticized as being negative and insular— the maintenance of neutrality between 1939 and 1945. That demonstrated, as nothing else could have done, the sovereignty of the new state. It was conducted with superb skill by Mr. de Valera. Perhaps at no time in his long career did he command such universal support as when he defended it against the attack of Mr. Churchill in a famous broadcast at the end of the war in Europe. But there were other consequences. The apparent imminence of invasion in 1940 led to a hasty expansion of the regular and volunteer defence forces. The volunteers came from all sides, from members of the pre-Truce IRA as from those in the National Army and post-Treaty IRA who had fought each other in the Civil War. They were joined by many others who had fought in the last campaigns of the Irish regiments. It was an impressive demonstration of an underlying unity: *idem sentire idem velle idem nolle de re publica.*

For too many years after the war that mood seemed to have been transitory. It was renewed and strengthened during the too few years when Pope John reigned in Rome and John Kennedy in Washington. These two men have left a deep impress on the present generation in Ireland. Perhaps the most attractive part of Irish nationalism has been its antipathy to sectarianism, and the new movement towards ecumenism satisfied a deep longing to be rid of the hatreds that were a legacy from past centuries. It has added a new dimension to life in Ireland, Pope John's memory will be recalled there not only with the affection which he inspired throughout the world but with a special gratitude.

It would be difficult even for a skilled and percipient writer to express what the election of John Kennedy to the American Presidency meant to Irish people. It was not simply that a descendant of Irish emigrants had now assumed the post of greatest power on the earth. Much more important was the lesson that even emigration, for so long a reproach and a symbol of weakness, had somehow worked for good. If such achievement could be plucked from poverty there was no reason

70. The mood is exactly described by Mr. Michael MacLiammoir when he writes of Ireland 'presented a little late in the day at the Court of a post-war world, at this stage very bored not merely with her, but with all the insignia of national entity she has been at such pains to acquire . . .', *Put Money in Thy Purse*, Methuen, London: 1952, p. 58.

why the future should hold any fear for those who lived in a more fortunate age.

There were other signs, during the earlier sixties, that the country was shaking itself free from the repressing and negative parts of its inheritance from history. Those years witnessed a sharply increased rate of economic development which, although it has since been interrupted (partially though not wholly by events outside Irish control), has shown for the future what can be done even in an economy that was stagnant for so long. In wider fields it may be fairly claimed that Ireland has contributed its share to the work of the United Nations. Lastly, and most nearly touching an unhealed wound, the meeting in 1965 between Mr. Lemass and Captain O'Neill, then Prime Minister of Northern Ireland, gave some promise that the bitterness which derived from the racial and religious struggles of the seventeenth century and persisted almost unabated into our own might yet be alleviated.

These hopes have been disappointed: those who live across the border now seem to be more deeply divided than at any time since they were separated from the rest of Ireland. It can only be hoped that the very urgency of the crisis will produce a new way of living together. But if we turn from the condition of our country to regard that of the state in which we live, firmer ground for confidence appears. There are economic difficulties. There have been failures of public policy in both economic and social matters. Nevertheless it may fairly be claimed that freedom has exercised some part of that beneficence which before 1922 it was believed to possess; that, if new issues now face the people of the Republic, at least the old divisions are disappearing, and that self-governing Ireland offers to-day to all its people a kindlier and more hopeful life than at any time in the eight centuries which have been so cursorily surveyed in the preceding pages.

CHAPTER TWO

Labour Force, Production, and National Income

AN EXAMINATION OF THE ECONOMIC GROUPING OF THE population must start from the census of 1926 when the distinction between an occupational and an industrial classification was first fully drawn.[1] Comparisons with earlier census years are, therefore, almost impossible; and it will be seen later that further changes have been made in the occupational classification between 1951 and 1961.

Broadly, the occupational classification covers all persons aged fourteen years and over, including those out of work or temporarily resident in institutions, who are grouped according to their usual occupations. In the industrial classification, gainfully occupied persons who were aged fourteen years and over and were at work on the date of the census are classified according to the industry in which they were engaged. A lorry driver, for example, who is employed by a builder is allocated to the building industry in the industrial classification but is included with road transport workers in the occupation classification.[2]

Table 2.1 shows the number of persons in each occupational group at each census between 1926 and 1951. For most practical purposes the figures are comparable.[3] The reader should be reminded that the total population has fallen during the last three decades. The impact of changes from one occupation to another is the more violent when they occur in a society that is not growing in numbers.

1. Irish occupational statistics have a tangled history which was summarized in *GR*, 1926, pp. 21–3.
2. This example is given in the notes to part ii of volume iii of the Census of 1951.
3. The most important change was that in censuses up to and including that of 1946 some groups employed in the postal services were included with persons in public administration and defence. In 1951 they were included in transport and communications.

TABLE 2.1

Numbers of persons engaged in principal occupational groups, 1926–51

	Actual numbers				Numbers per 100 gainfully occupied			
	1926	1936	1946	1951	1926	1936	1946	1951
Agriculture	670,076	643,965	593,653	512,510	51.3	48.1	45.7	40.3
Fishermen	5,751	4,385	3,647	2,775	0.4	0.3	0.3	0.2
Mining and quarrying	2,599	3,042	3,129	3,782	0.2	0.2	0.2	0.3
Other producers, makers, and repairers	165,236	196,104	187,621	239,014	12.7	14.6	14.5	18.8
Total producers, makers, and repairers	843,662	847,496	788,050	758,081	64.6	63.2	60.7	59.6
Transport and communications	64,873	69,043	59,179	72,645	5.0	5.2	4.6	5.7
Commerce, finance, and insurance	101,052	109,110	102,938	113,372	7.7	8.1	7.9	8.9
Public administration and defence (excluding professional occupations and typists)	37,332	30,840	42,867	31,502	2.9	2.3	3.3	2.5
Professional and technical occupations (excluding clerical staff)	54,656	61,213	70,154	74,654	4.2	4.6	5.4	5.9
Personal service (including institutions, clubs, hotels, etc.)	112,056	115,077	108,638	92,487	8.6	8.6	8.4	7.3
Clerks, typists, and draughtsmen (excluding civil service and local authority clerks)	30,000	37,629	43,720	53,244	2.3	2.8	3.4	4.2
Other gainful occupations	61,289	68,677	82,821	76,053	4.7	5.1	6.4	6.0
Total gainfully occupied	1,304,920	1,339,085	1,298,367	1,272,038	100.0	100.0	100.0	100.0
Total not gainfully occupied	859,995	866,434	884,982	886,489	65.9	64.7	68.2	69.7
Total persons, 14 years of age and over	2,164,915	2,205,519	2,183,349	2,158,527	165.9	164.7	168.2	169.7
Total persons under 14 years of age	807,077	762,901	771,758	802,066	61.8	57.0	59.4	63.1
Total population	2,971,992	2,968,420	2,955,107	2,960,593	227.8	221.7	227.6	232.7

Source: *Census of Population*

Occupational classification

It will be seen that there was a fall in the number of gainfully occupied persons during the period. This was appreciably greater than the fall in population: there was an increase in the number not gainfully occupied, for example housewives and children. The number of 'producers,

TABLE 2.2

Non-agricultural occupations in which more than 5,000 persons were returned in 1951

		Numbers occupied 1951
Over 20,000	Salesmen and shop assistants	46,751
	Unskilled workers (not elsewhere specified)	43,111
	Domestic servants (indoor) living in	39,207
	Clerks (excluding civil service and local authority clerks)	36,105
	Proprietors, managing directors, and managers in trading and in wholesale or retail businesses (excluding publicans)	33,862
	Contractors' labourers, road workers, navvies, etc.	31,818
	Builders', bricklayers', plasterers', and masons' labourers	24,249
	Domestic servants (indoor) living out	21,006
10,000–20,000	Carpenters and joiners	17,966
	Professed clergymen and nuns	17,607
	Teachers (not music teachers)	15,400
	Typists, shorthand typists, and secretaries (not company secretaries)	14,845
	Drivers of self-propelled vehicles and tractors (not agricultural)	19,944
	Civil service officials and clerks	12,025
	Packers, balers and bottlers (not elsewhere specified), and other warehouse assistants	10,141
7,500–10,000	Postmen, post office sorters, and post office assistants	9,001
	Trained nurses and midwives, except mental nurses	8,478
	Barmen and barmaids	7,763
	Messengers	7,561
	Motor and motor-cycle mechanics	7,535
5,000–7,500	Publicans	7,404
	Dressmakers and other light clothing makers	7,353
	Tailors	7,000
	Civic guard—sergeants and lower ranks	6,691
	Army—others	6,548
	Machinists	6,197
	Painters and decorators	6,013
	Articled clerks and pupils and other professional students (except agricultural students)	5,862
	Warehousemen and storekeepers	5,815
	Bakers, pastry cooks, biscuit makers, and ovenmen	5,311
	Waiters, waitresses, and stillroom hands	5,284

Source: *General Report, 1946–51*, Table 80

makers, and repairers' fell by 86,000 from 1926 to 1951. This was almost entirely due to the most striking feature of the table, the continuing decline in the number of those engaged in agricultural occupations, a decline which, as will be seen later, continued during the 1950s. This decline has not been fully offset by the increase of 73,800 in the number of 'other producers, makers, and repairers', the figure for which is given as 188,000 in 1946 and 239,000 in 1951. The figure for 1946, however, was recorded when many manufacturers were working below capacity on account of the shortage of raw materials. Equally, the figure for 1951 may include some unskilled workers who in 1946 were returned in the category of 'other gainful occupations'.

TABLE 2.3

Occupied persons, male and female, 14 years and over, per 1,000 total gainfully occupied, 1951

	Leinster	Munster	Connacht	Ulster (three counties)
Agriculture	236	450	674	603
Other producers	241	184	99	153
Total producers	477	634	773	756
Transport and communication	74	54	28	33
Commerce, finance, and insurance	103	88	63	70
Public administration and defence	36	18	11	12
Professions	69	54	47	40
Personal service:				
Domestic	56	50	26	37
Others	34	21	14	13
Clerks and typists	67	29	13	13
Others gainfully occupied	84	52	25	26
Total gainfully occupied	1,000	1,000	1,000	1,000

Source: *Census of Population, 1951.* vol. iii, part i. Table 3 (*a*)

With two exceptions the other occupational groups increased during these twenty-five years. The fall in 'public administration and defence' was due partly to the re-allocation of postal workers which has been noted and partly to the reduction in the number in the army after 1946. The other fall, in 'personal service' probably reflected the post-war trend out of domestic service.

Generally speaking, however, the period between 1926 and 1951 witnessed a fall in the number of producers, makers, and repairers and an increase in the number engaged in the provision of services. Among producers, there was a sharp fall in the number engaged in agricultural occupations and an increase in the number engaged in non-agricultural occupations.

These trends were not experienced in equal degree throughout the country. Statistics for the provinces are of no great value because the provinces do not correspond to distinguishable economic regions. County boundaries are even less economically distinctive than are the provincial; nevertheless, the reader will note the counties where the proportion of people engaged in agriculture was greatest in 1951.

TABLE 2.4

Numbers in each county of persons in agricultural occupations per 1,000 gainfully occupied

The counties are arranged in order of the figures for 1951

County	1926	1951	County	1926	1951
Leitrim	811	738	Meath	599	537
Mayo	801	712	Kilkenny	578	528
Roscommon	796	712	Tipperary	568	520
Cavan	749	663	Wexford	557	504
Galway	746	636	Westmeath	563	482
Clare	683	634	Carlow	533	477
Longford	733	632	Kildare	448	395
Sligo	704	593	Limerick[1]	457	395
Kerry	656	592	Cork[1]	438	371
Monaghan	685	586	Wicklow	485	358
Donegal	708	577	Waterford[1]	403	336
Laoighis	634	550	Louth	361	239
Offaly	613	541	Dublin[1]	53	34
			TOTAL	513	403

Sources: *Census of Population, 1926*, vol. ii. Table 3 (a); *Census of Population, 1951*, vol. iii, part i. Table 3 (a)

1. Including county borough

In Table 2.4. the counties are arranged in order of magnitude of the proportions of the gainfully occupied population in agricultural occupations. In the west, where the land is less fertile than in most other parts of the country, the proportions of the gainfully occupied population in agricultural occupations are highest, while along the east and south-east coasts the proportions in agricultural occupations are least. The table also shows that the fall since 1926 in the proportions of gainfully occupied persons in agricultural occupations was general throughout the country.[4]

The number of farmers returned at censuses is very much less than the number of occupiers of holdings returned at the annual inquiries for

4. Cf. E. A. Attwood and R. C. Geary, *Irish County Incomes in 1960*, Economic Research Institute, Dublin: Paper No. 16.

the purpose of obtaining agricultural statistics. In 1951,[5] for example, the number of farmers returned was 235,000 while the number of holdings was 379,000. By far the greater part of the discrepancy occurred in the smaller holdings. On holdings of between one and five acres, there were 6,000 farmers and 26,000 holdings; on holdings of between five and ten acres, the figures were 16,000 and 31,000; on holdings of between ten and fifteen acres, 22,000 and 30,000; and on holdings of between fifteen and thirty acres, 65,000 and 86,000. The implication is that many occupiers of small holdings work as agricultural labourers, road workers, etc., and are not full-time farmers. No doubt, the same thing happens at the other end of the scale in so far as large holdings may be occupied by people who are engaged in business or in the professions and are not farmers. But both from the point of view of the numbers involved and of the amount of land, it is well to remember that just under two-thirds of those who occupy land are in fact farmers.

According to the census of 1961, the total number of persons aged 14 and over who were gainfully occupied was 1,108,000. The largest occupational groups were:

Agricultural occupations, 393,000; Commerce, insurance, and finance occupations, 105,000; Service workers, 83,000; Professional and technical occupations, 79,000; Clerks and typists, 78,000; Transport and communication workers, 57,000; Labourers and unskilled workers (n.e.s.), 51,000; Building and construction workers, 49,000.

The grouping of workers in commerce, insurance and finance was largely composed of 44,000 shop assistants and 37,000 proprietors and managers in distributive trades. The total of service workers included 61,000 domestic servants and housekeepers. Professional and technical workers included 20,000 professed clergy and nuns, and 18,000 teachers.

The report of the 1961 census states that the occupational classification then used 'differs fairly considerably from that used at the 1951 Census, the changes being designed to make it possible to conform to international recommendations'.[6] It includes a comparison of occupations and occupational groupings for 1951 and 1961 in which the earlier

5. GR, 1951, p. 85. The figure of 379,000 includes 62,000 holdings of less than one acre or of unspecified size. The results of an experimental inquiry into these matters will be found in volume iii of the Census of 1961 in Tables 10 and 11. It appears that 12,918 farmers and 5,427 farmers' relatives assisting on farms had a subsidiary occupation, usually as labourers or road workers. The majority of them lived on farms of under thirty acres in Connacht and the Ulster counties.

It also appeared that 101,424 persons, not farmers, were landholders. About 78,000 held land in holdings of under five acres.

6. 1961 Census, vol. iii, Stationery Office, Dublin: Pr. 7415, p. iv.

results have been revised according to the 1961 practice.[7] This comparison shows that the total number of persons aged 14 years and over who were gainfully occupied fell from 1,262,000 in 1951 to 1,108,000 in 1961. Among the larger occupational groups there were increases from 68,000 to 79,000 in professional and technical occupations; from 70,000 to 78,000 in clerks and typists, and from 49,000 to 51,000 in labourers and unskilled workers (n.e.s.). Falls were shown in agricultural occupations from 509,000 to 393,000; commerce, insurance and finance occupations, 114,000 to 107,000; service workers 102,000 to 83,000; transport and communication workers, 62,000 to 57,000; and building and construction workers from 70,000 to 50,000.

Industrial classification

The industrial classification based on the 1951 Census is shown in Table 2.5. It will be remembered that it excludes those who were not at work, for example those who were retired or unemployed.

Apart from agriculture, the industrial groupings that contained most people in 1951 were:

Private domestic service	53,000
General building (not under local authorities)	42,000
Building, road repair, etc., for local authorities	33,000
Education	26,000
Retail grocery and provision trade	22,000
Persons in religious profession	18,000
Railways	15,000
Postal services	14,000

None of these groupings, it will be observed, fall under the heading of manufacturing industry. The most numerous subgroups under that heading were:

Handicraft, tailoring, dressmaking, and millinery	10,000
Bread and flour confectionery	9,000
Vehicle repair	9,000
Manufacture of sweets and jams	7,000
Factory manufacture of boots and shoes	7,000
Turf development and production	6,000
Men's clothing	6,000
General carpentry	6,000
Printing, other than newspapers and periodicals	6,000
Manufacture of chemicals, etc.	6,000

These figures will be considered more fully in the chapter dealing with non-agricultural production. It is sufficient to say here that they disclose an economy in which the main sources of employment, other than

7. Ibid., p. 11.

TABLE 2.5

Males and females, 14 years of age and over, at work, classified according to industrial group, 1951

	Thousands Total	Males	Females
Agriculture	493	425	68
Fishing	3	3	—
Mining, quarrying, and turf production	10	10	—
Manufacturing industries of which:	184	124	60
Manufacture of clothing (including boots, shoes)	35	13	22
Manufacture of food	35	24	11
Manufacture of transport equipment	20	19	1
Manufacture of textiles	16	6	10
Manufacture of metal products (excluding machinery, transport equipment)	11	10	1
Construction	85	84	1
Electricity, gas, water, and sanitary services	10	10	—
Commerce	138	90	48
Insurance, banking, finance	12	9	3
Transport, storage, communication	57	51	6
Public administration, defence	41	33	8
Professions	82	37	45
Personal service	85	16	69
Entertainment, sport	11	7	4
Other industries not stated	9	6	3
TOTAL ALL INDUSTRIES	1,220	905	315

Source: *Census of Population*

TABLE 2.6

Persons, males and females, at work, classified by industrial group, 1961

	Males	Thousands Females	Total	Percentage of total at work
Agriculture	334.2	42.1	376.3	35.8
Fishing	2.5	0.0	2.5	0.2
Mining, quarrying, and turf production	9.5	0.1	9.6	0.9
Manufacturing industries of which:	119.5	60.0	179.4	17.0
Food	26.5	10.7	37.2	3.5
Clothing (including boots and shoes)	10.0	18.8	28.8	2.7
Textiles	9.4	11.2	20.6	1.9
Printing and publishing	7.6	3.7	11.3	1.1
Metal products	9.3	1.1	10.4	1.0
Building and construction	58.6	1.0	59.6	5.7
Electricity, gas, and water supply	9.6	0.6	10.2	1.0
Commerce	94.7	48.5	143.2	13.6
Insurance, banking, finance	9.6	4.6	14.2	1.4
Transport, communication, and storage	47.3	6.9	54.2	5.1
Public administration and defence	32.7	7.9	40.6	3.9
Professions	35.0	51.0	86.0	8.2
Personal service	13.8	49.5	63.3	6.0
Entertainment and sport	5.8	5.2	11.0	1.0
Not stated	1.9	0.7	2.5	0.2
TOTAL ALL INDUSTRIES	774.5	278.0	1,052.5	

Source: *Census of Population*

the land, are largely based on construction, distribution, some services, and light industry.

The industrial classification in the census of 1961 is shown in Table 2.6.

The largest subgroupings were as follows: private domestic service 32,000; education 30,000; building and contracting not under local authorities 28,000; grocery and provision retailing 25,000; postal, telegraph, and radio communication 16,000; local authority engineering and construction 16,000.

The largest subgroupings in manufacturing industries were: ready-made outer clothing, 12,000; bread and flour confectionery, 8,000; printing and publishing (other than newspapers and periodicals), 7,000; woollen and worsted textiles, 6,000; boot and shoe manufacture, 6,000; hosiery and knitted goods, 6,000; milk products, 6,000; and turf production, 6,000.

International comparisons, especially if they are made with the countries of western Europe, show that the proportion of the occupied population that is engaged in agriculture is still high in Ireland. The following table shows the percentages of occupied manpower engaged in agriculture in 1967.

Greece	50.1	France	15.8
Portugal	32.3	Denmark	13.1
Ireland	29.6	Germany F.R.	10.2
Spain	29.4	Netherlands	7.5
Italy	22.5	Belgium	5.6
Austria	20.0	United Kingdom	3.1

A comparison of the percentage of the occupied manpower engaged in industry in the same year is equally striking:

Germany F.R.	48.2	Denmark	38.4
United Kingdom	46.7	Austria	40.3
Belgium	44.9	Spain	36.6
Italy	41.8	Portugal	36.2
Netherlands	41.3	Ireland	28.7
France	40.4	Greece	21.2

It will be seen that the number of employees in the labour force has increased both absolutely and relatively since 1926. This may be attributed to the growth of manufacturing and some services on one side and to the fall in the numbers in agriculture (which includes many self-employed and relatives assisting) on the other. Nevertheless, employees still constitute a much smaller proportion of the labour force in Ireland than in any other country in Western Europe, 59 per cent in 1961 compared with 88 per cent in the United Kingdom (1951), 79 per cent in the Netherlands (1960); 74 per cent in Denmark (1955); and 62 per cent in Austria (1961).[8]

TABLE 2.7

Employment status of persons fourteen years of age and over in 1961 with comparative figures for 1926 and 1951

	Thousands			Percentages		
	1926	1951	1961	1926	1951	1961
Employers	79	58	33	6.1	4.6	2.9
On own account	295	270	253	22.6	21.4	22.8
Relatives assisting	268	181	117	20.5	14.3	10.7
Employees	578	708	650	44.3	56.1	58.6
Out of work, etc.	85	45	55	6.5	3.6	5.0
	1,305	1,262	1,108	100.0	100.0	100.0

Source: *Census of Population.* The figures are not fully comparable on account of changes in classification

Unemployment

The figures in Table 2.8 should not be used to press comparisons between one period and another. The Unemployment Assistance Act of 1933 extended assistance to persons who had never been employed or gainfully

TABLE 2.8

Average numbers on the live register, 1930–68

	Claimants to benefit	Total live register
1930	12,080	22,176
1935	18,410	119,497
1940	23,318	84,054
1945	17,624	60,682
1950	16,632	53,793
1955	30,495	55,992
1960	28,412	52,668
1962	26,217	46,519
1963	28,352	50,202
1964	27,625	48,950
1965	27,660	49,669
1966	31,016	48,178
1967	31,660	55,067
1968	35,318	58,064

Source: *Reports of Department of Social Welfare*

occupied, as well as to a numerous class of persons who were working on their own account (for example, small farmers and relatives assisting them, whose means did not exceed a statutory limit) and would not

8. Cf. D. O'Mahony, *Economic Aspects of Industrial Relations*, Economic Research Institute, Dublin: Paper No. 24, p. 1.

TABLE 2.9

Population of each province classified by social group and numbers in each social group per 1,000 population in each province, 1961.

		Social group											
Area	Total	Farmers, farmers' relatives, and farm managers	Other agricultural occupations and fishermen	Higher professional	Lower professional	Employers and managers	Salaried employees	Intermediate non-manual workers	Other non-manual workers	Skilled manual workers	Semi-skilled manual workers	Unskilled manual workers	Unknown
Dublin County Borough and Dun Laoghaire Borough	585,240	1,462	5,355	19,985	20,993	27,958	17,389	119,220	88,451	114,899	89,635	56,564	32,329
Rest of Leinster	746,909	170,866	95,558	19,409	20,579	26,022	11,612	85,222	65,891	99,934	49,507	56,827	42,725
Munster	849,203	254,095	72,849	17,895	23,553	22,815	12,389	92,956	76,060	104,564	55,139	71,481	45,407
Connacht	419,465	244,066	12,961	7,097	11,472	8,318	3,391	32,207	20,677	28,007	10,716	22,788	17,765
Ulster (part of)	217,524	100,038	15,929	3,209	6,012	4,440	1,516	19,088	14,742	18,194	7,623	17,447	9,286
TOTAL	2,818,341	770,527	202,652	67,595	82,609	89,553	49,054	348,693	265,821	365,598	203,620	225,107	147,512

Numbers per 1,000 total population

Area	Total	Farmers, farmers' relatives, and farm managers	Other agricultural occupations and fishermen	Higher professional	Lower professional	Employers and managers	Salaried employees	Intermediate non-manual workers	Other non-manual workers	Skilled manual workers	Semi-skilled manual workers	Unskilled manual workers	Unknown
Dublin County Borough and Dun Laoghaire Borough	1,000	2	10	34	36	48	30	204	151	196	138	96	55
Rest of Leinster	1,000	229	128	26	28	35	19	114	88	133	67	76	57
Munster	1,000	299	86	21	28	27	15	109	90	123	65	84	53
Connacht	1,000	581	31	17	27	20	8	77	49	67	26	54	43
Ulster (part of)	1,000	459	73	15	27	20	8	88	68	83	35	81	43
TOTAL	1,000	273	71	24	29	32	18	124	95	130	72	79	53

Source: *Census of Population*

otherwise be regarded as unemployed according to the accepted meaning of the term. At certain times of the year between March and October unemployment assistance is restricted, so that comparisons between Live Register figures for different months of any year or between corresponding months of different years are vitiated to some extent. Under the Social Welfare Act of 1952 and amending legislation the number registering has been increased by the coverage of male employees in domestic service and agriculture. Further changes have been made by the Social Welfare (Miscellaneous Provisions) Act of 1965. A revised method of compiling the unemployment statistics was therefore introduced in January 1966. It is described in the issue of the *Irish Statistical Bulletin* for December 1965.

Socio-economic groupings

Reference should be made to an innovation in the census of 1951. This was an attempt to classify persons by the socio-economic group (e.g. higher or lower professions or skilled, semi-skilled, and unskilled wage-earners) to which they belonged or on which they were dependent. Thus persons who were or had been gainfully occupied were assigned to the social group to which their occupation was considered to belong. Persons not gainfully occupied were assigned to the social group of the head of the household if the head was gainfully occupied, otherwise to the social group of the principal breadwinner.

The experiment was repeated in the census of 1961; and the principal results are shown in Table 2.9. The variations between one area and another are a striking feature of this Table. For the country as a whole about 34 per cent of the population were in the agricultural social groups. The proportion in Leinster, exclusive of Dublin and Dun Laoghaire, was not greatly different: it was rather higher in Munster. But the proportions in Connacht and the Ulster counties are so much greater as to suggest a different type of society. The figures for other social groups show similar contrasts. If the figures for counties were set out, it would be seen that the counties of the west and north-west have the highest proportions in the agricultural social groups and the lowest proportions in the groups of skilled manual wage-earners and of non-manual wage-earners.

PRODUCTION

Agricultural

The definitions used in the measurement of agricultural output will be found in the prefatory notes to the agricultural section of the annual *Statistical Abstract*. Gross agricultural output is defined as:

that part of total agricultural production which is sold off farms or which is consumed by persons on farms during the year of enquiry. It may include the value of changes in livestock numbers during the year. It does not however include any part of the produce used for further agricultural production on the farm on which it was produced or which was sold by one farmer to another: for example, milk fed to calves, potatoes fed to pigs, turnips and mangels fed to cattle and livestock sold by one farmer to another.

Net output is obtained by deducting from the value of gross output the value of fertilizers and of feeds and seeds purchased from other sectors of the economy or imported.[9]

Estimates of the quantity and value of agricultural output for 1926–7 were given in a report entitled *The Agricultural Output of Saorstát*

TABLE 2.10

Estimated value of agricultural output (£ thousand), 1926–68

	Gross output	Farm materials purchased	Net output
1926–7	57,837	8,549	49,288
1929–30	61,387	9,924	51,463
1934–5	38,813	6,725	32,088
1938–9	52,223	8,698	43,525
1946	103,601	8,820	94,781
1953	171,924	29,537	142,387
1958	178,301	35,792	142,509
1960	191,407	32,257	159,150
1962	209,042	41,234	167,808
1963	211,437	43,524	167,913
1964	230,422	45,502	184,920
1965	232,407	53,848	178,559
1966	242,528	53,811	188,717
1967	272,248	57,350	214,898
1968	298,292	66,597	231,695

Including turf but excluding changes in livestock numbers

Source: *Irish Statistical Bulletin*

9. This figure should not be confused with 'income arising in Agriculture', for which further inputs (e.g. rates, fuel, depreciation of machinery, marketing costs, etc.) must be subtracted from net output. Again 'income arising in Agriculture' is not the same as 'profits of farmers and members of their families'. To arrive at the latter figure, wages and salaries of employees are deducted from income arising in agriculture.

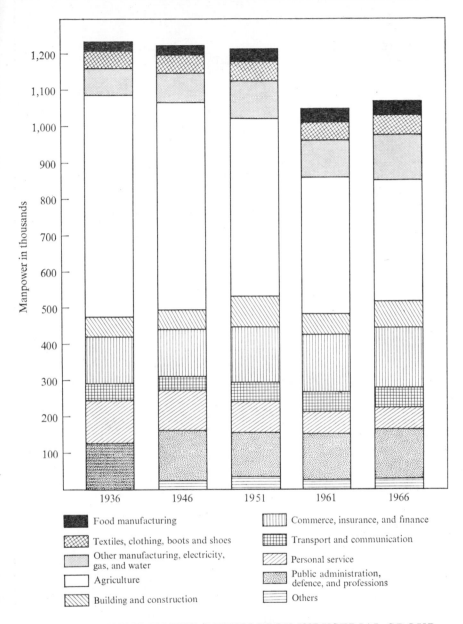

Manpower in thousands

| | 1936 | 1946 | 1951 | 1961 | 1966 |

Legend:
- Food manufacturing
- Textiles, clothing, boots and shoes
- Other manufacturing, electricity, gas, and water
- Agriculture
- Building and construction
- Commerce, insurance, and finance
- Transport and communication
- Personal service
- Public administration, defence, and professions
- Others

2. EMPLOYMENT IN THE REPUBLIC BY INDUSTRIAL GROUP

In 1936 Public Administration, Defence, the professions, and others, were grouped together statistically (see double hatching in col. 1) but were shown separately from 1946 onwards. There was no full census in 1941 or 1956. Figures taken from *Statistical Abstract of Ireland*.

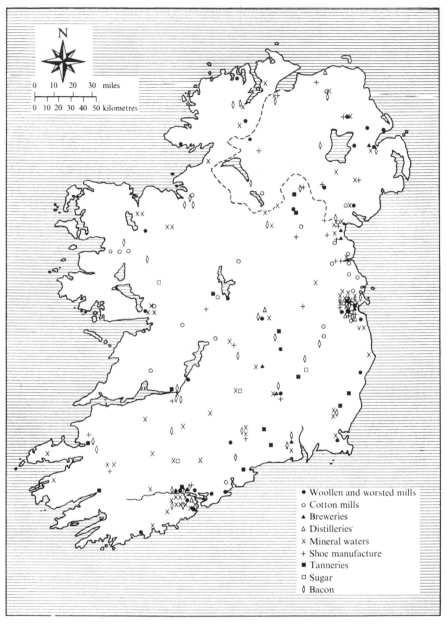

- ● Woollen and worsted mills
- ○ Cotton mills
- ▲ Breweries
- △ Distilleries·
- ✕ Mineral waters
- + Shoe manufacture
- ■ Tanneries
- □ Sugar
- ◊ Bacon

3. DISTRIBUTION OF INDUSTRY
AGRICULTURAL AND ASSOCIATED PRODUCTS

Woollen, worsted, and cotton industries are prominent in Dublin, Co. Cork, and Co. Donegal. Small-scale woollen industries exist in other towns and villages. Dublin, Cork, Dundalk, and Tullamore are the main centres for distilling and brewing. Leather industries have shown a marked advance in recent years not only in Cork, Dublin, Drogheda, and Dundalk, but also in many smaller towns and villages. The main sugar-beet factories are at Carlow, Thurles, Mallow, and Tuam. Bacon manufacture is scattered throughout the country.

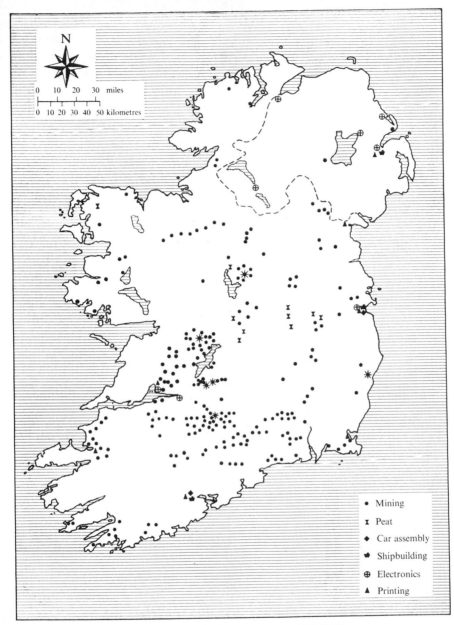

4. DISTRIBUTION OF INDUSTRY
SITES OF PRINCIPAL MANUFACTURING INDUSTRIES

Modern exploration has extended mineral mining, previously confined to the outcrop hills and the sea coast, to the plains of the midlands. The main metalliferous ore producing centres (star–dot) are Tynagh (lead–zinc–silver–copper), Gortdrum (copper–silver–mercury), Silvermines (lead–zinc–silver), Ballynoe (barytes), Keel (zinc–lead), Avoca (copper–iron). The main coal mining areas are Co. Tipperary, Co. Carlow, and Co. Tyrone. The newer electronics industries are based at Dublin, Limerick, Shannon, Antrim, Belfast, Enniskillen, Larne, and Londonderry.

Éireann, 1926–27.[10] Estimates were also made for 1929–30 and next for 1934–5. All the estimates of agricultural output from 1926–7 to 1956 have been included in a report entitled *Agricultural Statistics 1934–56.*[11]

TABLE 2.11

Index numbers of volume of agricultural output, 1926–68

	Livestock and livestock products	Crops and turf	Gross output	Farm materials purchased	Net output
		1938–9 = 100			
1926–7	99.4	90.8	97.2	89.5	98.8
1929–30	106.5	88.3	102.0	92.5	103.9
1934–5	100.2	97.8	99.6	83.2	102.9
1938–9	100.0	100.0	100.0	100.0	100.0
1946	90.3	126.3	99.2	51.1	108.8
1953	99.3	127.1	106.2	99.9	107.4
		1953 = 100			
1958	108.5	80.4	101.8	125.8	96.9
1960	114.9	105.5	112.6	126.3	109.8
1962	122.3	113.1	120.1	164.2	110.9
1963	126.4	103.6	121.0	173.1	110.2
1964	129.7	100.2	122.7	178.4	111.2
1965	129.7	89.4	120.1	201.8	102.9
1966	136.9	89.7	125.7	198.0	110.7
1967	146.1	101.2	135.4	208.4	120.2
1968	144.4	120.9	138.8	229.5	120.0

Including turf but excluding changes in livestock numbers

Source: *Irish Statistical Bulletin*

In the two preceding tables attention should be paid to the return of 'farm materials purchased'. This represents the estimated amount paid by farmers for fertilizers, feeding stuffs, and seeds purchased from merchants and used in producing the gross output for the year in question.[12] It was a long-standing characteristic of Irish agriculture that input into the soil was low.[13] During the Second World War, when imports were not available, the index number for farm materials purchased fell to exceptionally low levels, such as 18.1 in 1942–3 and 30.7 in 1943–4 (base 1938–9=100).[14] It will be seen that there has been a marked expansion under this heading in recent years.

10. P. 132, Stationery Office, Dublin.
11. Pr. 4335, Stationery Office, Dublin.
12. Cf. *ISB*, 1964, p. 72.
13. Cf. T. Walsh, P. F. Ryan, and J. Kilroy, 'A Half-Century of Fertiliser and Lime Use in Ireland', *JSSISI*, 1956–7, p. 104. T. K. Whitaker noted that in 1956 little more than half the hay crop and only 36 per cent of permanent pasture received any fertilizer whatsoever. *Economic Development*, Pr. 4803, Stationery Office, Dublin, pp. 61–8.
14. Cf. *ITJ*, 1947, p. 187.

Industrial

The first census of industrial production was taken in respect of the year 1926, the second for 1929 and the third for 1931. Censuses have been taken regularly since then but those for the years 1932–5 were restricted to certain manufacturing industries and those for the years 1939–42 covered transportable goods industries only. The census covers transportable goods (that is, manufacturing industries *plus* mining, quarrying, and turf) and building, construction, and service-type industries (for example, gas and waterworks, electricity, dyeing and cleaning). The two categories together constitute 'all industries' in Table 2.12.

TABLE 2.12

Value of industrial production (£ thousand): all industries, 1926–67

Year	Gross output	Cost of materials, etc.	Net output	Salaries and wages
1926	59,477	36,399	23,078	13,671
1938	89,996	53,964	36,032	21,429
1947	185,274	118,464	66,810	39,129
1953	393,019	268,476	124,543	73,138
1959	475,546	313,502	162,044	89,213
1963	679,398	436,927	242,471	133,290
1964	750,882	477,145	273,736	153,154
1965	805,917	507,926	297,992	162,235
1966	866,644	535,179	331,465	179,888
1967	976,969	600,275	376,694	195,906

Source: *Census of Industrial Production*

TABLE 2.13

Value of industrial production (£ thousand): transportable goods, 1926–67

Year	Gross output	Cost of materials, etc.	Net output	Salaries and wages
1926	49,360	32,953	16,407	7,865
1938	73,098	47,825	25,273	13,010
1947	156,943	107,151	49,792	25,737
1953	328,945	239,773	89,172	47,138
1959	406,861	285,095	121,766	62,892
1963	571,352	388,230	183,122	94,298
1964	628,373	422,504	205,869	107,430
1965	672,794	449,725	223,069	113,063
1966	714,577	466,746	247,831	124,186
1967	808,936	523,725	285,211	136,290

Source: *Census of Industrial Production*

The figures for 1926 are not strictly comparable with those for other years on account of changes in classification and coverage. The changes, however, were not so great as to make comparisons misleading.

In reading these tables, it will be remembered that the first tariffs protecting native industries were imposed in 1924, and that the policy of all-round protection dates from 1932. The effect of restricted access

TABLE 2.14

Indices of volume of industrial production, 1926–67

Base, 1953 = 100

Year	All industries and services covered by Census of Industrial Production	Transportable goods
1926	33.6	35.2
1938	54.7	53.6
1943	39.9	44.1
1947	62.1	65.2
1953	100.0	100.0
1959	110.9	117.5
1961	128.8	137.4
1963	146.0	153.5
1964	157.1	165.3
1965	163.6	172.2
1966	168.8	180.4
1967	182.2	195.8

Source: *Census of Industrial Production*

to raw materials during the war will be noted; much the same results flowed from the imposition of levies on imports, arising out of a balance of payments crisis, in 1956. Between 1946 and 1955 there was a period of rapid expansion followed by diminishing progress and actual retrogression until towards the end of the 1950s. But by 1965 industrial production in the transportable goods industries was 72.2 per cent greater than in 1953.

NATIONAL INCOME

The first estimate of national income covered the year 1926. It was made by Dr. T. J. Kiernan and was published in the *Economic Journal* for March 1933. Dr. Kiernan also communicated a paper on the national expenditure in the same year[15] to the Statistical Society.

The report of the 1938 Banking Commission included estimates of national income from 1929 to 1935, which were made by Professor George Duncan. Dr. Kiernan's estimate for 1926 was £164.5m. Professor Duncan's estimates showed national income at £161.7m. in 1929, falling to £140.1m. in 1933, and recovering to £149.2m. in 1935. The general accuracy of these estimates was endorsed by the Commission

15. T. J. Kiernan, 'The Net Expenditure of the Irish Free State in 1926', *JSSISI*, 1932–3, p. 91.

which remarked that 'the congruence of these estimates independently arrived at by different methods offer good grounds for the belief that they lie reasonably near the truth'.[16] In later papers to the Statistical Society, Professor Duncan provided further estimates, of £156.3m. in 1938 and £154.5m. in 1939.[17] He remarked on the disquieting failure of these totals to regain the levels of 1929.

The first official estimates covered national income and expenditure in the years 1938–44. These tables were revised in later years.[18] The concepts of national income and production which are employed in the Irish statistics conform to general practice. There are, however, some social and economic factors peculiar to this country and to its social framework which should be noted.

(1) A great deal of labour is either unpaid or paid at nominal rates.

There is still a high proportion of family labour on the farm and in the shop. Hospitals and schools are largely conducted by religious orders. There is a high proportion of self-employed persons, whose incomes are difficult to ascertain with accuracy. This difficulty arises also in the case of many who belong to more than one occupational group, for example, who combine ownership of a farm with the conduct of a professional practice or of a shop. Contractual employment is increasing and unpaid family labour is less general than it was even twenty years ago; nevertheless the presence of these factors must affect the total of national income.

(2) The proportion of persons in the young and elderly dependent age-groups is unusually high in Ireland.[19]

(3) Agriculture is conducted on family farms and is partly a subsistence economy.

A comparatively high proportion of production is consumed on the farm, without process of sale, either by the family or by livestock. In the

16. *BC*, 1938, paras. 116–17 and appendix 7.

17. G. A. Duncan, *JSSISI*, 1939–40, p. 1, and *JSSISI*, 1940–1, p. 140. See also, M. D. McCarthy and others, 'Symposium on National Income and Social Accounts', *JSSISI*, 1951–2, p. 473; Carter and Robson, 'Comparison of National Income and Social Accounts of Northern Ireland, the Republic of Ireland and the United Kingdom', *JSSISI*, 1954–5, p. 62. Also Broderick, 'Analysis of Government Revenue and Expenditure in relation to National Accounts', *JSSISI*, 1959–60, p. 132. More recent approaches have been made by P. M. Quinlan, 'A Dynamic Model of the Irish Economy', *JSSISI*, 1961–2, p. 1, and by R. C. Geary, 'Towards an Input-Output Decision Model for Ireland', *JSSISI*, 1963–4, p. 67.

18. *National Income and Expenditure, 1938–44*, Stationery Office, Dublin, P. 7356 and *Tables of National Income and Expenditure, 1938 and 1944–50*, Stationery Office, Dublin, Pr. 350.

19. On the other hand, the importance of the family in Irish society may mean that the level of family income is much higher than the sum of individual incomes may suggest. Cf. a fascinating paper by R. C. Geary, 'The Family in Irish Census of Population Statistics', *JSSISI*, 1954–5, p. 1.

Irish statistics the estimated produce so consumed is valued at current agricultural prices and is counted into agricultural income. In the 1962 estimates this figure amounted to £28m. out of a total of £124m. It is highly important to remember that so high a proportion of agricultural income is, in fact, non-monetary. The further point arises that there is 'a substantial non-monetary element' in the figure of personal savings.[20]

(4) There is an element of uncertainty in the figures for trade and balance of payments, which to some extent eludes estimation, such as the operations of Irish residents who conduct their stock exchange transactions through London stockbrokers.

The figures for these activities are, of course, more relevant to the trade and balance of payment figures, but they must necessarily influence figures of national income to some extent. These considerations should be borne in mind in comparisons of the Irish national income with other countries.[21]

The national income increased by 45.0 per cent between 1953 and 1962 since when growth has been high but fluctuating:

1959	1960	1961	1962	1963	1964	1965	1966	1967
6.0	7.0	8.0	7.2	5.8	12.9	6.3	3.4	8.0

The earlier performance was very different. In money terms, for example, the national income in 1956 was slightly lower than it had been in the previous year.

Valued at constant market prices the gross national product grew by only 2.5 per cent over the entire period between 1952 and 1958. Indeed, it did not exceed the 1955 level until 1959. Since then, however, there have been successive increases over the previous year as follows:

1960	1961	1962	1963	1964	1965	1966	1967
4.7	4.7	2.9	3.9	4.6	2.3	1.7	4.1

International comparisons in this field are notoriously dangerous; nevertheless, they are often used, for example during the discussions held in Brussels on the Irish application in 1962 for membership of the E E C. Here is a comparative table:

Gross national product per capita (U.S.A. dollars), 1968

U.S.A.	4,380	Germany F.R.	2,200	Italy	1,390
Sweden	3,230	Belgium	2,160	Ireland[1]	1,070
Switzerland	2,790	Netherlands	1,980	Greece	860
Denmark	2,540	United Kingdom	1,850	Spain	770
Norway	2,530	Austria	1,550	Portugal	530
France	2,360				

1. 1967

20. Cf. *National Income and Expenditure 1964*, Pr. 8716, Stationery Office, Dublin, p. 34, where definitions of national income etc. will be found.

21. It is not irrelevant that expenditure on defence in Ireland is almost negligible in contrast with other European countries.

When we turn to the *growth rate* of the gross national product, calculated at constant prices there are also interesting comparisons:

Growth rate of gross national product per capita, 1953–61

(Percentages)

Austria	62.8	France	32.6
Germany		Denmark	29.2
(Federal Republic including		Ireland	20.1
the Saar in 1961)	57.6	United Kingdom	19.9
Italy	54.2		

In reading this comparison it must be remembered that this period includes several years during which growth was severely limited in Ireland. During this same period the population of the Irish Republic declined while that of all other countries mentioned increased.

TABLE 2.15

National income (£ million), 1938–68

	1938	1948	1953	1966	1967	1968
Income from agriculture, forestry and fishing						
Wages and salaries[1]	6.7	15.5	15.6	21.0	20	21
Profits[2]	28.2	73.8	108.2	135.4	148	172
Non-agricultural income:						
Wages, salaries, pensions[1]	69.9	140.2	204.0	482.9	519	574
Other income	40.3	65.3	79.9	166.4	177	198
Net foreign income[3]	12.3	24.6	28.7	43.7	46	48
Stock appreciation	n.a.	−0.3	+2.9	−9.5	−8	−15
Total national income	157.4	319.1	439.3	839.9	902	998

Source: *National Income and Expenditure*

1. Including employers' contributions to social insurance.
2. Including income of farmers and members of their families.
3. Net inflow of profits, dividends, wages, pensions, emigrants' remittances, etc.

The proportion of income arising in the agricultural sector was 23.6 per cent in 1938 when that sector was only emerging from the economic war. It rose to 29 per cent in 1952 and in 1963 it was 21 per cent. The fact that much of the income attributed to the sector is non-monetary obscures the difficulties which are caused by increasing money costs.

Two related features of Table 2.17 are outstanding. The first is the very high proportion of national expenditure which is devoted to personal expenditure on consumer goods and services. This has altered very little in recent years, being 72.7 per cent in 1953, 72.1 per cent in 1961, and 72.0 per cent in 1962. In 1938, it was as high as 77.0 per cent but in that year, unlike more recent years, the country was not engaged in programmes of capital investment. The limitations within which

TABLE 2.16

Net national product at factor cost by sector of origin and gross national product at market prices (£ million), 1938–68

	1938	1948	1953	1963	1965	1966	1967[2]	1968[2]
Agriculture, forestry, and fishing A	37.1	92.2	15.6	16.7	19.2	19	171	196
B			111.1	125.1	147.5	140		
Industry A		72.1	88.2	157.9	192.6	208	288	323
B			26.1	48.2	55.3	57		
Distribution, transport, and communication A		53.8	42.5	74.8	91.2	100	151	166
B			22.9	38.9	42.5	43		
Public administration and defence A	108.0	17.3	24.9	39.2	50.9	54	56	61
Other domestic[1] A		58.9	47.8	87.7	109.7	118	198	219
B			28.2	53.2	61.8	64		
Adjustment for stock appreciation		−0.3	+2.9	−3.7	−5.1	−10	−8	−15
Rest of world: emigrants' remittances	3.0	8.4	10.7	12.8	14.1	15	46	48
Other	9.3	16.2	18.0	24.2	29.2	28		
Net national product at factor cost = national income	157.4	318.6	438.9	673.9	808.9	836	902	998
Plus provision for depreciation	4.2	13.5	21.8	59.7	71.6	77	83	91
Gross national product at factor cost	161.6	332.1	460.7	733.6	880.5	913	985	1089
Plus taxes on expenditure	24.1	52.4	78.4	131.5	168.5	190	157	171
Minus subsidies	−2.0	−19.6	−13.5	−28.5	−38.6	−42		
Gross national product at market prices	183.7	364.9	525.6	836.6	1010.4	1061	1142	1260

1. Including rent. 2. Estimated. A. Remuneration of employees. B. Other.

Source: *National Income and Expenditure*

such programmes must be conducted are indicated by the fact that the proportion of national expenditure represented by gross domestic capital formation was 15.4 per cent in 1953, 13.1 per cent in 1960, 14.5 per cent in 1961, and 15.4 per cent in 1962.[22]

TABLE 2.17

Expenditure on gross national product at current market prices (£ million), 1948–68

	1948	1958	1964	1965	1966	1967	1968
Personal expenditure on consumers' goods and services	292.1	459.3	665.9	704.4	739.2	772	849
Net expenditure by public authorities	42.6	70.7	118.9	129.6	135.5	146	164
Gross domestic fixed capital formation	40.9	79.8	174.2	198.1	195.0	215	255
Value of physical changes in stocks	+9.1	−7.7	+18.4	+22.5	+9.4	−6	+12
Exports of goods and services	135.0	205.0	338.0	353.0	383.3	429	493
Less imports of goods and services	−154.6	−206.0	−369.4	−394.8	−399.4	−414	−513
Gross national product at current market prices	365.1	601.1	946.0	1,012.8	1063.0	1,142	1,260

1. Estimated

Source: *National Income and Expenditure*

Comparable percentages for other countries in the period 1953–61 were 29.6 per cent in Norway, 23.3 per cent in the Netherlands, 22.9 per cent in Germany F.R., 22.6 per cent in Austria, 21 per cent in Sweden, 16.5 per cent in Belgium (1953–60), and 15.3 per cent in the United Kingdom.

Table 2.18 also shows the total sums available for capital formation. Ideally, however, the amounts should not be swollen by liquidation of external assets. To repatriate these assets may or may not be a proper policy on other grounds, but it is certainly not satisfactory that repatriation must occur simply because the volume of savings is insufficient. The volume of personal savings also has fluctuated very sharply in the past. Apart from changes shown in the table, there were swings from £20.2m. in 1951 to £41.0m. in 1953 and to £29.4m. in 1955. In the period 1950–5 current savings as a proportion of national income were 21 per cent in the Netherlands, 19 per cent in Norway, 14 per cent in Denmark. In Ireland they were 9.5 per cent against 7.8 per cent in the United Kingdom.

22. But it increased to 18 per cent in 1963, 18.5 per cent in 1964, and 19.5 per cent in 1965.

TABLE 2.18

Savings and amounts available for investment (£ million), 1938–68

	1938	1948	1958	1966	1967	1968
Savings before adjustment for stock appreciation						
Personal	7.4	9.4	17.9	85.7	107	
Companies	4.7	10.2	11.6	20.2	25	171
Public authorities	3.0	− 2.4	7.1	16.2	17	
	15.1	17.2	36.6	122.1	149	171
Stock appreciation	n.a.	−0.3	+0.7	−9.5	−8	−15
	15.1	16.9	37.3	112.6	141	156
Provisions for depreciation	4.2	13.5	33.8	75.7	83	91
Net foreign disinvestment	−2.0	+19.6	+1.0	+16.1	−15	+20
Gross domestic physical capital available for investment	17.3	50.0	72.1	204.4	209	267

Source: *National Income and Expenditure*

Table 2.18 must be interpreted with care. The general formula is that current savings, plus provision for depreciation, plus foreign disinvestment, equals gross domestic physical capital formation, but in the provision for depreciation the figure for depreciation in the agricultural sector is an allowance based on the National Farm Survey[23] covering machinery and farm equipment only. The figure for public authorities is again conjectural. The figure for foreign disinvestment should not be taken as firm. The figure for personal savings is a residual, moreover it contains a non-monetary element as it includes the effect of changes in livestock and certain other sections. Nothing has appeared to invalidate the substantial correspondence of these figures with the facts, but, as much emphasis has been laid on the figure for savings, and especially for personal savings, it is proper to point out that their reliability must be subject to some, though not to vital, qualification.

TABLE 2.19

Capital formation (£ million), 1938–66

	1938	1948	1958	1964	1965	1966
Building and construction	6.0	21.7	42.6	100.4	114.2	112
Other home produced capital goods (net of exports)	8.0 ⎱	19.2	12.8	23.6	24.4	25
Imported capital goods	3.1 ⎰		24.4	50.1	59.3	57
Value of change in numbers of livestock on farms	+0.2	+3.9	+3.2	+9.7	+20.1	+6
Increase in value of non-agricultural stocks and work in progress	n.a.	+5.5	−11.6	+19.1	+7.9	+13
Adjustment for stock appreciation	n.a.	−0.3	+0.7	−10.4	−5.1	−10
Total capital formation	17.3	50.0	72.1	192.5	220.8	203

Source: *National Income and Expenditure*

In interpreting Table 2.19 it should be remembered that the classification can be misleading. Thus, imported capital goods include heavy machinery but may also include lorries. The second point is the very great preponderance of building and construction in the table of capital formation which has been characteristic of the entire post-war period.

23. Pr. 6180, Stationery Office, Dublin.

PRICES AND EARNINGS

The course of prices may be traced through three indexes—(a) the agricultural price index; (b) the consumer price index which has replaced the old cost of living index; (c) the wholesale price index.[24]

Agricultural prices

The agricultural price index was originally based on the average of agricultural prices in the years 1911–13.[25] This index stood at 288 in 1920 but, on account of the world deflation, it had fallen to 132 by 1927. There was a small recovery to 139 in 1929 but thereafter there was a continued decline, to 98 in 1932, to 84 in the two years following, and to 83 in 1935. There was then a recovery to 105 in 1937 and 121 in 1939.

TABLE 2.20

Agricultural prices index, 1945–68

| | | 1953 = 100 | | |
	Livestock	Livestock products	Crops	Total index
1945	52	65	74	60
1947	65	76	80	71
1951	90	90	96	91
1955	106.9	100.3	96.3	103.1
1957	101.6	97.3	97.6	99.8
1959	106.9	95.2	99.1	102.4
1961	100.0	100.6	99.8	100.0
1963	102.8	104.3	96.8	102.2
1964	117.2	110.9	102.2	113.1
1965	122.0	111.7	113.8	117.7
1966	115.8	115.8	116.8	115.9
1967	117.8	121.1	115.2	118.3
1968	137.9	124.7	114.9	130.4

Source: *Irish Statistical Bulletin*

This fall was not equally shared between the various forms of production. The economic war and the depression brought a calamitous fall in the livestock price index from 139 in 1929 to 75 in 1935. The index for livestock products, which were partially supported by subsidies, fell from 144 to 94 in the same period. The crop price index fell from 135 in 1928 to 93 in 1933. It rose throughout the remainder of the decade to 139 in 1939 when the livestock index was 119 and the livestock products index was 123.

24. Indexes of import and export prices and of the terms of trade are also available.
25. A detailed review will be found in *ITJ*, 1931, p. 85.

A new index was adopted in 1941 which was based on the agricultural prices of 1938–9 being equal to 100.[26] This index covered the war years. On the 1938–9 basis the general agricultural price index rose from 105 in 1939 to 183 in 1943 and 190 in 1945. The livestock index in the same years rose from 106 to 184 and fell slightly to 179. Livestock products rose from 103 to 186 to 209 and crops from 107 to 181 to 195.

The agricultural price index at present in use is based on the agricultural price level of 1953 being equal to 100.[27]

Consumer price index

Until 1922 the cost of living index number was published by the Ministry of Labour. The first official retail price index for the Irish Free State related to March 1922 and was based on the price level of July 1914.[28] The weighting of this index represented the pattern of expenditure of working class families, as determined by a family budget enquiry taken in June 1922 in which 308 families gave usable returns.

In October 1922 this index stood at 189. The subsequent decline was at a slower rate than in the United Kingdom, the index averaging 176 in 1929 and 156 in 1935. Thereafter there was an increase to 173 in 1938. The war caused a rapid rise from 205 in 1940 to 226 in 1941, 250 in 1942, to 282 in 1943, and 295 in 1944. (It will be remembered that salaries and wages were generally frozen between 1942 and 1946 by an Emergency Powers Order.) After 1944 the increase was temporarily checked, the average for 1946 being 291, but the index reached 319 in August 1947.

At this point a new Interim Index was introduced. In Ireland, as elsewhere, the change was hastened by the growing difficulty of relating remuneration to the old index, but it cannot be denied that the construction of the old index had little relevance to the conditions of 1947. Accordingly, the Interim Cost of Living Index (Essential Items) was introduced in December 1947.[29] It was intended to serve until the results of a new family budget inquiry made possible the determination of an up-to-date and detailed consumption standard. It was retained until the results of the Household Budget Inquiry of 1951–2 became

26. For its construction see *ITJ*, 1943, p. 46.
27. See *ITJ*, 1957, p. 159.
28. *ITJ*, 1953, p. 222, which describes the cost of living index and the method of calculation of the index now in use. See also *Report on the Cost of Living in Ireland*, June 1922 and, for fuller detail the report of the *Committee on the Cost of Living Index Figure*, 1933, P. 992, Stationery Office, Dublin. A useful survey of the issues involved in the compilation of an index will be found in R. C. Geary, *The Official Cost of Living Index Number and its Critics*, Cork University Press, Cork, 1951.
29. See *ITJ*, 1947, p. 146 and *ITJ*, 1948, p. 93.

available.[30] It was replaced in November 1953 by the present consumer price index number, the construction of which differs in many respects from the old cost of living index. Its course in recent years may be seen from Table 2.21.

TABLE 2.21

Consumer price index. Annual average of all items, 1953–69

Mid-August	Mid-August 1947 = 100	1953 = 100
1953	125	99.8
1955	128	102.7
1957	143	111.5
1959	144	116.5
1960	146	117.2
1962	157	125.3
1963	159	127.3
1964	173	138.8
1965	181	144.8
1966	187	150.0
1967	192	153.3
1968	200	160.3
1969	—	173.8

Source: *Irish Statistical Bulletin*

Wholesale price index

The general wholesale price index was introduced in 1946 based on the level of wholesale prices in October 1938. This index was superseded in 1955 by the present series which is shown to base year 1953.[31]

The main conceptual difference between the old series and the new is that, in its weighting system and in the types of commodities included, the old series was based on the principle of *exchange* whereas the new series is based on the *economic flow* principle. According to the exchange principle the basic weights were the values of commodities exchanged at all stages of production: (raw materials, simply transformed materials, more elaborately transformed consumption goods and capital goods ready for use) with adjustments made to eliminate, as far as possible, double counting. . . . According to the flow principle on the other hand the whole economy is regarded as composed of several economic sectors and the index numbers purport to represent the trend of prices as they affect sellers and purchasers in the sector. According to this concept transactions between members of the same sector are ignored; it is the sector as a whole which is regarded as the transactor.

30. *Household Budget Inquiry*, 1951–2, Pr. 2520, Stationery Office, Dublin.
31. The first index is described in *ITJ* 1946, p. 54, with indexes covering the period 1939–46. The present index is described in *ITJ*, 1955, p. 2.

TABLE 2.22

Index numbers of wholesale prices, 1955–68

	General index	Personal consumption goods	Capital goods 1953 = 100	Materials for use in industry	Output of industry	Materials for use in agriculture
1955	101.6	100	102	99.2	98.4	96.6
1957	109.9	110.9	112.6	108.2	108.7	97.4
1959	113.5	114.2	112.9	104.8	112.8	93.0
1961	114.7	117.0	119.3	105.5	116.4	86.3
1962	118.3	120.8	124.1	106.8	120.8	87.0
1963	119.8	122.3	125.1	108.7	122.4	88.3
1964	126.8	128.2	132.7	114.8	128.1	89.6
1965	131.6	132.7	136.3	117.0	132.5	92.9
1966	134.2	137.1	141.6	122.0	137.9	97.1
1967	137.7	141.9	146.2	125.7	143.0	99.3
1968	145.9	148.9	152.0	132.4	149.4	104.3

Source: *Irish Statistical Bulletin*

Agricultural and industrial wages

Minimum agricultural wages are fixed by Orders under the Agricultural Wages Acts of 1936 and 1945 and vary according to area. They are highest in some parts of Leinster and the Cork City area and, generally, are lowest in Connacht and the Ulster counties.

Industrial wages were governed by Emergency Powers Orders from 1942 until 1946–7. Their general effect was to prohibit increases above

TABLE 2.23

Indexes of average weekly earnings in transportable goods industries and agriculture, 1957–68

	Industry October 1953 = 100	Agriculture July 1953 = 100
October 1957	117.0	118.7
October 1959	128.6	126.1
October 1960	138.3	134.7 (a)
October 1961	147.3	142.0 (b)
October 1962	162.0	150.3
October 1963	169.2	150.3
December 1964	189.5	178.2
December 1965	196.5	197.2
December 1966	219.8	221.5
December 1967	231.6	221.5
December 1968	255.1	246.3

(a) From 24 October 1960
(b) From 30 October 1961

Source: *Irish Statistical Bulletin*

the 'standard rates' in operation in April 1942.[32] These Orders ceased to operate in 1946–7. Since then, wages have advanced partly by the normal processes arising out of the circumstances of individual industries but also by a series of all-round wage-increases.[33]

32. See 'The Industrial Relations Act' by R. J. P. Mortished, *JSSISI*, 1946–7, p. 685.

33. The 'rounds' may be reckoned as follows. The first took place after the removal of the Wages Standstill Order and the establishment of the Labour Court in 1946–7; the second in 1948 (9 per cent); the third in 1951; the fourth in 1952; the fifth in 1955; the sixth in 1957; the seventh in 1959–60; the eighth in 1961; the ninth in 1964, and the tenth in 1965–6. A number of the 'rounds', notably the second, fourth, sixth, and ninth followed on the lines of agreements between the trade unions and the federation of employers.

See also D. O'Mahony, *Economic Aspects of Industrial Relations*, Economic Research Institute, Dublin: Paper No. 24, pp. 14–33.

NOTE

The census of 1966 showed that the number of gainfully occupied persons had grown to 1,118,000 from 1,108,000 in 1961. The numbers in the following occupational groups increased: professional and technical from 78,000 to 87,000; clerks and typists from 78,000 to 90,000; commerce, insurance and finance from 107,000 to 109,000; transport and communications from 57,000 to 58,000 and building and construction workers from 25,000 to 31,000. The following occupational groups decreased in numbers: agricultural occupations from 393,000 to 345,000 and labourers and unskilled workers from 75,000 to 72,000. The number of service workers remained at 83,000.

CHAPTER THREE

Trade and Balance of Payments

THE PRESENT SERIES OF TRADE RETURNS DATES FROM
1 January 1924. Ninety-nine years earlier, the last of the protective duties
imposed by the Irish Parliament had been terminated. Thereafter the
commercial union between Great Britain and Ireland was complete;
and no statistics were collected in respect of trade crossing the Irish sea.
Returns of cattle exports were provided in 1878, but no information in
regard to trade as a whole was available. In 1894 the eminent statistician,
Sir Robert Giffen, in giving evidence to the Commission on Financial
Relations between Great Britain and Ireland, estimated that in 1893
exports from (all) Ireland were £25.7m. and imports were over £20m.[1]
This, however, could be no more than an approximation.

The absence of firm statistics attracted the attention of the Department of Agriculture and Technical Instruction when it was established in
1899. It became the special care of the first Superintendent of Statistics,
W. P. Coyne, who died before the first estimates were produced. The
first estimate was for the year 1904 and was prepared by Coyne's successor, W. G. S. Adams[2] who recorded that it was 'the object of the late
Dr. Coyne to ascertain, as far as possible, what was the state of the
trade of Ireland, and the foundations of the work on which this is the
first report were laid by him'.[3]

1. *Minutes of Evidence*, C. 8008, HMSO, London: 1895, p. 3.
2. See his paper, 'Some Considerations relating to the Statistics of Irish Production
and Trade', *JSSISI*, 1909, p. 310.
3. Dr. Adams held office as Superintendent of Statistics from 1904 to 1909 followed by Thomas Butler, 1910–14, succeeded in turn by John Hooper who became
Director of Statistics under the Free State government and held the post until 1930.
His successors have been S. G. Lyon, 1930–47; R. C. Geary, 1947–57; M. D. McCarthy,
1957–67; and T. P. Linehan. The Statistics Branch formed a section of the Department of Industry and Commerce under the Free State government until 1949 when it
was enlarged into the Central Statistics Office and placed in the Department of the
Taoiseach.

Based on revised voluntary returns, these estimates, which appeared annually in the period 1904–21, attained substantial accuracy; they are summarized in Table 3.1.

TABLE 3.1

External trade of all Ireland (£ million),
1904–21

	Imports	Exports	Excess or deficiency
1904	55.3	49.8	− 5.5
1909	65.2	61.0	− 4.2
1914	74.1	77.3	+ 3.2
1918	126.0	152.9	+ 26.9
1919	158.7	176.0	+ 17.3
1920	203.8	204.8	+ 1.0
1921	119.0	129.6	+ 10.6

Source: *Reports of Department of Agriculture and Technical Instruction*

Recurrent export surpluses are shown in the table, particularly in the last four years of the period. It was a period of rising prices, especially of course in the years after 1914. The war must also have played its part in restricting imports. On the other hand, the onset of the slump in prices in 1920, which was to persist so calamitously for so long, will be seen plainly.

The table covers the trade of all Ireland; and it is worth noting how much of that trade originated in the north-eastern area. In the exports for 1921, for example, textiles at £32m. were the largest single item, followed by livestock at £28m., ships and machinery at £13m., and beer and spirits at £12m. The importance of the north-east, whence the textiles, ships, and machinery assuredly came, is unmistakable; and, as is remarked elsewhere, it did much to influence the course of modern Irish history. It should be added that the export surpluses of the war years have equally influenced that history. From them sprang the external assets which have enabled the Irish state to choose its policies without reference to their impact on possible foreign lenders.

The principles of free trade were pushed far in nineteenth-century Ireland. Linen and ship-building drew their raw materials from abroad and looked to the world for their markets. Ireland itself was of little or no importance either as a producer of raw materials or as a consumer of the final product. The industries that served the home market were comparatively small and unimportant.[4]

4. With the possible exceptions of brewing and distilling. But the export market took by far the greater part of the production of beer and stout and whiskey was a prestige product abroad.

Agriculture showed the same characteristics. World prices deflected the farmer out of grain and into livestock and, in a smaller degree, into livestock products. He produced for the export market: his own needs were satisfied by purchasing cheaper grades of what he sold. Thus imports were principally finished consumption goods and raw materials for the manufactures of the north-east. There were also heavy imports of agricultural produce. Irish bacon, to take an example, was exported while the farmer's family fed on the cheap American product.[5]

This was to sell in the dearest market and to buy in the cheapest. It exemplified the international division of labour. It maximized the farmer's income. It also meant that Ireland imported large quantities not only of grain and flour but also of butter and eggs, poultry and vegetables. This did not always command approval. Comment on the trade returns often emphasized the desirability of increasing home production so as to eliminate these imports. This approach missed the point; but it was to influence the controversies that raged in the 1920s and 1930s on the proper aims of agricultural policy.

The trade figures for the Twenty-six Counties fall into well-defined periods. The first 1924–31, the last free trading years; the second 1931–8, the years of the introduction of all-round protection, the promotion of the home market and the economic war; the third runs from 1939 through the war until about 1948 when both imports and exports began to revive. Recent years (see Table 3.2) have witnessed growing imports with some isolated peaks and a remarkable expansion of exports.

The trade returns show considerable fluctuations.[6] The slump in the value of exports between 1929 and 1933 and the fall in both imports and exports between 1938 and 1943 are cases in point. An even clearer example is the extreme fluctuation in imports and the trade deficit in the later 1940s and throughout the 1950s.

In no normal year is the balance of trade favourable: in 1928, for example, the value of exports was 77 per cent of the value of imports; ten years later it was no more than 58 per cent. In years of exceptionally heavy imports the ratio has been worse still: 30 per cent in 1947 and 40 per cent in 1951. In recent years, in spite of growing exports, the ratio has been no better than 71 per cent in 1957.[7] This throws so heavy a burden on invisible earnings that a deficit in the balance of payments seems almost built into the economy. The Central Bank has spoken of 'an

5. Cf. C. H. Oldham, *JSSISI*, 1916–17, p. 397. 'What we produce, we do not consume, we export it; and what we consume, we do not produce, we import it.'
6. Here, even elemental causes should not be overlooked. A bad harvest, as in 1954, 1960, or 1962 can lead to increased imports of wheat. The trade returns are also influenced by cattle prices and stocks.
7. In 1957 imports were affected by the special levies. The ratio in recent years has been 69 per cent in 1961, 64 per cent in 1962–4, 60 per cent in 1965, and 66 per cent in 1966.

exceptionally high propensity to import'.[8] This is not due solely to increased imports of consumer goods, reflecting an improving standard of living; it can equally be due to expanding industrial activity causing an increased importation of raw materials and capital goods, and both causes may operate at the same time. Thus an increased visible deficit is not necessarily a sign that the economic virtues have been neglected.[9] The true difficulty is that a large proportion of our industrial output is such that its growth will always call directly or indirectly for more imports.

TABLE 3.2

Value and volume of imports and exports, 1924–69

	Value (£ million)			Volume (1953 = 100)	
	Imports	Exports[1]	Deficit	Imports	Exports
1924	68.9	51.0	17.9	84.8	122.2
1929	61.3	47.3	14.0	86.4	118.0
1931	50.5	36.3	14.1	91.4	105.8
1933	35.8	19.0	16.8	71.6	77.2
1938	41.4	24.2	17.2	71.2	73.8
1943	26.4	27.8	−1.4	21.2	41.1
1948	136.3	49.3	87.0	90.5	54.9
1951	204.6	81.5	123.1	106.3	73.5
1955[2]	207.7	110.9	96.8	107.6	95.3
1959	212.6	130.6	81.0	109.6	109.6
1960	226.2	152.7	73.5	114.4	130.2
1962	273.7	174.4	99.3	137.2	149.1
1963	307.7	196.5	111.1	151.3	164.5
1964	349.3	222.0	127.3	170.0	175.3
1965	371.7	220.8	150.9	177.5	173.3
1966	372.6	243.4	129.2	176.0	190.0
1967	390.5	284.4	106.1	189.0	220.0
1968	489.0	332.0	157.0	216.0	239.0
1969	589.0	370.0	219.0	n.a.	n.a.

Source: *Trade and Shipping Statistics*

1. Including re-exports.
2. Small readjustments of classification were made in 1955.

The result has been that the importance of foreign trade in the Irish economy, already great in the 1920s, is now greater than ever. The OECD country studies for 1968 noted the proportions which exports and imports formed of the gross national product of the countries of western Europe. For Ireland, exports were 26 per cent and imports 40 per cent of the gross national product. These proportions were exceeded only in the Netherlands (33 and 37 per cent) and in Belgium–Luxemburg (38 and 39 per cent). They were approached in Norway (22 and 30 per cent), Denmark (21 and 26 per cent), and Switzerland (23 and

8. *CBR*, 1955–6, p. 37.
9. Which is not to say that there have not been times when they most obviously were neglected.

26 per cent). The proportions for the United Kingdom were 14 and 18 per cent. At the other end of the scale came Italy (14 and 14 per cent), France (10 and 11 per cent), and Spain (6 and 14 per cent).

TABLE 3.3

The terms of trade, 1959–68

1959	99.4	1965	98.2
1960	95.9	1966	100.0
1961	93.8	1967	100.6
1962	94.7	1968	99.5

Source: *Trade and Shipping Statistics*

The terms of trade

The relationship between the price of imports and the price of exports is set out in Table 3.3. The index represents the ratio of the index of export prices to the index of import prices multiplied by 100. The base year is 1953.

TABLE 3.4

Distribution of imports according to main use (£ million), 1938–68

	1938	1951	1963	1964	1965	1966	1967	1968
Consumers' goods								
Food, drink, tobacco		20.3	19.9	19.8	25.2	23.7	25.0	29.4
Other	12.9	36.9	45.3	51.4	56.8	60.5	62.8	82.2
Materials for further production[1]								
Agriculture	1.3	6.3	16.9	16.5	17.8	15.2	17.0	22.6
Industry	23.6	122.3	164.4	195.5	201.8	204.0	217.5	271.9
Producers' capital goods	2.9	15.8	47.3	52.2	60.3	57.9	58.8	72.0
Unclassified	0.7	3.0	13.9	14.0	11.8	11.4	11.1	11.4
	41.4	204.6	307.7	349.4	373.7	372.7	392.3	489.5

Source: *Trade and Shipping Statistics*

1. Imports of materials for agriculture (e.g. maize) which were processed before use in this country are classified as materials for industry.

Composition of trade

The balance between imports of consumer goods and imports of raw materials for further production will be seen to have changed greatly during the period covered by Table 3.4. The change is even more striking if the comparison is carried back to a year before the general tariff was imposed, such as 1929. In that year imports of consumer goods represented 45 per cent of all imports while imports of materials for further production represented 47 per cent. By 1938 these percentages had changed to 31 and 60 respectively. In very recent years they have remained at about 20 and 62. Imports of materials for further production in agriculture appear to be extraordinarily small in comparison with imports of raw materials for industrial production. This is probably partly due to the method of classification, and partly to the fact that the input of fertilizers, etc., has been traditionally small. The increased import of capital goods in recent years will be noted.

TABLE 3.5

Value of domestic exports (£ million), by groups of commodities, 1929–68

	Live animals	Food, drink, and tobacco	Other raw materials and manufactured goods
1929	19.7	20.6	5.8
1938	11.9	9.9	1.8
1951	29.8	34.5	14.2
1959	39.1	43.6	35.6
1961	55.4	62.7	46.8
1962	47.5	63.9	48.2
1963	52.8	72.6	55.3
1964	66.7	72.8	66.9
1965	56.3	77.1	84.6
1966	54.7	84.4	97.3
1967	52.9	110.0	112.7
1968	57.9	117.9	147.6

Source: *Trade and Shipping Statistics*

There have been, as Tables 3.4 and 3.5 show, considerable changes in the composition of both imports and exports. The encouragement of industrial production has been successful enough to diminish the proportionate volume of imported finished goods; but many of the new industries must go outside the country for sources of supply, so the volume of imported raw materials and of capital goods has grown. Thus both the standard of living and the maintenance of industrial employment depend much more than they did on the capacity to pay for imports.

Table 3.5 shows the marked increase, during very recent years, in the export of raw materials and manufactured goods. In the pre-war period the much smaller totals under this heading were composed almost entirely of raw materials, for example wool, rather than of manufactured goods. Nowadays, however, manufactures predominate in this category and cover a surprisingly wide field extending from electrical and other machinery to clothing, footwear, and printed matter.

Two points arise from the expansion in the food, drink, and tobacco group. The traditional trade in meat took the form of the export of livestock, consigned almost entirely to Great Britain. In 1957 exports of live cattle totalled 830,500 head while the total beef exported amounted to the equivalent of 207,000 head. Thus the live equivalent of the beef exported amounted to 20 per cent of the gross total. By 1960 the percentage had grown to 40 per cent. In 1963 it was 37 per cent, representing a gross total of 1,055,000 head and a beef export equivalent to 393,000 head. In 1964, which was regarded as an exceptionally good year for the cattle trade, live exports were 794,000 head and the equivalent of beef exports was 281,000 head. This represented a proportion of 35 per cent, still appreciably above the proportion of six years earlier which itself was far higher than anything recorded in the inter-war period.[10]

It is clear that a higher degree of processing of exports is to be desired on all grounds. This applies not only to meat but to the entire range of agricultural produce—dried milk and cheese, vegetables, etc. The economy would gain heavily from a greater intensity of production and employment and from a wider diversification of opportunities to export.[11]

Direction of trade

Trends in the direction of trade are difficult to trace over a long period because the classification has gradually been changed from the country from which goods are imported to the country of origin and from the country to which goods are exported to the country of ultimate destination. In each case, the adjustment involves a reduction of the stated trade with Great Britain. The voluntary trade returns for 1921, for example, showed that 78 per cent of imports came from Great Britain and 98 per cent of exports went to that country.

The first official statistics of the Irish Free State showed that in 1924 84 per cent of exports went to Great Britain and 14 per cent to Northern Ireland. In that year 69 per cent of imports came from Great Britain and 11 per cent from Northern Ireland.

The situation in more recent years is set out in Table 3.6.

This table brings out the unbalanced nature of Irish trade. With every area, except Northern Ireland, there is a deficit. The deficit is substantial with the EEC and other continental countries but surprisingly small with the dollar countries, which in this context means the United States and U.S. forces overseas and Canada. The relative percentages in 1965 were: of imports, 54 came from EFTA coun-

---

10. The provisions of the 1965 Anglo-Irish Trade Agreement concerning cattle and meat exports are summarized below on p. 79.
11. e.g. by increased earnings of currencies other than sterling.

tries; 15.3 from EEC countries; and 10.8 from the dollar countries, the balance being spread over the other headings while of exports 71.6 went to the EFTA countries; 12.7 to the EEC countries; and 6.1 to the dollar countries. Trade with Great Britain formed 46.6 per cent of imports and 59.3 per cent of exports. Trade with Northern Ireland formed 3.9 per cent of imports and 11.3 per cent of exports.

Incentives to export have been provided in recent years for manufacturers, beginning in the budget of 1956. The situation in 1967 was

TABLE 3.6

Trade (£ million), by areas, 1964–8

	Imports				Exports			
	1964	1965	1967	1968	1964	1965	1967	1968
Great Britain	160.5	173.3	179.5	227.6	129.8	130.7	169.8	187.8
Northern Ireland	16.0	14.6	17.5	19.9	29.2	26.5	35.0	42.9
Other EFTA	13.2	13.8	14.8	21.8	3.2	3.3	3.1	4.1
Total EFTA	189.8	201.8	210.7	269.3	162.2	160.4	207.9	234.8
EEC	54.2	56.7	56.9	80.3	25.4	28.4	24.2	29.6
Other OECD	3.8	3.8	3.8	3.8	1.4	2.3	1.6	2.2
Dollar countries	34.5	40.1	42.4	46.8	15.8	13.8	30.7	39.2
All other	56.9	61.0	69.6	81.6	8.8	8.5	12.4	18.9
Re-imports and temporary exports	8.6	8.2	7.2	7.7	8.8	10.6	7.5	7.8
	347.8	371.6	390.5	489.5	222.4	224.0	284.4	332.5

Source: *Trade and Shipping Statistics*

that for new industries there was total exemption from taxation of profits from exports for a ten-year period, followed by a further period of exemption on a decreasing scale. Already existing enterprises obtained comparable concessions. Agricultural products are excluded from these benefits.

Assistance to exporters is also provided by Coras Trachtála, known abroad as the Irish Exports Promotion Board. It was established by the State in 1952 as a non-profit making private company, controlled by a board appointed by the Minister for Industry and Commerce, and financed from State funds. Its function is to provide services such as surveys of foreign markets, trade missions, and general publicity abroad. It has also encouraged group marketing of exports such as whiskey, handwoven tweeds, and pedigree livestock. It advises on such matters as import regulations, tariff classifications, shipping and insurance, methods of payment, credit ratings, etc. These are facilities which individual firms could not easily provide from their own resources.

ANGLO-IRISH TRADE AGREEMENTS

No formal trading agreement existed between the Irish Free State and the United Kingdom during the ten years after 1922. None was needed. Few tariffs existed on the Irish side and practically none on the British. The tariffs imposed by the Irish government carried imperial preference rates for goods from the United Kingdom and its colonies and from the Dominions.

When Great Britain adopted a general tariff in 1931–2 the position was confused by the dispute between the British and Irish governments over the land annuities.[12] During 1932 this dispute developed into what was then called 'the economic war'. The Irish government sent a delegation to the Imperial Trade Conference at Ottawa in the summer of 1932. It concluded trade agreements with some of the Dominions; but no settlement was reached with Great Britain.

In 1935 and succeeding years, the economic war was modified by a succession of 'coal–cattle' agreements. Their nature and scope is suggested by their title, and they were renewed from year to year. In an attempt to dispose of all matters of contention between them formal negotiations between the two governments were commenced in January 1938, leading to the Anglo-Irish agreements of April 1938.

Irish goods were to be admitted free into the United Kingdom. The Irish government affirmed its willingness to co-operate with the British government's policy of ensuring orderly marketing of agricultural produce. The British government undertook that it would not regulate the quantity of imports from Ireland without regard to the special conditions of Irish exports and their course in the past. Irish exports to the United Kingdom would receive preferential treatment as compared with non-Commonwealth goods.

Equally, the Irish government extended preferential treatment to British goods entering Ireland. Free entry was to be given to British coal, iron and steel and other metal manufactures, machinery and chemicals; and a minimum duty was imposed on imports of coal from other countries. The Irish government undertook to review its protective duties and, if necessary, to replace them by duties which would allow British producers a chance of reasonable competition while affording adequate protection to Irish industries. This review was to be undertaken by the Prices Commission, to which British firms could appeal. It will be seen that these concessions on the Irish side, which were the prelude to the re-establishment of the export trade in agricultural produce, went far beyond the bounds of preferential treatment of British imports.

12. On the details and progress of this dispute, see p. 97 *infra*.

The foregoing is only a summary of a long and comprehensive instrument.[13] The Trade Agreement of 1948 reviewed and, in general, continued these arrangements. Provision was made also regarding the quantity and price of agricultural products to be supplied by Ireland. The revival of the cattle trade to its pre-war level was allowed for, three-quarters of the total exports to be store cattle. The quantity, and in some cases the prices, of other agricultural products which would be accepted by Great Britain were set out. Some dispute had arisen whether the term 'free entry' in the 1938 agreement excluded regulation by quota. The British government agreed without prejudice to review any such quotas, and it was further agreed that the Irish government would consult with the British if it proposed to place quotas on British imports hitherto enjoying free entry into Ireland. It was agreed that the review of Irish tariffs should be carried out in such order of priority as the two governments might agree upon. The circumstances of the time were reflected in a British undertaking to maintain supplies of coal and an Irish promise to economize in the use of hard currencies and to obtain the maximum amount of Marshall Aid so as to relieve the strain on the dollar pool of the sterling area.

The negotiations for the next trade agreement, which was reached in 1960, were carried out in changed circumstances. The EEC and EFTA were now in existence. In the field of Anglo-Irish trade the advantages hitherto enjoyed by Irish agricultural products had been largely destroyed by the system of British guaranteed prices for domestic production, which severely reduced the market for Irish supplies. In the case of cattle, exports to Great Britain were not subject to quantitative control. The price was linked to the British controlled prices which meant that in effect the Irish farmer shared in the benefits which the British producer received from State subsidy. This, however, applied to store cattle only, and did not extend to fat cattle.

The Irish government proposed an arrangement whereby Irish and British farm prices would be linked, thus in practice extending the advantages of the British support prices to Irish farmers, in exchange for widely increased preferences for British goods entering Ireland, but this proposal was not accepted by the British government. The trade agreement thereafter concluded renewed in general the preceding agreements, formalized the price link for store cattle, provided for a review of Irish tariffs at the request of the British government and allowed the Irish government to re-impose restrictions on imports of goods wherever a removal of a tariff might lead to exceptional imports which would be detrimental to Irish producers.

These arrangements were replaced by the Anglo-Irish Free Trade

13. For details of the 1938 and 1948 agreements see *Public Administration in Ireland*, vol. ii, F. C. King (ed.), published by the Parkside Press, Dublin: 1949, p. 247.

Area Agreement[14] which was signed on 14 December 1965. This Agreement came into effect on 1 July 1966 when British duties on Irish goods (with some exceptions) entering the United Kingdom were abolished. Irish duties on imports from the United Kingdom were reduced by 10 per cent and will be reduced by the same proportion annually until 1975. Each country has agreed to remove quantitative controls on imports from the other. This does not, however, apply to all Irish agricultural products entering the United Kingdom. Equally, the Irish government may use quantitative controls for particular products during the period of transition to complete free trade. The Agreement guarantees unrestricted access to the United Kingdom for Irish store cattle, store sheep, and store lambs. The waiting period for these animals before they qualify for guarantee payments under the British fatstock guarantee scheme was reduced from three to two months. The British government further undertook to extend the full benefit of the guarantee payments to 25,000 tons of carcase beef and 5,500 of carcase lamb each year. These payments are to be made directly to the Irish government: the use made of them will be the subject of consultation between the two governments. The Irish government undertook to use its best endeavours to provide not less than 638,000 store cattle and at least 25,000 tons of beef and 5,500 tons of lamb for export to the United Kingdom each year. In regard to other agricultural products, it was provided that trade should be subject to the needs of orderly marketing, but the British government undertook to consult with the Irish government when necessary, on account of the special relationship of the two countries. The targets set out in the Second Programme for Economic Expansion would be relevant to these consultations. The quota set for British imports of butter from Ireland was raised from 12,900 tons in 1965–6 to 23,000 tons in 1966–7.

INTERNATIONAL TRADING GROUPS

The Free Trade Area

In February 1957 the Council of the Organization for European Economic Co-operation initiated negotiations to establish a Free Trade Area in Europe within which there would be no tariff barriers or other restrictions to trade; although the already existing European Economic Community and each of the other countries within the proposed

14. The full text of the Agreement, together with annexes, 'exchanges of letters' and a 'record of understanding' (many of which may be of considerable importance) were published as a White Paper by the Irish Government: Pr. 8623. 1965.

Area would maintain protective defences against the rest of the world.

As a member of OEEC, Ireland joined in the negotiations, which took place during 1957 and 1958. Two points were especially important. The future of tariffs against agricultural products, in which the Irish government was specially interested, was never fully clarified before the breakdown of the negotiations in November 1958. The second point lay in the proposals to give special treatment to undeveloped countries (later known as countries in course of economic development) by extending the period in which tariffs might be eliminated and by providing financial assistance if required. Originally, the countries suggested for this treatment were Greece and Turkey; but it appeared that the Irish government hoped for the inclusion of Ireland in this category. No decisions had been made before the breakdown of the project of a Free Trade Area.

The European Free Trade Association

This association, consisting of Great Britain, Austria, Denmark, Norway, Portugal, Sweden, and Switzerland, was established in 1959. Ireland did not apply for membership, on the ground that participation would not offer any advantages in view of the pattern of Irish trade. Trade with the EFTA group consisted overwhelmingly of trade with Great Britain, which was already governed by special trade agreements. As Mr. Lemass remarked:

The other six members of the EFTA have not been important markets for us in the past and, while we must not of course neglect any market, it is doubtful whether the advantages we could hope to reap in those countries would justify acceptance of the Stockholm Convention, particularly as agriculture is expressly excluded from its provisions.[15]

The European Economic Community

The Irish government applied to become a full member of the community on 31 July 1961. In January 1962 Mr. Lemass presented the Irish case for membership to the Council of the Community. It was generally understood that the Irish application would not be considered until a decision had been reached regarding the position of Great Britain. In October 1962, however, the Council accepted the Irish application for further negotiation. Matters were at this stage when negotiations between the Community and Great Britain broke down in January 1963.

15. Speech in the Dáil on 16 May 1961, *PDDE*, pp. 189, 297. See also the White Papers issued by the Government on the European Economic Community; Pr. 6106 issued on 30 June 1961 and Pr. 6613 issued on 28 June 1962.

A parliamentary statement was then made by Mr Lemass, who emphasized the

'basic importance' of Irish trade relations with Britain. In the belief that the forces making for European unity must eventually prevail, the government would continue to prepare and plan for entry to an enlarged Community . . . Everything that had been done in preparation for membership of the European Economic Community had been worth doing for its own sake, and the necessary measures would have to be continued and, where necessary, strengthened 'in contemplation of our assuming by 1970 all the obligations of free trade which membership of the Community would then entail'.[16]

These matters were again reviewed by Mr Lemass during the debate in the Dáil on the Free Trade Area Agreement in January 1966. He said that:

Our aim is, of course, to achieve membership of the E E C and, if we should decide to explore EFTA membership, this aim should not be considered as modified on that account. It is, however, unlikely in the extreme that membership of the EEC will be feasible for us except in circumstances in which it will be feasible also for EFTA countries or arises from a situation in which the two European groups will amalgamate in one way or another. Deputies who have been following events in this respect will be aware that on the initiative of the British Prime Minister, efforts are being made to promote contacts between the two European groups with the ultimate aim, no doubt, of bringing about some arrangement of this kind. Membership of EFTA might become a matter of urgency as well as of importance to this country if these efforts should look like making progress.[17]

These views were reiterated by his successor, Mr. Lynch, when British interest in the Community was reaffirmed in November 1966.

BALANCE OF PAYMENTS

Few aspects of the Irish economy have been more consistently a cause for concern than the balance of payments. The Free State began its life under the shadow of a heavy fall in agricultural prices and a deficit in the balance of visible trade. By 1924 it was already obvious that the reserves accumulated during the war were being drawn upon. The first attempt at a statistical investigation was published in 1926.[18] It covered the financial year 1924–5, for which the following details were given:

---

16. *CBR*, 1962–3, pp. 14–15. Discussions on accession to the General Agreement on Tariffs and Trade were suspended in 1961 pending the outcome of the EEC negotiations. In the Budget speech of April 1964 it was announced that they would be resumed. Accession to GATT was approved by the Dáil in 1967.

17. *PDDE*, 219 , pp. 1147-8.   18. *ITJ*, 1926, p. 112.

Inward or credit movements	£ thousand	Outward or debit movements	£ thousand
Exports	48,838	Imports	66,992
Income from investments	11,000	Profits on foreign investment	3,340
Emigrants' remittances	2,250	Payments of land annuities	2,664
Pensions	2,347	Pensions paid to members of	
Adjustment of Post Office		Royal Irish Constabulary	1,332
balances	1,338	Payments from local loans	
Compensation from British		fund	798
Government	584	Other debits	520
Interest on banks' loans to			
London money market	250		
Net export of specie	231		
	66,838		75,646

Inevitably, this was not so exhaustive an investigation as is the modern statement of the balance of payments. Nevertheless it contained the three features which have become familiar; an over-all deficit in payments in which a surplus on invisible earnings does not fully balance the shortfall in visible trade.

The balance of payments was not prominent in the reports of the Banking Commission which reported in 1926. The second Banking Commission, which reported in 1938, had every reason to comment on the increased information which was available by then.

It pointed out that there were deficits on current account to the extent of £3.2m. in 1931, of £6.3m. in 1934, and of £3.7m. in 1935. On the other side, net external assets were comparatively ample; in 1936 those held by the banking system amounted to £86.0m. This figure, however, showed a fall from £95.7m. in 1932. The Banking Commission therefore issued the first of a long series of warnings against any assumption that the amount of the external assets was a sufficient safeguard against continued current deficits. It remarked that:

In each year there has been an adverse balance on the current account which has had to be covered either by encroachment on external capital assets or by increase of external liabilities. The loss of external income due to this cause increases the difficulty for the future of bringing the current account of the balance of payments into equilibrium and tends to make the country more dependent upon the maintenance of its export capacity.[19]

When these observations were published, the economic war had ended; and the prospects for the balance of payments had greatly improved. They were belied by the outbreak of war which greatly restricted trade. The war years brought a short succession of surpluses, but it was clear that this improvement was caused by forced savings and that it would end as soon as supplies became available again. This was fully shown in the balance of payments in 1947, which was the first of a

19. *BCR*, 1938, para. 153.

number of years of heavy deficits; table 3.7 shows how things have gone since then.

Table 3.7 does not disclose the very heavy deficits of £61.6m. in 1951 and of £35.5m. in 1955 but these were extremes of a general characteristic in which the visible account is normally in heavy deficit while the invisible account is, without exception, in heavy surplus. The last four years illustrate this pattern clearly.

TABLE 3.7

Balance of payments: summary of current account (£ million), 1947–67

	1947	1953	1957	1962	1963	1964	1965	1966	1967
Known deficit on merchandise trade	91.4	68.5	53.2	100.2	111.2	127.6	151.2	128.7	106.6
Known net invisible receipts	53.9	50.9	56.2	58.2	58.5	64.4	79.2	71.6	79.9
Other known current items[1]	—	—	—	17.5	18.5	24.0	27.5	31.3	36.9
Balance unaccounted for	7.7	10.6	6.2	11.1	12.1	7.8	2.7	9.7	5.0
Estimated current deficit	29.8	7.0	+9.2	13.4	22.1	31.4	41.8	16.1	+15.2

Source: *Irish Statistical Bulletin*

1. Including net trade between Shannon Free Airport and other countries.

Invisible earnings and outgoings have traditionally had four principal elements: tourism and travel, dividends, pensions and remittances from emigrants. The Banking Commission of 1938 commented that at least two of these (pensions and remittances) were clearly wasting assets and that a third (dividends) might well disappear if continued liquidation depleted holdings of investments abroad.[20] These items have not proved as precarious as was feared: they have all increased since the 1930s and the last ten years have brought further growth.

It should be remembered that the figures in the first item in Table 3.8 refer to 'travel' as well as to 'tourism'. They include the expenditure of those who cross and re-cross the Irish Sea and the border in the course of their business.[21]

The outgoings in respect of tourism and travel have increased in recent years and may be expected to increase still further. Rising incomes will probably lead to greater expenditure by Irish people going

20. *BCR*, 1938, paras. 145–52.
21. The figures are analysed each year in the *Irish Statistical Bulletin*. For State policy in regard to the tourist trade, see *Administration* (Autumn 1961) which contains a useful survey of legislation since the original Tourist Traffic Act of 1939 by Dr. T. J. O'Driscoll, Director-General of Bord Fáilte Éireann, the body now assigned 'the central position in the promotion and organisation of tourism'. See also a review of tourism in *IBR*, March 1960.

abroad for holidays. Nevertheless the table emphasizes the importance of the tourist trade which has become an important element of total earnings and is also capable of very considerable future expansion. A survey of tourism expenditure in 1964 included a calculation of tourist receipts in foreign currencies as a percentage of visible trade. The percentage for Ireland was 18, compared with 42 for Spain, 24 for Austria, 14 for Greece, and 12 for Italy and Switzerland.

TABLE 3.8

Some items of invisible trade (£ million), 1938–68

	1938	1952	1962	1965	1966	1967	1968
Tourism, travel							
Receipts	n.a.	27.9	45.6	67.7	65.1	70.3	75.7
Outgoings	n.a.	9.8	19.2	28.2	31.6	30.1	36.3
	2.4	18.1	26.4	39.5	33.5	40.2	39.4
Dividends, etc.							
Receipts	13.4	22.7	33.9	44.2	45.1	45.1	49.9
Outgoings	7.1	12.6	20.2	26.5	28.8	28.5	26.5
	6.3	10.1	13.7	17.7	16.3	16.6	23.4
Remittances							
Receipts	3.0	10.2	13.7	14.5	15.2	16.7	19.2
Outgoings	—	0.3	0.4	0.4	0.4	0.4	0.4
	3.0	9.9	13.3	14.1	14.8	16.3	18.8
Pensions							
Receipts	2.4	4.2	5.2	6.4	6.4	7.6	8.8
Outgoings	0.2	0.2	0.5	0.7	0.8	0.8	0.9
	2.2	4.0	4.7	5.7	5.6	6.8	7.9

Source: *Irish Statistical Bulletin*

The capital account in the balance of payments has become increasingly important in recent years, which have seen a considerable increase in foreign investment in Ireland. It will be seen from Table 3.9 that there are two major items in the capital account. The first is transactions in Irish and foreign securities arising between residents and externs. The two sides of the account roughly balanced each other in recent years. It should however be remembered that this item refers only to purchases and sales of securities through Irish stockbrokers and banks. It seems highly probable that a substantial business is done by residents in Ireland through London stockbrokers and banks. The second major item is 'other capital transactions'. This covers a wide field which includes activities which have increased greatly in recent years, in particular extern subscriptions to issues of the State and public corporations, direct investment by extern companies in their branches and subsidiaries and purchases of lands and buildings by externs.

TABLE 3.9

Estimated balance of international payments (£ thousand), in the years 1964–8

Category	Inward or Credit Movements (Exports) 1964	1965	1966	1967	1968	Outward or Debit Movements (Imports) 1964	1965	1966	1967	1968
Capital Items:										
1. Government transactions:										
(a) Changes in holdings of Trustee Savings Banks and Government Funds	14,784	—	1	15	—	—	—	—	—	—
(b) Indebtedness to Government of United States of America under European Recovery Programme	—	—	—	—	—	—	—	—	—	—
(c) Payments to International Institutions (IMF, IBRD, IFC, IDA)	—	—	8,036	—	7,260	836	1,086	1,119	1,240	1,647
2. Changes in external funds of the Central Bank	—	—	13,851	3,888	—	586	409	3,896	5,558	15,849
3. Banking transactions—changes in net external assets	8,500	4,161	4,050	—	15,949	28,479	—	33,458	45,519	—
4. Purchases and sales of securities by private holders through Irish stockbrokers and banks	17,505	17,337	16,604	27,607	30,188	17,537	15,133	18,619	24,265	32,928
5. Movements arising out of capital issues by companies										
(a) Public issues	3,696	838	2,156	10	160	—	—	—	—	—
(b) Private issues	2,268	3,217	2,857	4,353	5,874	—	—	—	—	—
6. Net capital payments in respect of life insurance	—	—	—	—	—	2,457	2,600	2,700	3,100	4,000
7. Withdrawals from British Post Office Savings Banks	575	586	551	519	447	—	—	—	—	—
8. Encashment of British Savings Certificates	41	53	56	60	38	—	—	—	—	—
9. Other capital transactions										
(a) Extern subscriptions to Central Government or Local Authority issues, prize bonds, Exchequer bills	63	2,379	18,358	2,889	2,919	80	—	—	—	—
(b) Borrowing by Semi-State Concerns and Trade Credits	9,461	2,243	471	2,830	3,687	—	—	—	—	—
(c) Net change in extern capital of Hire Purchase Concerns	2,800	2,300	30	2,887	—	—	—	—	—	10,824
(d) Other Direct Investment by externs	18,706	11,027	14,363	8,426	13,338	—	—	—	—	—
(e) Other transactions	2,939	2,989	8,337	10,972	7,646	—	—	—	—	—
Total: Capital Items	81,338	60,981	75,870	64,456	87,506	49,895	19,228	59,792	79,682	65,248
Balance on Capital Account	—	—	—	15,226	—	31,443	41,753	16,078	—	22,258

Current Items:										
10. Merchandise—Total exports (f.o.b.) and total imports (c.i.f.)[1]	212,257	211,362	234,422	273,404	318,376	338,386	362,612	363,625	379,978	484,623
11. Commission earnings of import agents	4,400	4,500	4,550	4,850	6,300	321	361	956	395	507
12. Coin and bullion	117	69	156	773	483	—	—	—	—	—
13. Transportation	8,235	8,783	12,069	12,766	15,531	—	—	—	—	—
14. Receipts and payments in respect of tourism and travel, etc.	58,800	67,700	65,100	70,300	75,700	25,900	28,200	31,600	30,100	36,306
15. Income from investment abroad and extern profits, etc.	38,766	44,231	45,129	45,088	49,875	25,661	26,461	28,814	28,468	26,498
16. Net outflow in respect of rental of films, etc.	—	—	—	—	—	780	800	910	840	1,115
17. Emigrants' remittances and legacies:										
(a) Great Britain and the Six Counties	5,607	5,726	7,017	5,766	5,676	—	—	—	—	—
(b) Other countries	7,865	8,789	8,164	10,999	13,498	375	400	400	425	450
18. Pensions and allowances:										
(a) Great Britain and the Six Counties	4,450	4,700	4,650	5,881	6,950	560	611	700	765	801
(b) Other countries	1,695	1,700	1,750	1,800	1,850	89	101	102	105	122
19. Payments to the British Government	—	—	—	—	—	250	250	250	250	250
20. Expenditure of Irish Lights Service	1,224	1,221	1,364	1,858	1,719	—	—	—	—	—
21. Posts, telegraphs, and telephone payments and earnings	289	280	248	202	178	390	724	453	692	591
22. Diplomatic, consular, and similar expenditure	480	550	600	645	650	561	683	662	754	955
23. Other known current items	11,963	15,308	15,759	19,799	25,223	799	949	1,227	1,148	744
24. Balance unaccounted for	7,580	5,409	12,714	5,035	8,689	—	—	—	—	—
Total: Current Items	363,748	380,378	413,692	459,146	530,698	395,191	422,131	429,770	443,920	552,956
Balance on Current Account	31,443	41,753	16,078	22,258						15,226

Source: *Irish Statistical Bulletin*

1. For balance of payments purposes the official trade figures have been adjusted in certain minor respects.

CHAPTER FOUR

Agricultural Production

THE PATTERN OF AGRICULTURAL PRODUCTION MAY BE attributed to three principal causes: climate and soil, the trend of prices, and the impact of public policy. Accordingly, this chapter begins with a note on the soil and climate of the country, and then proceeds to a review of price movements, especially during the years of free trade between the 1840s and the 1920s which was the formative period of modern Irish agriculture. The policies followed since 1922 are then described in some detail, because the general shape of economic policy has been largely decided by views of the proper aims of agricultural policy. The trends in agricultural production and its disposal during the last forty years are then considered and the chapter concludes with a short review of fisheries and afforestation.

CLIMATE AND SOIL[1]

About four-fifths of the country has an annual rainfall of between 35 and 50 inches. A small coastal strip extending northwards from Dublin has less than 30 inches. In the west, in the mountainous areas facing the Atlantic much greater totals are recorded, 94 inches in the Gap of Dunloe in Kerry and 99 inches in the Mweelrea mountains in Mayo. Still larger totals are recorded over extensive areas of Great Britain; but in Ireland the total is distributed over a remarkably large number of wet days, that is, days on which 0.1 inches or more of rain falls. Thus, in the south-east the mean number of wet days in the year is less than

---

1. This section is taken almost directly from Mr. J. P. Haughton's article, 'Physiography and Climate', in J. Meenan and D. A. Webb (eds.) *A View of Ireland*, published for the British Association, Dublin: 1957, pp. 1–15 and from paras. 5–13 of the (Smiddy) *Report on Agricultural Policy*, 1945, P. 7175.

200; in the eastern midlands between 200 and 225; in the western midlands between 225 and 250 and in the north-west and south-west over 250. The annual distribution of rainfall everywhere shows a minimum in the late spring, a maximum in August, a relatively dry September and a wet winter. At all times of the year, the frequent rainfall creates difficulties on account of poor drainage conditions.[2]

Extremes of heat and cold are very rare. The maximum July isotherm of 60 degrees is relatively low for western Europe. The January isotherm varies from 40 degrees in the north-east to 44 in the southwest, which is the highest in western Europe. To take a specific example, there is little difference in the total number of sunshine hours between Ireland and Denmark but there is appreciably more sunshine in Denmark than in Ireland in the months from April to September. These moist and mild conditions encourage the growth of grass but cause the harvesting of cereals to be more hazardous than is the case elsewhere in Europe.

No detailed soil survey of the country was undertaken until 1958, after the establishment of the Agricultural Institute.[3] The natural fertility of the soil is generally high over wide areas in the central plain and in the south and east. Equally, over large areas calcium and phosphate deficiencies in particular are widespread. The resultant contrasts were memorably expressed by Mr. G. A. Holmes in his report on the state of Irish land.[4]

Let me say, first of all, that there is no area of comparable size in the northern hemisphere which has such marvellous potentialities for pasture production as Éire undoubtedly has. The depth of loam in the plains and valleys, the abundance of limestone, the normally mild winter, and the reliability and distribution of the summer rainfall combine to make ideal natural conditions for growing grass and for raising and fattening livestock. In 8 of the 26 counties I have seen old permanent pastures with a density, colour, composition, and grazing capacity superior to anything in western Europe, their quality being proved by the excellence of the cattle on them. In some of the same counties, and in all the others which I visited, I saw hundreds of fields which are growing just as little as it is physically possible for the land to grow under an Irish sky.

These variations frequently occur within a very small area, thus aggravating the difficulty of imposing uniform policies, of specializing forms of production and of unifying methods of working.

2. See the *Report of the Drainage Commission*, 1940.
3. See the *Annual Reports* of the Soils Division of the Institute.
4. G. A. Holmes, *Report on the Present State and Methods for Improvement of Irish Land*, P. 9248, Stationery Office, Dublin: 1949, p. 8. Writing of some decades earlier, Moritz Bonn made the same point. 'Irish grass farming mainly consists in this, that Heaven causes the sun to shine and the rain to fall, and that Man sends the cattle to the pasture and gives himself no further trouble about them.' M. Bonn, *Modern Ireland*, Hodges & Figgis, Dublin: 1906, p. 38.

AGRICULTURAL PRICES

The history of agricultural prices has been exceptionally well documented.[5] Barrington's paper shows clearly how the prices for animals and animal products rose throughout the seventy years preceding the first war while cereal prices remained comparatively stable or, as in the case of wheat, actually declined. This contrast continued even after the heavy fall in agricultural and general prices in 1920. Comparing 1840 and 1925, the price of wheat rose in the ratio of 100 to 118 while the price of store cattle rose in the ratio of 100 to 443. The cause was the increasing ease of shipments to Great Britain, so that the prices paid at Irish fairs were ultimately determined by the state of the British market and Ireland became an exporter of livestock, not of meat. Again, the number of cows remained much the same over the whole period: dairying in Ireland did not develop to anything like the extent achieved in Denmark. This, in Barrington's view, was due to the different course of prices in the two countries. In the paper just cited he remarks that:

the statistics show that the price trend in cereals was relatively much more favourable to the farmer in Denmark than in Ireland, and hence no credit is due to the Danish farmer at the expense of his Irish confrère for maintaining with much greater success the area under cereals. The full effect of the contrast does not, however, end here. If, during the same period, the price of store cattle rose more in Ireland than in Denmark a further factor would operate to keep the Danish farmer in tillage and to force the Irish farmer out of it.

By this argument, the dominant factor in Irish farming was the price of store cattle. The fall in cereal prices forced the farmer out of possible cash crops such as wheat; and the number of the dairy herd was determined by the demand for stores rather than by the attraction of butter, cheese, and milk production. In this analysis the Irish farmer appears as a model Economic Man who followed prices with keenness and success.

This achievement did not command universal admiration. It entailed a system of grazing which, granted that so many pastures were kept intact, needed the least possible amount of labour. The Recess Committee of 1896 quotes a suggestion that work on the land was carried on during only 240 days of the year.[6] Moreover, the trend towards grazing was at the expense of dairying which would normally carry a greater rural population. These issues were formulated clearly by Horace Plunkett before the end of the nineteenth century. His views

5. Thomas Barrington, 'A Review of Irish Agricultural Prices', *JSSISI*, 1925–6, p. 249, in which there are references to earlier reviews. On trends of output, see H. Staehle, 'Statistical Notes on Irish Agriculture, 1847–1913', *JSSISI*, 1950–1, p. 444.
    6. Ibid., p. 340.

on them were shared by many others. T. W. Russell, who succeeded him as vice-president of the Department of Agriculture in 1907, declared that 'nobody ever intended that we were to abolish ranches in order to establish small grazing farms'.[7] The failure of mixed farming to develop meant that there were heavy imports of agricultural products; in 1913 Russell noted that, apart from livestock, agricultural imports were actually greater than exports.[8] Deeper instincts were involved. It may be generally true that production for the highest available prices with the least possible exertion and expense is highly desirable: but the truth of that generalization will not be readily admitted in a country where rural population is declining and its decline leads directly to a fall in total population. There was a deep resentment of the process by which cattle, as it was thought, were displacing people;[9] here and there, this feeling was coloured by opposition to every form of dependence, commercial as well as political, on Great Britain.

AGRICULTURAL POLICY

All these issues affected the problems of framing agricultural policy. They will now be studied against the background of the policy adopted in 1922 and of the policy which replaced it ten years later.

In January 1922 Patrick Hogan was appointed Minister for Agriculture in the Provisional Government which held office until December of that year. On the establishment of the Irish Free State in that month, he was confirmed in that office which he held until the change of administration in March 1932. This new minister in a new State inherited a department that had already had twenty years of life.[10] It was now, of course, a department of government in a sovereign state; its opportunities and its responsibilities were greatly increased.

So were its problems. Irish agriculture has survived many vicissitudes, but it can seldom have been in so unpromising a condition as it was in 1922. It had not yet begun to recover from the slump in prices which occurred in 1920. The agricultural price index had risen from 100 in 1911–13 to 288 in 1920; by 1924 it had fallen to 160. In the years of wartime prosperity many farmers had borrowed extensively from

7. *JDATI*, 9, p. 216.
8. Ibid., 15, p. 6.
9. The number of cattle first exceeded the population of Ireland in the early 1890s.
10. The Department of Agriculture and Technical Instruction was established in 1899, largely as a result of the report of the 'Recess' committee of 1896. See the report of that committee, published by Browne & Nolan, 1896, and W. P. Coyne (ed.), *Ireland, Industrial and Agricultural*, Browne & Nolan, Dublin: 1902, pp. 271 f. Useful summaries of its policies up to 1922 will be found in *JDATI*, 19, 160 (by T. W. Russell), and *JDATI*, 23, 38 (by T. P. Gill).

the banks: they now found themselves committed to repay out of shrunken earnings.[11]

During the war Irish agricultural products had been given the windfall of a near-monopoly of the British market, but this magnificent opportunity to acquire lasting good-will was thrown away. When the war was over and supplies from Denmark and overseas were again available, the British consumer had only too clear a memory of bad eggs and worse butter from Ireland.[12] To restore the good name of Irish produce was obviously the first move towards recovery: it was not one that could have immediate results.

The fact was that in the early 1920s Irish agriculture suffered a profound set-back after a period of expansion and prosperity. The effect on production was severe. Between 1918 and 1925, it contracted markedly. Even the weather fought against agriculture. The rains of 1924 led to widespread livestock disease; the distress of 1924-5 was described as the worst that the western counties had experienced since the famine of 1879. It was no matter for wonder that the 1926 Banking Committee should note that 47 per cent of sales of farms had been abortive in 1925-6[13] compared with 8 per cent in 1915-16.

Policy 1922-32

The Commission on Agriculture, the first to be established by a native government, was appointed in November 1922, when the civil war was still in progress and its outcome still seemed doubtful. The terms of reference instructed it

to enquire into and report on the causes of the present depression in Agriculture and to recommend such remedies as will secure for Agriculture, and for Industries subsidiary to it, an assured basis for future expansion and prosperity.

The chairmanship was filled by James MacNeill and later by Professor J. P. Drew.[14] It presented five interim reports; the first on tobacco growing; the second on the marketing of butter; the third on the marketing of eggs; the fourth on agricultural credit; and the fifth on the licensing of bulls. It is notable that all these reports, dealing with technical issues, were unanimous; but, although there was agreement on means, there was no agreement on ends. The Commission ended its

11. This experience is still vividly remembered and must not be ignored in any discussion of how agricultural credit can best be provided and used. Many references to the position of the farmers vis-à-vis the banks in the early 1920s will be found in the minutes of evidence before the 1938 Banking Commission.

12. See the Irish Statesman, passim, in the summer and autumn 1925.

13. Second interim report, para. 16. All this report (on agricultural credit) gives a vivid picture of the position of agriculture.

14. The other members were R. A. Butler, C. M. Byrne, Michael Doyle, Joseph Johnston, George O'Brien, and Sir John Keane (who signed the majority report), and Thomas Johnson and Michael Duffy, the signatories of the minority report.

labours in April 1924 by presenting majority and minority reports which were in sharp conflict on the aims of agricultural production.

In several fields the majority recommended sweeping measures of State intervention, for example in livestock breeding and in the marketing of butter and eggs. These measures were designed to improve the framework within which the producer worked. The majority report was opposed to the granting of direct assistance by tariffs, subsidies, or guaranteed prices. In Irish circumstances, they could be paid for only out of revenue, that is 'by the agricultural community itself by passing money from one pocket to another with the added expense due to the cost of administrative services'. There were, however, specific cases, such as tobacco-growing, sugar beet, industrial alcohol, and the reclamation of bog lands, where the State might properly take the initiative and assist 'to a limited extent' by means of direct subsidy. But in the last resort 'the main work of agricultural recuperation must rest with the individual farmer, whether working singly or organized in co-operation with his fellows'. In general, therefore, the positive recommendations were directed towards improvements in the existing system: in production by better breeding policies, in marketing by branding and standardization; and, to return to the point from which the survey began, these efforts were to be directed towards the recovery and expansion of the export market.

Legislation on these lines began with the first Dairy Produce Act in 1924, followed by the Agricultural Produce (Eggs) Act in the same year and the Agricultural Produce (Fresh Meat) Act in 1930. These Acts aimed at the establishment of standards of production and presentation for butter, eggs, and meat. The Livestock Breeding Act of 1925 eliminated breeding from animals of indifferent strains. There has been controversy from time to time whether the Department of Agriculture has been correct in its breeding policies, but at least the issues were set out and breeding ceased to be a matter of indiscriminate use of scrub bulls and boars.

The long-term results of this legislation, which was thought to be almost revolutionary at the time, were not obtained. Changes in agricultural policy by a new government, with a very different scale of values, reduced production for export to a position of secondary importance. The immediate results, however, were notable and deserve to be recalled today when there is so much pessimism about the future of Irish agriculture. Irish eggs quickly retrieved their wartime reputation and obtained the highest quotation on the British market. The trend of butter exports, which had fallen to less than half the 1914 level by 1925, was even more remarkable. Marketing of creamery butter on national lines began in the spring of 1928; the following summer showed an expansion of exports and the price gap between Irish and Danish butter narrowed from between fifteen and twenty shillings to between two and three shillings. The volume of total exports (then almost entirely agricultural in origin) rose between 1926 and 1929 in the ratio of 87 to 104. Their value in 1929 was £47m., a figure which, incredibly enough, was not again approached until 1948, and then in a sadly depreciated currency. This is a remarkable, and perhaps comforting example of the resilience of Irish agriculture.

The purpose of these policies was to improve the efficiency of production and marketing so that Irish farmers could sell profitably in the free and fiercely competitive British market. That market was transformed by the events of 1931 in Great Britain: the formation of a National government in August, the abandonment of the Gold Standard in September and the general election in October. These led to the installation of a reconstituted National government in which the Conservative party, by then committed to the creation of a British tariff, was preponderant. The first enactment against free imports became law in November, and at the end of that month it was announced that measures for the protection of British agriculture were contemplated. A general tariff was provided by the Import Duties Act which became law on 29 February 1932. It was understood that preference would be given on a reciprocal basis to members of the Commonwealth in return for preference to British goods in their markets. These matters were negotiated at the Imperial Economic Conference held at Ottawa from 21 July to 20 August 1932. The agreements concluded by Great Britain were enacted by the Ottawa Agreements Bill which became law in November 1932. Henceforward, within the limits of whatever marketing regulation might be imposed by the British government in the interests of its own farmers, the Commonwealth producer received more favourable treatment than others, such as the Danes.

The depression, which was the immediate cause of these fundamental changes in Great Britain had been felt in Ireland before the summer of 1931. It was mitigated to some extent by the fact that the fall in prices had been much more severe in cereals than in livestock, though livestock products suffered. Wheat, by 1931, had fallen to its lowest price for generations; but that did not affect the Irish farmer, who did not grow it. The world-wide glut, however, was so great that at the end of 1930 a prohibitive duty on imported butter was imposed by the Irish government in November 1930. A duty on imported oats and oatmeal followed in October 1931. In the next month an Act was passed to prevent dumping, under which a duty on bacon was imposed.[15] The changes in British policy were naturally studied and in January 1932 Hogan and

15. The Customs Duties (Provisional Imposition) Act. The debates show very clearly that Hogan had lost none of his belief in the need for efficiency and that he regarded protection as worthless and dangerous to an exporting industry.

the Minister for Industry and Commerce (Mr. McGilligan) visited London 'with the object of examining the trade relations between the United Kingdom and the Free State as a preliminary to the general discussion of inter-imperial trade at Ottawa'.[16] Their government was defeated in the general election of 16 February 1932; on 9 March Mr. de Valera, in forming his first administration, gave the Department of Agriculture to Dr. James Ryan. Thus Hogan left office, to which he was not destined to return, being killed in a road accident in July 1936.

Policy 1932–8

The incoming government was deeply committed to a policy of protection. From its foundation in 1926, when free trading was still in fashion, the Fianna Fáil party had emphasized the importance of the home market. In doing so they followed the lines of the Minority Report of the 1923 Commission.

The signatories of that submission[17] had stated that:

we dissent from the report of the majority in that it appears to view agriculture and all the operations connected therewith as a means of making money, and to test the prosperity of agriculture by the amount of the balance at the end of a period lying to the credit of the farmer. . . . We believe to be fallacious the theory that the maximum benefit to the nation will be achieved by encouraging every individual in the nation to pursue his own personal advantage; we are emphatically of opinion that State policy respecting agriculture must be guided by a clear recognition of the principle that in the utilization of the national resources, including the land, individual self-interest must be subordinated to the national welfare.

The national welfare, they held, would be best served by the direction of agriculture:

firstly, to satisfy the needs of the people of this country, and secondly to supply the demand from other countries for commodities of a quality or kind which we can produce to advantage, and to exchange these for commodities which we cannot produce or which we can only produce at an exorbitant cost.

This involved the positive encouragement of tillage, and especially of wheat-growing. They therefore recommended that rates on pasture land should be increased and that the State should guarantee a minimum price for limited quantities of wheat. The signatories of the minority report were ready to agree with their colleagues in recommending reforms in breeding policies and in marketing—both of them matters on which the fortunes of the export trade depended. But they refused to give any priority to that trade. Priority was to be given to the growing in Ireland of everything that the Irish people normally wanted for food,

16. *AR*, 1932, p. 123.   17. Messrs Thomas Johnson and Michael Duffy.

except where climatic conditions made that obviously impossible. Production was to be for subsistence, not (except in a most subordinate sense) for exchange.

The same line of thought emerges clearly in the opening lines of the minority report submitted after the next full-dress examination of agricultural policy—the report of the Select Committee on Wheat-growing.[18] 'The primary purpose of agriculture', it began, 'is to provide human food. Wheat is the raw material of the most important single article of food of the population of Saorstát Éireann. There is, therefore, a presumption in favour of the opinion that the first function of farming in Saorstát Éireann should be the production of wheat.' In fact, however, the domestic output of bread stuffs was 'not sufficient to supply our needs for twelve days every year'.

The signatories of the minority report rejected the view that the limited cultivation of wheat was the result of the Irish climate or the nature of Irish soil. 'This argument', they remarked:

is part of the general view that the policy forced upon us as individuals by the pressure of external competition is necessarily the wisest policy for us as a community. We would be justified in dismissing this contention as unworthy of consideration in view of the fact that Ireland is the only country in the world which for over eighty years has had a continually declining population and is still unable to check the decline.

The encouragement of wheat might not necessarily result in a great increase in the number of persons employed in agriculture but it would 'employ more fully the persons at present engaged in the industry, and help to retain them on the land'.

The majority report contested all these claims. It argued that wheat-growing was not as profitable to the individual farmer as other crops; and that, if the object were to secure maximum gross wealth, then potatoes or flax would be more efficacious and would also call for more labour. On that basis, it would be better to subsidize all tillage. That course would eliminate the high probability that the subsidization of wheat would lead only to the substitution of that crop for others that were not subsidized. It would also take care of the farmer whose land was not suitable for wheat. On the specific question of providing employment, it quoted Mr. Hooper's review of Irish agriculture[19] to support the argument that the problem of unemployment was more likely to be solved by the encouragement of dairy farming than by that

18. *First and Second Interim Reports on Wheat Growing and the Question of a Tariff on Flour*, Economic Committee, 1928. The signatories of the Majority Report were Messrs. Earnan de Blaghd, P. McGilligan, P. Hogan, M. O'Braonain, John Leonard, A. R. S. Nutting, and George O'Brien. The signatories of the Minority Report were Messrs. Eamon de Valera, Seamus O'Riain, Sean F. Lemass, Thomas Kennedy, and Richard S. Anthony (the last two subject to reservations).

19. *Agricultural Statistics, 1847–1926*, I. 22, 1928.

of cereal cultivation. The argument that the country should be self-sufficient in an essential foodstuff was countered by the claim that wheat could be produced easily enough in the event of an emergency and that, in that case, the real problem would not be to get food into the country but rather to get at least some proportion of our surplus food exported and to get it paid for. On both sides of the Economic Committee, the need for self-sufficiency in time of war must have seemed academic enough in 1929.

At the last annual conference of his party before its accession to office Mr. de Valera placed wheat-growing and the development of the home market for agricultural produce in the forefront of his programme. He said:

With regard to economic problems I hold more strongly than ever to our aim of making Ireland as far as possible self-sufficing. The countries which to-day are suffering most from the prevailing depression are those which are most dependent on foreign trade. Ireland, thanks to her soil and climate, is in the fortunate position of being able to produce all the necessaries of life for her own people. It is our intention to enable home producers to take advantage of that position by giving them security in the home market. In pursuit of this policy, we propose to protect every branch of agriculture.[20]

The trend towards self-sufficiency was strengthened by the Anglo-Irish dispute over the land annuities which broke out soon after the new government took office.[21] In July 1932 special duties were imposed on

20. As reported in the *Irish Press*, 28 October 1931.
21. The details of this dispute are perhaps best studied in Hancock, *Survey of British Commonwealth Affairs*, vol. i, 'Problems of Nationality', Oxford University Press, London: 1937, pp. 340–68. Its settlement, by the Anglo-Irish agreements of 1938, is described by Mansergh, *Survey of British Commonwealth Affairs, Problems of External Policy, 1931–1939*, Oxford University Press, London: 1952, pp. 312–13.
The land annuities were, and are, the annual repayments made by tenant-purchasers in respect of moneys advanced for the purchase of their holdings under the provisions of the Land Purchase Acts. Until 1932 the annuities were collected by the Irish government and transmitted to the British Commissioners of the National Debt for the discharge of the interest and sinking fund payments prescribed by these Acts. Sir Keith Hancock has described the controversy as 'a dispute between Irish lawyers, a dispute between Irish political parties, a dispute between successive Irish governments, a dispute between Mr. Eamon de Valera's government and the British government'. The campaign for the retention of the annuities was said to have been initiated by Colonel Maurice Moore and Professor William Magennis (see correspondence in the *Irish Statesman*—which described the campaign as 'organised hypocrisy'—for January and February 1927). It seems more likely that the true precursor was Mr Peadar O'Donnell who has recalled his activities in *There will be Another Day*, Dolmen Press, Dublin: 1963. He went much further than the colonel or the professor or (later) Mr. de Valera by claiming that the farmers should not pay annuities to any government, British or Irish. The issue was taken up by the Fianna Fáil party in the general election of September 1927. The political issues may be studied in a full-dress Dáil debate, see *PDDE*, 29, *passim*. The legal issues may be studied in a White Paper, P. No. 579, Stationery Office, Dublin: n.d., published by the (Cumann na nGaedheal) government which set out the advice of counsel that the annuities were properly payable to the British Commissioners of the National Debt and in a rebutting pamphlet

Irish livestock, dairy produce, and meat entering the United Kingdom. Some of these duties were increased later; and quota restrictions were also imposed.

The most detailed and coherent statement of the policies introduced in 1932 will be found in the minutes of evidence of the Banking Commission.[22] In December 1935, Mr. Daniel Twomey, then secretary of the Department of Agriculture, appeared before the Commission and sustained a prolonged interrogation on their nature and aims.

Mr. Twomey submitted a memorandum from the Department. It stated that:

Up to recent years the agricultural economy of the country had been governed by two factors—the existence of an unlimited market in Great Britain for cattle, butter, bacon, eggs, and other livestock products, and the low level of prices for grain crops on the world markets. As a result, large surpluses of livestock and livestock products were produced for export. At the same time the home production of grain was limited almost entirely to what was required for the feeding of livestock. The country's requirements of wheat for milling and of wheaten flour for bread-making were imported at prices which our farmers regarded as unremunerative. This state of affairs resulted in the agricultural industry of the country becoming largely dependent upon the continued existence of an outlet in Great Britain for livestock and livestock products. It also meant that the country was mainly dependent for a very important portion of its food supplies on wheat and flour imported from abroad. Moreover, it deprived the country of the employment that would result from the production of the wheat and other cereals required for the food of the population and for livestock. The defects of the system became apparent when the depression in world prices of livestock and livestock products set in followed by the imposition of Import Duties on such products and the quantitative restriction of imports of certain of the commodities into Great Britain.

For these reasons, policy as regards agricultural production was directed to

(1) making the country self-sufficient in respect of all agricultural commodities for the production of which the soil and climate are suitable or for which suitable substitutes can be grown in the country; and

(2) producing for export a surplus of such commodities over and above home requirements, equivalent to what the export trade can absorb at an economic price.

This would entail several changes in the traditional pattern of agricultural production. In particular it would involve a reduction in

published by the Fianna Fáil party containing an opinion by other counsel that the annuities might properly be retained by the Irish government. In the event, the Irish government announced its intention of retaining the annuities pending arbitration and the British government imposed the special duties in order to recoup itself. The dispute was not conducted on its merits by either government: it could not be separated from the other quarrels arising out of Mr. de Valera's policy of revising the Treaty of 1921.

22. Published by the Stationery Office, Dublin, vol. ii, pp. 1189–1306; 1330–68.

the production of cattle. On the other hand, although handicapped by the special duties, the export trade in butter, eggs, and bacon would not be seriously affected. The memorandum remarked that:

at the present stage of industrial development exports of agricultural products must be relied on mainly to offset necessary imports of raw materials for industrial purposes and of commodities which cannot be produced in this country.

The reduction in earnings from cattle exports would be balanced by the domestic production of agricultural products which previously had been imported. These were set out in the memorandum.

The principal agricultural commodities capable of being produced in this country which are still imported in large, though reduced, quantities, are (1) grain (wheat and maize); (2) fruit, principally apples and soft fruits and fruit juice and pulp; (3) vegetables, mainly onions and tomatoes, and (4) tobacco. In addition, mention should be made of sugar manufactured from sugar beet which can be grown in this country. Steps have been taken by the Government which will ultimately result in the displacement of these imports by home-grown produce to a very large extent. This displacement will involve a very considerable increase in the area under tillage.

These policies entailed state intervention in order to provide adequate prices. A minimum price was fixed for wheat; the difference between it and the average market price was paid out of State funds.[23] Legislation provided for the absorption of surplus oats and barley by mixing them with maize for feed. The growing of sugar beet and tobacco was encouraged by remissions of duty.[24] The growers of fruit and vegetables were protected by tariffs and quotas. Exports, even if directed to the United Kingdom, were subsidized. Attempts were also made to find alternative markets for agricultural produce; though they did not meet with striking success.[25]

Indeed, a reading of this exposition of the new policy leaves the impression that, with the great exception of the proposed reduction of cattle herds, it would have meant, even if it had been fulfilled, very little change in the pattern of agriculture. In the subsequent evidence given by Mr. Twomey, it appeared that an extra 500,000 (or, allowing for rotation, 1,000,000) acres of wheat would be needed to satisfy total

23. Professor Johnston suggested as a motto for the new policy—*cras aret qui nunquam aravit, quique aravit cras aret.*

24. The measures taken to encourage the growing of tobacco were eventually discontinued because the results were disappointing.

25. An agreement with Spain amounted to the exchange of a quota for Irish eggs in return for a quota for Spanish oranges. Belgium granted import quotas for cattle and butter. With Germany, from which much had been hoped, the trade agreement provided that the Reich would buy £1 of Irish goods for every £3 of German goods imported by the Free State. The 1930s were not a favourable period in which to develop new trading contacts; and these arrangements, it will be seen, did not open new channels of any importance.

requirements and another 400,000 acres for maize, tobacco, and vegetables. If all this were achieved, the increase in tillage would be of the order of 1,500,000 acres in any one year. This would certainly have been a considerable increase over the levels of 1931 and preceding years. Nevertheless, it represented just about 15 per cent, of the total area under pasture and hay, which was 9,900,000 acres in 1934. The witness agreed that:

we do not expect that, as a result of the present policy, there will probably be what you would call a profound change of economy. There will be adjustments. If we continue at the present rate, we will in time extend the acreage under wheat from 165,000 acres to 650,000 acres. Although that is very important in itself, one cannot say that it is going to bring about a profound change in our agricultural economy.

It would, however, have some far-reaching implications. The British market was no longer to be relied on.[26] Alternative markets might be found but hardly in a degree that would compensate for it. If exports were to be permanently reduced, a balance in payments could be achieved only by reducing imports. Greater self-sufficiency was therefore necessary, not simply as an emergency measure but as a permanent policy. This was the official attitude in the subsequent interrogation on the departmental memorandum.

It was, however, clear that self-sufficiency, even if attained, would not go far to meet the situation. If the proposed domestic production of wheat, animal feed, vegetables, fruit and tobacco was achieved, the saving of imports would amount to £5m. in a year. That sum represented 11 per cent of the annual imports of the time. It exactly equalled the then value of the exports of stout and porter. If, as Dr. Per Jacobssen pointed out, Messrs. Guinness were to move from the country, the effect of all the innovations in policy on the balance of payments would be offset.[27]

It was also accepted that, even if the new policy were operated successfully, some problems of surplus would remain. 'The policy is not to produce more than all our available markets will absorb.'[28] That was not too easy to bring about. In cattle and poultry the productive capacity of agriculture was much greater than that; but it was hoped that these difficulties would be solved by a continued fall in the number of cattle and, less consistently, by a recovery in poultry prices. Thus there were two strings to the policy. The way to solve inconvenient surpluses

26. Cf. the well-remembered phrase 'So far as I can see the British market is gone for ever' (Mr. de Valera in August 1933, *PDDE*, 49, 1610). The qualification is not often remembered; but then it was not often used by Mr de Valera's supporters.

27. *MEBC*, ii, 1206. At this time, Messrs. Guinness were building the Park Royal Brewery in London.

28. Ibid. 1287.

was not to have any, by reducing production. Self-sufficiency might raise internal costs and so affect export capacity; but that could and should be accepted in a system in which the export trade was to count for less than in the past. The new situation, in this view, called for a complete reversal of the values that had been accepted up to 1932. In the words used by the witness:

I think, in the new set of circumstances that now exist, that the new agricultural policy is better balanced than the policy it succeeded. At the same time, I want to make it quite clear that I consider the policy adopted in this country prior to the year 1930 or 1931 was suitable for the circumstances that existed at the time.[29]

The decision to reduce cattle herds was implemented in 1934 by the provision of a bounty on calf-skins and of a scheme for the free distribution of beef to the unemployed. This was perhaps the one part of the new policy which might have had far-reaching consequences; but the 'slaughter of the calves' was so severe a shock to public opinion that the scheme had a short life.[30]

The positions occupied by the Irish and British governments in the summer of 1932 had already been modified when Dr. Twomey gave his evidence in December 1935. The first of what were known as the Coal–Cattle pacts was announced on 3 January 1935. It had a duration of one year. The British government increased the quota of Irish cattle allowed to enter the United Kingdom. The Irish government undertook to allow purchases of British coal to an equivalent value, which meant in practice that virtually all Irish supplies of coal would be drawn from Great Britain. These were limited concessions. The British special duties on Irish agricultural produce and the Irish emergency duties on British coal were continued. The agreement, however, was of considerable importance in so far as it suggested that neither side was prepared to continue economic warfare indefinitely. It arrested, as was no doubt the intention, the tendency to reduce cattle herds and it gave hope that at some future date the restraints on Anglo-Irish trade would be removed.

Fulfilment was delayed for a longer time than was then expected. On 17 February 1936 the pact was renewed for another year. It was again renewed in February 1937 when the quota for cattle was increased. The next move was decisive. Negotiations over a wide field between the two governments were opened on 17 January 1938 and

---

29. Ibid. 1263. For further details see Dr. Twomey's evidence at *MEBC*, ii, 1193, and the contemporary annual reports of the Department of Agriculture.

30. The economic war has been studied in some detail by Johnston, *Irish Agriculture in Transition*, Hodges & Figgis, Dublin: 1951, pp. 31–55. In 'The Outlook for Irish Agriculture', *Studies*, 1939, pp. 195 and 375 he estimated that the cash income of farmers fell from £32m. in 1929–30 to £14m. in 1933.

were successfully concluded on the following 25 April. The first agreement concerned the transfer of the three ports retained by Great Britain under the provisions of the Treaty of 1921. By the second agreement the Irish government paid £10m. to the British government 'as a final settlement of all financial claims of either of the two Governments against the other'.[31] The third agreement covered trade between the two countries. This ended the British special duties and the Irish emergency duties and, in the words of the *Annual Register*, brought the commercial relations of Great Britain and Éire into line with those of the Dominions under the Ottawa Agreement.[32] In retrospect, the long delay between the first pact in 1935 and the final agreement in 1938 appears to have been most unfortunate. In the event, too little time was left for readjustment before the outbreak of war.

Policy in wartime

Irish agricultural policy was thus provided with an opportunity for revision to meet an altered situation. The agreement did not restore the situation to the *status quo ante bellum*: Great Britain now followed a policy of agricultural protection and was entitled to place quantitative restrictions on imports. Nevertheless, the principal market was again accessible; and the Irish contribution to it was so small, except in the case of livestock, that quantitative restrictions seemed to be a remote possibility, all the more remote as the European situation worsened. Policy could again be based on the development of the export trade: the ground lost for six years could be regained.

The need for some re-examination of agricultural policy appeared to have been realized when the appointment of a new commission of enquiry into agriculture was announced; the work of this commission, however, was overtaken by events. In September 1939 the outbreak of war and the declaration of Irish neutrality created an entirely new situation. The proceedings of the commission were therefore discontinued. During the six years that followed, agricultural policy depended on events that were far beyond the power of any Irish government to control: it could not be framed by deliberate choice.

A return to the older policy of free imports was now impossible and, even if it had been possible, undesirable. It was impossible because neither wheat nor maize were readily available abroad; if they had been available, and the currency to purchase them could be found, the prob-

---

31. It should be pointed out that the land annuities, which formed the principal item in question, amounted to nearly £3m. a year; and most of them had over thirty years to run in 1938.

32. *AR*, 1938, p. 117. The trade agreement of 1938 is more fully discussed in Chapter Three.

lem of finding shipping was almost insuperable. It was undesirable because reliance on imports would involve undue dependence on the goodwill of the belligerents who controlled the seas and shipping. Reduced supplies of wheat and other essential imports were made available even when the Battle of the Atlantic was at its height and shipping space was most precious to the Anglo-American cause, but there was clearly a limit to the degree to which a country which sought to preserve its neutrality could or should depend on the goodwill of belligerents; Ireland was now to experience self-sufficiency in earnest.

This was most notable in the increase of tillage which was expanded from 1,484,000 acres in 1939 to 2,463,000 acres in 1945. On the other hand, the output of livestock and livestock products fell away (largely on account of the shortage of feeding stuffs and also on account of an outbreak of foot-and-mouth disease in 1941) and in the last year of the war reached only 86 per cent of the 1938–9 level. In the 1930s the United Kingdom had adopted a policy of paying a higher price for domestically reared and fattened cattle than was available for similar cattle exported fat from Ireland. Irish exports of fat and store cattle were also limited by quota, so there was a discrimination against Irish cattle by price and by quantitative restriction. These measures were taken as part of British agricultural policy generally, and not specifically in pursuance of the 'economic war'. They were not affected, therefore, by the Anglo-Irish agreement of 1938. The quota restriction was indeed suspended but price differentiation remained and was continued throughout the war years. The picture of a neutral Ireland waxing prosperous on wartime prices is therefore grossly misleading.[33]

The true position was accurately described by the Smiddy Commission in 1945.

At the outbreak of the present World War our agriculture had not had time to recover from the adverse effects of the previous years. In order to provide an adequate supply of wheat and other crops for direct consumption by our human population our Government was obliged to intensify once more the emphasis on cash crop cultivation and diminish the emphasis on grass-land cultivation and the cultivation of tillage crops for animal feeding.[34]

33. For example, see Mr. Winston Churchill's memorandum to the Chancellor of the Exchequer, 1 December 1940: 'The straits to which we are being reduced by Irish action compel a reconsideration of the subsidies [to Ireland]. It can hardly be argued that we can go on paying them to our last gasp . . . Pray let me know how these subsidies could be terminated, and what retaliatory measures could be taken in the financial sphere by the Irish, observing that we are not afraid of their cutting off their food, as it would save us the enormous mass of fertilizers and feeding-stuffs we have to carry into Ireland through the de Valera-aided German blockade.' W. S. Churchill, *Their Finest Hour*, 1st edition, Cassell, London: pp. 534–5. The fertilizers and feeding-stuffs were, unfortunately, nearly as mythical as the subsidies.

34. *Committee of Inquiry on Post-Emergency Agricultural Policy*, P. No. 7175, Stationery Office, Dublin, para. 87.

This new committee of inquiry was appointed on 8 September 1942 with the following terms of reference:

to consider and report on the measures best calculated to provide for the situation which may be expected to exist in the agricultural industry at the end of the Emergency with special reference to measures for increasing the fertility of the land, promoting efficiency in the industry and making the various branches of the industry self-supporting.

Three interim reports, on the cattle and dairying industry, on poultry production and on veterinary services were issued. The majority report, which was signed on 1 June 1945,[35] argued that agriculture was the basis of the national economy and that it was essential even to industrial development 'to the extent that the latter requires the import of essential raw materials and agricultural exports are, in the last analysis, the principal means by which industrial raw materials may be acquired and paid for'. It was reasonable to suppose that British policy would require increasing imports of agricultural products from this country. Moreover,

the post-Emergency world will be one that has been devastated and impoverished by more than five years of war. . . . Restrictionist policies cannot seriously be entertained in a world of acute scarcities. Common sense as well as common humanity will suggest the need for expanding the production of every kind of agricultural produce.[36]

What was good ethics and good politics would also be good economics. If the country did not develop its export capacity it would not easily find markets when the period of scarcity had passed.

The first minority report opened with two observations which presented a strongly dissenting view.[37] The first was that 'the primary function of agriculture in this country is to provide food for the people'. The second was that 'agriculture is not only an industry—and in this country by far our greatest industry—but is also a way of living'. It suggested that the depression of the early 1930s was 'but the final phase of the collapse of a programme which, for so many years, had for its object the supplying of foreign markets with food and other primary products at prices which, by suicidal international competition, eventually fell below cost of production'. Re-entry into international competition could not be contemplated. The home market was of primary importance to the producer and it could be increased. But the export market should not be wholly abandoned.

35. The membership was Professor T. A. Smiddy (chairman); Mr. R. C. Barton and Professors C. Boyle, J. P. Drew, and Joseph Johnston (who signed the majority report), Professor E. J. Sheehy and Mr. J. Mahony (who signed the first minority report), and Dr. Henry Kennedy, who signed a second minority report.
36. Ibid., para. 92.
37. The second Minority Report by Dr. Henry Kennedy agreed in principle with the Majority Report.

Increased production from our land is imperative. A potential market at home awaits the produce of some of this increased production. The remainder must be exported and every effort should be made to extend up to the limit which is profitable, the volume of our agricultural produce reaching the export market. Nor should any measure be adopted which would limit the exportation of produce up to the availability of a remunerative market abroad.[38]

Post-war policy

The choice between these two points of view was dictated by events. In July 1947 the Irish government accepted the invitation of the British and French governments to meet in Paris to elaborate the European Recovery Programme. The manner in which Ireland could best contribute to reconstruction was summed up in the first paragraph of the study of Ireland prepared for Congress by American technicians.

Ireland's principal problem is the restoration of agricultural production and Ireland's main contribution to European recovery will take place through the production of more food for export. Since the economy of Ireland is closely related to that of the United Kingdom the major part of increased food exports will probably go there. To expand its exports of agricultural products, Ireland needs to mechanize its agriculture, obtain more fertilizers and animal feedstuffs, increase its imports of fuel and overhaul its transportation system. [39]

In the following year, 1948, the Irish long-term programme covering the years 1949–53, was published in a White Paper.[40] Its primary aim was described as 'the improvement and intensification of agricultural production'. It went on to state that:

Agriculture will naturally continue to play the major role in our national economy.

We must continue to rely on our agricultural production for the exports which, supplemented by our invisible earnings, enable us to pay for the things we must import. Our long term programme envisages an increase in the volume of agricultural output of 22 per cent over production in 1947, and 11 per cent over that in the year 1929–30. Our export programme for the year 1952–53 assumes an increase in the volume of our agricultural exports of over 100 per cent over 1947, which is equivalent to about one quarter higher than the pre-war level. In terms of value, this represents, on account of price increases, a level of exports in 1952–3 approximately 138 per cent higher than in 1947.

Thus policy was turned again towards the export market. The revision in 1948 of the trade agreement with Great Britain, which removed much of the wartime discrimination, appeared to prepare the way for a notable increase in agricultural produce for export.

38. Minority Report, para. 90.
39. *The European Recovery Programme*, published as a White Paper by the Minister for External Affairs, P. 8792, Stationery Office, Dublin: 1948.
40. P. 9198, Stationery Office, Dublin: 1948. This policy was vigorously pursued by Mr. James Dillon who became Minister for Agriculture in 1948.

The aims and methods of agricultural policy were again reviewed in the White Paper on Economic Expansion in 1958. The following summary will indicate the lines of approach.[41]

There is little scope for increased home consumption of farm produce; the average standard of nutrition in Ireland is high and the population is not rising. Increased agricultural production will for the most part be for sale abroad. It must, therefore, be competitive, which for many products means that costs must be reduced per unit of output. The test of agricultural policy, therefore, is whether in the long run it enables output to be increased at costs which make exports profitable without subsidization. . . . The main objective of agricultural policy in the years to come is not only to maintain but to intensify the welcome upward trend in agricultural output which has been evident in recent years . . .

Policy is then considered under the following general headings:

> (a) the improvement of grasslands,
> (b) dairying,
> (c) pigs and bacon,
> (d) poultry and eggs,
> (e) tillage,
> (f) agricultural education,
> (g) credit, trade, and marketing.

It is pointed out that:

by far the greatest proportion of our agricultural land has always been and will continue to be under grass . . . It is highly unlikely that, even in times of emergency, more than about 20 to 25 per cent of our total land will be tilled. The use of phosphates on grasslands is to be a main objective of policy. This will make it possible to carry much larger numbers of livestock; and a target of 1,500,000 cows by 1964 is set out. Granted the difficulties of the dairying industry (to which only a limited subsidization of exports is promised) these extra cows should be bred for beef rather than for milk. The difficulties of the trade in pigs and bacon and in poultry and eggs are attributed to the collapse of the export trade on account of British domestic agricultural policies, production in small units and problems of marketing. It is proposed to maintain the extent of the tillage area and to provide cash crops such as wheat, malting barley, and sugar beet.

In 1963 the Second Programme remarked that:

the fundamental problem confronting Irish agriculture at the present time is that, while the capacity exists to expand production substantially, current international conditions favour the profitable disposal of only certain forms of additional output. The conditions prevailing in the export markets in which we must seek outlets for the greater part of our increased produce are not favourable for some of our food products, notably dairy products, pigmeat and other grain-derived produce.[42]

41. Pr. 4796, Stationery Office, Dublin: 1958, pp. 11–26.
42. *Second Programme for Economic Expansion, 1963*, Pr. 7239, Stationery Office, Dublin: para. 32. See discussion of this Programme on pp. 261–2.

The Programme therefore stressed the need for concentration on three aspects of agricultural policy: a search for an improved and stable access to export markets, a more rapid rate of improvement in productive efficiency and, in areas where small holdings predominate, the creation of viable family units.

More specifically an average annual growth rate of gross agricultural product of 2.9 per cent in the decade 1960–70, or 3.8 per cent in the period 1964–70, was envisaged. This general approach was elaborated in a further and very comprehensive White Paper which surveyed the entire field of agricultural activity[43]. It contemplated an increase in the output of cattle from 1,126,000 in 1963 to 1,500,000 by 1970. The number of cows would grow from 1,323,000 to 1,700,000 in the same period. The output of sheep was to grow from 1,900,000 to 2,500,000. For pigs, an output target of 2,030,000 was set, representing an increase of about 20 per cent over the 1963 output.

In regard to milk production, the Programme stated that the quantity of milk likely to be supplied to creameries in the closing years of the decade might amount to around 550 million gallons as against the 1963 intake of 337 million gallons. This would involve a surplus for disposal abroad in one form or another of 340 million gallons, an increase of 200 million gallons. This would raise, as the Programme pointed out, considerable financial problems. Assistance was, therefore, to be given to the Irish Agricultural Organization Society[44] to enable it to consolidate the co-operative creameries and agricultural co-operation in general.

STRUCTURE OF AGRICULTURE

Area of agricultural land

The acreage of agricultural land (that is the acreage under crops and pasture was returned at 12,004,000 in 1851, at 12,520,000 in 1901, and at 11,514,000 on the average of the three years 1958–60. It is not surprising to find such a contraction in a period when the rural population declined so heavily. The magnitude of the reduction, however, especially in the present century, has been used to support arguments that a larger number of families might be settled on the land if more energetic policies were adopted. The following note is relevant.

43. *Agriculture in the Second Programme*, Pr. 7697.
44. The Irish Agricultural Organization Society was founded in 1894 for the organizing and servicing of the agricultural co-operative societies which had been established throughout the country. The majority of these societies have been creameries, although there has been a noticeable extension of activity during the last twenty years. At the end of 1966 there were 341 co-operatives affiliated to the IAOS with a membership of about 127,000 and a trade turnover of £127m.

It should be recognized that it is impossible to . . . draw precisely and on a consistent basis the line between good grazing and rough grazing, the latter of which is regarded as non-agricultural land . . .[45]

No objective definitions of what constitutes agricultural land have been laid down, and a great part of the decline seems to be the result of re-assessments. The greater part of this apparent contraction has occurred in five counties (Wicklow, Kerry, Galway, Mayo, and Donegal), where the land merges easily from one classification into another. It would therefore be rash to suppose that there is a reserve of land which could be brought back into cultivation and used to support more families.

Number and size of holdings

In 1960, 50 per cent of all holdings of over one acre could be classified as holdings of not more than thirty acres (see Table 4.1), and 71 per cent were less than 50 acres; but the proportion of smaller holdings has been decreasing thoughout this century. The number of farms of 30–50 acres has remained constant in the last half-century, and the number of 50–200 acres has increased; the reduction falls almost exclusively among the smaller farms.[46] It is notable that a great deal of this reduction occurred between 1912 and 1931, but it will be seen that the rate of decline appears to have been greater in the 1950s than it was in the two preceding decades.

Taking only agricultural land, 62 per cent of the total was on holdings of under 50 acres in Connacht and 55 per cent in the Ulster counties; but only 25 per cent of the agricultural land in Leinster, and 27 per cent of it in Munster, consisted of holdings of that size. A high proportion of the smaller farms are on the poorer soils and a high proportion of the larger farms are on the richer.

45. *Agricultural Statistics, 1934–1956*, Pr. 4335, Stationery Office, Dublin: 1960, p. viii. The note goes on to recall that the amount of agricultural land was consistently under-reported to the enumerators when Compulsory Tillage Orders were in operation.

46. Summaries of all agricultural statistics will be found in (a) *Agricultural Statistics, 1847–1926*, I. 22, 1928; (b) *Agricultural Statistics, 1927–1933*, P. 1577, 1935; (c) *Agricultural Statistics, 1934–1956*, already cited; and (d) the results of the 1960 census of agriculture which were subsequently published as *Agricultural Statistics, 1960*, Pr. 7540. Agricultural statistics have been collected by the police yearly since 1847, with the exception of the period 1919–24. Since 1956 the returns have been based on samples except in 1960. See 1962 SA 57.

A further survey made in 1965 showed the number of holdings to be as follows:

Above 1 acre and not exceeding 15	67,956
Above 15 acres and not exceeding 30	68,769
Above 30 acres and not exceeding 50	61,238
Above 50 acres and not exceeding 100	55,197
Above 100 acres and not exceeding 200	23,325
Above 200 acres	6,971
Total holdings above 1 acre	283,456

The Irish farmer is as likely as not to be the holder of not more than 50 acres; but, if one counts by acres rather than by holders, Irish land is much more likely than not to be part of a relatively large farm. Table 4.1 shows that in 1960 the total number of holdings over 1 acre was

TABLE 4.1

Number of agricultural holdings (thousands), according to size, 1912–60

Year	1–14 acres	15–29 acres	30–49 acres	50–99 acres	100–99 acres	Over 200 acres	All holdings over 1 acre
1912	164	105	59	49	20	9	406
1931	104	90	62	50	21	8	336
1949	89	87	62	51	22	7	319
1960	71	73	62	54	23	7	290

Source: *Agricultural Statistics*

290,000 and of this total 206,000 were 50 acres and under. In that year the total farm acreage under crops and pasture was 11,200,000. It was distributed as follows:

52,521 acres were on farms of		under 1 acre
492,045 ,,	,,	1–15 acres
1,449,496 ,,	,,	15–30 acres
2,060,641 ,,	,,	30–50 acres
i.e. 4,054,703 ,,	,,	of 50 acres and under
3,098,368 ,,	,,	of 50–100 acres
2,472,690 ,,	,,	of 100–200 acres
1,573,925 ,,	,,	of over 200
i.e. 7,144,983 ,,	,,	of over 50 acres

The perplexities of agricultural policy will be readily perceived.[47]

47. Cf. paras 10–12 of the Smiddy Report. More recent surveys have been J. J. Byrne, 'Some Provincial Variations in Irish Agriculture', *JSSISI*, 1958–9, p. 60, which notes a widening gap between trends in Leinster and Munster on one hand and Connacht and the Ulster counties on the other. Also R. C. Geary, 'Variability in Agricultural Statistics', *JSSISI*, 1956–7, 1, who refers to 'fantastic variability'. Cf. also Attwood, 'Agriculture in the Irish Economy'; *IBR*, June 1962, p. 20 who notes that 'in the National Farm Survey . . . the average output per man was found to vary from under £200 on the small subsistence farms in the West to over £1,000 on the large mixed dairying and cash cropping farms on the better land. Even within farms of the same size and type the average productivity of the best one-third of farms in the sample was found to be about double that of the farms in the lowest income groups in a number of the farming systems.'
Reference may be made to the *Final Report of the National Farm Survey 1955/6 1957/8* (Pr. 6180). This was undertaken with the object, *inter alia*, of establishing the level of income from agricultural activity for individual farms and the variation in such incomes; the extent of the differences, in financial terms, between farms of different sizes and in different regions; and the differences between farms of similar size and location following different patterns of farming.
The number of farms covered was 2,620, of which 1,174 were covered throughout the Survey. It is apparent from the Report that returns for individual farms showed a

5. DISTRIBUTION OF FARMS BY SIZE, 1966

The dots have been placed as far as possible in the areas actually farmed. Gaps include the major uplands and lowland peat bog. Table 4.1 shows the decline in the number of small farms since 1912. Note that there are certain differences in the collation of statistics between the Republic and Northern Ireland. Sources: *Ulster Year Book* and *Statistical Abstracts*.

Interrelation of farms

A survey made in 1957 made the following observations:

The livestock industry is the integrating force in Irish farming. Surplus animals bred on dairy and small farms are sold to the big farms to be finished and fattened for home consumption or for export. From this domestic trade in animals a close interdependence has developed between the various sizes of holding and the different regions of the country. The fattening region is roughly a triangle of counties stretching from Galway in the west to the eastern seaboard. The dairying industry is concentrated mainly in the south and south-west, while the north-western and western counties contain large numbers of small farms ... The fortunes of all sections of agriculture are linked to livestock production and the general prosperity of the economy is associated with the cattle export trade. It is therefore considered desirable that the integrated system of livestock production should be preserved. But the pattern of production in Irish agriculture is essentially extensive, yielding a relatively low output per acre and affording limited scope for employment. It is based on permanent pasture, which involves a low ratio of input to output, and it has a small and falling labour content as the experience of recent decades clearly shows. Furthermore the mutual dependence of the various sectors does not necessarily represent mutual benefit. The pool of immature stock provided by dairy and small farms is of undoubted advantage to the larger farms and enables them to exploit the opportunity presented by the British market, but it is questionable whether the production of these young animals is profitable to the farms concerned. Existing trends suggest that it is not and that the breeding and rearing farms bear a disproportionate share of the cost of cattle production.[48]

Nevertheless, the economy of the small farms tends to change towards carrying more dry cattle. Another writer in 1957 remarked on the change in their activities:

In the years preceding 1939 the small farms supported a relatively dense population. Many of the very small units gave only part-time employment but a considerable number were farmed sufficiently intensively to provide a living for fairly large families. The economy of the latter farms was based on pigs and poultry, with dairying in some areas, though not in all. The farm-yard livestock were fed mainly on potatoes, milk and imported maize. In the absence of mechanization the provision of the home-grown part of the ration required a large labour force, particularly because the fuel to cook the potatoes had also to be produced from the adjoining bogs.

Though this type of husbandry managed to support a virile population it was of course subsistence farming in the truest sense and was carried on due to lack of more remunerative employment elsewhere. The advent of World

very high degree of variation. In general the pattern for the East and Midland Region was intermediate between that for the South Region, which showed the highest returns, and that for the North and West Region, which showed the lowest. Cf. an article by Dr. R. C. Geary in *Administration*, Spring, 1957.

48. See J. J. Byrne in the chapter on agriculture in *A View of Ireland*, J. Meenan and D. A. Webb (eds.), pp. 103–4. Further information on the pattern of land use in 1960 will be found in a supplement to the *Irish Trade Journal*, June 1961, and in Attwood 'Some Economic Aspects of Land Use in Ireland', *JSSISI*, 1964–5.

War Two had a profound change on all this. Employment opportunities opened up both at home and abroad and family members who heretofore would have remained on their small farms left for other employment.[49]

The writer went on to remark on the changes in the pattern of farming between 1931 and 1949. He pointed out that on the smaller farms there were decreases (per acre of crops and pasture) in the density of dairy cows, calves, pigs, and poultry. On the other hand, there was an increase in the density of older cattle.[50]

Persons engaged in agricultural occupations

The number of persons in agricultural occupations was given as 670,000 in 1926, 594,000 in 1946 and 513,000 in 1951. The percentage of all those gainfully occupied represented by these totals fell from 51.3 in 1926 to 45.7 in 1946 and to 40.3 in 1951.[51] The census of 1961 showed a further sharp decline under both headings. The total number engaged in agricultural occupations was returned as 393,000 or 35.4 per cent of all those gainfully occupied.[52]

TABLE 4.2

Status of persons at work in agricultural occupations (thousands), 1926-61

	1926	1936	1946	1951	1961
Employers and workers on own account	269	260	252	236	211.7
Relatives assisting	264	244	204	171	108.0
Employees	122	113	124	97	56.6

Source: *Census of Population*

Of this 393,000 the number returned as at work on the date of the census was 381,000. The composition of this total has changed very significantly over the last thirty-five years. In 1926, 41 per cent of those at work were employers or persons working on their own account, another 40 per cent were relatives assisting and 19 per cent were employees. In 1961 the percentage in the first category had risen to 56, the percentage in the second category had fallen to 28 while the third category had remained relatively unchanged at 16. The totals are shown in Table 4.2.

49. See O'Connor, *A View*, p. 114.
50. The position of the small farms may be studied further in three more recent surveys—*The Report of the Inter-Departmental Committee on the Problems of Small Western Farms*, Pr. 6540, Stationery Office, 1962; E. A. Attwood, 'Agriculture and Economic Growth in Western Ireland', *JSSISI*, 1961-2, 172; R. Fennell, *Industrialization and Agricultural Development in the Congested Districts*, An Foras Taluntais, Rural Economy Division, Economic Research Series, No. 2, 1962.
51. *GR*, 1951, Table 88.
52. 1961 Census, vol. iii, Table 1. The totals in this paragraph refer to all persons engaged in agricultural occupations. Table 4.2 omits those who were out of work at the time of the Census. The 1966 Census returned 201,700 employers and workers on own account, 83,300 relatives assisting and 46,200 employees.

A detailed examination of the fall in the numbers at work in farming and stock-rearing between 1926 and 1946 was made in paragraphs 85–93 of the Emigration Report. Therein, Table 20 shows that the total number at work fell by 85,400 in the period; 44,700 men and 40,700 women. This fall occurred principally in the category of relatives assisting (59,200). Comparing 1926–36 with 1936–46, the loss of workers

TABLE 4.3

Density of population engaged in farming and stock-rearing on different sizes of holdings, 1926–61

Persons engaged per 1,000 acres of crops and pasture

Size of holding			1926	1936	1946	1951	1961[1]
1 and under	5 acres		181	187	112	96	70
5	,,	10 ,,	175	157	110	94	92
10	,,	15 ,,	133	121	95	87	87
15	,,	30 ,,	83	81	73	59	54
1	,,	30 ,,	106	100	82	69	62
30	,,	50 ,,	57	59	57	49	42
50	,,	100 ,,	39	41	41	36	29
100	,,	200 ,,	26	27	28	25	19
200 acres and over			18	18	18	20	13
All holdings			53	52	49	42	33

Source: *Agricultural Statistics*

1. On account of a revised method of treatment of divided holdings the figures for 1961 are not fully comparable with those for previous years. In 1951 and 1961 the figures refer to farmers, assisting relatives, and labourers: earlier years include market-gardeners, etc.

was much the same in each period, 39,000 in the first and 46,400 in the second. In the earlier period, however, the loss of men was more marked and in the later the loss of women. In the earlier period, again, the fall was spread over all categories (farmers, relatives, and employees), in the later there was an increase in the number of employees while the loss was almost wholly among relatives assisting.

This decline was felt especially severely on the smaller farms. The decline of 44,700 men between 1926 and 1946 was the sum of a fall of 42,700 on farms under 15 acres, of 14,900 on farms of 15 and under 30 acres, counterbalanced by an increase of 12,900 on farms of 30 acres and over. For women, there were declines in all three classes, of 16,700 on farms of under 15 acres, of 9,600 on farms of 15 and under 30 acres and of 14,400 on farms of 30 acres and over. Thus, 70 per cent of the total fall between 1926 and 1946 occurred on farms of under 15 acres, of which one-half were relatives assisting and most of the remainder were farmers.

These tendencies are clearly shown in Table 4.3.

I.E.—10

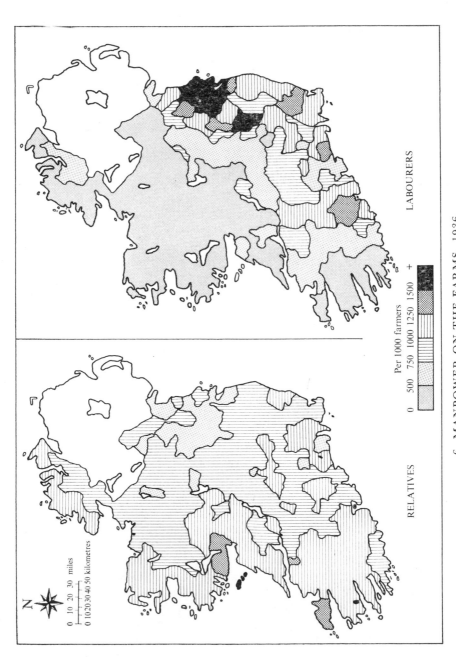

RELATIVES　　　　　　　　　　　　**LABOURERS**

Per 1000 farmers

0　　500　750 1000 1250 1500　　+

6. MANPOWER ON THE FARMS, 1936

The left-hand map shows that 'assisting relatives' were as numerous as farmers in virtually the whole area of the western seaboard but less numerous in the rest of the country. The right-hand map shows that farm labourers were employed chiefly on medium-sized and

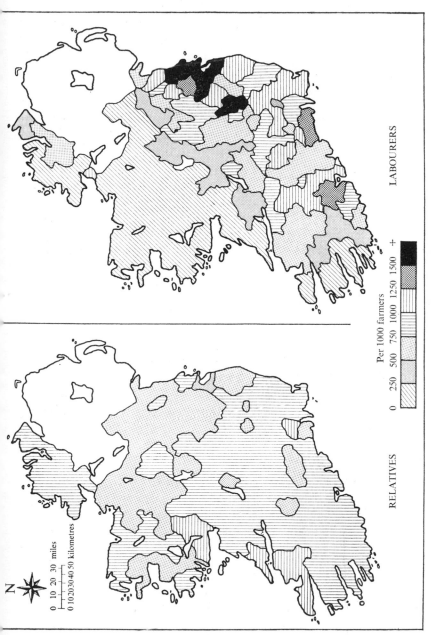

RELATIVES

LABOURERS

Per 1000 farmers

0   250   500   750   1000   1250   1500   +

7. MANPOWER ON THE FARMS, 1946

These maps show the marked changes since 1936. 'Assisting relatives' had left in large numbers. The number of labourers remained fairly constant. But as Table 4.2 shows, the numbers of both had halved by 1961.

Below 30 acres, the smaller the farm, the greater was the loss; above 30 acres, there was reasonable stability. The density on the smaller farms is still, however, appreciably greater than on the larger farms. A great deal of the statistics of population and emigration may be explained by this table.

TABLE 4.4

Males (over 17) engaged in farm work (thousands), 1955–68

	Members of Family	Other Males Permanent	Temporary	Total
1955	297.6	56.7	40.2	394.5
1957	285.3	50.5	39.1	374.9
1959	281.8	48.1	35.8	365.7
1961	280.3	44.6	30.2	355.1
1962	266.8	41.4	28.2	336.4
1963	264.1	39.3	28.5	331.9
1964	260.3	36.6	25.5	322.4
1965	249.6	35.0	25.8	310.4
1966	248.0	32.6	21.9	302.5
1967	242.5	30.0	21.3	293.8
1968	238.7	28.6	20.3	287.6

Source: *Irish Statistical Bulletin*

Table 4.4 shows the trend during more recent years; but it applies only to males engaged in farm work.[53]

AGRICULTURAL PRODUCTION

Area under crops

In this section and in the two that follow, it is necessary to indicate trends over an extended period. The choice of what years should be included in tables is particularly difficult in the case of agriculture. In this survey the following years have been chosen: 1851, because it stands almost at the beginning of post-Famine trends without being directly affected by the Famine itself; 1931, because it was the last year of free trading in agricultural products and of a strongly marked agricultural policy; 1939 and 1945, as marking the effects of the Second World War. It does not seem that any major fluctuation is ignored by this choice apart from the passing effects of the First World War and the exceptionally low levels of 1947 which were due chiefly to weather and shortages of almost everything that farmers needed.

The area under tillage (including fruit after 1906) fell almost continuously after 1851, though with interruptions in the middle 1850s, and the later 1860s, 1870s, and 1880s until the early years of the present century. There was a temporary revival during the First World War on

53. *I T J, passim.*

account of the encouragement given to tillage. The acreage then rose to 2,383,000 in 1918, the highest recorded since 1877. It fell away immediately after the war, declining again throughout the twenties to its nadir of 1,425,000 in 1932. The policy of encouragement of tillage during the thirties, followed by the compulsory tillage orders during the

TABLE 4.5

Area under crops (thousand acres) at various dates, 1851–1968

	1851	1931	1939	1945	1964	1965	1966	1967	1968
Wheat	429	21	255	662	214	182	131	189	224
Oats	1,585	623	537	834	289	284	243	238	218
Barley	312	116	74	170	454	464	462	451	454
All corn crops	2,377	763	868	1,680	965	939	841	884	904
Potatoes	666	346	317	388	182	174	168	160	146
Turnips and mangels	331	266	227	240	139	147	142	139	137
Sugar beet	—	5	42	85	80	66	54	64	64
All root and green crops	1,072	656	612	750	460	443	411	408	392
Total tillage	3,509	1,425	1,492	2,474	1,438	1,395	1,262	1,302	1306
Hay {First-year		331	286	425	302	295	283	273	257
{Other	1,060	1,982	1,776	1,526	1,610	1,659	1,723	1,775	1827
Pasture	7,435	7,989	8,052	7,130	8,147	8,270	8,465	8,458	8467
Total crops and pasture	12,004	11,727	11,606	11,555	11,233	11,413	11,656	11,747	11,868

Source: *Irish Statistical Bulletin*

war years, brought the area to its maximum in modern times of 2,567,000 in 1944, the highest recorded since 1872. There has been a renewal of the decline since then: the acreage fell below 2,000,000 in 1949, and the largest acreage tilled since then has been 1,808,000 in 1954. This tendency for the tilled area to contract except under the pressure of exceptional circumstances seems to be one of the most persistent features of Irish economics. It may be noted, however, that at no time in the period covered by statistics was the percentage of land under tillage very great. In the year of greatest recorded tillage, 1851, the percentage ploughed was only 29 per cent,which is very low when set against the normal proportion tilled in continental countries. After the famine, at any rate, Ireland was never a tillage country in the sense in which that term is normally used. The tradition that it was such may be derived from the coincidence between the decline in the tillage area and the decline in population, and also from the fact that some of the best tilled counties in 1851 are, in modern times, the grazing counties.[54]

54. In the summer of 1849 Macaulay, then preparing his *History of England*, travelled from Drogheda to view the battlefield of the Boyne. He was impressed by the rich fields of wheat which he passed in the valley. See G. Trevelyan, *Life and Letters*, 1876, vol. ii, p. 220.

Oats have traditionally been the greatest tillage crop. The greatest acreage under oats was 1,662,000 in 1852 followed by a decline until the First War in which there was a temporary expansion to 1,129,000 in 1918. A further decline was followed by another wartime expansion to 945,000 in 1944. Since the introduction of feeding barley the area under oats has contracted.

Wheat acreage decreased continuously and very steeply from its maximum of 671,000 acres in 1847. There was an almost continuous decline from 1868 to the end of the nineteenth century. During the First World War the acreage rose to 135,000 in 1918 but fell away immediately to 59,000 in 1919. It continued to decline during the 1920s and reached its lowest point at 21,000 acres in 1931 and 1932. These were the last years of free prices; and the policy of fostering wheat-growing, introduced in 1932, restored the area to 255,000 acres by 1939. The wartime maximum was 662,000 acres in 1945. Since the war, the area has declined again.

The area under barley reached 314,000 acres in 1849. It fell heavily to 151,000 acres in 1866 and did not change greatly until the First World War. In 1920 the acreage was 202,000. It declined again thereafter and fell to 103,000 acres in 1932. The extent sown depended largely on the amount contracted for by the brewing and distilling companies and was confined to certain counties. The introduction of feeding barley has led to a considerable extension.

Apart from some expansion during the wars, the area under root and green crops has shown a steady decline. The largest crop was, of course, the potato which was at its lowest recorded level of 220,000 acres in 1847 and recovered to its maximum of 923,000 acres in 1859. Thereafter there was a decline to 413,000 acres in 1914. There was a rebound to 520,000 acres in 1917 but the highest level recorded since then was 428,000 acres in 1941 and the acreage in recent years has contracted and was no more than 168,000 in 1966. Turnips had a recorded maximum of 317,000 in 1853 but the greatest extent in recent years has been 159,000 in 1947. Mangels occupied 12,000 acres in 1848 but increased greatly afterwards. The greatest acreage in recent years was 96,000 in 1941; it was 40,000 in 1965. Sugar beet came into the agricultural statistics in 1926. Its maximum has been 88,000 in 1963. The acreage under fruit was first separately recorded, at 6,000, in 1906: it has grown to 12,000 since the Second World War. Flax had a maximum acreage of 95,000 in 1864. It increased from 9,000 acres in 1914 to 34,000 acres in 1920. During the Second World War it increased again from 4,000 acres in 1939 to 33,000 in 1945 but has become negligible in recent years. The acreage under hay was 959,000 in 1847 and expanded without interruption to 1,862,000 in 1905. In the next year the total was divided between first-year and other hay; and the distinction was made permanent in 1926. In that year the acreage of first-year hay was 366,000 which had fallen to 254,000 in 1935. The acreage grew during the Second World War, reaching 444,000 in 1947 and has since fallen away. Other hay was 2,009,000 acres in 1929 (the highest figure recorded) and fell to 1,757,000 in 1938. The decline continued during the war and has persisted during the last decade.

The area under pasture was first returned in 1851, at 7,435,000 acres. Here also there was a steady rise to a maximum of 9,058,000 in 1902. There was a contraction during the First World War, but when enumeration was resumed in 1925, the acreage was found to be 8,411,000. There was a decline during the next ten years, followed by an increase in the later 1930s and a new decline during the period of compulsory tillage in the 1940s. Since the war, there has been an almost continuous increase. Minor fluctuations are unimportant because it seems that pasture is the residual factor in Irish agricultural statistics and its reported area is directly affected by any revision of the concept of agricultural land.

A final point may be made—the extraordinarily small extent to which the use of land has varied even under the pressure of war and State compulsion. In 1918 the area tilled was 685,000 acres greater than in 1913: in 1944 it was 1,075,000 acres greater than in 1939. These figures should be set beside the background of 11.5 million acres of agricultural land.

Crop yields

Variations in the extent of tillage and pasture have often been the subject of discussion and even of political controversy. In quite recent decades an unfounded antithesis between tillage and grass has been one of the disputed frontiers of party politics. The result has been that the highly important trends in crop yields have been obscured until lately. In 1928 Hooper wrote:

Attention in the past has been too much focused on areas and too little attention has been paid to increasing yields of crops and to the total production of crops. Changes in yields per acre were as great and as important from the point of view of total production as changes in areas.[55]

Table 4.6 should be interpreted with reserve. Apart from the innate difficulties of estimating yields, standards of husbandry vary so greatly that averages can be misleading. The figures should be regarded as representing trends rather than absolutes. At the same time, it is believed that the modern figures for wheat and beet may be taken as being reasonably accurate: the same cannot be claimed for oats, root crops, and hay.

55. *Agricultural Statistics, 1847–1926*, p. xxxvi.

Mixed farming with considerable tillage	Sheep raising and fattening with some stock raising
Mixed farming with stock raising and feeding for the store cattle trade	Cottage farming
Graze and fattening country with some highly specialised large farms	Peat bogs, mountain pastures, and uninhabited areas
Dairying predominant, for creameries and local milk supply	×[×]× Market gardening

8. TYPES OF FARMS, 1946
Adapted from the *Geographical Journal*, 110, 1947, page 45.

Pasture yields have not been examined until very lately.[56] The following figures for 1951-2 which show the estimated average output of pasture here and in three other countries speak for themselves:

	cwt.	(Starch extract per acre)
Netherlands	26.2	,,
Denmark	22.3	,,
England and Wales	16.7	,,
Ireland	14.0	,,

Turning to Table 4.6, yields per acre vary so greatly as to reduce the value of averaged figures. It has been suggested that they vary from 14 to 30 cwt. for wheat, from 12 to 30 cwt. for oats and from 12 to 35 cwt. for barley. Sugar beet varies from 6 to 18 tons, mangels and turnips between

TABLE 4.6

Estimated annual average rates of produce of crops per statute acre, 1850–1959

	Wheat	Oats	Barley	All corn crops. Starch	Potatoes	Sugar beet	All root and green crops. Starch	Hay 1st year	Other
	cwt.			lbs.		tons	lbs.	cwt.	
1850–9	13.0	13.4	16.7	967	4.6	—	1,978	38.6	
1920–9	19.0	16.6	18.3	1,169	5.2	—	2,324	38.7	
1930–9	19.8	19.3	19.8	1,363	7.6	10.1	2,972	40.9	42.8
1940–9	16.9	17.4	17.7	1,265	7.8	8.7	2,872	42.1	43.6
1950–9	21.4	19.3	23.1	1,542	8.5	10.7	2,098	44.5	44.5

Source: *Irish Statistical Bulletin*

10 and 30 tons, and potatoes between 6 and 13 tons. Variations over so wide a range suggest that there is room for an immense improvement in output if the standards of farming are raised.

Even on the basis of Table 4.6 the improvement in fertility has not been general. The following figures have been calculated to show the percentage increase in crop yields when the average yields of 1952–6 are compared with those of 1847–51.

Percentage increase per acre

Wheat	77	Turnips	7
Oats	43	Mangels	6
Barley	37	All root and green crops	39
All corn crops	56	Hay	3
Potatoes	60		

56. The following passages are taken from Dr. T. K. Whitaker's *Economic Development*, pp. 53–4 and 61–8. See also R. O'Connor, 'The Economic Utilization of Grassland', *JSSISI*, 1959–60, p. 71 on the potential increase of yield.

Hooper might claim, with much justice, that 'the statistics indicate that this country during the present century has been producing larger quantities of food for beast and man than at any time during the nineteenth century'.[57] These figures suggest that production, even if increased, fell far short of what might have been achieved.

Livestock

The contraction of the area under tillage is often associated with the increase in livestock, especially in cattle.[58] In fact a considerable part of the post-Famine increase was concentrated in the period between 1849 and 1859 when the area ploughed fell very little. In those nine years the total number of cattle rose by 66 per cent; from 1,848,000 to 3,062,000. There were fluctuations in succeeding decades but from 1889 onwards there was a fairly continuous increase which culminated in 1921 when the numbers reached 4,419,000, the highest recorded until then. Then they fell, reaching 3,947,000 in 1926, but recovered to 4,137,000 in 1929. There was a further fall in the 1930s and another increase during the war followed by a fall to 3,921,000 in 1948. In recent years there has been a marked increase.

The number of milch cows has remained notably constant in the last hundred years. It reached 1,324,000 as early as 1859, a level which was not surpassed until the 1930s. In recent years, numbers have risen sharply.

The increase in total numbers of cattle, recently and in the past, was largely achieved by reducing the slaughter and general mortality of calves. This also reflects the degree in which post-Famine, and more recent, trends have favoured beef production rather than dairying. Hooper brings out this point in a table which shows that the number of calves per 1,000 milch cows rose from 449 in 1854 to 801 in 1920 and 783 in 1926. The 1920 figure coincided with the peak years for cattle and in 1921, there were 1,022,000 calves in the country. The number fell to 884,000 in 1935, and at the end of the Second World War it was even lower still at 851,000 in 1947. In recent years it has risen to new peaks.

Numbers of cattle of one to two years showed much the same trend in recent years, being at a low point of 742,000 in 1948 and rising to a new peak of 1,349,000 in 1967. Cattle of two to three years were first enumerated in 1926 and rose to 672,000 in 1929. By 1937 they had fallen to 509,000 and had recovered to 710,000 in 1946. They reached a

57. Loc. cit., p. xxxvii.
58. The standard work on livestock is *The Economic History of Livestock in Ireland*, J. O'Donovan, Cork University Press, Cork: 1940. Also H. Kennedy, 'Our Dairying and Cattle Industries', *JSSISI*, 1946–7, p. 705. See also *ITJ*, 1955, p. 154.

peak of 922,000 in 1967. Cattle over three years, also first enumerated in 1926, showed the same general trends.

Heifers in calf were first enumerated in 1908 when they were 72,000. They were 80,000 in 1929 and 57,000 in 1937. The numbers have been much greater in recent years.

TABLE 4.7

Numbers of livestock (thousands) at various dates, 1851–1968

	1851	1931	1939	1945	1965	1966	1967	1968
Horses[1]	400	450	445	465	119	104	89	80
Milch cows	n.a.	1,222	1,260	1,222	1,547	1,582	1,568	1,607
Heifers in calf	n.a.	78	84	96	193	166	178	183
Cattle under 1 year	418	995	1,026	945	1,359	1,382	1,337	1,364
Cattle 1–2 years	461	856	927	921	1,216	1,325	1,349	1,295
Cattle 2–3 years ⎫		619	565	709	808	896	992	897
over 3 years ⎬ 1,448		237	171	291	221	224	219	213
Total cattle	2,327	4,029	4,057	4,211	5,539	5,590	5,586	5,572
Ewes[2]	n.a.	1,507	1,298	1,058	2,197	2,083	1,936	1,882
Total sheep	1,971	3,575	3,048	2,581	5,014	4,661	4,239	4,077
Sows[3]	n.a.	125	95	44	139	95	98	105
Total pigs	902	1,227	931	426	1,266	1,014	985	1,063
Total poultry	5,882	22,782	19,551	18,314	11,405	10,793	10,593	10,492

Source: *Irish Statistical Bulletin*

1. Figures up to and including 1945 relate to all horses. For 1962 and later they relate to working horses only.   2. For breeding.   3. Including gilts.

Sheep rose rapidly in numbers between 1849 and 1854, from 1,698,000 to 3,507,000, an expansion of 107 per cent. In the late 1860s there was a new rise which brought the numbers to their highest level of 4,580,000 in 1868. There were subsequent variations, leaving numbers at a comparatively low point of 2,666,000 in 1923. There was an increase to a minor peak of 3,575,000 in 1931, followed by a decline to 2,931,000 in 1934. The post-war period began with one of the smallest enumerations of the series in 1948—2,058,000. Lately, there has been an increase which brought the numbers to 5,014,000 in 1965.

The number of pigs has changed violently. It grew from 530,000 in 1848 through many fluctuations to its peak of 1,325,000 in 1871. The herd dropped during the years of the First World War to 844,000 in 1917. The inter-war period brought minor peaks of 1,186,000 in 1923 and of 1,227,000 in 1931. The Second World War brought an even greater contraction than the First World War, the numbers falling to 381,000 in 1944.[59] The highest post-war figure has been 1,266,000 in 1965.

59 Articles on pig numbers and the trade in pigs appear at regular intervals in the *Irish Statistical Bulletin*.

Poultry increased steadily from 4,490,000 in 1849 to 20,228,000 in 1914. There was a wartime fall to 17,047,000 in 1917. After the First World War, the increase was resumed and the peak was reached in 1930 at 22,900,000. It fell from that to 19,485,000 in 1935; and, as in the case of pigs, the Second World War brought a further contraction, numbers falling to 17,097,000 in 1943. In the years just after the war, there was a sharp increase and numbers reached 22,077,000 in 1949. The contraction of the export market has since led to a steady decline.

Agricultural output

Estimates of the quantity and value of agricultural output were first published for the year 1926–7.[60] Similar estimates were made for 1929–30 and again in 1934–5, since when they have been published annually. In Tables 4.8 and 4.9 the returns given cover the two earliest years, the last pre-war year, 1947 which was an exceptionally difficult year and the latest years for which returns are available. This selection omits some important fluctuations such as the relative peaks reached at the end of the 1920s, the heavy fall in the middle 1930s and the great expansion in tillage products in the 1940s. Wherever possible, reference will be made to them in the following commentary.

For example, the figures available show the heavy fall in cattle production, doubtless as the result of the heavy fall in prices occasioned by the 'economic war', which appears when 1934–5 is compared with 1929–30. In the very next year, however, which followed the first Coal–Cattle pact (see page 101), there was a rebound to former levels. Output remained at comparatively low levels during the war and reached the lowest level recorded at 692,000 in 1948. There has been a marked expansion in recent years. The great increase in milk production should be noted, especially in view of the fact that the number of cows remained relatively stable until very recent years.

Output of sheep and lambs fell away in the years after 1942. The middle 1950s showed a revival which has brought output well above levels of thirty years ago. The output of pigs fell so heavily during the war that in 1948 it was not much more than one-third of the average of the early and middle 1920s. There has been a recovery in the last ten years. The output of poultry followed on much the same lines.

The great bulk of this increased production must go for export. The marketing of several agricultural exports is organized by the State. Thus, Bord Bainne (established in 1961) caters for the export of butter, cheese, and milk powder. The Pigs and Bacon Commission (organized

60. *The Agricultural Output of Saorstát Éireann 1926–27*, p. 132. *ITJ*, September 1952, provides an account of the series, accompanied by a summary of the principles and methods of estimation. Detailed figures of output for all years available are appended.

TABLE 4.8

Estimated output of some agricultural products, 1926–68

		1926–27	1929–30	1934–5	1938–9	1947 (thousands)	1953	1966	1967	1968
Horses	Nos.	12	10	14	10	23	18	25	27	21
Cattle, Calves	,,	754	928	777	937	903	821	1,169	1,468	1,308
Sheep, Lambs	,,	1,005	1,085	1,030	1,135	731	947	2,015	1,753	1,692
Pigs	,,	1,337	1,450	1,511	1,371	628	1,197	1,767	1,554	1,772
Turkeys	,,	800	1,000	1,000	990	953	1,435	485	458	465
Other Fowl	,,	11,200	11,400	9,200	8,530	7,688	9,310	14,757	14,969	16,996
Milk										
(a) Consumed by persons	Gals.	82	82	88	92	98	113	135	134	133
(b) Used in industry	,,	168	197	217	197	157	233	415	467	516
Wool	lbs	14,459	14,747	12,936	13,033	9,574	12,302	18,295	16,597	16,069
Eggs	120s	10,791	11,709	9,915	8,978	7,011	8,926	6,554	6,250	5,988
Wheat	cwt.	233	221	1,444	3,356	4,277	7,407	3,403	5,606	8,043
Oats	,,	2,753	2,521	2,564	2,553	2,093	1,669	748	799	767
Barley	,,	2,256	1,313	2,253	1,312	591	2,980	8,628	9,032	10,455
Sugar Beet	tons	86	141	484	395	451	809	693	941	1,075
Potatoes	,,	652	650	661	639	678	550	471	475	495
Hay	,,	109	101	84	73	67	44	32	32	31
Turf	,,	3,567	3,567	3,310	3,339	3,991	3,132	1,395	1,275	1,307

Source: *Irish Statistical Bulletin*

TABLE 4.9

Estimated value of output of some agricultural products (£ thousand), 1926–58

	1926–7	1929–30	1934–5	1938–9	1947	1953	1966	1967	1968
Horses	1,235	1,382	604	794	2,647	2,799	3,850	4,124	3,893
Cattle, Calves	12,791	14,960	5,519	11,920	24,709	39,502	69,064	88,666	94,152
Sheep, Lambs	2,634	2,911	1,683	1,980	4,186	6,536	12,111	11,648	12,948
Pigs	8,271	8,717	5,120	6,549	8,875	21,894	29,572	27,551	31,811
Turkeys	560	630	500	590	1,544	2,595	1,115	1,051	920
Other Fowl	1,740	1,715	1,150	1,412	2,913	3,843	5,107	4,836	5,472
Milk									
(a) Consumed by persons	3,196	3,258	2,756	3,538	7,602	12,967	17,646	18,678	18,718
(b) Used in industry	4,228	5,305	3,734	4,596	9,370	19,599	42,754	51,416	57,299
Wool	685	822	377	494	1,005	2,525	3,040	1,729	1,984
Eggs	6,690	7,113	4,273	4,666	10,158	14,782	9,187	9,375	9,569
Wheat	142	111	703	1,972	4,686	11,851	5,747	9,017	13,618
Oats	1,066	809	962	853	2,433	2,024	835	872	869
Barley	902	514	827	577	591	4,252	10,354	10,732	12,522
Sugar Beet	259	360	820	918	2,058	5,187	5,863	7,819	8,819
Potatoes	3,334	2,530	2,656	3,268	8,045	5,997	8,925	8,115	7,240
Hay	316	347	230	258	671	311	331	356	339
Turf	3,377	3,377	2,813	3,687	8,990	7,398	4,998	4,846	4,968
Total (all agricultural output)	57,837	61,387	38,813	52,180	112,271	171,924	242,528	272,248	298,292

Source: *Irish Statistical Bulletin*

in its present form in 1961) is concerned with the marketing of bacon and pork. Erin Foods (established in 1959) is concerned more particularly with the processing of foodstuffs. The establishment of a national meat board to control exports has been under review from time to time.[61]

The most striking point in the output of crops is, of course, the great increase in wheat production. It has fallen away from the peaks of the war and some post-war years but remains above the pre-war level. The output of both oats and barley declined during the war. Since then the growing use of feeding-barley has led to a greater output of barley than of oats, in reversal of the traditional relationship. Sugar beet output remains at a level higher than before the war, as may be seen from Table 4.8. The production of potatoes and turnips remained largely unchanged over the period. On the other hand, the output of hay has fallen heavily and in recent years has been less than half that of 1926–7.

The estimated value of agricultural produce has, of course, been heavily affected by changes in the value of money over the last thirty years. It should also be remembered that agricultural income, even disregarding these changes, has not uniformly increased over that period. On the contrary, there was a severe fall from the £61m. of 1929–30 to £39m. in 1934–5 and the earlier level was not regained until 1940–1 in much less favourable circumstances for good farming. Here again, the impoverishment of the 1930s, too often forgotten nowadays, becomes apparent. The discouragement and the disincentive to greater production which is the inevitable result are also too quickly put out of mind. The very great increase in income from what may be termed cash products, such as milk, wheat, and sugar beet, should also be noted. This represents a substantial redistribution of income which was unknown thirty years ago.

61. In 1958–9 an Advisory Committee on the marketing of agricultural produce was established under the chairmanship of Dr. Juan Greene. It published reports on the export of bacon and other pig-meat (Pr. 5060); of livestock and meat (Pr. 5224); on general aspects of the export trade (Pr. 5225), on the export of dairy produce (Pr. 5236); on turkeys (Pr. 5393); and on poultry other than turkeys (Pr. 5271). In 1961 a White Paper was issued by the Government on the marketing of Irish butter in Britain (Pr. 6333). In 1962 survey teams were established by the Minister for Agriculture to examine the efficiency of the more important processing industries. Reports were made on dairy products (Pr. 6960); on the beef, mutton, and lamb industry (Pr. 6993); and on bacon and pig-meat (Pr. 7080).

FORESTRY

The report of the Recess Committee, which was published in 1896, remarked:

No one can inquire with any thoroughness into the subject of forestry without being convinced that this is one of the most important of all the directions in which, with the aid of the State, the wealth of Ireland may be increased.[62]

Then, and now, Ireland was the least wooded country in Europe. None of the original forests had survived a succession of wars and changes in the ownership of land. Most of the woodland existing towards the end of the nineteenth century dated from the plantings made by landlords in the eighteenth century.[63] Even this small area was in danger when the operation of the Land Purchase Acts broke up the large estates and distributed the land among a number of tenant-purchasers.

Forestry was one of the activities entrusted to the Department of Agriculture and Technical Instruction when it was established in 1899. Policy was laid down in 1908 by the report of a departmental committee of which the President and Vice-President of the Department (T. W. Russell and T. P. Gill) were members.[64] It aimed at an afforested area of one million acres in all Ireland. It suggested that an area of 300,000 acres might be achieved by the end of ten years.[65]

Whatever chances might have existed of this programme being fulfilled were destroyed by the outbreak of war and the subsequent troubles in Ireland. It was not until 1924 that the new State could begin to take stock of its woodlands, which had been further depleted between 1914 and 1918. Forestry ranked low on the list of projects for which money was available. The price that could be paid for land purchased for afforestation was £4 an acre, the same as before the First World War. It remained at that figure until after the Second World War, until it was doubled in 1949. Under these circumstances it is not surprising that the greatest area planted in any one year was 7,600 acres in 1938–9.

A fresh start was made in 1948–9 when the Long Term Programme for economic development was drawn up in connection with the Marshall Plan. It was noted that the wooded area at that time consisted of 280,000 acres, of which 40 per cent was in State plantations and the rest, mainly in small lots, was in private ownership. The new programme envisaged a target of one million acres under woods and it was hoped to increase annual plantings to a rate of 25,000 acres a year.

62. *Report of the Recess Committee*, Browne & Nolan, 2nd edition, Dublin: 1896, p. 24.
63. The largest area under woods returned seems to have been 283,989 acres in 1881, out of a total area of 17,000,000 acres.
64. Cd 4027, 4028, 1908.
65. For a survey of the development of State forestry, see H. J. Gray 'The Economics of Irish Forestry', *JSSISI*, 1963–4, p. 18. Generally, see *Report of FAO Forestry Mission to Ireland*, 1951, Pr. 664.

This rate has now been achieved. The acreage in the State plantations was increased from 237,000 in 1957 to 637,000 in 1969. It seems, however, that there has been a reduction (partly through transfer) in the acreage of privately owned woodlands.

The White Papers on Expansion of 1958 and 1964 repeated the programme of 1949 for the amount of annual planting. Thus, performance in the past has been far below what seemed desirable to the Recess Committee. In retrospect that should not be surprising. It is one thing to maintain and gradually extend an already existing area of woodland. To build up an afforested area, almost from scratch, is quite another. Some of the difficulties are inevitable. In an agricultural country, there will always be competition for the use of land; and in Ireland, with so slight a tradition of forestry, it is almost certain that livestock will be preferred to trees. Thus, afforestation is limited to marginal land which may be as undesirable for planting as it is for grazing. Other difficulties are more easily remedied, if the cost will be faced. The acquisition of land for planting would have been eased in the past if the sums available for the purpose had been larger. It is, however, only since the war that funds have been available in any quantity and even now afforestation is not high among the objects of public expenditure. (Compulsory acquisition of land for planting has always, and almost certainly rightly, been ruled out.) There has also been, and perhaps there still is, a variety of opinions on the purpose of afforestation policies; whether they should be pursued in order to provide native sources of timber and to promote auxiliary industries, or in order to provide employment in areas of poor agricultural land, or to conserve and improve soils. After a point, these objectives are not reconcilable. The language of the White Paper suggests that present policies are directed towards the growth of industries using timber.

SEA FISHERIES

The fisheries were described by the Recess Committee, with what now seems an excessive optimism, as 'another of our immediately workable resources'.[66] It rehearsed the decline of the sea fisheries in the second half of the nineteenth century. It pointed out that income from the Scottish fisheries in 1895 was eight times that obtained from the Irish; and argued that a great deal could be done to modify such comparisons. At that time, the value of fish (excluding salmon) landed on Irish coasts was £281,000. That figure, of course, was for all Ireland. Forty years later, the value of fish landed on the coasts of the Twenty-six Counties was £134,000.

66. *Report of the Recess Committee*, Browne & Nolan, 2nd edition, Dublin: 1896, p. 30.

Between the 1890s and the 1930s, however, there was a period of growth. The improvement of the sea fisheries was a major aim of the Congested Districts Board during the period of its existence between 1891 and 1923. It was concerned only with the fisheries of the west coast; but it did a great deal to make them an important source of income. Sea fishing all round the coast, however, suffered a major collapse after 1918. Prices at home fell heavily and major markets, in the United States and in Russia, were closed. What was still more serious in the long run, the marketing organization (which was largely dependent on Scottish participation) was broken up and was never restored.

The losses suffered between 1918 and 1920 were not made good between the First and Second World Wars. Between 1923 and 1938 the number of men engaged regularly in fishing fell from 2,262 to 1,463 and the number of those engaged part-time fell from 8,970 to 5,888. New measures were introduced as a result of the Commission on the Gaelteacht and a deep-sea fishing industry was contemplated, but this project later was abandoned. Gradually, attention was concentrated on the home market where there were, and still are, difficulties in distribution and in marketing.

An Bord Iascaigh Mhara, a statutory body established in 1952 and reorganized in 1963, applies State grants to finance grants and loans for purchases of boats and gear. Certain harbours have been designated as fishing centres and canning and fish-meal factories have been established with varying success. Schemes of training and apprenticeship have been put into operation.[67]

These measures have succeeded in so far as landings of fish have improved between 1948 and 1968; in amount from 385,243 cwt. to 836,000 and in value from £595,000 to £1,669,000. The comparable figures for 1938 were 172,000 cwt. and £134,000. The impression remains that the slow growth of the sea fisheries is not only a matter of providing facilities or training schemes. Relations between those engaged in fishing and distributors appear to be traditionally bad. This may be influenced by the uncertain division of sea fishing between a full-time occupation and a form of livelihood ancillary to farming. It is possible that development of sea fisheries on a commercial basis cannot be achieved without specialization. On the other hand there are areas where part-time fishing is an important source of income. Finally, there is the major question of policy, whether the sea fisheries are to be directed at this stage towards the needs of the home market or whether the old export of cured fish should be revived.

67. See a symposium on the fisheries in *Administration*, Autumn, 1959, and the report of the American Survey Team (Pr. 7983), 1964.

CHAPTER FIVE

Industrial Production

THE FIRST OFFICIAL SURVEY OF IRISH INDUSTRIES IN THIS century was made in the census of production taken in 1907.[1] This census covered the then United Kingdom of Great Britain and Ireland. The totals showed that gross output was valued at £1,490m. in England and Wales, £208m. in Scotland, and £67m. in Ireland; the net output in each area being valued at £603m., £86m., and £23m. respectively. The numbers employed ranged from 5,808,269 in England and Wales to 885,403 in Scotland and 291,304 in Ireland. Net output per person employed was £104 in England and Wales, £98 in Scotland, and £78 in Ireland. Another figure given was the horse-power of machinery used in industrial production, which was reported as 9,097,869 in England and Wales, 1,397,733 in Scotland and 259,407 in Ireland. Thus the census showed how far Ireland, even with the north-east included, fell behind the rest of the United Kingdom in productive capacity.[2]

Excluding outworkers there were 291,304 in employment in Ireland in 1907, of whom 92,355 were attributed to the production of textiles, 42,408 to clothing, 37,811 to iron, steel, engineering, and shipbuilding, 35,583 to the production of food and drink, 32,423 to public utilities, 18,545 to building and contracting, and 12,559 to printing, paper, stationery, and allied trades. The results of a second enquiry made in 1912 were never published, but a summary table covering industrial

1. Cd 6320, 1912. See also, W. P. Coyne (ed.), *Ireland, Industrial and Agricultural*, Browne & Nolan, Dublin: 1902; *The Ireland of To-day*, reprints from articles from *The Times*, London: Murray, 1913; and E. J. Riordan, *Modern Irish Trade and Industry*, Methuen, London: 1920.

2. Of an estimated total export in 1907 valued at £59m., industrial products were valued at £25m., of which the principal items were: piece goods, £13.1m.; beer, spirits, minerals, £4.3m.; machinery, ships, £3.3m.; yarns, thread, rope, cordage, £2.7m.

TABLE 5.1

Industrial production (£ thousand), 1926–67[1]

	Gross output	Cost of materials, etc.	Net output	Salaries and wages	Average number engaged
			All industries		
1926	59,477	36,399	23,078	13,671	102,515
1931	54,884	29,282	25,602	14,041	110,588
1936	81,405	47,467	33,938	18,723	154,056
1946	155,143	98,966	56,177	31,157	169,788
1956	405,691	267,100	138,591	83,045	227,858
1963	679,398	436,927	241,826	133,290	246,308
1964	751,007	477,145	273,736	153,154	252,105
1965	804,389	507,652	296,737	162,234	255,692
1966	866,644	535,179	331,465	179,888	260,533
1967	976,969	600,275	376,694	195,906	263,748
		Transportable-goods industries			
1926	49,360	32,953	16,407	7,865	57,768
1931	44,125	25,907	18,218	8,129	62,608
1936	68,048	43,151	24,897	11,879	100,575
1946	133,975	91,177	42,798	21,165	116,294
1956	335,439	236,032	99,407	55,090	154,361
1963	571,352	388,230	183,122	94,298	177,732
1964	628,373	422,504	205,829	107,430	181,805
1965	671,265	449,746	221,813	113,061	182,662
1966	714,577	466,827	247,831	124,186	184,652
1967	808,936	523,725	285,211	136,290	187,448

Source: *Census of Industrial Production*

1. Data for 1926 and 1931 are not directly comparable with later years.

TABLE 5.2

Index numbers of industrial production, 1936–67

1953 = 100

	Volume of production	Value of Gross output	Net output	Salaries and wages	Average number engaged	Vol. of output per wage-earner engaged
			All industries			
1936	52.1	20.7	27.3	25.6	67.4	77.9
1946	56.2	39.5	45.1	42.6	74.3	75.9
1956	104.0	103.2	111.3	113.5	99.8	104.5
1963	146.0	172.9	194.7	182.2	107.8	133.8
1964	157.1	191.1	219.8	209.4	110.4	140.8
1965	163.6	204.7	238.3	221.8	111.9	144.9
1966	168.8	220.5	266.1	246.0	114.1	149.4
1967	182.2	248.6	302.5	267.9	115.5	158.0
		Transportable-goods industries				
1936	54.0	20.7	27.9	25.2	66.8	78.0
1946	60.8	40.7	48.0	44.9	77.2	76.9
1956	105.3	102.0	111.5	116.9	102.5	103.8
1963	153.5	173.7	205.4	200.0	118.0	131.2
1964	165.3	191.1	230.9	227.9	120.7	138.3
1965	172.2	204.1	248.7	239.9	121.3	143.7
1966	180.4	217.2	277.9	263.5	122.6	148.5
1967	195.8	245.9	319.8	289.1	124.5	157.9

Source: *Census of Industrial Production*

production in the Twenty-six Counties will be found in the reports on the census of industrial production in 1926 and 1929, in which it is emphasized that the figures for 1912 were incomplete:

in so far as a number of schedules which were issued were not returned to the Board of Trade, and the extent to which this defect applies varied from trade to trade. The figures for 1912 while of some interest are accordingly given just for what they are worth and with the utmost reservation.[3]

They returned the value of gross output at £29,740,000 and of net output at £9,377,000. The number of persons employed was 67,374, while 11,724 were employed by exempted firms. By far the greatest net output was returned for brewing and malting (£3,903,000). The only other trade groups with a net output of over £½m. were printing, publishing, and engraving (£545,000), grain milling (£533,000), and bread, flour confectionery, biscuits, sugar confectionery, and fruit preserving (£531,000). The groups employing more than 5,000 persons, exclusive of outworkers, were brewing and malting (7,076); clothing, millinery, and hats (6,538); bread, flour, confectionery, etc. (5,534); and printing, etc. (5,508).

The first census of industrial production in the Free State was taken for the year 1926,[4] the second in 1929 and the third in 1931. Partial enquiries were made in the years 1932–5. Thereafter, with the exception of restricted enquiries in the years 1939–42, an annual census has been taken; the results are set out in Tables 5.1 and 5.2.

The volume of production index for transportable goods industries has moved upwards steadily since 1936 with two exceptions. The first was in 1942–4 when the shortage of raw materials seriously restricted output in industries such as bacon curing, timber, soap, candles, and especially vehicle assembly and repair. The second was in 1956–8, when output fell below the level of 1955; again largely due to the altered conditions of supply of raw materials caused by the import levies imposed in 1956.

Any measurement of the expansion of employment must allow for changes in its scope and the Introduction to the 1926 Census of Production is at pains to point out that small concerns were omitted altogether from the scope of the survey. Some part of the apparent increase in industrial employment since 1926 is due to the gradual extension of the coverage of the census and to the changes in the economy which have caused many self-employed skilled tradesmen to become 'wage-earners'.[5]

3. *Census of Industrial Production*, 1926, p. iii.
4. Ibid.
5. On this, see G. Fitzgerald, *Studies*, 1959, pp. 145–7, where he contrasts employment in transportable goods industries as measured for (*a*) the Census of Production and (*b*) the Census of Population. The first shows an increase from 61,000 in 1926 to 149,000 in 1957, the second an increase from 123,400 to 196,000 in the same period; thus, the first shows an increase in employment of 144 per cent, the second an increase of 59 per cent.

The increase in net output and in employment has been experienced throughout the country; nevertheless Table 5.3 shows that both continue to be highly concentrated in Leinster and in Dublin City and county.

TABLE 5.3

Location of industrial production, 1931, 1946, and 1962

	Net output (£ thousand)			Average number of persons engaged		
	1931	1946	1962	1931	1946	1962
Dublin city and county	13,877	27,675	95,308	44,665	69,843	99,193
Rest of Leinster	2,458	7,489	33,581	15,954	26,436	38,124
Leinster	16,335	35,164	128,889	60,619	96,279	137,317
Cork C.B.	2,235	4,069	14,257	7,259	11,364	14,236
Limerick C.B.	680	1,098	3,388	3,164	3,600	4,468
Waterford C.B.	495	647	3,311	2,187	2,265	4,026
Rest of Munster	2,134	5,466	29,551	16,352	22,851	32,428
Munster	5,544	11,280	50,507	28,962	40,080	55,158
Connacht	766	2,291	7,703	6,875	10,093	12,764
Ulster counties	427	1,333	5,907	5,081	6,687	8,859
Totals	23,072	50,068	193,006	101,537	153,139	214,098
	Percentages					
Dublin city and county	60.1	55.3	49.4	44.0	45.6	46.3
Other county boroughs	14.8	11.6	10.8	12.4	11.2	10.6
Leinster	70.8	70.2	66.7	59.7	62.8	64.1
Munster	24.0	22.5	26.2	28.5	26.2	25.8
Connacht	3.3	4.6	4.0	6.8	6.6	6.0
Ulster counties	1.9	2.7	3.1	5.0	4.4	4.1
	100.0	100.0	100.0	100.0	100.0	100.0

Source: *Census of Industrial Production*

Note: The following industries are not included in this table—electricity undertakings, railways, canals, docks and harbours, Government departments, turf production and bog development. In 1962 their total net output was £28,329,000 and the average number of persons engaged was 24,547.

The industries showing a net output of £10m. and over in 1965 were: building, £26.8m.; electricity, £21.8m.; local authority construction work, £16.7m.; brewing, £13.9m.; metal trades, £13.1m.; printing, etc. £11.3m.; clothing (wholesale factories), £10.9m.

Those employing 10,000 persons and upwards in 1965 were: building and construction, 27,850; local authority construction work, 24,452; clothing, 16,169; and metal trades, 10,492. Industries employing between 7,000 and 10,000 persons were: bread, biscuit, and flour confectionery, 9,623; electricity, 9,537; printing, etc., 9.081; electrical machinery, 7.766.

The preponderance of service-type industries in the preceding two paragraphs will be noted.

Some industries have shown a remarkable increase in employment since 1926. Boot and shoe factories then employed 967 persons and hosiery 849. Employment in electricity undertakings has grown from 1,319; in woollen and worsted goods from 2,332; and in clothing from 4,001. On the other hand, a major industry such as brewing employed 4,625 persons in 1926 and 4,922 in 1965.

If the sometimes misleading criterion of net output per person employed be applied, many contrasts appear. The industries with the greatest net output per person engaged in 1965 were brewing, £2,819; margarine, compound cooking fats, and butter blending, £2,413; electricity, £2,288; fertilizers, £2,212. At the other end of the scale were shirt-making, £650; mens and boys' clothing, £664; and local authority construction work, £683.

Of the volume of production in manufacturing industries in 1965, 18.6 per cent was attributed to the output of producers' equipment and materials for capital goods, 11.0 per cent to consumers' capital goods, and 70.4 per cent to goods currently consumed or materials therefor. This breakdown is sometimes cited[6] as a sign of growing capacity to produce capital goods. It should be remembered that the first category includes:

manufactures of wood and cork except furniture other than church, school, and office furniture and fittings for shops, etc., structural clay products, asbestos goods, plaster, concrete products, slate and cement; metal manufactures except household utensils . . .

Attention should be directed to a valuable analysis of the material contained in the census of industrial production.[7] Some of its salient results will now be briefly recapitulated. They relate solely to manufacturing industry, and do not include very small establishments. It appears at once that the great majority of Irish manufacturing establishments do not have a large number of persons engaged. Just over 50 per cent of the 3,106 establishments surveyed engaged less than 15 persons. Another 40 per cent engaged between 15 and 99 persons. Only 31 establishments, or 1 per cent of the total, engaged over 500 persons. On the other hand, this 1 per cent of the establishments accounted for 27.7 per cent of the total net output and for 20.9 per cent of the total persons engaged. By contrast, the establishments employing on average less than 15 persons (which, as has been said, were just over 50 per cent of the total number of establishments surveyed) accounted for 5.9 per cent of total net output and for 7.6 per cent of the total employment.

International comparisons suggest that in general Irish manufacturing establishments are of much the same size as in countries such as

6. See *Report of the Commission on Emigration and Population*, para. 114.
7. See T. P. Linehan, 'The Structure of Irish Industry', *JSSISI*, 1961–2, p. 220. The passages above are a brief summary of some aspects of this paper and should be read subject to the qualifications which are set out therein.

France, Italy, Belgium, and Norway though they are much smaller than in countries such as the United Kingdom and Western Germany. It also appears that Irish establishments tend to increase in size. A comparison between 1938 and 1958 showed a considerable decline in the number of establishments employing small numbers. On the other hand, the number employing between 100 and 499 persons rose from 210 to 273 and the number employing over 500 persons increased from 15 to 31.

Over half (56.8 per cent) of the establishments had a net output of less than £10,000. Taken together they represented 4.5 per cent of the remainder of net output. On the other hand, only 0.7 per cent of establishments had a net output of £500,000 and over, but they accounted for 32.2 per cent of the remainder of net output.

A comparison of industry groups by average number engaged and by net output repeats a pattern that has been already seen. The food group employed 33,900; next came metals and engineering with 21,100 and clothing and footwear with 20,800. Drink and tobacco employed 9,800. The order of groups when viewed by net output was food, £25.8m.; drink and tobacco, £15.2m.; and metals and engineering, £14.8m. Viewed by number of establishments, food again was greatest with 972, followed by clothing and footwear, 377; wood and furniture, 363; and metals and engineering, 354.

Perhaps the most striking feature of this survey was the extraordinary variability between establishments in the same industry group. In the food group, for example, 410 establishments had a net output, per person engaged, of less than £500, while 17 establishments had a net output per person of £2,000 and over. In the 'bread, biscuits, etc.', industry (admittedly a localized trade) 22 establishments had a net output per person engaged of less than £200. Twelve establishments had a net output per person engaged of £1,000 and over; one establishment reported over £2,000. Similarly, in the mineral water industry 7 establishments reported a net output per person engaged of below £200, 10 reported £1,000 and over, one reported over £2,000. Mr. Linehan remarks with justice that:

the variability shown here is similar to that obtained for output per acre within size-region groups in the National Farm Survey.

PROTECTION FOR INDUSTRY

The narrowly limited powers which the Home Rule Bills of 1886 and 1893 proposed to concede to an Irish Parliament did not include control of customs and excise. These were to remain within the competence of the Imperial Parliament. The Home Rule Act, which was placed on the Statute Book in 1914, though its operation was suspended for the duration of the war, followed the same pattern. Any claim for fiscal autonomy would have been resisted at Westminster on account of its political implications and in Belfast, not only for that reason, but also through fear that a Dublin Parliament would impose tariffs which would increase the costs of northern industries.

The clash of interest between Dublin and Belfast was illustrated in the proceedings of the Irish Convention in 1917. The report signed by the Ulster Unionist delegates may be cited. Referring to a memorandum signed by the Nationalist leaders, it remarked:

In this document the Nationalists again emphatically insisted on their demand for Ireland's fiscal independence and crystallized their argument in the following terms. 'We regard Ireland as a Nation, an economic entity. Self-government does not exist where those nominally entrusted with the affairs of Government have not control of fiscal and economic policy.'

It is therefore clear that Fiscal Autonomy including the control of Customs and Excise and National Taxation is valued by the Nationalists not only on the grounds of supposed economic advantage but as an essential symbol of National independence. In opposition to this Ulster takes a firm stand on the basis of the people's common prosperity, and maintains that the Fiscal unity of the United Kingdom must be preserved intact, carrying with it as it does the sovereignty of the Imperial Parliament and due representation therein.[8]

The Government of Ireland Act 1920, which provided for the establishment of parliaments in Dublin and Belfast, reserved all powers under customs and excise to the Parliament in Westminster. This Act governs the constitutional position of the Government and Parliament of Northern Ireland to the present day. The rest of the country (which is now the Republic of Ireland) adhered to its claims for full fiscal powers. These were considered in the Anglo-Irish negotiations of 1921.

The proposals made by Lloyd George, then Prime Minister of Great Britain, in July, provided that there should be no protective barriers on 'the flow of transport, trade and commerce between all parts of these islands'. This marked an advance, but the proposals were rejected. No specific reference to customs and excise will be found in the Treaty which was eventually signed in December 1921, although full powers over them were surrendered to the new Irish government. They were included in Articles 1 and 2 which set out that the constitutional status of the new Irish Free State and its position in relation to the 'Imperial Parliament and Government' should be the same as that of the Dominion of Canada. It appears that the concession of fiscal independence was gained by the Irish plenipotentiaries at the very end of the negotiations.[9]

8. *Report of the Proceedings of the Irish Convention*, Cd 9019, HMSO, London: 1918, p. 32.
9. Cf. Pakenham, *Peace by Ordeal*, Cape, London: 1935, appendix iv, and P. Colum, *Arthur Griffith*, Browne & Nolan, Dublin: 1959, p. 302.

Accordingly, the customs and excise system of the Irish Free State came into existence on 1 April 1923. In the Finance Act of that year, the protective duties[10] and the revenue duties, then imposed in the United Kingdom, were continued. These revenue duties were levied on tobacco, wines, spirits, beer, tea, coffee, sugar, cocoa, cinematograph film, and dried fruits. In June 1923 the government appointed the Fiscal Inquiry Committee to investigate and report:

(a) as to the effect of the existing fiscal system, and of any measures regulating or restricting imports or exports, on industry and agriculture in the Saorstát, and
(b) as to the effect of any changes therein intended to foster the development of industry and agriculture, with due regard to the interests of the general community and to the economic relations of the Saorstát with other countries.[11]

The Committee produced two interim reports and a final report in November 1923. In some quarters it was hoped that these reports would provide arguments for a policy of thoroughgoing protection. These hopes were belied. The Committee's line of approach was clearly marked out by Mr Cosgrave when he announced its appointment.

It is facts and not policy which the Committee is intended to determine . . . The Committee is not expected to advocate policy. That will be a matter for the people and the Government when they have the facts before them.[12]

To use the description of one of its signatories:

the keynote of the report was the necessity of caution in framing a fiscal policy; precipitate or ill-considered action might, it was pointed out, produce injurious reactions. One industry might be assisted at the expense of others, and the possibility of damage being inflicted on exporting industries, especially agriculture, must be constantly borne in mind. The general conclusion to be drawn from the report was that fiscal changes should not be undertaken without mature deliberation and a full examination into their possible reactions.[13]

Thus, the report made no recommendations in favour of protection for industries though, as will shortly be seen, it provided a valuable examination of the major disabilities from which they suffered. Many industries presented a case for protection by tariff; the most important

10. The protective duties were imposed under (a) the Dyestuffs Act, 1920, passed to safeguard the dye-making industry in the United Kingdom and (b) the Safeguarding of Industries Act, 1921, passed to protect certain industries of special importance and more generally to protect employment against dumping and imports from countries with depreciated currencies. There were also the 'McKenna duties', imposed in 1915 on clocks and watches, motor-cars and motor-cycles, musical instruments, and their component parts.
11. The membership of the Committee comprised T. A. Smiddy (Chairman), C. F. Bastable, R. M. Henry, George O'Brien, and J. G. Smith.
12. PDDE, 3, 2024.
13. George O'Brien in The Irish Free State Official Handbook, Talbot Press, Dublin: 1932, p. 138.

being flour-milling and tobacco-manufacturing which complained of British competition. The margarine manufacturers stated that they had been adversely affected by a price-cutting war conducted by British and Dutch firms.

There were many other, much smaller, concerns that hoped for protection; providing between them a varied assortment of confectionery and clothing, boot and shoe and furniture makers, coach-builders and paper manufacturers, fertilizers, glass bottles and pottery. In almost all cases, these concerns were small and looked only to the home market. Very often, their existence was due to the resurgence of interest in Irish industry which marked the early years of the century; very often again, their survival was largely due to the small scale of their production. They were industries whose hopes of continuance depended largely on some measure of State assistance. Many industries owed their weakness to their failure to provide for changing tastes or to adapt themselves to new techniques. Of these, the Committee remarked that 'such industries can more fairly be described as debilitated than as infantile'.[14]

On the other hand, the industries that were then regarded as the major industries showed no desire for protection. The maltsters, the biscuit industry, and the jute industry, went so far as to oppose any application of tariff protection to their activities. The brewing and distilling industry and other industries with a high agricultural content, such as bacon-curing and butter-making, did not even appear before the committee. This reflected, no doubt, the clash between industries that looked to export markets and industries which, in the circumstances of the time, were thankful to hold what they could of the home market. The clash would have been intensified had it not been for the partition of the country and the consequent exclusion of the industries of the north-east from the survey of the committee. Lastly, the powerful influence of the Chambers of Commerce was cast decisively against any interference with the existing channels of trade. In these circumstances the caution shown by the committee becomes understandable.

Selective protection

Nevertheless, the next budget (in April 1924) imposed protective duties on five categories of goods—boots and shoes; soap and candles; sugar confectionery; cocoa preparations; table waters and glass bottles for beer, wine, or spirits. This first essay in protection was not to be taken as a portent for future policy. The Minister for Finance, Mr. Blythe, stated that:

The Government takes up no doctrinaire attitude on the question of free trade and protection. It regards the matter as one of expediency which may be

14. Ibid., para. 96.

variously decided in different circumstances . . . The Executive Council is convinced that the matter is one on which the country should feel its way. We are not prepared, on the one hand, to recommend anything approaching a general tariff with the substantial rise in the cost of living which would inevitably follow, bringing other and serious economic problems in its train. Neither are we prepared to let the industrial drift continue, and content ourselves with preaching efficiency and the virtues.[15]

The Finance Act of 1925 brought duties on personal clothing, blankets and rugs, and on furniture and bedsteads. In the 1926 budget a duty was imposed on oatmeal. In that year, also, the Tariff Commission was established. This body was intended to assist the framing of what Mr. Cosgrave described as a policy of selective protection. It was composed of a chairman nominated by the Minister for Finance and two others nominated respectively by the Minister for Industry and Commerce and the Minister for Agriculture. This body was charged with the duty of examining the applications for protection.

It remained in formal existence until 1939 when the Act establishing it was repealed. Its activity largely ended with the change of government and of fiscal policy in 1932. In all, it received fifteen applications for protective duties, a significantly small number as one authoritative observer has noted.[16] It published full reports on these applications, which covered not only the condition of the applicant industry but also the possible effects on other industries. The reports provide a fascinating picture of the degree to which, even then, industrial production was interrelated. Twelve of these fifteen applications were approved. A protective tariff was accordingly imposed in all but one instance of these twelve.

The Commission was intended to consider applications for protection in a quasi-judicial manner. This assumed that the government possessed full liberty of choice to grant or to withhold a tariff. The assumption was justifiable enough in 1926 and in the short period thereafter when it was still possible to believe that the world was progressing away from the dislocations of the First World War. As the depression deepened throughout 1930 and 1931 policy was forced into new channels. The victory of the National Government at the General Election in Britain in October 1931 provided the turning-point. It was

15. *PDDE*, 7, 40.
16. R. C. Ferguson, Secretary of the Department of Industry and Commerce, 1940–5, in *Public Administration in Ireland*, ed. F. C. King, Parkside Press, Dublin: n.d., vol. i, p. 41. This article is a valuable review of industrial development between 1922 and 1939.
The change of policy is particularly associated with the names of Mr. Sean Lemass who was Minister for Industry and Commerce from 1932 to 1948, again from 1951 to 1954 and again from 1957 to 1959 and of Mr. John Leydon who was Secretary of the Department from 1932 to 1939 and from 1945 to 1955, being Secretary of the wartime Department of Supplies in the interval.

obvious that within a short while a British tariff would be created, and there was a world-wide rush to export goods to the United Kingdom before that happened. The industries of the Free State faced the threat of dumping on an unprecedented scale. In November 1931 therefore, the Customs Duties (Provisional Imposition) Bill was introduced and rapidly carried into law. It authorized the Executive Council[17] to impose or vary duties for a limited period whenever such action appeared necessary to prevent dumping of goods or other injury to Irish industries. The Executive Council was also empowered to refer to the Tariff Commission any questions arising out of its action. Hitherto, the Executive Council had no such power of reference; it could now impose or vary a duty and later take the opinion of the Tariff Commission. Any order of the Executive Council had to be confirmed by resolution of the Dáil within ten days or by a bill within twenty days—the principle that tariffs should not be imposed without immediate discussion was still upheld. In the event only three orders were made under this Act before the change of government (in March 1932) brought a complete reversal of tariff policy and an abandonment of the principles on which it had been founded during the 1920s.

Full protection

The procedure of the incoming Fianna Fáil government was the exact reverse of 'selective protection'. It was well described later in 1932, by the new Minister for Industry and Commerce, Mr. Lemass, when he said: 'We had to proceed by a system of trial and error if you like, but we have the duties there'; and again 'the disposition is in favour of protection ... protection is given unless facts coerce us to modify them in some particular way.'[18] After March 1932, the onus of proof was transferred from the applicant for a tariff and placed on those who opposed the application. But to speak of the onus of proof is to imply a degree of judicial survey that was not attempted. In the article already cited, R. C. Ferguson has a revealing passage:

Broadly speaking, the attitude of the Government was that any firm or group of firms or individuals prepared to establish a new industry or to extend an existing industry could make application for the grant of the duties necessary to give ample protection and so create conditions in which external competition was, to a large extent, eliminated. The work of examination was done principally in the Department of Industry and Commerce and generally in consultation with those interested in the application. Owing to the necessity of preventing forestalling, it was not generally possible to consult the trades interested in the import or sale of the goods in question.[19]

17. i.e. the Government.
18. *PDDE*, 42, 876, 886.
19. *Public Administration*, vol. i, p. 43.

Thus the budget of 1932, presented two months after the new government took office, contained a list of forty-three duties. The move towards all-round high protection was greatly strengthened by the outbreak some months later of the dispute between the British and Irish governments over the annuities. This caused the passing of the Emergency Imposition of Duties Act of 1932 which, in the words of Mr. MacEntee, the new Minister for Finance, gave

powers essential to deal with the situation created by the action of the British Government proposing to impose penal duties on Irish agricultural produce.[2]

This Act empowered the government to impose, vary or revoke by order customs duties on any class of goods, subject to the order being confirmed by the Dáil within eight months after the making of the order. Hitherto, no duty had been imposed without parliamentary discussion either prior to or (under the Provisional Imposition Act) within twenty days of imposition. There could now be a long delay between imposition and a discussion which might well lose a great part of its urgency in the interval. This Act greatly increased the power and influence of the Department of Industry and Commerce. As a measure for times of emergency, in which swift action might be essential, it was justifiable. The fact remains that the great majority of duties since then and up to the present day have been imposed under this Act so that the Oireachtas has lost a great part of its control over fiscal policy.[21]

All these measures changed the position of the Free State dramatically. For a few months at the turn of 1931 into 1932, between the introduction of the British tariff and the change of government in Dublin, it was the last surviving example of a predominantly free-trading state left in the world. Within another few months it had passed to being one of the most heavily tariffed countries that could be found. At the end of 1931, the list of tariffs covered 68 articles including 9 revenue tariffs. At the end of 1936 it covered 281 articles including 7 revenue tariffs. These figures do not include a profusion of quotas and other restrictions. At the end of 1937 it was calculated that 1,947 articles were subject to restriction or control.[22]

Another measurement may be cited, taking the level of tariffs rather than their number. An examination on these lines suggests that the

20. *PDDE*, 43, 998.

21. The Imposition of Duties Act, 1957, provides that orders imposing or amending duties under its provisions must be confirmed by the Dáil within the calendar year following that in which they were imposed. This, of course, weakens parliamentary control still further.

22. *The Economist*, 1938, p. 433. In 1954 the Revenue Commissioners informed the Committee of Inquiry into Taxation on Industry that there were then some four hundred Tariff Reference Numbers, each relating to a particular class of goods. Well over three hundred related to protective duties. *Report of Committee on Taxation on Industry*, p. 110.

tariff level index was 9 per cent in 1931, 45 per cent in 1930, and 35 per cent in 1938. Measurements of this nature cannot be exact, but it would be difficult to find fault with the mode of calculation shown by the author. Another table showed the relative tariff levels of eighteen countries in 1937. In this table the Free State occupied fifth highest place, the level of its tariffs being exceeded only in Spain, Turkey, Germany, and Brazil. The British tariff was two-thirds as high, the French rather less than half as high; the Dutch and Swedish one-fifth as high.[23]

The zenith of protectionist policy in this period was touched in 1936–7. Thereafter further duties were imposed but their effect on the tariff level was outweighed by various influences which are noted by Dr. Ryan in the paper cited. The Anglo-Irish Trade Agreement of April 1938 did not, as he points out, contribute directly to a fall in the level. Nevertheless, its provision for a review of tariffs against British goods suggested a contraction rather than an expansion of protection.

The outbreak of war and the growing scarcity of goods enforced a revision of policy. The protective duties were suspended for all practical purposes in 1942. They were gradually revived as supplies became more freely available in the post-war period.

In November 1953 the Dáil was informed by Mr. Lemass, then Minister for Industry and Commerce, that a systematic review of the operation of the protective tariffs would be held:

It will be directed to investigating the efficiency with which productive operations are carried on here and the need for protection at existing rates or the possible consequences of its modification in some instances.[24]

In the following July a new Minister for Industry and Commerce, Mr. Norton, told the Dáil that he had decided that:

a review of tariffs should be instituted immediately and I have entrusted this task to the Industrial Development Authority.[25]

In the event, no observable consequences followed these decisions; tariffs and quotas continued to be imposed. Protection was intensified by the events of 1956–8. As a result of the increasing deficit in the balance of payments, special import levies were imposed on a wide

23. W. J. L. Ryan, 'Measurement of Tariff Levels in Ireland', *JSSISI*, 1948–9, 109. See also Nevin, *The Irish Tariff and the E.E.C.: A Factual Survey*, Paper No. 3, 1962. In this paper Table I sets out the incidence of import duties (i.e. the percentage of total value of merchandise imports represented by the amount received in import duties) in some countries towards the end of the 1950s. The percentage for Ireland is 6.5 against 11.1 in Portugal and 9.4 in Italy. It was 5.9 in Holland and Austria, 5.1 in France and 3.8 in Belgium–Luxemburg. But the table must be taken subject to the reservations expressed by the author. See also E. T. Nevin, *The Irish Price Level*, Economic Research Institute, Dublin: Paper No. 9., 1962.
24. *PDDE*, 143, 1107.
25. Ibid., 146, 1098.

range of goods in March 1956. Further levies were imposed in the following July.[26] These charges were designed to discourage imports. They were not intended to provide further protection for Irish industries many of which, indeed, were gravely embarrassed by the increased cost of raw materials. When the payments crisis had abated, it was declared, the levies would be withdrawn.

In the event, levies were withdrawn from many categories of goods and in a small number of cases the normal customs duties were also abolished. But in an almost equally large number of cases, customs duties were imposed when the levies were withdrawn and this was done in a number of instances where there had been no previous customs duty charged. Finally, customs duties were imposed on a number of categories of goods which had not previously been subject either to levies or to customs duties. In some other cases again, the existing duties were increased. The result was a substantial addition to protection.

It is proper to add that most of this addition occurred during 1958, when the original plan for a European Free Trade Area was under discussion. There might well have been some design of increasing tariffs so as to obtain a better bargaining position when freer trade became obligatory. But the higher duties survived the plan for a free trade area.

Recent tariff policy

Subsequent events abroad have had some influence on tariff policy. In June 1959, Mr. Lemass returned to the subject of protection in one of his speeches. He said:

Our pre-war industrial development was based on home market requirements and protection, and it served the purposes of that time. I think it was the only practical industrial policy then. Because of it, we have secured a basis of industrial organization, a pool of managerial competence and industrial skill on which we can build for the future . . . There is need now to raise our targets and, I believe, also to change our methods.[27]

In 1961, as entry into the EEC appeared to become imminent, a succession of ministerial speeches foreshadowed a thorough revision of protective measures. These culminated in an official announcement that tariffs would be reduced by 10 per cent on 1 January 1963, with further reductions in succeeding years; and that quotas, which would be replaced by tariffs similarly to be reduced, would be ended on 1 July 1963. The first reduction was duly made; and was shortly followed by the collapse of negotiations at Brussels for entry into EEC.[28] Thus a

26. The levies were charged at a rate of 37.5 per cent *ad valorem*; British goods were charged at a rate of 25 per cent.

27. *PDDE*, 175, 937.

28. Actually, the collapse of the British negotiations; but a definitive consideration of the Irish application for membership had been postponed until a decision was reached on the position of the United Kingdom.

new situation was created and policy was again adjusted. In the event, some quotas were abolished; but others were increased during 1963. A further reduction of 10 per cent in tariffs took place in January 1964.[29]

The further reductions contemplated for January 1965 were not made on account of the imposition of import levies in the United Kingdom during the balance of payments crisis of autumn 1964. Special import levies (at a rate of 15 per cent, with a 10 per cent preferential rate for British and Canadian goods) were imposed by the Irish government in November 1965. They were removed in September 1966. The position as regards tariffs on Anglo-Irish trade is now governed by the provisions of the Anglo-Irish Trade Agreement of December 1965.

The change of outlook is symbolized by the establishment of Adaptation Councils in the principal sectors of industry. Their function is to maintain a sense of urgency regarding the problems to be expected from freer trade, to co-ordinate the plans of individual firms, to promote co-operative action within branches of industry and generally to seek out trading opportunities and use them to the best advantage.

At the end of 1962, in the 22 industries surveyed by the Committee on Industrial Organization the usual tariff rate was 75 per cent with a Preferential Rate of 50 per cent.

LONG-TERM PROBLEMS

In 1924 the Fiscal Inquiry Committee noted that the Irish industries long-term problems might be gathered under five main headings:

1. The supply of capital.
2. The supply of labour and skill.
3. Transport facilities.
4. Access to fuel and power.
5. Raw materials.

Each of these will now be surveyed, with a short account of what has been done to provide a solution.

Capital for industry

In paragraph 74 of their report the Fiscal Inquiry Committee remarked:

Capital for the promotion of industrial enterprise is not readily obtainable in Ireland. The number of new companies which have been floated in recent years is comparatively small and in many cases these have been nothing more than conversions of private firms. The Committee is aware that the policy of

29. Some quotas were also enlarged in January 1964.

Irish banks has been to afford sufficient credit facilities to well established enterprises. Indeed it seems that in this matter they have gone as far as the limits of safety will allow . . . On the other hand, there has been some investment of outside capital in certain Irish industries and this tendency will no doubt increase if general conditions in the country improve.

Even in its unabbreviated form, the paragraph is not long, and the reader may infer that the supply of capital was not one of the more pressing problems of Irish industry in 1924. Probably it was not, if only for the fact that the times were not propitious for the launching of new enterprises. At home, a civil war had only recently ended. Abroad, the post-war fall in prices was still in progress and trade was still disturbed by currency fluctuations.

In the 1920s whatever risk capital was available for investment in Ireland had little outlet. The Irish investor had little opportunity or inducement to place his money at home. Very few concerns in the Irish Free State had floated their shares on the market. In the ten years after the report of the Fiscal Inquiry Committee's report there was only one public issue by an industrial company, the amount involved being £15,000. In 1933 there were only twenty-four public industrial companies quoted on the Dublin Stock Exchange, with a total issued capital of £4.8m. Matters changed with the introduction of protectionist policies. Between 1932 and 1957 capital issues by Irish industrial concerns which were quoted on the Dublin exchange amounted to £19.5m., relating to eighty companies.[30] In recent years, the annual reports of the Central Bank have repeatedly drawn attention to the small amount of industrial issues compared with the total raised by the State, State companies, and local authorities. Thus, during the fifteen years 1951 to 1965 the total new capital raised by public issue was £376m. Of that amount, £256m. was raised by the State, £24m. by local authorities, and £60m. by State companies. Only £36m. was raised by industrial and commercial concerns.

The private rather than the public company is characteristic of the Irish scene. Table 17 of the *Report of the Committee of Inquiry into Taxation on Industry* shows the number of companies registered as engaged in mining and manufacturing in various years between 1938 and 1954. The total number of these companies increased in this period from 1,037 to 2,290 and their paid-up share capital increased from £23.9m. to £65.6m. The

30. The total issued between 1932 and 1957 was £21.6m., of which the largest issue was £2.1m. and the smallest £8,000. The total comprised rather less than 90 companies. Thirty companies had issues for less than £100,000 each; 32 for sums between £100,000 and £250,000; 19 for sums between £250,000 and £500,000; 4 for sums between £500,000 and £1,000,000; and 4 for sums over £1,000,000.

On these matters, see C. H. Murray, 'Some Aspects of the Industrial Capital Market', *JSSISI*, 1959–60, p. 97. On sources of industrial capital generally, see *IBR*, September 1960, p. 10.

number of public companies grew from 137 to 169 and their paid-up share capital from £13.6m. to £29.4m. On the other hand, the number of private companies increased from 900 to 2,121 and their paid-up share capital from £10.3m. to £36.3m.

TABLE 5.4

Legal status of establishments in transportable goods industries, 1952

Legal Status	Establishments		Gross output %	Net output %	Average number of persons engaged %
	Number	%			
Public limited companies	287	8	45	43	35
Private limited companies	1,600	47	41	44	47
Total limited companies	1,887	55	86	87	82
Individuals and partnerships	1,281	37	5	7	11
Co-operatives	225	7	8	3	3
Statutory bodies	39	1	1	3	4
Others	18	—	—	—	—
	3,450	100	100	100	100

These figures are based on the Census of Industrial Production. The Register of Companies, which is not fully comparable, shows that the number of public companies rose from 137 in 1938 to 169 in 1954 and of private companies from 900 in 1938 to 2,121 in 1954.

It seems reasonably certain that the growth in private companies represents a large number of family businesses which have become limited companies. In many cases, no doubt, these concerns are so small that an issue of shares to the public would be impracticable. It is equally true that there are many family companies where an issue of shares has been ruled out on account of the possible loss of control. In either case, working capital is obtained by bank advances which, however terminable in theory, have in practice become long-term loans.

The position is illustrated by Table 37 in the report of the Committee on taxation on industry which covers eighty-three manufacturing companies. It is based on a submission from the Federation of Irish Manufacturers. In 1953 the fixed assets of these companies totalled £4,778,000 and their current assets £8,791,000. The grand total of £13,569,000 was financed as follows:

Preference capital	£980,000	7%
Ordinary capital	£3,572,000	26%
Retained profits	£4,193,000	31%
Debentures and loans	£410,000	3%
Creditors	£2,407,000	18%
Bank overdrafts	£2,008,000	15%

These figures have been compared with a similar examination of the sources of industrial capital in the United Kingdom published in the Radcliffe Report. The point of greatest difference lies in the fact that in the United Kingdom bank overdrafts and loans accounted for only 3 per cent of industrial capital.[31]

It may be added that in January 1939 bank advances to mining and manufacturing totalled £3,200,000 or 5.9 per cent of all advances. In January 1967 they were £48,857,000 or 14.3 per cent.

State action to facilitate the provision of capital to industry commenced with the first of a series of Trade Loans (Guarantee) Acts in 1924. The Minister for Industry and Commerce was empowered, on certain conditions, to guarantee repayment of the principal, and payment of the interest, on loans of the character defined in the Act. The Minister was given power to make a direct loan, but this power was never exercised, and the loans have been raised from the banking system. Being State-guaranteed, they have enjoyed a preferential rate of interest. The operation of these trade loans was examined by the Banking Commissions of 1926 and 1938. The latter reviewed their history at some length, and with little sympathy. It emphasized the then unimpressive record of repayment and argued that as advances for working capital were a normal banking activity, they should not be created 'by means external to the system and in circumstances where the tests ordinarily applied by bankers are in abeyance'.[32] Moreover, it felt that State policy might be embarrassed if the State possessed a financial interest in the success of particular undertakings. It recommended that the scheme of trade loan guarantees should be terminated forthwith. This recommendation was not adopted.

The demand for long-term industrial and commercial credit was examined by the 1926 Banking Commission in its third Interim Report.[33] It noted that, on the evidence available, the business community was content with the facilities provided by the banks; and it quoted a submission of a special committee of the associated Chambers of

31. See an article, 'Finance for Industry', by Dr. J. P. Beddy in the Irish Supplement of the *Financial Times*, April 1960. More recent, and detailed, surveys are 'Capital in Irish Industry', by E. W. Henry and L. J. Heelan, *JSSISI*, 1962–3, p. 135; and *The Capital Stock of Irish Industry*, by E. T. Nevin, Economic Research Institute, Dublin: Paper No. 17.

32. *BCR*, 1938, para. 97, 445–56.   33. Paras. 2–3.

Commerce to this effect. It felt, nevertheless, that some special provision should be made for new or struggling industries and it indicated that this could best be done by the Industrial Trust Company, which had been founded earlier that year with a capital of about £163,000 of which £50,000 was provided by the State. This company however, 'owing to an imprudent policy in external investments . . . was forced eventually to go into liquidation with an almost total loss of the capital provided for it by the State and by private interests'.[34]

A second attempt was made by the Industrial Credit Act of 1933, under which the Industrial Credit Company was set up. The facilities offered by the Company to industrialists include the underwriting of capital issues, subscription for shares or other securities with a view to their disposal by offer for sale or otherwise, issuing house services for capital flotations, the provision of long-term and medium-term secured loans, advisory services in regard to industrial capital and hire-purchase finance for new industrial plant and machinery. In short, its services range over a wide field which in more developed economies would be covered by a variety of agencies.[35] Between 1933 and 1967 it has been responsible for the provision of capital for industry to the extent of approximately £57m.

Industrial capital is also provided by grants from the State. Originally, these grants had a social as well as an economic purpose. The Undeveloped Areas Act of 1952 established a statutory body known as An Foras Tionscal to deal, *inter alia*, with the encouragement of industrial undertakings in the province of Connacht, the counties of Donegal and Kerry, and part of the counties of Clare and Cork. This area, which was later extended, corresponded very closely with that served by the Congested Districts Board between 1891 and 1923. Foras Tionscal was empowered to assist industrial enterprise in this area by providing suitable factory buildings or by making grants to the full amount of the cost and/or a grant not exceeding two-thirds the cost of fixed assets or such smaller assistance as seemed proper. It was also empowered to make grants towards the cost of training workers and was given powers regarding the remission of charges such as rates and electricity costs.

Subsequent legislation has widened the scope of the operations of Foras Tionscal. Its grants are available on different terms according to their purpose and the area in which the enterprise is situated. In what are termed the Undeveloped Areas (i.e. the province of Connacht and counties Kerry, Clare, Donegal, Cavan, and Monaghan), they run at higher levels than elsewhere in the country. Grants are either 'ordinary'

34. *BCR*, 1938, para. 51.
35. See *Twenty-one Years of Industrial Financing*, published by the ICC, which covers the period 1933-54. Mr. J. P. Colbert was chairman and managing director from 1933 to 1952, when he was succeeded by Dr. J. P. Beddy. See also M. M. Connor, 'Financing of Industry', *JIBI*, 1964, p. 33.

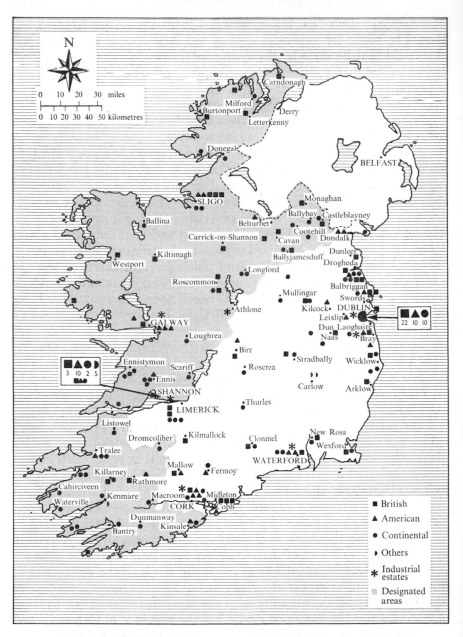

9. PRINCIPAL INDUSTRIAL PROJECTS WITH FOREIGN PARTICIPATION IN THE IRISH REPUBLIC

The shaded portion of this map shows the parts of the country designated for special industrial development (see pages 145–53). Based on information supplied by the Industrial Development Authority, Dublin.

or 'adaptation', the latter being designed for industries catering for the home market which wish to prepare for competition from abroad under freer trade. The report of Foras Tionscal for the year 1966–7 showed that adaptation grants to a grand total of £13,897,000 had been approved. Grants for industries in the undeveloped areas totalled £9,852,000 since 1952. Grants outside the undeveloped areas totalled £15,475,000 since 1956.

Projects requiring capital additional to that provided by Foras Tionscal may obtain unsecured loans, interest-free for seven years and at a negotiated rate thereafter, from Taisci Stáit (State Holdings Ltd.). This body was established in 1963 to enable the Minister for Finance to make funds available for the purposes mentioned in the establishing Act. In effect, this applies to any grant-aided industry, or to any company to which a grant or guarantee has been given for the encouragement of tourism.

Public policy towards the employment of foreign capital has been sharply reversed in recent years. The adoption of all round protection was accompanied by measures intended to deter foreign investment in the newly established concerns. The Control of Manufactures Acts 1932–4 required that before a new manufacturing company could begin operations, one-half of the issued capital and at least two-thirds of the capital with voting rights should be in the beneficial ownership of persons born in Ireland, or qualified by residence, and that a majority of the directors, other than whole-time managing directors, should be Irish nationals.[36]

These stringent provisions were explained by Mr. Lemass when he introduced the 1934 Act. He stated that, without them, there was a strong probability that the new industries would be almost exclusively in the hands of foreigners (scilicet, in British hands). This would happen because of (a) the comparatively small number of Irish people with the technical competence to establish factories, (b) the degree to which the distributive trade, under free trading conditions, had become associated with British firms, (c) the close ties of geography, language, etc., with Great Britain. Under such circumstances, he argued, protection by itself would mean that British firms would establish themselves behind the tariff wall and, quite probably, extinguish Irish firms who were the intended beneficiaries of protection.

There can be little doubt that these calculations were well based. As long before as 1928, Mr. Lemass had attributed the lack of enthusiasm among manufacturers for tariffs to the fear that British concerns would

36. Provision was made for the issue of 'new manufacture licences' to external firms, exempting them from compliance with the general provisions of the Act. Between 1932 and 1939 ninety-six licences were granted: one hundred and ninety-four between 1945 and 1958.

be established behind the tariff wall and drive the surviving Irish firms out of business.[37] It might perhaps have been added that the danger was all the greater on account of the form that protected industrialization took—of discouraging imports of consumer goods in favour of importing the raw materials and processing them here. If industrialization had been based on such agricultural and industrial raw materials as were available in Ireland both the opportunities and the temptations for British firms would have been fewer.

In practice, it seems to be very generally agreed that the Control of Manufactures Act succeeded only up to a point. In a free society, its prohibitions were evaded by all kinds of personal agreements and understandings.[38] Nevertheless, its presence on the statute book suggested that foreign capital would receive only a qualified welcome from the State. This did not matter greatly in the 1930s, still less during the Second World War. It mattered a great deal when, from 1949 onwards, the Industrial Development Authority began to canvass abroad for investment in Irish industrialization.[39] In the then state of international affairs, there was much in the Irish scene to attract capital from an insecure continent. It was not easy, however, to explain to inquiring foreigners why their first move in Ireland must be to engage legal advisers skilled in the arts of evading the law. The more reputable the foreign firm was, the more reluctant it was to begin its career in such a manner. A reform of the law was clearly needed. This was done by the Industrial Development (Encouragement of External Investment) Act of 1958.[40] This measure is a highly complicated example of legislation by reference. A straightforward repeal of the Acts of 1932 and 1934 might have been preferable; but it was felt that this course would break faith with enterprises that had been established under the protection of their provisions. Very generally, the effect of the 1959 Act was to exclude from the principal Acts companies which are incorporated, managed, and controlled in Ireland, which have exports as a principal object and which offer not less than half of their voting shares to the Irish investing public. The safeguards against abuse appear to be exceedingly thin, but it was admitted that the prize of large-scale foreign investment was so great that risks should be accepted.[41] Certificates of exemption may be given to smaller companies, and companies with fixed assets of less than £5,000, or not using mechanical power, are also exempt. To

37. *PDDE*, 22, 210.
38. In the debates on the amending Act, Mr. Norton pointed out that no prosecution had ever been initiated for breach or evasion of these provisions.
39. The Industrial Development Authority is a State body established in 1949 for promotional activities such as the creation of industries in specified fields and the attraction of foreign industrial firms.
40. The measure was originally introduced as the Control of Manufactures (Amendment) Bill. The title was presumably changed for psychological effect.
41. See speech by Mr. Sean Lemass, *PDDE*, 165, 531 f.

balance these and other relaxations, some of the loop-holes in the major Acts were closed but the tone of the debate showed that public policy had been sharply reversed.[42]

Labour and skill

The Fiscal Inquiry Committee reported that a further obstacle to industrial development was the inadequate supply of labour. At first sight this might appear surprising in a country of emigration, but it is a case where cause and effect become indistinguishable. The findings of the Committee may be summarized under the headings of (a) the small supply of skilled labour; (b) its tendency to emigrate; (c) the high level of Irish wages; (d) the inefficiency of labour.[43]

The Committee remarked that Irish industry:

has not the advantage, enjoyed so widely in other countries, of being able to call upon a constant supply of workers endowed with a hereditary aptitude for certain forms of skilled labour . . . Certain employers have had the extra burden placed on them of having to train their own skilled workers, many of whom, especially in periods of depression in Ireland, emigrate to the great external labour markets . . . This difficulty might in part be met by adequate technical instruction; but, up to the present, financial and administrative difficulties, combined in some cases with a reluctance on the part of the workers to avail themselves of the instruction provided, seem to have retarded this most desirable development.

The provision of a developed system of technical instruction dates only from the recommendations of the Recess Committee in 1896 and the establishment of the Department of Agriculture and Technical Instruction in 1899.[44] Thereafter there was a rapid development which was arrested by the outbreak of war in 1914. In 1924 technical instruction was transferred to the Department of Education. The situation was examined by a Commission on technical education under the chairmanship of Mr. John Ingram, which was appointed in 1926 and reported in 1927.[45] The great majority of its numerous recommendations were adopted, in the views of some authorities, on an inadequate scale.[46]

42. In 1963 the *Second Programme for Economic Expansion* stated (para. 57) that the Control of Manufacturers legislation would be repealed. This has now been done, with effect from 1 January 1968.

43. Ibid., paras 71–3.

44. See W. P. Coyne (ed.) *Ireland, Industrial and Agricultural*, Browne & Nolan, Dublin: 1902, pp. 271–94. For the position before 1900, see the same publication, pp. 155–75.

45. A useful article in the *Irish Statesman* for 12 September 1925 reviews the situation when the Commission was appointed and a second, in the issue for 3 March 1928, considers its recommendations. The second article states that, when the Carlow sugar-beet factory was set up, operators for its main switchboard could not be found in Ireland and had to be brought in from Belgium.

46. See addendum to the *Report of the Commission on Emigration and Population* by Fr. T. Counihan S.J., pp. 191–7.

The Vocational Education Act of 1930 was the legislative expression of these recommendations. It established 38 local vocational education committees whose funds are provided by the State and by the local rating authority. A recent survey points out that in 1929–30 there were 67 technical schools with 2,500 whole-time students.[47] This had grown by 1966–7 to well over 900 schools with 39,800 whole-time and nearly 80,000 part-time students.

The Apprenticeship Act of 1931 was a logical sequel. This was a permissive measure with no element of compulsion. At the request of the workers and employers in a trade, an apprenticeship committee, representative of both sides, might be established to regulate the conditions of apprenticeship. Its provisions applied to only four trades—hairdressing, furniture manufacture, house-painting and decorating, and brush and broom manufacture. A number of trades, however, sponsored apprenticeship schemes of their own.

The position was reviewed by the Commission on Youth Unemployment[48] which recommended a National Apprenticeship Council, an extension apprenticeship scheme, and more effective measures for the training, instruction, and testing of apprentices. The Apprenticeship Act of 1959 followed these lines. It does not apply to the professions, agriculture, horticulture, the dairying industry, or clerical occupations. A National Apprenticeship Board was established in 1960 composed of representatives of employers and workers with some nominees of the Minister for Education without voting power.

A further approach was made by the Industrial Training Act in 1967. In effect, this repeals the 1959 Act and establishes a body—An Chomhairle Traenála—to provide and promote training for any activity of industry. The new body will therefore deal not only with apprenticeship but also with all other types of industrial and commercial training, including the retraining of adults and the training of unemployed and redundant workers.

It is one thing to train labour and quite another matter to retain it. The Fiscal Inquiry Committee commented on the mobility of Irish workers. Nothing has happened to diminish that mobility in the last forty years and many things have combined to increase it. In the 1920s the choice lay between the United States and a depressed British labour market. Today, the outlet is towards Great Britain. The existence of full employment there places the Irish employer at an immense disadvantage. Every Irish worker can take advantage of such opportunities without the least hindrance on either side of the Irish Sea. He has no barrier

47. T. Ó Raifeartaigh, 'Changes and Trends in our Educational System since 1922', *JSSISI*, 1958–9, p. 42.

48. Pr. 709. Stationery Office, Dublin. The Commission, under the chairmanship of the Most Reverend Dr. J. C. McQuaid, Archbishop of Dublin, reported in July 1951.

of race, of immigration restrictions, or union regulations. This is the point where the opportunities which an ability to emigrate affords the Irish people are most apparent. It is also, less happily, the point where individual good fortune conflicts with the interest of the community in economic development.

This mobility is, of course, of long standing, although the attraction of work in Great Britain has become much greater in the last ten or fifteen years. In 1938, the Banking Commission noted[49] that the rates of pay for skilled labour in Dublin were on the same level as those in the major English cities. That position still obtains. There is the one labour market; there is the single rate within that market. National boundaries are of no importance. In Great Britain, moreover, there is very often the opportunity to bring home still larger sums through overtime, and so far as unskilled labour is concerned both the basic rates of pay and the chances of overtime are much more favourable in Great Britain than anything available in Ireland.

The result is that despite the undeveloped state of the economy, the cost of labour in Ireland is not low. This emphasizes the necessity to increase its efficiency. Admittedly, a large proportion of workers who receive technical instruction and training at the expense of the Irish community will, so long as mobility continues, give the benefit of their acquired skill to the British economy. In doing so, they act no differently from many university graduates whose courses are subsidized to some extent by the public purse. Both types of emigration of skilled labour stem from the position of the Irish people and their inherited ability to move without difficulty to the richest labour markets in the world. It is one of the data of the economic situation which has to be accepted.[50] But the fact that labour may be lost this way would be a foolish reason for neglecting schemes of improved training from which those who remain may benefit. The matter has become more urgent on account of the large number of processes, previously unknown in Ireland, which have been developed by the foreign firms established in recent years.

On the employers' side, the Irish Institute of Management was founded in 1952. Its first task has been to counter the comparative lack of a tradition of management in a country where the scale of business has been small and enterprises have long been controlled by families. Its second task has been to disseminate the knowledge of modern managerial techniques. These aims are pursued by a series of conferences and short courses, or seminars, on special subjects and by the publication of a journal.[51]

49. Ibid., para. 100.
50. But it might be added that an avoidance of sharp fluctuations in industries such as building and construction would have assisted them to retain skilled labour.
51. See a useful article on the work of the Irish Institute of Management in the *Irish Banking Review*, June 1961.

The formal organization of labour relations may be appropriately mentioned at this point. The Irish Trades Union Congress was established in 1894. It had to deal not only with the multiplicity of unions which existed in Ireland, as in Great Britain, but also with the fact that in some cases labour was organized by purely Irish unions, while in others it was organized by Irish branches of British unions. Nevertheless, the trade union movement grew in strength during the early years of the present century and in 1922 the affiliated membership of the Irish Trades Union Congress was 189,000. It declined in the subsequent decade and was only 92,000 in 1929. From 1933 onwards, however, there was a marked recovery. In 1945 dissensions in the movement led to the establishment of the Congress of Irish Unions which catered solely for Irish-based unions. Following negotiations presided over by Professor John Busteed, reunion was achieved in 1959 when the ITUC and the CIU merged to form the Irish Congress of Trades Unions. Since 1961 the ICTU has explored means of reducing the number of unions.[52] Its estimated affiliated membership in the Republic was 364,000 in 1966.

Arising out of the labour troubles of the time, the Dublin Employers' Federation was formed in 1911. Much later, and in different circumstances, the Federated Union of Employers was established in 1942, aiming at the organization of employers throughout the country.

In 1946 the Industrial Relations Act was passed, providing machinery for the regulation of conditions of employment. This Act established the Labour Court which is composed of representatives of workers and employers with an independent chairman. Its recommendations are not binding, and in recent years there has been a growing tendency to by-pass it when the issues involved in a labour dispute are so important as to carry political implications.[53] This was particularly evident in the very disturbed period which began in 1964 and continued into 1966. For many years the record relating to industrial disputes had been relatively good. A comparison among eighteen countries of the number of working days lost through industrial disputes per thousand workers in the period 1955–64 showed Ireland with 495 working days so lost, roughly in the middle of a table which was headed by the United States with 1,044. The comparable figures for 1964 showed the Irish record far in advance of any of the other countries with 1,580, the next highest being Italy with 1,270. The position

52. For the history of organized labour in Ireland see *The Irish Labour Movement* by W. P. Ryan, Talbot Press, Dublin, 1919; generally, Chapter 3 of the *Report of the Commission on Vocational Organisation*, which reported in 1943, and 'Trades Union Organisation in Ireland' by Ruaidhri Roberts, *JSSISI*, 1958–9, p. 93.

53. See R. J. P. Mortished, 'The Industrial Relations Act', *JSSISI*, 1946–7, p. 671. Also, D. O'Mahony, *Industrial Relations in Ireland*, Economic Research Institute, Dublin: ERI Paper No. 19, 1964. Periodical surveys of industrial disputes are published in the *Irish Statistical Bulletin*.

in 1965 was worse still, the Irish figure being 1,770 and the next highest (for the United States) being 860. The return of total man-days lost, which comes from the Labour Court, shows a total of 104,000 in 1962, 234,000 in 1963, 545,000 in 1964, 556,000 in 1965, 784,000 in 1966, 183,000 in 1967, and 406,000 in 1968.

International comparisons can be misleading in so far as they are based on the duration of strikes and the number of workers involved and do not take account of the total number of strikes. For example, the figure for 1965 was very largely the consequence of only three disputes. Nevertheless it is not surprising that an extension of the powers of the Labour Court has been widely discussed. In the event a new Department of Labour was set up in July 1966.

The employer and worker organizations have been brought together with increasing frequency in recent years. In 1959 the National Productivity Committee was established. It comprises representatives of employers, the unions, the universities, and technical schools. It provides a common ground for the study of productivity methods. In 1962 a National Employer–Labour Conference was held with the intention of providing a general discussion of economic trends and the hope of making such discussion a regular event. In 1963 the National Industrial Economic Council was established on the initiative of the Government. It is composed of members nominated by the Government, the Irish Congress of Trades Unions, the Federated Union of Employers and other employers' organizations, State boards, and the Federation of Irish Industries.[54] The Taoiseach, Mr. Lemass, defined the Council's work at its inaugural meeting:

The Council is charged with the task of preparing reports from time to time on the principles which should be applied for the development of the national economy, and for the realization and maintenance of full employment at adequate wages, with reasonable price stability and reasonable long-term equilibrium in the balance of external payments. In these reports the Council will have regard to the level and trend of incomes, from whatever source. The Council will not deal with agricultural matters. Some explanation may be expected for the decision to make a distinction between agriculture and the rest of the economy. The explanation lies in the fact that agricultural policy is determined to a large extent by external conditions, which we cannot hope to alter by decisions taken here. There would also be some practical difficulties in setting up a Council, which would be workable in size but fully representative in character, to deal with agriculture, industry and the rest of the economy. If, however, in the light of experience of the working of this Council, or for some other reason, it should appear to be beneficial to have this decision reconsidered, this could be done.[55]

54. The Federation of Irish Industries was founded in 1932 as a national organization, consisting exclusively of manufacturers, for the general advancement and defence of Irish industry.

55. Reported in the Press of 10 October 1963. The subsequent activities of the Council are described in *The Work of the N.I.E.C., 1963–6*, Pr. 9090.

The Committee on Industrial Organization was set up in 1961. Its members were recruited from the Federation of Irish Industries, the Federated Union of Employers, the Irish Congress of Trades Unions and, the Government service. Its function was defined as providing an examination of the industrial structure and to recommend how it could be prepared for international competition. At that time, the admission of Ireland into the European Economic Community was thought to be imminent; the work of the Committee, however, continued after the suspension of the negotiations for entry. Specialist survey teams were constituted to examine each sector of industry. Each team included a senior official of the Department of Industry and Commerce, an economist and a representative of the industry under survey, if so desired. The Reports were published as they became available.[56]

Mention may appropriately be made here of the Institute for Industrial Research and Standards. It was established by an Act of 1946 which provided for a State grant. This grant has been increased by subsequent legislation. The functions of the Institute were defined as the promotion of scientific research and investigation of natural resources, the improvement of technical processes used in industry, the testing of commodities placed on sale and the formulation of standard specifications. It has formulated over a hundred specifications and, among other activities, has investigated the production of bread with a greater proportion of native wheat and new production processes for the Irish Sugar Company.

Transport

The Fiscal Inquiry Commitee observed that:

all the evidence given points to the conclusion that transport charges in Ireland are excessive, and that Irish industry, in nearly all its branches, is hampered from this cause, especially in competition with imported commodities which have the benefit of through rates. The Committee is impressed by the serious nature of this disadvantage, and is led to the conclusion that the development of all means of transport, whether by land or water, and its organization upon economic lines, are urgently required in the interests of industrial progress.[57]

Forty years on, the reader will recognize an apt summary on the contemporary problems.

Railways

In 1923 the difficulties of the railway system were not yet realized. What was only too obvious was the extent of the losses in business,

56. See article on the CIO in the issue of the *Irish Banking Review* for June 1963, also, 'The CIO Industrial Survey' by Miss C. Brock, *JSSISI*, 1963-4, p. 176.
57. Ibid., para. 70.

permanent way and viaducts, and in rolling stock, that they had suffered in the civil war.[58] It was not so apparent that the system had become unable to face the growing competition from road transport.

During the First World War the Irish railways, like the British, were under State control. Wages were increased by amounts varying from 27 per cent to 80 per cent; conditions of service were improved and working hours reduced. When de-control came in 1921 expenditure on wages and salaries was three times the pre-war level.

At that time, there were forty-six railway companies in operation, controlled by twenty-eight different managements, with a total capital of nearly £47m.[59] Of the total track, 2,705 miles lay in the Irish Free State and 773 miles in the Six Counties of Northern Ireland. Some of these companies were highly prosperous, others operated on a precarious balance; others again were light railways which had been constructed in the south and west in the 1890s and worked under a Government guarantee. As a whole, however, they had paid their way; in 1913, receipts had been £4,920,000 and expenditure £3,071,000.

The structure of ownership and control was most complicated, having developed through a succession of mergers and agreements. Thus the Dublin South-Eastern Railway comprised, among other companies, the Dublin and Kingstown Railway, the Dublin and Wicklow Railway, and the Dublin, Wicklow, and Wexford Railway. It followed that some railway shares were much more valuable than others. In the example given, the Dublin and Kingstown profited from the use of its line by the other companies. The contrast was to produce much hardship when railway capital was reduced indiscriminately.

Even before 1914 the railways faced difficulties. Planned for a population of seven million, they served half that number. The character of the economy did not suit railway traffic; there was little carriage of coal or other minerals which were remunerative. In 1905, a typical pre-1914 year, of goods receipts in Ireland 14 per cent came from the carriage of coal and minerals, 16 per cent from livestock, and 70 per cent from general merchandise. In England the proportions were 48 per cent; 2 per cent; 50 per cent.[60] Even at that, in the stagnation of agriculture,

58. e.g. the report of the Chairman of the Great Southern and Western Railway in March 1923 stated that *inter alia* there had been 467 cases of damage to the permanent way, 291 cases of damage to bridges, 103 signal cabins damaged or destroyed, and 468 locomotives, carriages, or other rolling stock derailed or destroyed.

59. *A History of Railways in Ireland* by J. C. Conroy, Longmans Green, London: 1928, covers events up to the 1924 Act. Developments after 1922 are fully described in the Report of the Tribunal on Public Transport, 1939. See also Inquiry into Internal Transport, 1957 (Pr. 4091), and papers by B. F. Shields, covering the working of railway companies from 1924 onwards, *JSSISI*, 1937–8, p. 87; 1945–6, p. 541; and 1953–4, p. 19.

60. D. J. Reynolds points out that in 1960 the load factor on Irish railways was the lowest in Europe. *Inland Transport in Ireland: A Factual Survey, ERI* Paper No. 10, 1962.

there was no constant increase in the volume of trade. A further weakness, which became acute when competition appeared, was the large staff. This numbered 19,000 in 1926.

The Railways Act of 1924 amalgamated twenty-six companies which operated exclusively in the Irish Free State into the Great Southern Railway Company. The new company had a capital of £26,008,707, which represented a capital reduction of £1,445,027. It was thought that the benefits of a unified direction would be sufficient to place the railways in a sound position. This soon proved to be mistaken. Operating costs remained high. More important was the rapid growth of road transport of passengers and goods.[61] Passenger buses or lorries could operate wherever the demand was to be found. They could make their own charges; they could move from one place to another with the minimum of difficulty. A new group of bus companies among whom there was intense competition emerged to serve Dublin and suburbs. The railway companies, on the other hand, were obliged to maintain services even where they were unremunerative, to maintain scales of charges which could not be quickly varied and to accept whatever goods were offered them for carriage. From an early stage, they were left with the less remunerative forms of traffic.

The Railways (Road Services) Act of 1927 gave the railways power to provide road services. The provision, however, was subject to complex formalities and the more flexible competitors were still able to capture traffic. Then and later, it was also claimed, the railway managements were unable to adjust themselves to the special conditions of road transport which they regarded only as a feeder to rail services and not as a service in its own right. Certainly one factor in delaying a solution to the problem was the division, within the successive boards of management of the railway, between 'road-minded' and 'rail-minded' directors.

A further approach to the problem was made in 1932 by the Railways Act and the Road Transport Act. The first empowered the Minister for Industry and Commerce to close down unremunerative branch lines. The second imposed a measure of control on all road passenger services by obliging them to publish timetables, etc., thus putting them on the same basis as the Great Southern Railway and the Dublin United Tramways.

61. The number of private motor-cars registered rose from 9,246 in 1923 to 48,599 in 1938, 52,401 in 1939, 229,125 in 1963, and 296,372 in 1966. Table 59 of the 1957 Transport Report showed that in 1954 the number of private cars in relation to national income was markedly greater in Ireland than in any other country of Western Europe—274 per million pounds of national income against, e.g. 228 in France, 205 in Great Britain, 159 in Denmark and 134 in Italy. The number of commercial vehicles rose from 3,507 in 1923, which included tractors, to 10,406 in 1938 and 45,433 in 1963, 46,928 in 1964, and 48,276 in 1965. Nevertheless, Reynolds (op. cit.) points out that in 1959 there were about 5 motor vehicles per mile of road in Ireland, against 33 in Great Britain and 27 in Western Germany.

These, however, were overshadowed by two Acts of 1933. The Railways Act provided for a drastic reduction of capital to £11,574,290. Debentures were reduced by 15 per cent and ordinary shares by 90 per cent. It is a useful example of the manner in which investment may have to be written off and of the risks to which the entrepreneur is exposed. The hardship imposed on those whose income was derived from formerly safe railway shares should not be forgotten. Power was also given to the Great Southern Railway to discontinue or reduce train services provided that adequate services by road were substituted.

The Road Transport Act of 1933 dealt with competition from the roads. It provided that road transport of goods for reward should be confined to those who were operating at the time of the Act. Licences to operators were transferable, in practice only to members of the same family. The railways were given powers of compulsory acquisition, and the number of licences for goods transport fell from 1,356 at the time of the Act to 886 in 1938.[62] The same powers applied to the non-statutory road passenger undertakings which decreased from 107 to 48. The railways complained that the sums paid out in purchase were excessive and that the carrier who transported his own goods was left untouched.

Succeeding years, which covered the depression of 1931 and Economic War period of 1932–8, brought no solution. The next step was the appointment, in December 1938, of the Tribunal of Inquiry on Public Transport, which published a report in August 1939.[63] It pointed out that railway traffic losses continued to mount and, a point of increasing importance, maintenance and renewal of permanent way and rolling stock were becoming more difficult. A majority report recommended:[64]

1. The establishment of a National Transport Council for the review of all forms of transport; 2. The establishment of a Board of three to govern the Great Southern Railway in the period, of whom one should be appointed by the Government; 3. Increased duties on all motor vehicles not operated by the statutory companies; 4. The issue of a Government guaranteed debenture of £1¼ millions for the Great Southern Railway; 5. Dublin traffic should be pooled between the Great Southern Railway and the Dublin United Tramway Company.

A minority report advocated:

1. The taking of the Great Southern Railway into state ownership; 2. The subsidization of the Great Northern Railway and 3. Opposition to any restrictions on road transport.

62. The number of licensed hauliers was 903 in 1962, 900 in 1963, and 908 in 1965.
63. P. 4866. The Chairman of the Tribunal was Mr. John Ingram and the members J. P. Beddy, H. Kennedy, J. P. O'Brien, and D. O'Hegarty.
64. The two following paragraphs are a summary of the principal recommendations.

The outbreak of war created fresh difficulties. In 1942 an Emergency Powers Order was made in respect of the board of the Great Southern Railway. The chairman of this board was appointed by the Government and given exceptional powers, while four directors were elected by the shareholders. This presaged the Transport Act of 1944 by which the Great Southern Railway and the Dublin United Tramway Company were amalgamated into a new company—Coras Iompair Éireann.[65] The Board consisted of a chairman appointed by the Minister for Industry and Commerce, with other directors elected by shareholders. No meeting of the board might be held in the absence of the chairman; no decision might be reached without his approval and by himself he might constitute a quorum at a meeting. An issue of new railway stock, guaranteed by the State, to be redeemed in 1960, replaced Great Southern Railway and Dublin United Tramway Company stock. The initial capital of the company was about £13.4m. The definitions of 'carriage of goods for reward' was tightened.

These drastic measures did not prevent further decline. The railway was handicapped by dear and inferior coal supplies and, after 1946, by higher wages and the resumption and extension of road transport. In addition, the deterioration of its equipment had reached a serious point. On average, the age of locomotives was fifty-one years, passenger coaches forty-eight years, and wagons thirty-five years.

In 1949 the Milne report on transport made a number of recommendations on organization and policy. The Transport Act 1950 accepted the principle of state ownership. The Grand Canal Company was amalgamated with Coras Iompair Éireann which was henceforward under the direction of a board appointed by the Government, being not fewer than three, or more than seven, in membership. There was a further reorganization of capital while the new board was empowered to borrow for permanent work by the issue of stock to an amount not exceeding £47m. A new transport tribunal had the function of decision on applications to close branch lines.

The next few years were delusively encouraging. A switch to diesel traction combined with operational economies to produce not only better results but even an increase in passenger traffic, in spite of an adjustment of fares to more realistic levels. But the decline in freight continued, and wages, which constituted 56 per cent of operating costs continued to increase.[66] By 1956 Coras Iompair Éireann had fallen into fresh difficulties; for twenty-eight weeks of that year it reported a loss of almost £500,000.

The Committee of Inquiry into Internal Transport was appointed

65. Transport Company of Ireland.
66. 1957 Report, para. 339. The proportion of wages on the Great Northern Railway was 64 per cent.

in July 1956 and reported in May 1957.[67] The report rehearsed conclusions which had become only too familiar—that the causes of the crisis were the low volume of traffic, an excess of transport facilities, over-staffing, over-capitalization and, on the part of the public, a distrust of rail management which was rooted in the past. Above all, it stressed that the railway system was much too large. Its survival was due principally to the windfall surpluses during the war, to State aid of some £12m. since the war, and the writing down of £13.5m. capital in 1933 and of £700,000 in 1950. The Committee recommended that the capital of the company should be written down by £11.6m. and that the interest on State advances should be waived.[68] It also recommended a drastic reduction of the rail system of Coras Iompair Éireann by the closing of 145 stations out of an existing 194 and reducing the track from 1,918 to 850 miles. There should also be a severe reduction of staff.[69] Finally, the company should be relieved of its obligations as a common carrier. If all this were done, the company might be given a further chance to prove its capacity to survive. On that point, the committee were not unduly optimistic.

As now constituted and operated we see no reasonable justification for the continuance of the railway undertaking of CIE but equally we consider it cannot be demonstrated clearly at present that under changed circumstances the railway undertaking would fail to justify its continued existence ... Railways should be given a limited number of years in which to show that their continuance can be justified in the national interest.[70]

This report led to further legislation, for CIE and for the Great Northern Railway, in 1958. Altogether, seventeen Transport Acts were passed between 1924 and 1958, a record surpassed only by the series of Land Acts. The capital of Coras Iompair Éireann was written down by £10m. to £13.5m. and repayable advances made by the Exchequer, totalling £6.6m., were also written off. Capital advances made by the Exchequer to the Great Northern Railway were also written off and the part of the Great Northern Railway within the State was amalgamated with Coras Iompair Éireann. The company was relieved of its liability as a common carrier.[71] It was given the objective of eliminating loss by 31 March 1964. To this end, the State engaged to provide monies from which redundant staff might be compensated. Finally, annual grants of

67. Pr. 4091. The committee was composed of Dr. J. P. Beddy (Chairman) with Messrs. J. F. Dempsey, J. N. Greene, J. J. Stafford, and S. F. Thompson.
68. In the event route mileage in the Republic of Ireland (including the Great Northern Railway which did not come within the survey of the Committee) fell from 2,440 in 1951 and 2,218 in 1957 to 1,458 in 1964.
69. The CIE board later estimated that 30 per cent of the railway staff were redundant.
70. Para. 354.
71. Commercial traffic on the Grand Canal was ended in 1959.

£1,175,000 were made to Coras Iompair Éireann in each of the five financial years ending March 1964.[72]

A new board of management was appointed in 1958 with Dr. C. S. Andrews as chairman and managing director. The goal of eliminating loss by 1964 was not achieved. This was due to the railway system which, although pruned of a further 621 miles of track during the period, incurred losses which more than offset the profits from other activities.

Accordingly the Transport Act of 1964 increased the annual grant up to £2m. each year up to 1969. The Minister for Finance was empowered to advance sums not exceeding £6m. for capital expenditure, provided it was economic. This legislation, it seems, was intended as a holding operation; it is accepted that the railway system cannot pay its way but capital expenditure will not be incurred in order to maintain it at all costs.

Shipping services

The dimensions of Irish shipping services will be seen from the following table.

TABLE 5.5

Number and net tonnage of vessels registered in Ireland, 1926–67

| | Number registered | | | | Net tonnage | | | |
	1926	1937	1948	1967	1926	1937	1948	1967
Steam	152	141	78	39	51,965	61,326	29,585	18,438
Motor	232	352	320	660	4,355	7,780	12,182	63,933
Sail	166	92	50	33	8,746	5,026	4,395	3,108

Source: *Irish Statistical Bulletin*

Fishing vessels, not included in the above Table, totalled 1,207 in 1967 with a tonnage of 7,900.

At the beginning of the 1920s Irish shipping was almost extinct. As virtually all trade was with Great Britain there were few opportunities for the development of ocean-going tonnage. The services across the Irish Sea were almost completely in the hands of British-controlled companies whose vessels were British-registered. The weakness of this position was at once apparent in 1939 when many ships were withdrawn by the British Government from Anglo-Irish services for use elsewhere. The carriage of raw materials, foodstuffs, and oil needed for the maintenance of essential services within the Republic became a vital national interest. In 1941, therefore, Irish Shipping Limited was established by the Government as a State company. Operating, in the early stages, on bank

72. From 1949 to 31 March 1964 State assistance to the transport system totalled £45.3m. *PDDE*, 210, 749.

overdraft, it succeeded in acquiring some fifteen vessels. Granted the then intense demand for shipping, some of these vessels were in very poor condition and their ages varied between thirty and sixty years. Nevertheless, the company was able to maintain essential supplies and also to accumulate a considerable working surplus. Since the end of the war in 1945 there has been a succession of building programmes and at the end of the year 1966–7 the company possessed fifteen modern ships with a dead-weight tonnage of 139,000.

This tonnage is mainly engaged in tramp and charter services and the cargo lifted in 1965–6 amounted to 1,672,629 tons. About three-quarters of the freight carried is between overseas ports. Only one-quarter arises from Irish-overseas trade. Only about one-quarter of Anglo-Irish trade is carried in ships of Irish registration and about one-half of the trade between the Republic and European ports is carried in ships registered in the Republic.[73]

Air transport

The geographical advantages of the Republic in the sphere of air transport are obvious. The first non-stop crossings of the North Atlantic by aeroplane ended and began in Ireland.[74] In the event, however, the early development of Irish air services took place towards Great Britain and the Continent.

This development was initiated by Aer Lingus which was incorporated as a private company in May 1936 at the instance of the then Minister for Industry and Commerce, Mr. Sean Lemass. This was done pending the passage of the Air Navigation and Transport Act 1936 which authorized the formation of a national air transport company. Under the Act, Aer Rianta was registered as a public company in 1937. Its capital was subscribed by the Minister of Industry and Commerce and until 1966 it held a majority of the shares in Aer Lingus, the operating company. It is now concerned with the administration of the airports.

The latter began operations in May 1936 and operated some routes

73. This situation has often incurred criticism especially as about one-half of Irish imports and three-quarters of exports are carried across the Irish Sea. The first step towards participation in Anglo-Irish trade must be the provision of port facilities and ancillary services which, under present circumstances, would be highly expensive. It is, of course, also true that the carriage of so much trade in British ships constitutes an important adverse item in the balance of payments. On these issues, see the Dáil debates on the Irish Shipping Limited Act, 1959, at 173, *PDDE*, 182, 206. Also a symposium on Irish Shipping in *Administration*, Winter, 1954–5.

In 1965 the British and Irish Steampacket Company was purchased by the State from Coast Lines Ltd.

74. The first non-stop west–east crossing of the North Atlantic by airplane was made in June 1919 by Alcock and Brown. They landed near Clifden in County Galway. The first east–west flight, by Huenfeld, Kohl, and Fitzmaurice, in April 1928, commenced at Baldonnell, County Dublin.

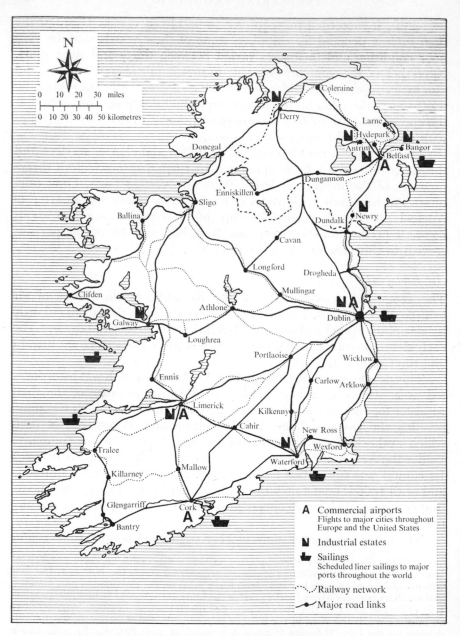

10. MAJOR COMMUNICATIONS NETWORK AND PRINCIPAL
INDUSTRIAL SITES

Based on information supplied by the Industrial Development Authority, Dublin, and
Ministry of Commerce, Belfast.

across the Irish Sea conjointly with a British air services company. In the first full year of operation, 1937, some 2,700 passengers were carried, but development was severely restricted by the outbreak of war in 1939. Up to the end of 1944, the number of passengers carried never exceeded 7,000 in any year. Thereafter, expansion was rapid, being greatly helped by an agreement reached in 1946 between the British and Irish governments. This gave Aer Lingus exclusive rights to operate services scheduled between the two countries and admitted British European Airways and British Overseas Airways to a 40 per cent share in its capital (which was increased from £100,000 to £5,000,000) and direction.[75] This advantageous position enabled the company to dispense with operating subsidies though its capital needs have still to be met by the Minister out of the Central Fund of the Exchequer. It also opened a number of services to the Continent. In 1956–7 it carried 448,000 revenue passengers on scheduled services, of whom 412,000 were on routes between Ireland and Great Britain.[76]

In 1956 the agreement governing services between the two countries became due for revision. A new arrangement admitted British European Airways (whose share of the capital was reduced to 10 per cent) to a fifth share of the traffic on the three major routes from Dublin—London, Birmingham, and Manchester. Aer Lingus responded by an extension of its Continental routes. In 1968–9 it carried 1,142,000 revenue passengers.

Transport of cargo by air was negligible before 1939 but reached 5,000 tons in 1951. In 1968–9, 33,600 short tons were carried on scheduled and chartered flights.

The progress of Aer Lingus seems to depend largely on success in keeping its administration tightly knit and to good judgement in its purchasing of suitable aircraft. These advantages were the more necessary on account of some inherent weaknesses. The company's routes, especially the most important ones to Great Britain, are exceptionally short. The use of the system is highly seasonal. A huge proportion of the passenger traffic is concentrated into the summer and Christmas holidays. As has been remarked, there is 'a summer harvest and a winter famine'. This traffic, again, is very largely composed of Irish travellers or people who have lately emigrated from Ireland to Great Britain. Their support has been a great source of strength to the company. Nevertheless, the smallness of the potential passenger traffic from the continent to Ireland and the seasonal nature of total traffic is only too obvious. From the

75. British Overseas Airways Corporation relinquished their holding in Aer Lingus to the British European Airways Corporation. They in turn relinquished their holding to Aer Lingus in 1964.

76. A useful account of the early years of the air services will be found in *Civil Aviation in Ireland*, Castle Publications, Dublin: 1956. See also 'The Finance of Air Transport Services in Ireland', by Peter Brennan, *JSSISI*, 1950–1, p. 379.

point of view of Aer Lingus, the geographical position of the country presents little advantage.

This position, however, is quite altered if the country is seen as a link between the two sides of the Atlantic. The transatlantic service dates only from 1958 but its origins go back much further. In November 1935 agreement was reached between the British, Canadian, and Irish governments to operate jointly a transatlantic air service. The Irish government assumed the obligation to provide an air base with the necessary facilities and a suitable site was chosen at Rineanna in Clare—now known as Shannon Airport. In the meantime, Foynes, on the Limerick side of the Shannon estuary, was used as a base for the flying-boat service which began in 1939.

The outbreak of war in 1939 ended the plans for an internationally operated service. The base at Foynes was used until October 1945 since when all services have used Shannon Airport. In 1947 Aerlinte Éireann[77] was established as a subsidiary company of Aer Rianta to operate a transatlantic service. A change in government in 1948 brought also a change in government policy and the service, which was planned to have begun that year, was abandoned. Following a further change of government and policy in 1951 it was decided to commence a service using leased aircraft. This project also fell through, but it was revived again in 1958 and the first service opened in April of that year with craft leased from Seaboard and Western Airlines. In the first full year of operation, 1959, some 23,000 passengers were carried. In October 1960 Aerlinte took delivery of its own craft for the service. In 1968–9 it carried 220,000 passengers.

In 1946, its first full operating year, Shannon Airport was used by 4,126 craft carrying 108,000 passengers. In 1954 these numbers had risen to 8,207 craft carrying 304,000 passengers. The number of passengers rose to a peak of 498,000 in 1958; then it declined but had recovered to 469,000 in 1966–7. The number embarking or disembarking at Shannon has risen from 53,000 in 1955 to 239,000 in 1966–7. Transit freight totalled 17,700 tonnes in 1966–7 while terminal freight totalled 6,900 tonnes.[78]

A customs-free area was established at Shannon Airport as early as 1947 but it remained almost unused for a number of years. An Act of 1958 provided for the relief of customs procedure and restrictions on the importation of raw materials for goods manufactured within the airport area. Further legislation empowered the State to advance moneys to the Shannon Free Airport Development Company (established in 1959) for the construction of factory buildings which may be leased out, and to provide grants covering half the cost of machinery and all the cost of

77. Now known abroad as Irish International Airlines.
8. A tonne is equivalent to 0.984 of a U.K. ton.

labour training. An Act of 1958 empowered the Minister for Finance to grant exemption from taxation on profits from exports to firms operating with the customs-free area for a period ending in 1983. The Control of Manufactures Acts do not apply to foreign investment in this area. In March 1969, 4,300 workers were employed in factories on the industrial estate at Shannon.

Fuel and power

The Fiscal Inquiry Committee stated that:

The most important source of industrial power cannot be obtained as cheaply in Ireland as in most European countries. The supply of Irish coal at present available is utterly inadequate for the needs of Irish industry, and the necessary supply of imported coal can only be obtained at a higher price than it costs in its country of origin. This disability is especially serious in the case of industries situated at a distance from the ports. In some cases water power has been substituted for coal. But it is not yet certain that water power or wind power can be relied upon as a substitute for coal except in small scale industries.[79]

The Shannon Scheme

The provision of electricity from water power represented the first great enterprise undertaken by the new State in 1925 and the Electricity Supply Board is by far the largest capital investment undertaken in Ireland in the last forty years. The Shannon Scheme was of immense psychological importance because it stimulated public self-confidence when encouragement was badly needed.

The circumstances in which the Shannon Scheme was first considered were described to the Dáil by Mr. Cosgrave, then President of the Executive Council.[80] In December 1923 Dr. T. A. McLaughlin, then an engineer employed by Messrs. Siemens-Schukert in Berlin, was introduced to him to discuss a proposal to harness the water-power of the River Shannon. The idea of obtaining hydro-electric power was not novel in itself, indeed, several schemes for harnessing the Liffey were under discussion at that time. The possibilities of the Shannon had been previously considered with discouraging conclusions but observations of its flow had been taken by Mr. J. Chaloner Smith over a period of thirty years. These observations were to prove of great value. Dr. McLaughlin, however, had gone much further by drafting a scheme which had attracted the interest of Messrs. Siemens-Schuckert. The high standing of

79. Ibid., para. 69. The importance of coal supplies has diminished since then. Imports (reckoned in thousands of tons) were 2,405 in 1928; 2,484 in 1938; 1,772 in 1951; and 1,022 in 1967. There has been a further change. In the pre-war years practically all coal came from the United Kingdom, though there was some contraction of imports during the economic 'war'. Since 1960 a high proportion of coal imports has come from the United States.

80. Speech of 3 April 1925, *PDDE*, 10, 2015.

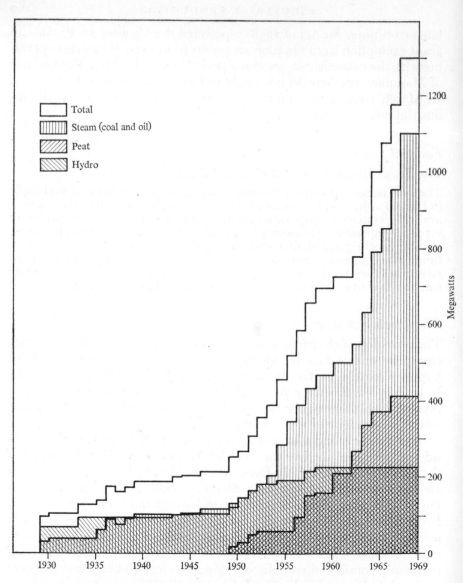

**11. ELECTRICITY SUPPLY GENERATION
IN THE REPUBLIC, 1930–69**

This graph illustrates the vast increase in the generation of electricity since 1945, and the increased use of peat as fuel. Imported fuels must be used to meet the rising demand for electric power. Source: Electricity Supply Board, Dublin, *Annual Report, 1969*.

Key to map:

1 SHANNON BRIDGE	11 Francis St
2 FERBANE	12 Carrick mines
3 Athlone	13 Milltown
4 PORTARLINGTON	14 RINGSEND
5 ALLENWOOD	15 INNISCARRA
6 Newbridge	16 MARINA
7 Maynooth	17 Trabeg
8 LEIXLIP	18 Haulbowline
9 Inchicore	19 ARDNACRUSHA
10 Sean McDermott St	In this key generating stations are shown by capital letters

Legend:

- ◰ Hydro stations
- ◼ ◉ Steam stations
- ▢ Steam stations projected
- ▽ Pumped storage station projected
- △ 220 kV transformer station
- ○ 220 kV transformer stations projected
- ● 110 kV transformer stations
- ◔ 110 kV transformer stations projected
- ▬▬▬ 220 kV lines
- ▬ ▬ ▬ 220 kV lines projected
- ▬▬▬ 110 kV lines
- ▭ ▭ ▭ 110 kV lines projected
- ▬·▬·▬ 275 kV lines
- ▬ ▬ Other high voltage lines

12. ELECTRICITY SUPPLY DISTRIBUTION NETWORK

Based on information supplied by the Electricity Supply Board, Dublin, and the Electricity Supply Board, Belfast. All transformer stations in Northern Ireland connected to 275 kV lines also have 110 kV equipment.

this firm put what had previously been vague hopes into an altogether new perspective. The result of this first interview, however, was that the scheme was 'turned down', to use Mr. Cosgrave's phrase. A second interview was obtained in January 1924, largely through the interest of the Hon. Gordon Campbell (later Lord Glenavy) who was then Secretary of the Department of Industry and Commerce. At this interview Mr. Blythe and Mr. McGrath were also present.[81] There was a third in early February, attended by representatives of Messrs. Siemens-Schuckert.

The result was a White Paper which was laid before the Dáil on 7 March 1924. It consisted of a letter, drafted by Mr. Campbell, to the German firm and their reply accepting the proposals of the Irish Government. Mr. Campbell's letter set out thirteen points under which Messrs. Siemens-Schuckert would work out a detailed plan for the development and distribution of electrical power from the Shannon and would make a binding estimate as to costs. The scheme would be submitted to experts selected by the Irish government. If it was finally approved, the government would either promote it as a State project or give the firm the first option to carry it out. Thus the German company was committed while the Irish Government retained its liberty of action.

The scheme was submitted to four experts nominated by the Government, the directors of the State electrical schemes of Sweden and Norway, and two Swiss authorities. On 19 December 1924 Mr. McGilligan made a long statement to the Dáil from which it emerged that the cost of the proposed scheme would be £5,200,000.[82] The report of the experts, which endorsed the scheme in all significant points, was published in March 1925. In April Mr. McGilligan moved that legislation to implement the scheme should be introduced. After a two-day debate this resolution was passed without an opposing vote.[83] Accordingly the Shannon Electricity Bill was introduced in May and became law before the summer.

The reader will note the great care with which proposals involving the spending of £5m. were set out and examined. The scheme proposed by Siemens ran to 186 large pages. It was examined by a committee of experts. It was debated on three separate occasions by the Dáil. Larger sums have been spent since with less consideration. Equally, the reader will note the rapidity with which the scheme was elaborated, examined, and approved in the sixteen months between February 1924 and June 1925. Another point should be noted, the strength of the opposition to

81. Mr. Blythe was Minister for Finance 1922–32. Mr. McGrath was then Minister for Industry and Commerce, from which office he resigned in March 1924. Mr. McGilligan was appointed as his successor in April and was responsible for the parliamentary conduct of the project. Mr. McGrath was later appointed director of the labour employed on the Scheme, which was no sinecure, as the readers of contemporary newspapers will observe.

82. *PDDE*, 9, 2791 f.   83. *PDDE*, 10, 1753 f.

the scheme. One must go through not only the parliamentary debates but the columns (and the leading articles) of the principal newspapers to appreciate how widespread and virulent this was.

It came, naturally enough, from the sponsors of the Liffey hydro-electric scheme then under consideration. It came, less comprehensibly, from distributors of electrical appliances. A number of eminent civil engineers stated that the Shannon could not be safely banked. Members of the Farmers' party in the Dáil claimed that the State could not afford an expenditure of £5m. Other opponents argued that the production of the Shannon would be grossly in excess of demand as the consumption of electricity then amounted to 35 million units a year. Another interest disliked the possible introduction of German influence and, pointing to the position of Great Britain as Ireland's best customer, argued that it would be necessary to borrow abroad for the cost of the scheme and that British capital would not be forthcoming. A final argument, used indiscriminately by the various groups of the opposition, was that the embankments of the river or the transmission lines might be blown up or destroyed by those hostile to the State.[84] It is proper to recall that the then principal opposition party, the Labour Party, supported the scheme from the beginning and its leader, Thomas Johnson, insisted on a roll call being taken on the April resolution so that the decision might be placed beyond all doubt. Thereafter, work proceeded rapidly. The Shannon Scheme went into operation in 1929.

Special reference should be made to the transmission system which was constructed to distribute power throughout the country. It was the first example of its kind in these islands, ante-dating the British national grid by some years. It was planned and executed by Irish engineers.

In 1927 the Electricity Supply Act was passed for the purpose of supervising the distribution of electricity supply. Mr. McGilligan stated that the Government was unwilling to accept proposals that distribution should be leased to private interests.[85] Equally it did not favour control by a department of State. Accordingly, he proposed the establishment of a board of management 'as independent of Parliament and the Government as far as that could reasonably be arranged'. Thus the Electricity Supply Board was established. Its members are appointed by the Government and are eligible for reappointment. The Board submits an annual report and accounts to the Minister, to be laid by him before the Oireachtas. It is also obliged to furnish such statistics and returns as the Minister may require. Its function is to generate, transmit, and distribute electricity. It must so arrange its tariffs so that

84. All these prophecies may be read in the parliamentary reports, and in the principal newspapers. At this distance of time, it would be unfair to particularize more closely.

85. PDDE, 18, 1894 f.

revenue will be sufficient (and, as near as may be, only sufficient) to meet working expenses, interest, repayments of advances, and such sums as should be set aside for reserve fund, extensions, renewals, depreciation, loans, and other like purposes. The Board is placed in exactly the same position as a commercial undertaking and must organize its activities to achieve this object.[86]

TABLE 5.6

Output and sale of electricity

Year (ending 31 March)	Units generated and purchased (million)	Units sold (million)	Revenue from sales of energy (£ thousand)	Average price p. unit sold (pence)	Total consumers
1929–30	60.9	43.2	478	2.66	48,606
1939–40	407.0	318.6	1,946	1.47	172,545
1949–50	784.8	626.2	4,774	1.83	310,639
1954–5	1,461.7	1,192.2	9,522	1.92	461,901
1959–60	2,096.0	1,692.2	14,724	2.09	610,946
1962–3	2,714.9	2,238.5	19,445	2.08	659,932
1963–4	2,900.8	2,375.9	20,383	2.06	678,054
1964–5	3,240.2	2,682.6	22,488	2.01	697,491
1965–6	3,546.2	2,953.3	24,077	1.96	716,113
1966–7	3,851.0	3,238.1	26,690	1.98	726,561
1967–8	4,246.4	3,570.1	29,898	2.01	745,430
1968–9	4,749.0	4,012.3	34,457	2.06	765,213

Source: *Reports of the Electricity Supply Board*

These figures are an adequate commentary on the fears that the production of the Shannon Scheme would exceed demand. They do not, however, show the problems of policy which must be faced by the Electricity Supply Board. The uncertain factor is the trend of industrial demand.[87] This is one-third of the total while domestic demand increased from 25 per cent in 1936 to 44 per cent in 1966–7. This increase presumably reflects factors such as urbanization and better housing and general living conditions. On the other hand, a sharp

86. This description of the position of the Electricity Supply Board is taken from 'Statutory Corporations and Commissions' by R. F. Browne, published in *Public Administration in Ireland*, vol. i. On State companies generally, see G. FitzGerald, *State-Sponsored Bodies*, Institute of Public Administration, Dublin: 2nd edition, 1963; also Bristow, 'State Enterprise and Planning in the Irish Republic', *JSSISI*, 1964–5, p. 77.

87. On this, and other matters relating to the Electricity Supply Board, see 'The Electricity Supply Board', by R. F. Browne, Chairman of the Electricity Supply Board, 1931–60, in *JSSISI*, 1951–2, p. 564. See also the issue of *Administration* devoted to the Electricity Supply Board, Autumn, 1957. See further the paper written by J. L. Booth and published by the Economic Research Institute on *Fuel and Power in Ireland*, Part ii.

expansion of industrial demand has become apparent. A programme for the new generating plant, covering the period until 1969, is now in hand.[88]

These matters are closely connected with the question of the motive powering of future stations. Originally, the output of electricity (apart from existing coal plants in Dublin and Cork) was derived from hydro-power. After the Shannon, the next scheme was the Poulaphouca scheme on the Liffey which was opened in 1939: the Erne followed in 1952. Further stations were erected on the Liffey, the Lee, and at Clady in County Donegal. It is understood that the possibilities of hydro-power are now virtually exhausted so that, as is reflected in the last table, the cost of current has been increasingly influenced by the cost of other sources of power. The Electricity Supply Board's report for 1968–9 shows that the electricity supplied to the system was provided as to 17 per cent by water-power; 11 per cent by sod peat; 26 per cent by milled peat; 1 per cent by native coal; and 45 per cent by oil or coal.[89]

Another problem facing the Electricity Supply Board is the programme of rural electrification. Aided by State subsidies, this programme was begun in 1946. The State assistance was discontinued in 1955, when less than one-fifth of the programme had been completed. It was restored in 1958 but the effect of the suspension has placed a burden on the Electricity Supply Board's finances which must be borne by urban and industrial consumers. Even with a subsidy of 50 per cent, the further progress of rural electrification is increasingly unremunerative as the more isolated and sparsely populated areas are tackled; 'each new area completed involves an additional and continuing annual loss to the Board.'[90] At 31 March 1969, the number of consumers connected under this programme was 327,629 and the total amount invested in the scheme was £43m.

Development of peat resources

Schemes to use the bog-lands have a long and, until lately, discouraging history. The very first of all the numerous Commissions which have examined Irish economic problems was the body which 'enquired into the Nature and Extent of the Several Bogs in Ireland and the Practicability of Draining and Cultivating them', between 1809 and 1814. This commission, as a most valuable paper by Dr. C. S. Andrews pointed out,[91]

88. See Booth, *Fuel and Power in Ireland*, ERI Paper No. 30, Part i.
89. These proportions vary to some extent with the weather. In a wet year more power will be derived from water-power; in a dry year, from turf. But these factors are not necessarily compensating.
90. *Report of Electricity Supply Board for 1959–60*, p. 10.
91. 'Some Precursors of Bord na Móna', *JSSISI*, 1953–4, p. 132. Dr. Andrews was in charge of turf development from 1933 to 1958.

was inspired by Sir Arthur Wellesley, then briefly Chief Secretary for Ireland before embarking on his Peninsular campaigns.

Various attempts, which are described by Dr. Andrews, were made during the nineteenth century to develop the bogs. In 1917, the (British) Department of Scientific and Industrial Research initiated a further inquiry. This was accomplished by a committee composed of Sir John Purser Griffith, Professor Pierce Purcell, Professor Hugh Ryan, Professor Sydney Young, and Mr. George Fletcher. Their report, which was published in 1918, has since proved to be of great value, but it was disregarded at the time. Three years later, the Dáil Commission of enquiry, under the chairmanship of Professor Ryan, submitted a further report.

The present development of turf resources dates from 1933. The Turf Development Board was established in 1935, and land was acquired for experimental mechanical working in the following year. Further development was delayed by the war but in 1946 Bord na Móna was established as a statutory body to produce fuel from the bogs. Its borrowing powers, which are met out of the Central Fund, have been progressively extended by a succession of Turf Development Acts. Its market is provided by the Electricity Supply Board whose stations were for some years planned and sited to allow turf, machine-won and more lately milled, to be used on the site. In 1968–9, a year of unusually sunny weather, the production of machined and milled turf was 4,754,549 tons, of briquettes 270,978 tons; and of peat moss, 649,368 bales. The electricity generating stations absorbed 2,500,000 tons of turf. The briquettes and peat moss, in which there is now an export trade, were sold to the public.[92]

Mineral resources

The Fiscal Inquiry Committee remarked that many Irish industries suffered from the difficulty of obtaining raw materials.[93] They also pointed out that the most important raw materials of the woollen industry, the paper-making industry, the jute industry, the manufacture of fertilizers, brushes, pottery and clay pipes, the coach-building industry, and the furniture industry had all to be imported.

Thirty years later the Commission on Emigration summarized the position as follows:[94]

Several metallic ores, notably copper, lead, zinc, and iron pyrites were mined in Ireland early in the 19th century. Most of these operations were discontinued because of mining difficulties and a reduction in the world price of metals caused by the development of sources of supply in other countries. Copper,

92. The activities and organization of Bord na Móna are described in detail in *Administration*, Spring 1959.
93. Para. 68.   94. Para. 63.

lead, zinc and silver are widely distributed but in relatively small quantities; small amounts of iron ore also exist. The development of non-metallic minerals, particularly gypsum, limestone, slates, clays, gravel, brick clay and road metal is much greater than that of metallic minerals. Fireclay is worked in the coalfields, ornamental marble is being utilized to a small extent and there are small deposits of low quality rock-phosphate. Sulphur ore, barytes, glass and ochre are also found. It is possible that the limits of profitable development may be extended by improved methods of surveying or of exploitation.

The foregoing passage was intended as a summary of the position as it then existed.[95] It was in its turn, founded largely on two publications which had appeared in the previous decade. One was *Irish Mineral Resources* by D. W. Bishopp, published by the Stationery Office in 1943. The other was *The Natural Resources of Ireland* published a year later.

It will be worthwhile to expand these references. In 1843–4 Robert Kane delivered a series of lectures under the auspices of the Royal Dublin Society on the sources of industrial power in Ireland. These lectures were published by the Society in 1844 under the title of *The Industrial Resources of Ireland*. A modern authority has remarked that:

it is impossible to do justice to this great book in any brief manner . . . it represents the first and most important attempt to apply scientific methods to the evaluation and use of our industrial resources.[96]

The commemorative volume of 1944, to which Mr. Bishopp was an important contributor, represented an assessment of Kane's survey in the light of a greatly increased power to develop the natural resources of the country. In the greater part of the intervening century, however, little or nothing had been done to advance development. Kane's work was so acclaimed that a second edition was called for within a year. But there has never been a third. The year of the second edition was also the first year of the Famine. Years afterwards, giving evidence in 1885 to the Select Committee on Irish Industries[97] Kane stated[98] that the Famine had obliterated interest in the development of Irish resources; moreover

95. For greater detail see *Ireland* (3rd edition) by T. W. Freeman, Methuen, London: 1965, which is the definitive work of general and regional geography. It contains a valuable bibliography.

96. Professor T. S. Wheeler, *The Natural Resources of Ireland*, Royal Dublin Society, Dublin: 1944. This book contains a symposium organized by the Royal Dublin Society to commemorate the centenary of Kane's *Industrial Resources of Ireland*.

97. 1884–5, PP, HMSO: vol. ix, i.

98. See his answer to Q. 2705: 'Circumstances do not seem to require it, and a very short time after 1845 the condition of the country was very materially changed by the occurrence of the dreadful famine of 1846, which made such a profound alteration in the condition of the country, and of the people, that the subject of industry fell, I may say, out of sight.' And again, Q. 2905: 'There was much more interest taken in the development of industries when you published your book than there has been since; you are of opinion that the famine broke the spirit of the people in regard to industries?—I think so: I think at that time there was very much more tendency towards industrial enterprise than there has been since.'

he added, the growth in overseas sources of supply had brought prices below the level at which Irish deposits might be profitably worked.[99]

It is not surprising, however, that a belief in the importance of Irish natural resources was vigorously fostered as the nationalist movement grew in strength. On 18 June 1919, the following resolution was moved in Dáil Éireann by Arthur Griffith and seconded by Terence MacSwiney:

That a Select Commission be appointed to inquire into the natural resources and the present condition of manufacturing and productive industries in Ireland, and to consider and report by what means these natural resources may be more fully developed and how these industries may be encouraged and extended.[100]

The tone of the resolution is that of a sovereign legislature such as, six months earlier, the Dáil had proclaimed itself to be. But there was more to it than that. The text is copied word for word from the House of Commons resolution of 1885 which set up the Inquiry just mentioned. The deliberate symbolism may confidently be attributed to Griffith.

The body thus established was more a National Economic Council rather than a committee of inquiry; and its members were not drawn exclusively from the ranks of Sinn Féin. Two committees were formed; one on Food, of which Mr. Thomas Johnson was chairman; the other on Power, with Professor Hugh Ryan as chairman. These travelled around the country and collected evidence. Their activities attracted the unfavourable attention of the Crown forces, and after February 1920 the proceedings were subject to interruptions which have been vividly described by the secretary.[101] Nevertheless in the years 1920 and 1921 it published reports on coal resources; milk production; cattle-breeding; industrial alcohol; and water-power; an achievement that might be envied by subsequent commissions which deliberated in more peaceful circumstances.

After the Treaty, interest was concentrated, as has already appeared, on water-power and later on turf. The wartime shortage of supplies acted as a spur to further action in a wider field. The Minerals Development Act of 1940 was intended to stimulate prospecting and mining and enabled the State to acquire mineral deposits that were not being worked. A State-owned company, Mianraí Teo., a successor to previous ventures in this field, was established in 1945 to explore and develop lands for the purpose of ascertaining the nature and quality of

99. Answer to Q. 3094, that the prices of the principal metals were not half, sometimes less than one-third, of what they were in 1844.

100. Dáil Éireann, *Minutes of Proceedings*, 1919–21, p. 123 gives an abbreviated text of the resolution. The full text will be found in the book by Darrell Figgis which is quoted in the next footnote, and in the Commission's interim report on milk production which is dated March 1920.

101. Darrell Figgis, *Recollections of the Irish War*, Benn, London: 1927.

minerals thereon and the advisability of working them. Its field of action was extended by the Minerals Company Act of 1947. The investigations, conducted with up-to-date methods of prospecting, greatly increased the volume of information available. In particular, they gave ground for believing that extensive quantities of copper ores, with zinc and lead, remained in the Avoca mines which had long been worked in the eighteenth and early nineteenth century but had been almost derelict for over half a century. Two Acts of 1956 provided tax remissions for mining.[102] These incentives encouraged exploration by Canadian and other interests. In 1962, however, the workings at Avoca were suspended. Some months earlier, the location of rich mineral deposits had been reported from County Galway. The contrast symbolized the chequered history of mineral research in Ireland.

Developments since then have been remarkable. The mineralization in County Galway, at Tynagh, proved to be composed of lead, zinc, and copper. It was brought to the production stage at the end of 1965 by Irish Base Metals Ltd., a wholly owned subsidiary of the Canadian company, Northgate Exploration.

The same company is also engaged in the development of other copper deposits at Gortdrum in County Tipperary. The largest venture of all is the project now being carried through by Consolidated Mogul (which was connected with the Avoca mine) at Silvermines, also in County Tipperary.

102. The foregoing is a highly condensed account of a variety of enterprises which were amply discussed by the Dáil in the debates on the Finance (Profit of Certain Mines) Act, 1956. *PDDE*, p. 154, *passim*.

CHAPTER SIX

Population and Emigration

THE FIRST RELIABLE IRISH CENSUS WAS THAT TAKEN ON 6 June 1841.[1] Its director was Thomas Larcom, a captain of engineers who had been previously engaged in the organization of the ordnance survey of the country.[2] Under his inspiration, the census included life-tables for urban and rural areas, and analyses of the fertility of marriage which were not prepared in England and Wales until 1911. The census also provided tables of overseas migration. An inquiry into agriculture foreshadowed the institution in 1847, largely through Larcom's initiative, of annual returns of crops and livestock. All round, the census of 1841 was a most notable achievement. It is proper to recall the tribute paid to its sponsors when the task of enumeration was first discharged under an Irish government:

It is possible, of course, to criticize the methods of some of these enquiries and their results, indeed the Commissioners themselves were their own severe critics; but after a passage of nearly a century no student of this great Census can fail to recognize the statistical virtuosity of the census-takers judged by the standards of any age.[3]

The precedent of inquiring into matters not usually covered by a census has been followed on many occasions since 1841. Their wide

---

1. For a general survey of previous attempts, see *GR*, 1926, 1 f. They are discussed at much greater length and from a new angle by K. H. Connell, *The Population of Ireland, 1750–1845*, Clarendon Press, Oxford: 1950. Comments on the development of the census after 1841 will be found in W. J. Thompson, 'The Development of the Irish Census', *JSSISI*, 1910–11, p. 474, and C. H. Oldham, 'The Reform of the Irish Census', *JSSISI*, 1925–6, p. 197.

2. Later Sir Thomas Larcom, 1801–79, Under-Secretary for Ireland, 1853–68. See notice in *DNB*, xi, 584, and memoir on pp. 54–7 of the *Centenary History of the Statistical and Social Inquiry Society of Ireland*, ed. R. D. Black, Eason, Dublin: 1947. Sir Thomas was a founder of this society.

3. *GR*, 1926, 4.

range testifies to the strong tradition of versatility which derived from Larcom and has been maintained by his successors to the present day.[4] At no time have purely demographic matters been isolated from the general pattern of the economy; and this practice seems to be peculiarly appropriate to a country whose economic development has been so profoundly influenced by violent changes in the size and distribution of its population.

Until 1911 the census was taken on the same night as in England and Wales and in Scotland, thus ensuring conformity in the statistics of the United Kingdom. It was impossible to organize a census in 1921 and no enumeration was made until 1926, when a census was taken simultaneously in the Irish Free State and Northern Ireland. A census was next taken in the Free State in 1936 and in Northern Ireland in 1937; and a further census was taken in the south in 1946. In 1951 it was again found possible to hold a census on the same night in both parts of the country; simultaneously, a census was taken in England and Wales and in Scotland for the first time in twenty years: thus conformity between the several divisions of the two islands was restored after a break of forty years. In 1961, however, the census was taken in the Republic on 9 April and in Northern Ireland on 23 April. It is not, therefore, strictly accurate to combine the results to obtain a total population for all Ireland as has been done in Table 6.1.

Registrations of population in 1941 and in 1943 inquired into name, sex, date of birth, and conjugal condition; detailed returns were published for 1941 but only totals for 1943. In the commentary to the tables of the 1945 *Statistical Abstract*, it was remarked[5] that 'experience has shown that the 1943 Register was remarkably accurate'.

The census of 1951 was confined to a classification of the population by area, sex, marital condition, age, occupation, industry, and employment status. The census of 1956 was a simple count of heads, which grouped the population only by area and sex. Thus the census of 1961 was the first complete inquiry in fifteen years, a period in which the rate of social and economic change was exceptionally rapid.

In 1841 the population of Ireland was more than half that of England and Wales and much larger than that of Scotland. Between 1841 and 1961 the population of England and Wales increased from 15,914,000 to 46,072,000 and that of Scotland from 2,620,000 to 5,178,000. Another contrast is provided by the experience of Belgium. In 1851 the population of Ireland was 6,552,000 and that of Belgium

---

4. A very useful table of the questions asked, added, or discontinued at each census since 1841 will be found in Dr. M. D. McCarthy's 'The 1961 Census of Population', *JSSISI*, 1960–1, p. 73.

5. *SA*, 1945, 9.

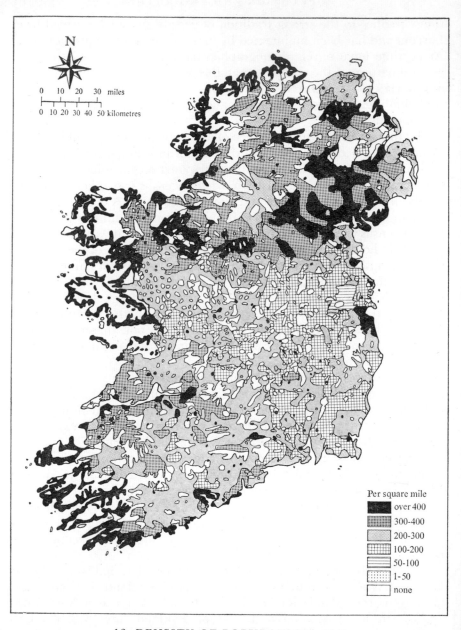

Per square mile

▓	over 400
▒	300-400
░	200-300
⊞	100-200
☰	50-100
·	1-50
□	none

13. DENSITY OF POPULATION, 1841

Much of rural Ireland had at least 200 persons to the square mile at this time and substantial areas had over 400. The lowest densities were in the eastern 'grazing districts' of Meath and Kildare. Adapted from *Pre-Famine Ireland*, by T. W. Freeman, Manchester University Press, 1957, page 18.

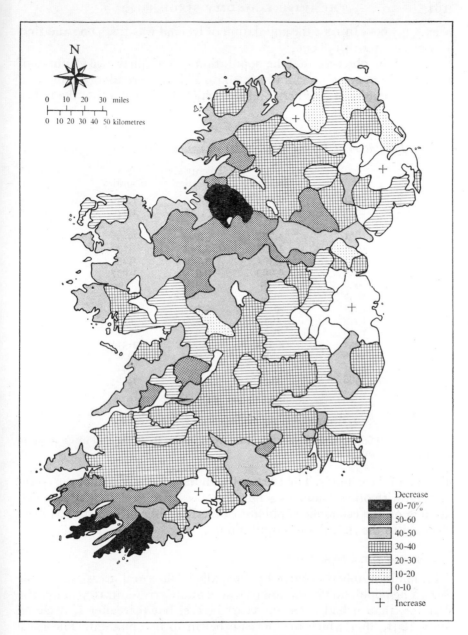

14. INCREASES AND DECREASES IN POPULATION, 1891–1961

Decreases are heavy in the north-west and south-west. Increases are found around growing
urban areas and in rural areas of Co. Dublin, Co. Meath, and Co. Cork.

was 4,337,000. In 1961 the population of Ireland was 4,243,000 and that of Belgium was 9,178,000.

It will be observed that the population of the Thirty-two Counties of Ireland is now larger than it was in 1926. This is the result of a growth in the Six Counties of Northern Ireland which more than offset the fall in

TABLE 6.1

Population of Ireland (thousands) at various dates, 1841–1966

	Ireland	Twenty-six Counties	Six Counties
1841[1]	8,175	6,529	1,646
1851[1]	6,552	5,112	1,440
1891	4,705	3,469	1,236
1901	4,459	3,222	1,237
1911	4,391	3,140	1,250
1926	4,229	2,972	1,257
1936	n.a.	2,968	n.a.
1937	n.a.	n.a.	1,280
1941[2]	n.a.	2,992	n.a.
1943[2]	n.a.	2,950	n.a.
1946	n.a.	2,955	n.a.
1951	4,332	2,961	1,371
1956	n.a.	2,898	n.a.
1961	4,243	2,818	1,425
1966	n.a.	2,884	1,485

Source: *Census of Population*

1. Army and Navy excluded.   2. Registration.

Note: In 1966 the Census was taken in April in the Republic and in October in Northern Ireland.

the rest of the country. The contrast with the other division of the country and with other countries generally, goes far to explain why so much writing on the economic problems of the Republic of Ireland has been devoted to the statistics of population.

Town and rural population

This fall in numbers occurred principally in the rural areas (see Table 6.2). The population in the towns was actually greater in 1851, after the Famine, than it had been ten years before, but thereafter it declined until 1891, after which an increase began to be apparent. The rural population, on the other hand, has fallen at each enumeration since 1841.

The first part of Table 6.2 shows the populations at the respective censuses within the 1936 boundaries of towns of 1,500 population or over in 1936. The second part shows the populations within the 1951 boundaries of towns of 1,500 population or over in 1951. The third part shows the populations in 1951 and 1956 within the 1956 boundaries of aggregate town areas in 1956. The fourth part shows the populations in 1956 and 1961 within the 1961 boundaries of aggregate town areas while the fifth part shows the populations in 1961 and 1966 within the 1966 boundaries.[6] The difficulty springs from changes in town boundaries.

TABLE 6.2

Town and rural population (thousands), at various dates, 1841–1966

	Total		Leinster		Munster		Connacht		Ulster (3 counties)	
	T	R	T	R	T	R	T	R	T	R
1841	1,100	5,429	530	1,444	429	1,967	110	1,309	31	709
1891	888	2,581	518	670	296	876	53	671	21	363
1901	911	2,311	547	606	290	787	53	594	22	324
1911	942	2,197	574	588	295	740	52	559	21	310
1926	959	2,013	595	554	288	682	54	499	22	278
1936	1,055	1,914	672	549	298	644	62	464	23	257
1936	1,099	1,869	701	519	313	629	62	464	23	257
1946	1,161	1,794	756	525	317	600	64	429	25	239
1951	1,227	1,733	814	523	323	576	66	406	25	228
1951	1,272	1,688	841	495	332	567	72	400	28	225
1956	1,285	1,613	855	484	333	545	70	376	27	209
1956	1,287	1,611	858	481	332	545	71	375	26	210
1961	1,299	1,519	871	461	331	518	72	347	25	193
1961	1,307	1,512	876	457	333	516	72	347	26	191
1966	1,419	1,465	960	455	357	503	76	326	27	182

Source: *Census of Population*

In almost every other European country the rural population increased during the nineteenth century; even where it fell, the decline was proportionately smaller than in the Twenty-six Counties.[7] The rural population also decreased in the Six Counties; this led the Commission on Emigration to remark[8] that 'in all rural parts of Ireland there existed some special factors making for rural depopulation which operated over the country as a whole'. It is hardly necessary to point out that the town population in the Twenty-six Counties increased more slowly and in a

6. Very small towns are closer in character to purely rural areas than to urban areas. The practice has been to assign towns of less than 1,500 population to 'rural areas'. But in determining whether a town with legally defined boundaries falls into the 'town' or the 'rural' category, the population of its environs is included. When such a town qualifies for inclusion in the aggregate town area the population of the environs is also regarded as belonging to the aggregate town area. Cf. 1956 Census Report, Pr. 3983, Stationery Office, Dublin: pp. xvii–xviii.

7. As in England and Wales, Scotland and France. 8. Para. 22.

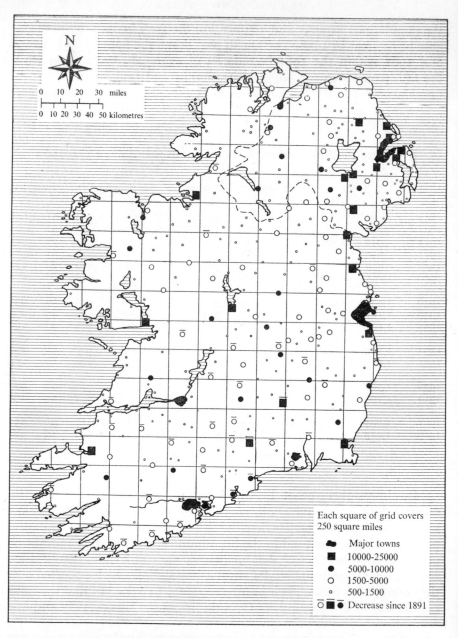

Each square of grid covers
250 square miles

    Major towns
■   10000–25000
●   5000–10000
○   1500–5000
∘   500–1500
Ō ▄ ● Decrease since 1891

15. TOWNS OF IRELAND, 1966

Munster, Leinster, and the east of Ulster have more towns than the remaining area of Ireland.
It is important to note the large number of towns with populations of less than 1500.
See Table 6.2.

smaller degree than the town population of the Six Counties or of other countries.

Between 1926 and 1961 by far the greatest proportionate increase in the population of towns was reported in the conurbation of Dublin and Dun Laoghaire which, in the later year, held no less than 51 per cent of the total number of people living in towns. Towns of over 10,000 population (the county boroughs of Cork, Limerick, and Waterford, and Galway, Dundalk, Drogheda, Sligo, Bray, Wexford, Tralee, Kilkenny, and Clonmel) also increased at each census. Towns with smaller populations decreased during the period 1911–26 and, often, the smaller the town the greater was the loss of population. In some cases, the fall was due to the departure of British troops from garrison towns.[9] After 1926, however, there was a marked change; and all sizes of town showed an increase at each census, with the exception of towns with a population between three and five thousand, which increased only in the period 1926–36. The totals involved are so small that percentage changes can be misleading. The broad conclusion is that since 1926, the capital has gained greatly, not only in relation to the total population of the state but also in relation to the population in other towns and villages. A growth in the population of the capital city is normal and the rate of growth of Dublin is not unusually rapid. Nevertheless, a situation in which the rural population is falling while cities and towns other than the capital increase only slightly in population is very different from the pattern found elsewhere. The growth of Dublin has aroused misgivings and the Commission on Emigration felt itself obliged to suggest measures which might reverse, or at least weaken, this trend.[10]

The territorial divisions of provinces and counties differ in the extent in which they have lost population, but these differences largely reflect the contrast between town and rural population. In 1841, as the Commission on Emigration pointed out[11] 'the population was distributed among the provinces in proportions roughly corresponding to their areas'. This may have reflected the acute sub-division of land which was then prevalent all over the country. In the hundred years since then, each province has lost population heavily; but there is a clear contrast between Leinster and the others. In Connacht and the three counties of Ulster there has been a loss of population at each census in the present century, while the first increase in Munster occurred in 1966. In Leinster, the first post-Famine increase was recorded in 1911. The census of 1926 showed a decrease but it is probable that the effects of the withdrawal of the British administration and armed forces in 1922

---

9. For example, in Fermoy and Droichead Nua (Newbridge), both garrison towns, the population in 1926 was only two-thirds of the total in 1911.

10. *Report of the Commission on Emigration and Population*, paras. 25–31.

11. Ibid., para. 15.

were greater in Leinster than elsewhere. The province showed an increasing population at each subsequent census up to and including that of 1951. In 1956, while other provinces lost population appreciably, it showed a minimal gain: and in 1961 it showed the smallest loss.

TABLE 6.3

Provincial populations (thousands), at various dates, 1841–1966

	Leinster	Munster	Connacht	Ulster (3 counties)
1841	1,974	2,396	1,419	740
1851	1,673	1,858	1,010	571
1891	1,188	1,172	725	384
1901	1,153	1,076	647	346
1911	1,162	1,035	611	331
1926	1,149	970	553	300
1936	1,220	942	525	280
1946	1,281	917	493	264
1951	1,337	899	472	253
1956	1,339	877	446	236
1961	1,332	849	419	218
1966	1,415	859	402	208

Source: *Census of Population*

The counties show a relative similarity over the whole period since the Famine but a divergent experience in recent times. Apart from the counties of Dublin, Kildare, Louth, and Wicklow (where the proportionate fall was much less or, as in the case of Dublin, there was a gain), the loss over the whole period varied between 59 per cent and 78 per cent. Five counties in 1956 showed a loss approaching 75 per cent of their 1841 population—Leitrim (76.1), Roscommon (74.8), Cavan (74.6), Monaghan (74.0), and Clare (73.0). In six other counties the population had fallen by two-thirds—Kilkenny (68.3), Laoighis (69.4), Longford (71.4), Tipperary (70.2), Mayo (65.7), and Sligo (68.5). But in the period 1911 to 1961 there is a well-marked group of counties where the loss is regularly appreciable. Thus, in 1956–61, the counties with the greatest proportionate loss were, in descending order, Leitrim, Monaghan, Cavan, Mayo, Longford, and Roscommon. These counties appear in each comparable table for all the inter-censal periods since 1911. These are proportionate figures; and too much should not be drawn from them when, as in several cases, the totals involved are small. Moreover, it would be difficult to discern any one feature of their economy which distinguishes them from the other counties. Nevertheless it will be noted that the counties in which the greatest proportionate loss of population has been reported in modern times are contiguous and lie along the border and in the west and north-west.

Density of population

The density of population has passed, in the last hundred years, from being one of the highest in Europe to being one of the lowest. In 1841 the density per square mile was 241. It was even higher, at 302, in what is now Northern Ireland. With that exception the density was exceeded only by Belgium (308) and England and Wales (273). Today the density is 104, well below the 791 of England and Wales or the 251 of Northern Ireland. It is greater only than Sweden (44) and Norway (29). In the same period, density has increased from 225 to 896 in Holland, from 142 to 361 in Switzerland and from 82 to 276 in Denmark.

TABLE 6.4

Population, area, and rateable valuation, 1961

	Population	Acreage	Valuation	Population per 1,000 acres	Valuation per head
Leinster	1,332,149	4,851,403	£7,928,749	275	£5.9
Munster	849,203	5,961,806	4,244,600	142	5.0
Connacht	419,465	4,230,720	1,736,311	99	4.1
Ulster (3 counties)	217,524	1,979,768	956,836	110	4.4
TOTAL	2,818,341	17,023,697	£14,866,496	166	5.3

Source: *Census of Population*

The contrasts shown in Table 6.4 are largely explained by differences in the proportion of town populations. In 1961, 55.4 per cent of the total population lived in towns.[12] For the provinces, the percentages varied from 72.2 in Leinster to 49.8 in Munster, to 27.7 in the Ulster counties and to 27.5 in Connacht.

The latest figures for the density of rural population per 1,000 acres of agricultural land are from the 1951 census. The overall figure for the Republic was 132. It was 116 in Leinster, 122 in Munster, 152 in Connacht, and 182 in the Ulster counties. By county, the greatest densities were 250 in Donegal and 199 in Mayo, which were in a class by themselves.[13] Other high densities were in Kerry (167), Galway and Monaghan (147), and Louth (144). The lowest densities were Kilkenny and Meath (101), Tipperary (100), Offaly (98), and Westmeath (96).

Sex ratio

In 1966 there were 1,449,032 males and 1,434,970 females in the population. The male majority, which is quite unusual among long

12. Town population includes persons living in all towns containing twenty or more occupied houses. This is not an exigent definition.
13. The density for county Dublin was 202; but that figure was almost certainly governed by the definition of urban boundaries.

settled peoples, has arisen since the Famine. In 1841 there was a ratio of 1,026 females to every 1,000 males. This was not a high ratio: in 1961, for example, the ratio in Northern Ireland was 1,052 and in England and Wales 1,067. The Irish ratio, after some fluctuation, reached its highest point of 1,034 in 1871 and then declined; a male majority first appeared in 1911. In the Republic as elsewhere there is an excess of male births but this is not balanced to the same degree as elsewhere by a greater female expectation of life. The natural increase of the male population was greater than that of the female in every inter-censal period after 1871, but that disparity gradually diminished after 1891 and practically disappeared in the period 1936–46. Since 1946 the natural increase of females has been greater than that of males. At various periods the number of women emigrating has been greater than that of men,[14] but this factor has not been so consistent as to account for the present male majority. Absolutely, the number of males increased at the census of 1936 (for the first time since 1841), and again in 1951, but it reached the lowest figure so far recorded in 1961. The number of females rose at the census of 1946 (also the first increase since 1841) but it fell thereafter until 1966. For the population as a whole, the ratio has varied in modern times between 952 women to every 1,000 men in 1936 and 990 in 1961, which represented the nearest approach to parity since 1911. It was 990 in 1966 also.

There have been more women than men in the town population since 1841 when the highest ratio, 1,180, was recorded; recent figures, following many fluctuations, have been 1,169 in 1946, 1,120 in 1951, 1,124 in 1956, and 1,103 in 1966. In the rural population, there was an exact balance in 1841, which was followed by a steady decline in the ratio. The 1951 ratio of 868 was the lowest recorded since the Famine; the 1956 ratio was 881 and the 1966 ratio was 892. It is notable that the same developments occurred in the Six Counties though, as a whole, women outnumber men there; a reflection of the higher proportion of town population.

Age-groups

It is inevitable that the age-grouping of a declining population should differ from what is regarded as normal elsewhere.

The impression of an ageing population[15] will be strengthened by the reflection that between 1841 and 1961 the total population fell by 3,710,000 while the number of persons aged 65 and over increased by 110,000. Elsewhere, absolute and relative increases in the numbers in the older age-groups are usually the result of a long-continued fall in the

14. See Table 6.13, below.
15. The average age of the community was 24.8 years in 1841, 32.5 years in 1951, and 32.8 years in 1961.

birth and death rates. In Ireland, the exceptionally high proportion of persons aged 65 and over is the result not only of an increased expectation of life at the later ages but also of the fact that such persons are survivors from a larger population. But, as the birth rate has not fallen appreciably, the proportion of children in the population is greater than

TABLE 6.5

Percentage distribution of population by age-groups, 1841–1966

	0–14	15–44	45–64	65+
1841	38.1	45.9	12.9	3.1
1901	30.2	46.0	17.3	6.5
1926	29.2	42.8	18.9	9.1
1936	27.6	43.1	19.6	9.7
1946	27.9	42.4	19.1	10.6
1951	28.9	41.0	19.4	10.7
1961	31.1	36.4	21.3	11.2
1966	31.2	36.7	20.9	11.2

Source: *Census of Population*

would be expected in an ageing population. Consequently, the proportion of persons in the 15–64 age-group is exceptionally small. In addition, the impact of emigration, as will be seen, affects, almost exclusively, the 18–40 age-group. Thus the weight of the two dependent groups, the young and the elderly, is exceptionally heavy. Absolutely, the number of persons aged 65 and over rose from 272,000 in 1926 to 323,000 in 1966. The number of children under 15 fell from 868,000 in 1926 to 820,000 in 1936 but increased to 900,000 in 196.6

A comparison of twenty-seven countries shows[16] that in 1951 the Republic of Ireland had the highest percentage proportion in the dependent age-groups: 39.6 against 37.5 in the Six Counties, 34.6 in Scotland, and 33.2 in England and Wales. The percentage proportion of 28.9 in the age-group under 15 compared with 27.6 in the Six Counties, 24.6 in Scotland, and 22.2 in England and Wales. Among other European countries, it was exceeded only in Holland, Portugal, Finland, Italy, Yugoslavia, Greece, and Poland. The percentage proportion of 10.7 in the age-group 65 and over compared with 9.8 in the Six Counties, 10 in Scotland and 10.9 in England and Wales. Elsewhere, it was exceeded only in France, 10.9, and it was equalled in Belgium. Further, the percentage proportion in the age-group 15–44, at 41 was greater only than Austria 40.6, but less than the Six Counties 42.5, the Federal Republic of Germany 43.1, Sweden 43.1, France 43.7, and Italy 43.8, Scotland 42.7, and England and Wales 42.7.

The contrast between the age-grouping of town and rural areas is marked.

16. *GR*, 1951, p. 47.

This, as the Emigration Commission pointed out[17] has obvious implications for the marriage rate in these areas. The greater burden of dependency must also affect the economic strength of the rural areas.

TABLE 6.6

Percentage distribution of population by age-groups in town and rural districts, 1951 and 1966

Age-group		Percentage distribution	
		Town areas	Rural areas
Under 15 years	1951	29.3	28.6
	1966	32.2	30.2
15–29 years	1951	24.6	19.6
	1966	22.8	18.3
30–44 years	1951	19.6	19.2
	1966	17.0	15.3
45–64 years	1951	18.3	20.2
	1966	18.9	22.9
65 and over	1951	8.2	12.4
	1966	9.1	13.3

Source: *Census of Population*

Marriage rate

Firm statistics for marriages (and for births and deaths) date from 1864 when registration became compulsory. The rates recorded immediately after compulsory registration were much higher than in any succeeding period, with the exception of some years after each of the major wars in this century. There was a steep fall in the marriage rate during the 1880s. Six times in that decade, it fell below 4 per 1,000; and the annual average for the period 1881–90 was 4.02. Thereafter, there was a modest improvement but the first sustained approach to the present level did not occur until the later 1930s. Between 1872 and 1936 the rate rose above 5 per 1,000 only in eight years, 1911 and 1912, 1914 and 1915, 1919 and 1920, and 1922 and 1923. Since 1937, however, the rate has never fallen below 5 per 1,000. Its peak, in the whole period was 5.91 in 1946. Another contrast, in terms of absolute figures, yields a curious result. In the census year of 1891, the population numbered 3,469,000; in the census year of 1961 it was 2,818,000. Nevertheless in 1891 the number of marriages was 14,371 and in 1961 it was 15,140.

But the recent improvement in the marriage rate fluctuates around a very low point. In 1960–4, for example, the annual average marriage rate was 5.5, which was high by previous standards. It was much below the comparable figures elsewhere: 6.8 in Belgium, 6.9 in France, 8.1 in

17. Para. 41.

Denmark, 7.4 in England and Wales, and 7.7 in Scotland. The Six Counties rate was 7.0.

It will be seen in Table 6.8 that the proportions unmarried at all ages up to 45 have fallen away from the levels reached at the censuses of 1926 and 1936. They are in fact lower than anything recorded since 1881. But the general pattern is still quite exceptional.

TABLE 6.7

Number of marriages and marriage rates, 1864–1968

	Average annual number	Average rate per 1,000
1864–70	21,150	5.10
1891–1900	14,805	4.45
1901–10	15,325	4.84
1911–20	15,785	5.11
1921–30	14,245	4.76
1931–40	14,359	4.86
1941–50	16,585	5.59
1951–5	16,011	5.44
1957	14,657	5.08
1958	15,061	5.28
1959	15,420	5.42
1960	15,465	5.46
1961	15,329	5.44
1962	15,627	5.52
1963	15,556	5.46
1964	15,941	5.64
1965	16,664	5.90
1966	16,727	5.8
1967	17 605	6.1
1968	18,792	6.5

Source: *Reports of Registrar-General*

This trend cannot be directly attributed to the influence of emigration. In all groups the proportions unmarried increased after the Famine, particularly at the younger ages. This continued almost without interruption until 1936 although the rate of emigration fell away considerably. Again, the marriage rate remained high throughout the 1950s although it is clear that the rate of emigration sharply increased. This suggests that other forces besides emigration must be considered when these figures are examined; and it will be suggested later that among these other forces the structure of post-Famine society in the countryside must be given a high place.

Several significant contrasts appear when the figures for the entire population are broken down. In 1961, no less than 71.7 per cent of men aged between 25 and 34 in the rural areas were still unmarried. The percentage in Dublin and Dun Laoghaire was 42.6 and it was 47.1 in towns, not being county boroughs, which had populations of over

TABLE 6.8

Percentage of single persons in certain age-groups, 1841–1966

	20–24 Male	20–24 Female	25–34 Male	25–34 Female	35–44 Male	35–44 Female	45–54 Male	45–54 Female	55–64 Male	55–64 Female
1841	n.a.	n.a.	43.3	28.0	15.4	14.7	10.0	11.7	n.a.	n.a.
1891	95.8	86.0	67.3	48.1	33.0	23.1	19.7	16.6	15.6	15.8
1911	96.6	88.4	74.5	55.5	44.5	31.0	28.6	24.0	22.7	20.8
1926	96.0	87.0	71.7	52.6	45.0	29.5	31.4	23.9	26.2	23.6
1936	96.2	86.4	73.8	54.8	44.2	30.2	33.5	25.1	28.2	23.7
1946	95.0	82.5	70.4	48.3	43.0	30.0	32.1	25.6	30.0	24.4
1951	94.9	82.3	67.4	45.6	40.5	27.6	31.0	25.7	28.8	24.7
1961	92.5	78.2	58.0	37.1	36.2	22.7	29.7	23.1	28.1	25.0
1966	89.6	74.8	49.8	31.0	33.4	20.4	29.1	20.8	27.7	24.4

Source: *Census of Population*

In 1841 the age-groups were 26–35, 36–45, 46–55 and 56 and over

10,000. Among women of that age-group, however, the percentage unmarried was 37.5 in the rural areas, 39.1 in Dublin and Dun Laoghaire and 38.7 in the larger towns. The General Report of the Censuses of 1946 and 1951 remarks[18] that:

the large percentage of men in rural areas who are assisting relatives and, therefore, are not in an economic position to marry, is an important contributory cause of the low marriage rate and the late marriage age in this country where persons living outside towns and villages constitute over half the total population.

Taking the rural areas of each county, there is a clear contrast between the eastern and the western counties. Of men living in rural areas and aged between 30 and 34 years in 1961 the percentage unmarried was 72.1 in Galway, 70.5 in Leitrim, 69.9 in Cavan, 69.8 in Monaghan, 69.6 in Roscommon, 69.1 in Longford, and 68.4 in Clare. The percentages were 46.8 in Dublin, 51.5 in Kildare, 52.9 in Meath, and 54.6 in Wicklow. The variations relating to unmarried women are not at all as great; but there again, the percentage unmarried tends to be higher in the west than in the east.

Average age at marriage

The average age at marriage has fallen in recent years. In 1925–6 it was 34.9 years for grooms and 29.1 for brides, the corresponding average ages being 29.1 and 26.6 in England and Wales.[19] In 1945–6 the Irish ages were 33.1 and 28.0 against 29.7 and 26.6 in England and Wales. The average ages in Northern Ireland in 1948 were 30.4 and 26.8.[20] Ages at marriage have been notified since 1957 in accordance with a recommendation of the Emigration Commission. The average ages in 1967 were 28.5 and 25.3 years.

Throughout the community the age at marriage and the proportion of people who never marry, is exceptionally high. But this generalization conceals some variations. In general, the lower paid occupational groups tend to marry earlier than the higher paid; but the proportion who ultimately marry is highest among those who are in better paid and more secure occupations. The age at marriage is highest among farmers: it was estimated at 36.9 years for grooms by the Emigration Commission. But, in 1951 for example, 71 per cent of all male farmers were married in contrast to 47 per cent among all occupied males.[21] It

18. GR, 1951, p. 56. And see ibid., p. 159, '. . . only 4 per cent of farmers' brothers assisting are married or widowed in the age-group 55 to 64 years'.

19. GR, 1926, p. 84.

20. Report of Commission on Emigration and Population, para. 146.

21. Ibid., paras 151–9, and GR, 1951, p. 160. It may be added that the proportion of farmers unmarried increased at each census between 1926 and 1951. Also, on farms under 30 acres, the average age of farmers, the percentage over 65 years and the percentage single are all higher than the general average for all sizes of farm.

seems clear that both the proportion married and the average age at marriage come closer to the norm among town dwellers than among the rural population.

Birth rate

In contrast to the marriage rate, the birth rate is not exceptional, though it is rather higher than in most countries of western Europe.

TABLE 6.9

Number of births and birth rates, 1864–1968

	Annual average number	Annual average rate per 1,000
1864–70	106,926	25.79
1891–1900	73,995	22.20
1911–20	66,507	21.50
1921–30	60,406	20.21
1931–40	57,105	19.34
1941–50	65,010	21.90
1951–55	62,844	21.34
1957	61,242	21.23
1958	59,510	20.86
1959	60,188	21.15
1960	60,735	21.45
1961	59,825	21.23
1962	61,782	21.84
1963	63,246	22.20
1964	64,008	22.39
1965	63,443	22.11
1966	62,143	21.6
1967	61,027	21.1
1968	60,785	20.9

Source: *Reports of Registrar-General*

The average annual birth rate (per 1,000) in the period 1960–4 was 21.9. This was exceeded in Northern Ireland (22.8) but was much higher than in Scotland (19.8) or in England and Wales (17.9). Birth rates in some countries regarded as being predominantly Catholic, in the same period, were Portugal 24.1, Spain 21.6, Italy 18.5, and Austria 16.8.[22]

The level of the Irish birth rate is the result of two unusual and opposing forces. The sex ratio, the age-grouping of the population, and the low marriage rate, combine to produce the result that the number of married women of child-bearing age, 15–45 years, is exceptionally low in Ireland. In 1951 it was 85 per 1,000 of the population which was the lowest figure in a comparative table[23] covering twenty-seven

22. The rates in this paragraph are based on live births only.
23. *GR*, 1951, T 36.

countries in Europe or of European settlement. The next lowest was 97 per 1,000 in the Six Counties. Comparable figures were Spain 108, Portugal 109, Austria 116, Italy 118. It was 126 in Scotland and 141 in England and Wales.

Nevertheless, another table[24] which covers all but one of these twenty-seven countries and shows the annual average number of total births per 1,000 married women of child-bearing age, shows an equally pronounced divergence in the opposite direction. In this table the figure for the Republic is very markedly the greatest, at 254. The figure for the Northern Counties is the fifth highest at 208. The figure for Italy is 194 per 1,000, Spain 187, and Austria 130. It is 141 for Scotland and 111, the lowest in the table, for England and Wales.

Fertility of marriage

In 1946 there were 451,331 families in the Republic. It proved possible to use rather more than 98 per cent of the returns covering them for further investigation. In the 443,636 families thus covered there were 1,568,186 children born alive. Of these 3.8 per cent were in families of one child, 7.8 per cent in families of two children, 35.2 per cent in families of three to five children, 37.7 per cent in families of six to nine children and 15.5 per cent in families of ten children and more. Taking only families of completed fertility (that is marriages of thirty or more years' duration) 96.2 per cent of the children were in families having three or more children. It is apparent that in Ireland the small family is still the exception.[25]

The fertility of marriage has been investigated on three occasions. The first, a pioneering inquiry in this field, was in the great census of 1841. The second was in 1911 at the same time as the census commissioners of England and Wales followed in the path of Larcom and his colleagues seventy years earlier. Both these inquiries, of course, covered all Ireland. Further inquiries were made in the censuses of 1946 and 1961.[26]

24. Ibid., T 201.

25. Equally, the family of 'man, wife, and three young children' is by no means as typical as is often assumed. Cf. R. C. Geary, 'The Family in the Irish Census of Population Statistics', *JSSISI*, 1954–5, p. 1.

The census of 1961 showed that there were then 468,228 families in the State. There were 1,607,627 children in the 455,394 families which could be further investigated. Of them, 3.4 per cent were in families of one child, 8.3 per cent in families of two children, 39.9 per cent in families of three to five children, 35.8 per cent in families of six to nine children, and 12.6 per cent in families of ten children and more. It would appear further that the decline in legitimate fertility which appeared in the first ten years after the war (and was possibly exaggerated by the fact that the figures for 1945–7 represented a peak) had been arrested. Cf. Leser, 'Recent Demographic Developments in Ireland', *JSSISI*, 1964–5, p. 179.

26. The results of an inquiry made in the census of 1926 were not published.

Comparisons of these figures suggest that there was little difference in fertility between 1841 and 1911. Geary notes:

Having regard to the somewhat different ages at marriage in the two years, the figures for durations (of marriage) 5–10 years indicate a small but real increase in the natural fertility in the 70 years. For durations under 3 years the fertility seems to have been appreciably greater in 1841. Compared with other countries, however, the most remarkable fact is the constancy of the rates over so extended a period, during which so many changes, both economic and social, took place.[27]

Comparing the returns of 1911, which related to all Ireland, with those of 1946 for the Republic alone, the General Report of the census of that year notes that the modal size of family among marriages of completed fertility fell from eight children to five during the period. The percentage of such marriages having ten or more children fell from 23.8 to 9.8 while the percentage having four children or fewer rose from 26.7 to 47.5.[28]

The General Report goes on to note that at each age of wife, fertility rates were lower in 1946 than in 1911, except in the case of marriages of less than five years' duration where fertility was higher. The rate for all durations and all ages of wife at marriage fell by 20 per cent—from 4.14 children per married woman in 1911 to 3.31 in 1946.[29]

Comparing the fertility rate for different ages of wife at marriage and using the rates standardized for duration of marriage, there was a fall in fertility between 1911 and 1946 in all age groups. The rate of decline increased with increased age. In the 15–19 age-group the percentage fall was twelve; 20–4, sixteen; 25–9 years, twenty; 30–4 years twenty-two; 35–9 years, thirty-one; and 40–5 years, fifty-two.

In the years 1870–2, the average annual number of legitimate births per 1,000 married women of childbearing age was 278.[30] It fell slightly to 275 in 1880–2, thereafter rising to a peak of 307 in 1910–12. Since then, there has been an almost uninterrupted decline; 272 in 1925–7, 258 in 1935–7, 261 in 1945–7, and 248 in 1950–2.

The fall in fertility has been more apparent in the towns than in the rural areas. In 1935–7, the fertility rate per 1,000 married women of child-bearing age was 263 in the towns and 266 in the rural districts. In 1949–51, the urban rate had fallen to 239 but the rural rate was only slightly changed at 263. The crude birth rates in town and country have tended to come together. In 1935–7, the urban birth rate was 23.2 and the rural was 17.6. In 1949–51, the urban rate had fallen to 22.4 while the rural rate had risen to 20.9. A study of the provincial birth and

27. R. C. Geary, 'The Future Population of Saorstát Éireann', *JSSISI*, 1935–6, pp. 15–35.
28. *GR*, 1946 and 1951, p. 211.   29. Ibid., p. 212–14.
30. Ibid., p. 219. These are the standardized rates.

fertility rates provides a further example of this divergent tendency. In 1950–2, Leinster had the highest birth rate (22.9) and the lowest fertility rate (252) while Connacht, with the second lowest birth rate (19.6), had the highest fertility rate (261). In noting these figures, the Commission on Emigration remarked:[31]

It is evident, therefore, that crude birth rates are to a large extent a reflection, not of fertility or family size, but of changing patterns of age-composition and marriage.

Death rate

The death rate, which was also first ascertained in 1864, rose during the 1870s and reached its highest point at 19.7 per 1,000 in the famine year of 1879. The subsequent decline was slow: in 1911–20 the annual average was 16.6; a steady decline followed, accelerating in the late 1940s.

TABLE 6.10

Deaths and death rates, 1864–1968

	Average annual number	Average annual rate per 1,000
1864–70	67,323	16.23
1891–1900	58,994	17.70
1911–20	51,453	16.64
1921–30	43,203	14.45
1931–40	41,841	14.17
1941–50	41,450	13.97
1951–55	36,875	12.52
1957	34,311	11.89
1958	34,248	12.00
1959	34,243	12.03
1960	32,660	11.53
1961	34,766	12.33
1962	33,838	11.96
1963	33,795	11.86
1964	32,473	11.40
1965	32,778	11.49
1966	34,725	12.1
1967	31,002	10.7
1968	32,800	11.3

Source: *Reports of Registrar-General*

The changing age-grouping of the population should not be ignored in any comparison of death rates over a period. This factor also affects the trend of urban and rural rates. For example, the average annual rural death rate in 1959–62 was 12.7 per 1,000, markedly higher than the urban 10.5, but in the 1920s the rural rate averaged 14.08 against the urban 15.42. On the other hand, the expectation of life is much greater in rural areas than in urban.

31. Ibid., para. 208.

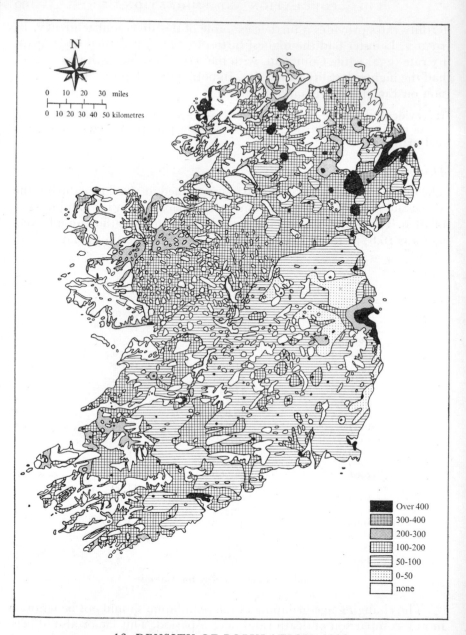

■	Over 400
	300-400
	200-300
	100-200
	50-100
	0-50
	none

16. DENSITY OF POPULATION, 1936

In the rural areas the density per square mile ranged from under 50 to more than 400, and was generally higher in the north and west than in the south and east. First published in the *Geographical Journal*, vol. 110, 1947, page 52.

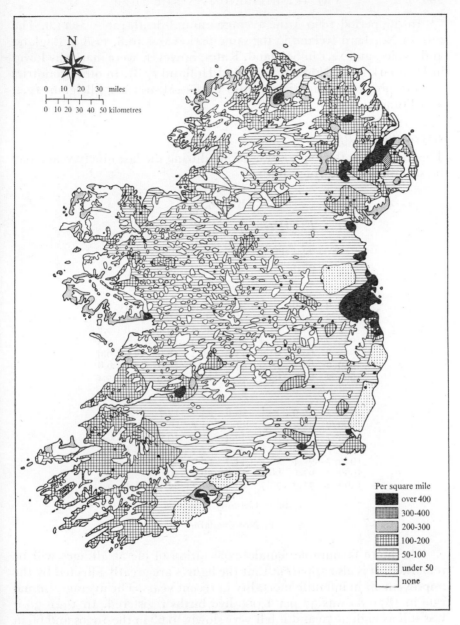

Per square mile

■	over 400
▦	300–400
▨	200–300
▦	100–200
▤	50–100
░	under 50
□	none

17. DENSITY OF POPULATION, 1961

Comparison with the map opposite shows heavy losses in Cavan (26 per cent), Mayo (24 per cent), Roscommon (24 per cent), Monaghan (23 per cent), Donegal (20 per cent), Longford (20 per cent), Sligo (20 per cent), Clare (17 per cent), Kerry (17 per cent). These movements are associated not with areas of marked poverty, but rather with those divided mainly into small farms. See also Map 5, page 110.

In the period 1960–4 the average annual death rate was 11.8. The rate in Northern Ireland in the same period was 10.8, 11.8 in England and Wales, and 12.1 in Scotland. Rates, however, were markedly lower in Denmark (9.5), Norway (9.5), and Holland (7.8). In other countries cited in previous comparisons, rates were—Austria 12.5, Belgium 12.2, and France 11.2.

Expectation of life

The increase in the expectation of life during the last ninety years may be seen in the following table:

TABLE 6.11

Expectation of life, 1870–1962

Average expectation of life at age indicated

	Birth	1	25	45	55	65	75
			Males				
1870–2	49.6	—[1]	39.0	24.4	17.5	11.1	6.5
1890–2	49.1	—[1]	37.8	23.4	16.5	10.5	5.8
1925–7	57.4	61.2	42.4	26.5	19.1	12.8	7.7
1935–7	58.2	62.2	42.7	26.3	18.8	12.3	7.3
1945–7	60.5	64.4	43.5	26.4	18.6	12.0	6.9
1950–2	64.5	66.9	44.8	27.0	19.0	12.1	6.8
1960–2	68.1	69.3	46.4	27.8	19.5	12.6	7.1
			Females				
1870–2	50.9	—[1]	39.8	25.0	17.7	11.2	6.6
1890–2	49.2	—[1]	37.7	23.2	16.2	10.3	5.9
1925–7	57.9	60.8	42.4	27.0	19.6	13.4	8.4
1935–7	59.6	62.6	43.2	27.2	19.6	13.1	8.4
1945–7	62.4	65.5	44.7	28.0	20.1	13.1	7.7
1950–2	67.1	68.8	46.6	28.9	20.6	13.3	7.6
1960–2	71.9	72.7	49.5	30.7	22.1	14.4	8.1

Source: *Census of Population*

1. Not available

The more favourable female expectation of life at all ages will be remarked. It is also apparent that the figures are greatly affected by the improvement in infantile mortality in recent years. The average annual rate in 1871–80 was 97 per 1,000 live births registered. In 1921–30 it was still as high as 70 and it fell very slowly to 68 in the 1930s and 66 in the 1940s. There was a pronounced fall in the last years of that decade; and it continued to drop to the lowest rate recorded, in 1965. This may be set against rates for the years 1960–4 of 80 in Portugal, 42 in Spain, and 40 in Italy, but it must also be compared with rates of 27 in Northern Ireland, 26 in Scotland, and 21 in England and Wales, while still lower rates have been reported in Holland and elsewhere.

Natural increase

The natural increase of population declined throughout the closing decades of the nineteenth century and then slightly increased. In recent years it has expanded sharply.

TABLE 6.12

Natural increase of population, 1891–1968

	Average annual number	Average annual rate per 1,000
1891–1900	15,001	4.50
1901–10	17,803	5.63
1911–20	15,054	4.86
1921–30	17,203	5.76
1931–40	15,264	5.17
1941–50	23,560	7.94
1951–5	25,970	8.82
1957	26,931	9.33
1958	25,262	8.85
1959	25,945	9.12
1960	28,075	9.92
1961	25,062	8.89
1962	27,944	9.88
1963	29,451	10.34
1964	31,535	10.99
1965	30,665	10.62
1966	27,418	9.9
1967	30,025	10.4
1968	27,985	9.6

Sources: *Census of Population* and *Reports of Registrar-General*

Here again, the contrast with the past is startling. Absolutely, the average annual natural increase was greater in the 1950s than in any decade since the 1870s. It was markedly greater than in the 1880s (19,600) when the total population was larger by a million. Relatively, the average annual rate of natural increase in the 1950s was the greatest since the later 1860s. A declining population and an expanding natural increase, a remarkable conjunction indeed. The average Irish rate in the period 1960–4 was 10.0 per 1,000 against 11.9 in Northern Ireland, 6.1 in England and Wales, and 7.6 in Scotland. There were rates of 7.3 in Denmark, 8.6 in Italy, 6.8 in France, 4.8 in Belgium, and 5.9 in Austria.

Forecasts of population trends

These have been made on several occasions. They are subject to the fluctuations of the major factor of emigration.[32] Three of them have appeared very recently: one made by Dr. Leser, another by the Survey

32. Cf. Geary, 'Irish Population Prospects considered from the viewpoint of Reproduction Rates', *JSSISI*, 1940–1, p. 91; EPC, paras 467–9; Leser, 'Recent Demographic Developments in Ireland', *JSSISI*, 1964–5, p. 179; *ISB*, 1965, p. 85; *Investment in Education* (Pr. 8311), pp. 24–33.

Team on Investment in Education and another by the Central Statistics Office. The assumptions on which these are made differ in a number of respects and should be consulted. On the assumptions stated in his paper, Dr. Leser suggests that population may be expected to grow by more than 100,000 in the decade 1961–71, reaching a total of 2,925,000 in the latter year. This total would differ in two important respects from what has been the recent norm: the male excess would disappear and there would be an increase of 150,000 or more in the number of people aged between 15 and 30 years. The Survey Team's approach includes the assumption made in the Second Programme for Economic Expansion that emigration will be reduced to 10,000 a year by 1970. They suggest a population of 2,939,000 in 1971 and of 3,041,000 in 1976. The Central Statistics Office project population at 2,974,000 in 1971, at 3,152,000 in 1976, and at 3,392,000 in 1981.

EMIGRATION

We may now turn to the other dominant factor in Irish demography —emigration. An invaluable source of reference for its study is provided by the *Report of the Commission on Emigration and other Population Problems.* This Commission was appointed, under the chairmanship of Dr. J. P. Beddy, in April 1948 to:

investigate the causes and consequences of the present level and trend in population; to examine, in particular, the social and economic effects of birth, death, migration, and marriage rates at present and their probable course in the near future; to consider what measures, if any, should be taken in the national interest to influence the future trend in population: generally, to consider the desirability of formulating a national population policy.

The Commission presented its report in March 1954.[33] It provided an exhaustive review of the statistical material relating to emigration, and also of the vital rates. It also made a broad survey of economic and social development and its connection with the level and trend of population. The Report will long remain the accepted source for studies of the Irish economy in the middle of the twentieth century.[34]

The most significant feature of emigration is that there are no firm figures for it, and there never have been.[35] For overseas emigration (which in practice means emigration to the United States) there are returns of the passenger movement from Irish ports since 1825. There is no account of the numbers who, in the last century and in this, sailed

33. Pr. 2541, Stationery Office, Dublin.
34. See also the symposium with a discussion on the report in *JSSISI*, 1955–6, p. 104.
35. On this see *Report of the Commission on Emigration and Population*, chapter vii.

from British ports such as Liverpool or Glasgow. Emigration to Great Britain is covered only in the period 1852–1921 and again between 1939 and 1952, and there is good reason to believe that the figures in each period are not definitive.

An indication of present trends is provided by the returns of passenger movements by public transport between the Republic and the United Kingdom (including Northern Ireland) but it will be seen at once that these cannot be firm figures of migration.[36] This lack of dependable figures is a result of the freedom of movement from the Republic. Thus, the volume of emigration can be ascertained only by comparing the total population at one census with that shown by the previous census and making allowance for the natural increase during the interval. Even then, the result is a figure of *net* emigration only. It is probably reliable enough, granted that comparatively few emigrants return. But, although this was certainly true of the nineteenth-century emigration to the United States, it may not be always equally true of the present emigration to Great Britain.

It has been argued that between 1891 and 1936 there was a continuous decline in the average annual net emigration. The small increase shown between 1911 and 1926 was very far from being anything like an 'average annual': for some years overseas emigration was suspended because of the First World War and it was certainly affected by the Anglo-Irish conflict thereafter. Moreover, no small part of the apparent emigration could be attributed to the evacuation of the Twenty-six Counties by British forces in 1922 and the change of regime in that year. The increased emigration in 1936–46 might reasonably be explained by the Second World War. When the census of 1951 showed the first censal increase for 110 years, observers might be pardoned for believing that a period of stability was now being replaced by a return to the normal condition of increase. It was not, perhaps, sufficiently appreciated that the expansion in the natural increase was almost balanced by a growth in the volume and rate of emigration. The outburst of emigration in the 1950s, which represented the highest rate since the exceptional period of the 1880s, came as a shattering blow to these optimistic beliefs.

Features of emigration
The validity of both optimism and pessimism will be discussed elsewhere.[37] Here, it is enough to examine the characteristics of emigration. There is a sense, of course, in which the Irish emigration is simply one instance of that great movement of peoples out of Europe where labour

36. The size of this movement should be noted. It is estimated that in 1966 the number of visits to Ireland made by persons resident elsewhere was 16,579,000.
37. See below, pp. 340–1.

was abundant and cheap, to the overseas countries where it was scarce and dear. But, in the first place, the migration to North America from Ireland was earlier than any other except the English and Scottish. In the second place, it has consistently disclosed features which do not appear in the emigration from any other country.

TABLE 6.13

Natural increase, net emigration and sex-ratio of net emigration in inter-censal periods, 1891–1966[1]

Annual Averages

	Natural increase	Rate per 1,000	Net emigration	Rate per 1,000	Female emigrants per 1,000 male emigrants
1891–1901	14,954	4.5	39,642	11.9	951
1901–11	17,940	5.6	26,154	8.2	1,223
1911–26	15,822	5.2	27,002	8.8	938
1926–36	16,318	5.5	16,675	5.6	1,298
1936–46	17,380	5.9	18,712	6.3	662
1946–51	25,503	8.6	24,384	8.2	1,365
1951–6	26,887	9.2	39,353	13.4	817
1956–61	26,416	9.2	42,401	14.8	935
1961–6	29,253	10.3	16,121	5.7	1,143

Sources: *Census of Population* and *Reports of Registrar-General*

1. The reader should be reminded that the periods are of unequal length. These periods, also, run from one census to the next; the natural increase, therefore, is not comparable with the figures in Table 6.12 which relate to calendar years.

The most obvious of these has been that only in the case of Ireland has emigration been associated with a decrease of population. It is clear that emigration did not offset the natural increase before the Famine; but it has done so ever since, except in very exceptional years.[38] The number of Irish-born living abroad steadily rose while the number living at home declined. This produced the fantastic result that in 1881 the number of persons of known Irish birth living abroad amounted to 60 per cent of the number who lived in Ireland.[39] It may not now be true that there are more people of Irish birth living in New York than in any Irish city; but it may yet come to pass that some such distinction will be true of Birmingham or London. In these respects, the Irish are unique among the emigrating races; nothing remotely comparable can be found in the statistics of Germany or Italy, of Great Britain or Scandinavia.

38. The annual estimates of the Registrar-General, which cannot be precise, showed increases of population in 1877, 1918, 1919, and 1920, 1931–4 inclusive, 1940 and 1941, 1945–8 inclusive and since 1962.
39. *Report of the Commission on Emigration and Population*, para. 268.

An important result has been to create a constant gap in the continuity of generations which, elsewhere, has been the consequence only of a major war. The Emigration Commission referred to what it called the 'survivorship ratio'.[40] It noted that of each 100 males aged between 15 and 19 in 1936, 21 emigrated in the following decade. Of each 100 males then aged 20–4, 19 emigrated in the same period. The corresponding figures for women in the same age-groups were 16 and 12. Figures for the period 1946–51 show[41] that in Connacht 30 of every 100 men aged 15–19 in 1946, and 25 of every 100 men aged 20–4, had left the province by 1951. The figures for women were 42 and 20. No doubt, even these figures can be easily surpassed in Irish demography. For example, only 46 in every 100 men who were aged between 15 and 19 in 1841, and only 47 in every 100 women of the same ages, were still alive and in Ireland in 1851. Nevertheless, they show how heavily emigration continues to affect the natural succession of the generations in the country as a whole, particularly in an area of heavy emigration such as the province of Connacht.[42]

A further characteristic of Irish migration is the unusually high proportion of women emigrants. Statistics for gross emigration, covering the period 1852–1921, shows 973 females to every 1,000 males.[43] The comparable figure for the Six Counties was 769. The figure for the Twenty-six Counties conceals several fluctuations; thus, the ratio was 996 in 1852–60 and 840 in 1861–70. Thereafter the proportion of women rose sharply. The ratio was 891 in 1871–80 and 977 in 1881–90. In the last three decades of the period more women than men emigrated. The ratio was 1,183 in 1891–1900, 1,092 in 1901–10, and 1,110 in 1911–21. This characteristic is not to be found in the records of emigration from any other European country. The highest ratio reached in the emigration from the Six Counties at any time in these seventy years was 960 in 1891–1900.

Between 1891 and 1921, two-thirds of all emigrants were aged between 20 and 24. This concentration in the younger age-group can be traced further back in the emigration returns: it has been equally apparent in statistics for later periods. The report of the Emigration Commission showed that in overseas emigration between 1924 and 1939, 61 per cent of males and 71 per cent of females were aged under

---

40. Ibid., para. 265.

41. *GR*, 1946 and 1951, p. 67. These figures make no allowance for mortality or for migration to other parts of Ireland. The comment is added that an allowance of about 1.5 per cent for men and of about 1.7 per cent for women should be made for mortality in the two age-groups combined. Migration, as will be seen, is unimportant.

42. e.g. the age-grouping shown for that province by the Census of 1961, vol. ii, p. 30: 5–9 years, 42,287; 10–14 years, 44,584; 15–19 years, 34,427; 20–4 years, 18,420.

43. *Report of the Commission on Emigration and Population*, T 90.

24.[44] More recently still, in the three years 1957–9, 60 per cent of males and 68 per cent of females to whom new passports were issued to go to employment or permanent residence were also aged under 25.[45] A further point which is suggested by these figures is that the Irish emigration has been composed of young people who are unmarried. Except possibly in the years immediately after the Famine there has been comparatively little of the emigration of families which has been characteristic of other peoples.

Exceptional mobility is perhaps the most striking feature of Irish emigration. Between 1841 and 1925, 5,814,000 people are known to have gone overseas from all Ireland.[46] Of these, 4,699,000 went to the United States, 669,000 to Canada, and 374,000 to Australia and New Zealand. The Canadian emigration was at its peak in the 1840s and 1850s and revived again in the first decade of this century. Emigration to the Antipodes fell heavily after the 1880s. At all times, by far the greater part of overseas emigration was directed to the United States which, as a percentage of the whole, rose from 69.8 in the 1840s to 84.4 in the 1860s and thence to a peak of 92.7 in the 1890s, falling to 75.3 in 1911–20 and 68.7 in 1921–5. Over the whole period 1841–1925, 80.8 per cent of the emigration overseas from (all) Ireland went to the United States, 11.5 per cent to Canada, 6.4 per cent to Australia and New Zealand, and 1.3 per cent to other countries. These percentages have not varied much in subsequent years; in the period 1924–52, 80 per cent went to the United States, 9.1 to Canada, 5.1 to Australia and New Zealand, and 5.8 elsewhere.

In more recent years the direction of emigration has been violently deflected. Irish immigration was not greatly affected by the quota restrictions introduced by the United States after the First World War.[47] The quota for the then Irish Free State was fixed at 28,567 in 1924 and 17,853 in 1929. It was not, however, filled in any year although there was then a period of exceptional prosperity in the United States. An observer in the late 1920s might have been excused a belief that the end of emigration, or at the least its reduction to manageable proportions, was then within sight. That belief would have been strengthened by the developments of the next few years. Under the impact of the depression, overseas emigration fell away and was replaced by a movement homewards of emigrants who could find no work. In the seven years 1931–8 emigrants overseas numbered 8,480 while immigrants from overseas numbered 15,859. But by 1938, emigration had regained its accustomed

44. Para. 263.   45. SA, 1960, 45.
46. In 1954 Dr. R. C. Geary and Dr. M. D. McCarthy estimated overseas emigration from the Twenty-six Counties at 5 million since the Famine. Report of the Commission on Emigration and Population, addendum no. 2, p. 201.
47. Cf. ibid., appendix v.

volume though it had now found a new outlet, to the United Kingdom. The change and its subsequent development may be studied in Table 6.14.

TABLE 6.14

Net emigration by main destination, 1926–61

	1926–36	1936–46	1946–51	1951–6	1956–61
Overseas	91,186	([1])	19,381[2]	20,072[2]	14,155[2]
Europe and United Kingdom	75,565	187,111	100,187	176,691	197,848
	166,751	187,111	119,568	196,763	212,003

Sources: *Report of Commission on Emigration* and *Irish Statistical Bulletin*

1. Negligible.   2. By sea only, calendar years.

A last individual characteristic remains to be noted. The change of country was almost always permanent. Links with home were indeed closely maintained: from the earliest days of the American migration it was noted that the Irish saved their earnings so that they might send back enough to pay the passage money for others of their family. To the present day the receipt of emigrants' remittances and legacies is appreciable. But there was little sign of the intention, common in the countries of southern Europe, of going abroad to make and save enough money to settle down comfortably at home again. Certainly, the 'returned Yank' was a figure in the Irish countryside; but that was because he was uncommon. As yet it is too early to discern if the emigration to England will be equally permanent. In several ways, such as the preponderance of women and in age-grouping, it closely resembles the earlier American emigration, and its absorption in the larger cities seems to be no less complete. But the ease of passage between Ireland and Great Britain may permit a larger returning movement than was customary when the intervening distances were so much greater and the ease of transport so much less.

It is reasonably certain, though it cannot be proved in the absence of precise statistics, that the bulk of emigration has proceeded from the rural areas. Neither in the period since the Famine to the present day, nor in the more recent period since 1926, has any increase in urban population offset the fall in the rural population.[48] The rate of net emigration has been greatest in the provinces that are least urbanized.

Net emigration in Table 6.15 may be, of course, affected by immigration from other parts of the country. But this type of migration,

48. Emigration from the urban areas has increased considerably since 1951. But in the present century, as in the second half of the last, it is clear that the great majority of emigrants came from the rural areas.

though certainly larger than it was, is still comparatively small in Ireland. In 1861, for example, only 336,000 in a native population of 4,310,000, or 7.8 per cent, were living outside the county of their birth. In 1961, a greater number in a smaller population—398,000 in a native population of 2,818,000, or 14 per cent, lived outside the county of their birth.[49] This was largely due to a movement into Dublin city and county

TABLE 6.15

Rates of net emigration and natural increase per 1,000 average population in the provinces, 1891–1961

	Leinster		Munster		Connacht		Ulster (3 counties)		Total	
	N.I.	E.	N.I.	E.	N.I.	E.	N.I.	E.	N.I.	E.
1891–1901	2.5	5.6	5.0	13.6	6.9	18.3	4.4	14.7	4.5	11.9
1901–11	4.4	3.6	6.2	10.1	7.4	13.1	4.8	9.1	5.6	8.2
1911–26	4.7	5.5	5.6	9.9	6.1	12.8	4.0	10.6	5.2	8.8
1926–36	6.4	0.4	5.3	8.2	5.0	10.1	3.4	10.2	5.5	5.6
1936–46	7.8	2.9	5.0	7.7	3.9	10.3	3.7	9.7	5.9	6.3
1946–51	10.7	2.1	7.5	11.7	6.3	15.1	6.2	14.6	8.6	8.2
1951–6	11.7	11.4	7.9	12.8	6.3	17.4	5.4	19.6	9.2	13.4
1956–61	12.2	13.1	7.7	14.2	5.9	18.3	4.5	20.7	9.2	14.8

Source: *Census of Population*

where in 1961 nearly one-fifth of the population was born outside the county area and within the State. Apart from Dublin, internal mobility has been slight. The contrast between the extraordinary mobility of the Irish people throughout the world and their relative immobility within their own country is striking; and it reflects an important feature of Irish emigration.

The same pattern will be discerned in the counties. Between 1956 and 1961, the highest rates of net emigration per 1,000 average population were found in Monaghan 26.5, Leitrim 22.7, Cavan 21.3, Longford 20.8, and Mayo 20.3. The lowest rates were in Dublin 10.1 and Cork 11.2.

It is reasonably certain that most emigrants 'came from agricultural occupations or else were unemployed and unskilled'.[50] A classification of overseas emigrants between 1924 and 1939 showed that 68 per cent of male emigrants were agricultural labourers and labourers not in transport and communications while 64 per cent of female emigrants were in the group 'domestic, hotel, etc., service'.[51]

A broadly similar picture is given by information derived from applications for travel permits, etc., between 1939 and 1952 and, later

49. *Census of Population, 1961*, vol. vii.
50. *Report of the Commission on Emigration and Population*, para. 272.
51. Ibid.

still, from applications for new passports. Certainly, occupations may be roughly described; and a prospective emigrant may put down the occupation which it is hoped to follow abroad rather than the occupation actually followed at home. Nevertheless, it is clear that unskilled workers preponderate in the Irish emigration; though during the 1950s there was notable growth in the number of emigrants possessing professional or technical qualifications.

TABLE 6.16

Geographical distribution. Persons born in all Ireland, 1841–1951

	Ireland	U.S.A.	Canada	Australia	Eng. & Wales	Scotland
1841	8,141	n.a.	122	n.a.	289	126
1851	6,502	962	227	n.a.	520	207
1891	4,581	1,872	149	227	458	195
1911	4,233	1,352	93	139	375	175
1931	n.a.	924	108	79	381	124
1951	n.a.	520 (1950)	81	45	627	89

Source: *Report of Commission on Emigration*

The American emigration was overwhelmingly to the larger cities. This feature was noticed from the time of the Famine; though it seems to have been present even earlier still. In 1950, when the movement of population had almost ceased, the Census of Population of the United States showed that 92 per cent of those born in the Twenty-six Counties lived in urban areas. This pattern is repeated in the more recent emigration to Great Britain. The census of 1961 there showed that one-third of those born in the Twenty-six Counties and living in England and Wales were living in Greater London and that two-fifths of the emigrants to Scotland were living in Glasgow. There is some reason to believe that a greater proportion of emigrants to Canada settled on the land. Nevertheless, the conclusion is inescapable that those who left the Irish countryside were, and are, well content with the opportunities of city life and were not attracted by the empty lands of North America and the Antipodes. It is possible that this characteristic of Irish emigration has restricted its long-term consequences in the countries of immigration. The number of persons of Irish birth who live abroad is still, however, amazingly large in relation to the population of the country. The figures in Table 6.16 cover persons born in all Ireland; no distinction can be made between the Six and the Twenty-six Counties. The figures returned for 1891 are the peak for the United States and for Australia. In Canada the highest figure was 286,000 in 1861.

The number of persons of Irish origin living abroad eludes precise measurement. In the United States census of 1950, the number of persons described as of 'Irish origin' (that is born in Ireland, exclusive of the Six Counties, or possessing at least one parent who was born in Ireland) was 2,396,865. In an addendum to the report of the Commission on Emigration, Dr. Geary and Dr. McCarthy spoke of the Irish race abroad as numbering between 15 and 20 million, covering those who live in Ireland and the descendants of emigrants since the Famine.[52]

Immigration is and has been of negligible proportions. In 1946 the number of residents in the State who were born outside it was 98,900 of whom 33,500 were born in the Six Counties. The comparable figures for 1961 were 98,951 and 27,129. Of the remaining 72,000 in 1961, some 54,000 were born in Great Britain (46,000 in England and Wales and 8,000 in Scotland) and 6,000 in the United States.

52. *Report of the Commission on Emigration and Population*, p. 203.

CHAPTER SEVEN

Banking and Currency

THE OLDEST OF THE BANKS NOW IN EXISTENCE IS THE BANK of Ireland. Established under charter in 1783 pursuant to an Act of Grattan's Parliament in the previous year, it was entrusted with the Government account and the management of the National Debt. It also received a valuable monopoly because the Act provided that no other persons exceeding six in number might take up or owe any sums on their bills, etc., payable on demand or for a less period than three months. This monopoly did not affect the many private banks which issued notes at that time, but these banks were reduced in number by a succession of crises during the Napoleonic war and its aftermath. A panic in 1820 left the country without banks outside Dublin, Belfast, Cork, Wexford, and Mallow.

This situation led to legislation (1821) which permitted banking companies with more than six partners to carry on business at a distance of fifty Irish miles from Dublin and to borrow, owe, or take up any sum on their notes or bills payable on demand. Amending legislation, in 1824 and 1825, was necessary to give effect to the purpose of the Act of 1821. Thereafter new banks appeared quickly: the Northern, the Hibernian, and the Provincial were established in 1825; the Belfast in 1827, the National in 1835, and the Royal and the Ulster in 1836. The Hibernian and the Royal commenced business in Dublin and were therefore precluded by the monopoly of the Bank of Ireland from issuing notes. From an early date the new banks, led by the Provincial, established branch offices throughout the country, and their example was followed by the Bank of Ireland, which up till then had followed the practice of the Bank of England in refusing to open branches.[1]

1. F. G. Hall, *The Bank of Ireland, 1783–1946*, Hodges & Figgis, Dublin: 1949, p. 172.

The Bankers' Act, 1845

In 1845 the Bankers (Ireland) Act was passed, withdrawing the monopoly of the Bank of Ireland in the Dublin area but confirming its functions of Government banking and management of the National Debt in Ireland. The right of note-issue was attached to the six banks that already enjoyed it—the Bank of Ireland, Belfast, National, Northern, Provincial, and Ulster. Each of these banks was required to provide the information necessary to calculate its circulation of notes in the year ending 30 April 1845, and was empowered to issue notes up to a certified amount thus derived. It might issue notes in excess of that amount provided the excess was fully covered by gold or silver coin—the silver coin to be not more than one-fourth the amount of the gold. The issue of each bank possessing the right to issue notes was therefore composed of (a) the permitted issue, ascertained as described, which was known as the 'fiduciary' issue, and (b) the 'secured' issue, in excess of that figure, which had to be covered by gold and silver coin. The total fiduciary issue was £6,354,494, of which the Bank of Ireland's quota was about 60 per cent, the two next largest shares being those of the Provincial and National. The secured issue could, of course, be increased up to any amount provided the backing was provided and maintained.

These rights of issue in Ireland were of considerable importance throughout the nineteenth century, because the cheque-system was not developed as in England. This reflected the difference between an urban and commercial community and one in which money circulated chiefly at country fairs and markets.[2] Thus, the Act of 1844 in England assisted the gradual centralization of the banknote issue at the Bank of England: the Act of 1845 in Ireland permitted an indefinite growth. This had further effects, noted by Dr. Hall:[3]

Undoubtedly, this variation in procedure accounted for the difference in development of Irish and English banking. In England, the banks of issue—which were for the most part small and local concerns—were gradually eliminated or lost the right of note issue through amalgamation with other banks. The great English joint stock banks came into being largely as a result of these amalgamations. In Ireland, on the contrary, the privilege of unlimited circulation discouraged the formation of new banking ventures, so that the Irish banking system developed within the framework of the existing joint stock banks. In fact, the Irish banking system to-day consists of the six banks which were granted the privilege of circulation in accordance with the terms of the Act, the two Dublin banks which were refused the right of issue, and only two concerns which were subsequently established.

2. In spite of pressure from England against the issue of notes for smaller amounts than £5, they were issued by the Irish banks for the convenience of traders at fairs and markets. F. G. Hall, op. cit., p. 207.
3. F. G. Hall, op. cit., p. 210.

The system established in 1845 survived for just over eighty years, and its abolition was much more a consequence of political changes than of any inherent weakness. It was open to the criticism that those banks which had enjoyed the right of issue before 1845 were confirmed in their advantage over those that had not—the Hibernian, Royal,

TABLE 7.1

Bank-note circulation and deposits in banking system (£ thousand): all Ireland, 1850–1920

At 31 December	Bank-note circulation	Joint stock banks	Deposits and cash in Trustee Savings Banks	Post Office Savings Bank[1]
1850	4,512	8,269	1,292	—
1870	7,432	24,366	2,055	583
1890	7,098	33,325	1,973	3,723
1910	7,553	54,936	2,515	11,931
1920	25,815	182,949	3,502	14,074

Source: *Report of the Banking Commission, 1938*

1. The Post Office Savings Bank was established in 1861.

and the Munster and Leinster, which was established in 1886. A more fundamental criticism was that as trade increased the gradual expansion of the note issue could be effected only by immobilizing an equal amount of gold and silver.[4] Nevertheless, the progress of the Irish banks in the second half of the century was one of the few aspects of the economy on which observers commented with approval. An enviable record of stability was acquired: the last failure of an Irish bank was that of the Munster in 1885 and in that case all creditors were soon paid off in full by its successor, the Munster and Leinster. Deposits grew with increasing prosperity and there was an increasing inclination to use the services provided by the banks.

TABLE 7.2

Assets of banking system (£ thousand): all Ireland, 1890–1920

At 31 December	Cash	Call	Investments	Bills and advances	Total
1890	9.1		17.1	28.8	56.1
1900	11.7		17.7	37.5	67.9
1910	8.4	5.4	23.2	44.2	82.1
1920	35.4	11.3	71.8	120.1	240.4

Source: *The Economist*

The total includes other assets not shown in the table.

Much of the great increase between 1910 and 1920 was, of course, due to the depreciation in the value of money during the First World War; but Table 7.1 shows that there had already been an appreciable growth in the amount of savings entrusted to the banking system. Table 7.2 summarizes the use made of these deposits.

4. *Banking Commission Report*, 1926, Final Report, paras. 35–6.

It may be taken that all the investments were British gilt-edged securities, Ireland being then still part of the United Kingdom.[5]

The number of offices maintained by the banks increased as business grew, from 180 in 1844 to 859 in 1913, both figures being for all Ireland. The Trustee Savings Banks originated in 1817. By 1836 their number had risen to thirty-six; but owing to various causes, principally perhaps the institution of the Post Office Savings Bank in 1861, there was a subsequent decline, and by the 1920s there were eleven in operation, five in the Irish Free State and six in the Six Counties area.[6]

At the time of the 1845 Act the United Kingdom was, of course, on the gold standard and gold coin circulated freely. Notes were not legal tender although at one time there had been argument about the status of Bank of England notes. The Bank of Ireland maintained that these notes were not legal tender in Ireland and this claim was expressly approved by the 1845 Act, although the notes continued to circulate and were accepted in payment of revenue.[7]

This situation remained unchanged until 1914. The Currency and Bank Notes Act, passed two days after the declaration of war, authorized the British Treasury to issue notes with legal tender status and provided that the notes of Irish banks of issue should be legal tender in Ireland except for payments by the Head Office of the issuing bank, which were to be made in British Treasury notes. It also provided that this arrangement should continue until revoked by proclamation, which took effect on 1 January 1920.[8]

The Currency Act, 1927

Thus the currency and banking systems were in an exceptionally confused condition when the Irish Free State was established on 6 December 1922. The circulation consisted of British coin, British Treasury notes (Bradburys), Bank of England notes, and Irish bank notes. It was certain that neither the notes of the Irish banks nor the notes of the Bank of England were legal tender. Treasury notes issued before the establishment of the State did enjoy that status; but, as they bore no

5. As long ago as 1862, W. N. Hancock, in his 'Report on the Supposed Progressive Decline of Irish Prosperity', noted that 'it is a matter of grave enquiry why the farmers of Ireland should lend such large sums to the different banks . . . to be employed in the large towns, and much of it in London, instead of expending it in agricultural improvements . . .'. He returned to the point in his paper, 'Complaints against Bankers in Ireland', *JSSISI*, 1875–6, p. 523.

6. See C. Eason, 'Trustee Savings Banks of Great Britain and Ireland', *JSSISI*, 1929–30, p. 1. Also *MEBC*, 426.

7. F. G. Hall, op. cit., p. 207.

8. Of the gold held by the Irish banks, £2m. were released to the British Government in October 1915. In September 1917 they agreed to place 90 per cent of their remaining stock (i.e. about £3,663,000) at the disposal of the Treasury. The balance was transferred in June 1920. See F. G. Hall, op. cit., pp. 320–7 and 333.

date of issue, they could not be identified. In practice, remarkably little difficulty arose: in theory the position was unacceptable. The partition of Ireland introduced a further complication in that the Government of Ireland Act, which established the parliament of Northern Ireland, reserved legislation on 'coinage, legal tender; negotiable instruments (including banknotes)' to the Imperial Parliament.[9] Partition also created great difficulties for the Irish banks generally as almost all of them had branches on both sides of the border and some had Head Offices outside the new Irish Free State. For example, the Bank of Ireland, the Hibernian, the Royal, and the Munster and Leinster were incorporated within the Free State. The Northern, the Ulster, and the Belfast had their Head Offices at Belfast, while the National and Provincial had their Head Offices in London. Quite apart from any consideration of national prestige, the establishment of a new legal tender and the clarification of the position of the banks were clearly matters of prime importance.

It is well to recall the state of public opinion when the regularizing of banking and currency was taken in hand. At home, the country was still only four years away from the Civil War. When the Currency Act was first introduced, the principal opposition party, the new Fianna Fáil led by Mr. de Valera, still refused to acknowledge the legality of the Dáil.[10] Great Britain had returned to the Gold Standard in April 1925, successfully as it then appeared. Public opinion was still impressed by the great German inflation a few years before. Even on the innocuous proposals contained in the Coinage Act, one of the most enlightened members of the Dáil warned the Government that:

when once you begin tampering with coinage you go on to tampering with currency, and once you begin to tamper with currency you begin to operate an inflation that leads to national disaster.[11]

Similarly, the debates on the Currency Bill contained many suggestions that no innovations were necessary as the existing bank note issue was fully adequate to the need.

The first step was taken by the passage of the Coinage Act of 1926 which provided for a distinctive issue of token coin. The new coins, issued on 12 December 1928, originally contained 75 per cent silver, this being a higher content than the contemporary coinage in Britain

9. Sect. 4 (12) of 10 & 11 Geo. V. c. 67. Thus the reduction and redistribution of the fiduciary issue in Northern Ireland was effected by the Bankers (Northern Ireland) Act of 1928, passed at Westminster.

10. The measure was first introduced in March 1927 but its progress was halted by the first dissolution of that year. It formed the principal business of the Dáil when Fianna Fáil took their seats, on 12 August. The first speech made for the party in the Dáil was on this measure, by Mr. Sean T. O'Kelly who stated that it had no responsibility for the bill which would need amendment later.

11. Major Bryan Cooper. *PDDE*, 14, 169.

which was 50 per cent. Since 1950 the silver has been replaced by cupro-nickel (of which the threepenny and sixpenny coins were made from the beginning) but even in that undistinguished material the coinage continues to honour its designer, Percy Metcalfe, and those who were so discriminating as to approve it.[12] In sharp contrast to our stamps, the Irish coins have acted, in a characteristic phrase of Yeats, as 'the silent ambassadors of national taste'.[13]

Wider issues were touched by the appointment, in March 1926, of the first Banking Commission:

to consider and to report . . . what changes, if any, in the law relative to Banking and note issue are necessary or desirable, regard having been had to the altered circumstances arising out of the establishment of Saorstát Éireann.

The chairman was Professor Henry Parker-Willis of Columbia University, who had served for some years with the Federal Reserve Board. The first interim report was signed in April 1926, and the final report was signed in the following January.[14] The Currency Act of 1927, which still governs the issue of legal tender notes, was based on the recommendations of this Commission.

The Act provided for a new unit of value to be known as the Saorstát pound, to be maintained at parity of exchange with the pound sterling.[15] Legal tender notes were to be issued by the Currency Commission which was now established and entrusted with the administration of the Act. The eight banks operating within the State[16] subscribed the capital of the Commission and elected three banking members of the Commission. Three other members were nominated by the Minister for Finance, and the chairman was elected as a seventh by the other six.[17] The Act provided that the legal tender issue should be backed 100 per cent by a reserve composed of gold, British legal tender or sterling

12. The advisory committee was composed of W. B. Yeats, Dermod O'Brien, P.R.H.A., Thomas Bodkin, Lucius O'Callaghan, Barry Egan, T.D., and Leo T. McCauley. For details of designs submitted, which included 'a kneeling angel pouring money from a sack', see *The Coinage of Saorstát Éireann*, the Stationery Office, Dublin.

13. *PDSE* 6, 501.

14. The interim reports covered agricultural credit, long term business credit, and Government financial business.

15. For a study of the Act, see Joseph Brennan, 'The Currency System of the Irish Free State', *JSSISI*, 1930–1, p. 23. A more recent survey of the system, as it has evolved since the Central Bank Act of 1942, will be found in a lecture 'Our Currency and Banking System' by J. S. Oslizlok, *JIBI*, 1963, 266. Also Hein, 'Institutional Aspects of Commercial and Central Banking in Ireland', E R I, Paper No. 37.

16. The Bank of Ireland, the Hibernian, the Munster and Leinster, the National, the Northern, the Provincial, the Royal, and the Ulster, known since 1942 as the Associated Banks.

17. The Commission was established on 23 September 1927. Its first chairman was Mr. Joseph Brennan who held office (from 1943 as Governor of the Central Bank) until 1953. He was succeeded by Mr. J. J. McElligott who in turn was succeeded by Mr. Maurice Moynihan in 1961 and by Dr. T. K. Whitaker in 1969.

balances, or British Government securities maturing within twelve months.[18] It was made mandatory on the Commission to redeem its notes in London in British legal tender and optional to redeem them in Dublin. The Commission was obliged to issue notes when presented with British legal tender. The first legal tender notes were issued on 10 September 1928.

In all essential points, these provisions followed the recommendations of the Parker-Willis Commission. It expressly advised against the establishment of a Central Bank 'at the present time' on the grounds of the existence of a well-organized banking system and the absence of a money market.[19] In the absence of a Central Bank, it advised against any kind of fiduciary issue.[20] Events have made irrelevant the possibility, considered by the Commission, of a return to the use of gold; and Part II of the 1927 Act, which provides for the minting of a gold coin with a fineness equalling that of the sovereign, remains a dead letter. Wider issues such as those raised by the choice of parity with sterling will be considered in Chapter Fifteen.

The 1927 Act made a number of changes in the bank-note issue. The existing issue, dating from 1845, was terminated. A new issue of consolidated bank-notes of the Currency Commission was provided. In determining the aggregate issue of these notes and their allocation between the banks, the Commission was required to have regard to liquid sound advances made by shareholding banks within the State.[21] The concept of 'liquid sound advances' was severely criticized as being inapplicable to Irish conditions;[22] and it was never used in practice. In the event, the Currency Commission required the banks to make formal transfers to it of Government securities adequate to cover all outstanding consolidated bank-notes.[23]

The aggregate limit of the consolidated bank-note issue was fixed at £6m. This figure originated in a tentative suggestion of the Parker-Willis Commission[24] which was adopted by the Currency Commission. It remained unchanged during the existence of the consolidated bank-note issue. Participation in the issue was shared between the eight banks which subscribed the capital of the Currency Commission; and thus the

18. The time limit arose out of an amendment moved in the Senate. It was repealed in 1930.

19. First Report, para. 16, and Final Report, para. 42. In a minority report Mr. McElligott, then Secretary of the Department of Finance, suggested that the question of setting up a Central Bank should be re-examined after a period of five years' smooth working of the new arrangements.

20. Final Report, para. 38.

21. Sect. 52 (2).

22. e.g. by Mr. Andrew Jameson in a statement accompanying the first interim report and generally in the Senate debates on the Bill.

23. Cf. BCR, 1938, para. 244.

24. First report, para. 20.

three banks which had been excluded from the right of issue under the 1845 Act (the Hibernian, the Royal, and the Munster and Leinster) now were admitted to it. The right, however, was by no means as profitable as it had been because each bank was made subject to a charge, supplemented in 1932, on the value of its notes whether they were in circulation or not. Thus, the valuable right of free till money disappeared; and with it, much of the attraction of the right of note issue.[25] The first consolidated bank-notes were issued on 6 May 1929.

The 1927 Act worked smoothly from the start although the banks most adversely affected by the changes in note issue might not have agreed with the statement that it was 'not a change in fact but a change in form'.[26] Its provisions were amended in 1930, when the limitation to British government securities maturing within twelve months was removed on account of the growing scarcity of such issues.[27] The amending legislation gave the Oireachtas an opportunity to review what had been done. It did not do so, although Mr. MacEntee, speaking for the Opposition, alluded to the risks that might be incurred through a change in the backing of the currency.[28] When Great Britain went off the Gold Standard in September 1931, thus depriving holders of legal tender notes of the opportunity to obtain gold,[29] there was considerable criticism of Irish acquiescence in the British lead. But the banking system took the depression and the economic war in its stride; and, in 1932, its deposits were swollen by the transfer, providently as it turned out, of monies to it from the less secure banks of the United States.[30]

The Banking Commission, 1934–8

The next development was the appointment of a new Banking Commission in November 1934. The terms of reference were:

to examine and report on the system in Saorstát Éireann of currency, banking, credit, public borrowing and lending and the pledging of State credit on behalf of agriculture, industry and the social services, and to consider and report what changes, if any, are necessary or desirable to promote the social and economic welfare of the community and the interests of agriculture and industry.

25. An advantage often claimed for the Act was that it would provide a source of revenue for the Exchequer which the Parker-Willis Commission estimated at about £300,000 p.a. First report, para. 27.

26. Professor Thrift, PDDE, 19, 1180.

27. The Currency Amendment Act of 1930 also provided machinery whereby the form of asset held in the legal tender note fund might be varied. See below, p. 224.

28. PDDE, 35, 1180.

29. Between 1927 and 1931 the Free State was on what was then termed the 'gold exchange standard': i.e. its currency was directly convertible, not into gold but into a currency (sterling) which was itself convertible into gold—in units of £1,700 which was then the price of a bar of gold.

30. Cf. T. A. Smiddy, 'Some Reflections on Commercial Banking', JSSISI, 1935–6, p. 53, and BCR, 1938, para. 160.

An official statement issued at the time referred expressly to the resolution of the World Economic Conference in 1933 in favour of the establishment of Central Banks, to the steps towards that end taken in India, New Zealand, and Canada and to the need to examine the special difficulties and problems of establishing a Central Bank in the Free State.

The composition of the Commission excited the admiration of *The Economist*.[31]

It was presided over by the Chairman of the Currency Commission. It included the permanent head of the Department of Finance, the Chairmen of the Industrial and Agricultural Credit Corporations, the Chairman of one bank and Directors of two others, the Professors of Economics of the three University Colleges of the country, a Roman Catholic Bishop, representatives of Labour, and finally two external experts . . .[32]

This notice went on to stress, with much justice, the chairman's achievement in obtaining sixteen signatures to the majority report in a membership 'of such a varied, nay, variegated character' that totalled twenty-one.

The majority report was signed on 23 March 1938 and, with appendices and addenda, it ran to over 350,000 words; the three minority reports (one signed by three members, the other two by one member each)[33] ran to another 60,000; two volumes of minutes of evidence totalled 1,448 pages. The evidence given on behalf of government departments[34] is of the greatest value to the student of economic policies in the 1930s. Other evidence provides instructive examples of the panaceas which enjoyed a vogue during the depression. The appendices to the majority report included a study of the national income by Professor G. A. Duncan, a criticism of the schemes of social credit then in fashion, and an exposition of Catholic teaching on the use and control of credit.

The majority report was largely composed of an examination (not conducted with undue sympathy, as Mr. de Valera was later to remark)[35]

31. Ibid., 13 August 1938, p. 312. A different description was given by Mr. W. T. Cosgrave, then Leader of the Opposition, speaking on the Central Bank Bill: 'This Banking Commission was indeed a heterogeneous collection, picked from here, there and everywhere, some with theories, others with an open mind, some with a knowledge of the subject, hardly a Commission that would be selected by anybody other than the Government of the country at the time.' *PDDE*, 86, 224.

32. These were Dr. Per Jacobsson, Economic Advisor to the Bank for International Settlements 1931–56, Managing Director and Chairman of the International Monetary Fund until his death in 1963 and Professor (later Sir) Theodore Gregory, Cassel Professor of Economics, London, 1927–37, and Economic Advisor to the Government of India, 1938–46.

33. One of whom, it is said, was asked how he spelt 'hesitancy' when he presented his report.

34. It is notable that no evidence was given on behalf of the Department of Finance nor of the banks.

35. *PDDE*, 87, 403.

of the use of public credit to assist the growth of agriculture and industry and the extension of the social services. The lapse of time has inevitably affected the relevance of part of the discussion but it can be read with profit even today.[36]

The opinions of the majority report on the system of banking and currency may be summarized as a recommendation to leave things as they were. The report considered that in Irish conditions the scope for open-market operations by a central banking organization would be limited and it advised strongly against any attempt to build up a money market on the basis of Treasury bills. On the other hand, the growing scope and importance of State policy called increasingly for the provision of advice to the State by an independent monetary authority. The Currency Act did not provide for advice to the Government by the Currency Commission and no habit of consultation had grown up. This should be changed although the most suitable means could be left to develop by experience. The report stated that the Currency Commission had worked with a great measure of success in spite of the difficulties presented by the depression and the economic war. It stated that greater flexibility would be achieved if the monetary authority had power to rediscount bills (other than Treasury bills) and to make advances on the collateral of Government securities to other credit institutions out of the General Fund. Power should also be given to fix and publish minimum rates for these transactions. The monetary authority should also be authorized to buy and sell fixed interest-bearing securities of a gilt-edged nature; but any Government securities so bought should have been outstanding for at least two years. When this had been done, section three of the 1930 Act (providing a means of varying the assets in the Legal Tender Note Fund) should be repealed. It further recommended that the new monetary authority be empowered to receive non-interest-bearing securities from public authorities, banks, and other credit institutions.

The name of the Currency Commission should be changed so as to emphasize the fact that, once these powers had been conferred on it, it would become a central banking institution. No change of importance in its capital or in its general constitution was recommended. It was also reported that the existing arrangements for the Exchequer account (that is, its operation through the Bank of Ireland) were satisfactory and no change was recommended. The new monetary authority should establish a research department for comprehensive studies of economic and financial data; it should use all opportunities for direct contact with its counterparts elsewhere; in particular, it should be empowered to hold shares in the Bank for International Settlements.

36. Mention should be made of the chapter on 'The Economic Background' while the chapters on credit and on social aspects of currency and credit are still valuable in a wider context than the Irish economy.

The report found nothing to alter in the link with sterling. It surveyed the basis of the consolidated bank-note issue, noted the difficulties that had been found in the definition of 'liquid sound advances', and recommended the gradual termination of the issue. The new monetary authority, therefore, would be the sole issuer of notes in the State, and the issue of coinage was likewise to be transferred to it from the Department of Finance.

The Central Bank Act, 1942

Although the majority report was signed in March 1938, the Central Bank Bill, which was largely based on its recommendations, was not introduced until March 1942. In the interval, the outbreak of war had emphasized the need for a monetary authority with wider powers than were possessed by the Currency Commission.[37] The Bill became law on 4 November 1942.[38]

In its original form it impressed one Senator[39] as 'one of the most amazingly conservative pieces of proposed legislation that one could possibly imagine'. Some of its proposals, however, even in the original text, went beyond the recommendation of the Banking Commission; others were added during its progress through the Oireachtas. The capital of the Bank was to be subscribed by the Minister for Finance, not, as had been the case with the Currency Commission, by the commercial banks. The Bank was empowered[40] to require licensed bankers to effect their clearances through it. This point was not even considered by the Banking Commission. The powers of rediscounting were extended beyond the Commission's recommendations to include first-class commercial bills, bills drawn for agricultural purposes, Exchequer bills, and bills of local authorities.[41] The Bank was empowered to buy Irish government securities or any securities of public authorities possessing trustee status which had been offered for public subscription before being bought by the Central Bank and had been quoted on the Stock Exchanges of Dublin and Cork. These facilities were designed to provide a means whereby the Central Bank might act as a lender of last resort if the banks could not obtain legal tender in the ordinary manner on

37. e.g. in June 1940 when the liquidity of the banking system might have been seriously affected by the state of the gilt-edged market in London. But it should be remembered that any emergency could have been met by the use of the 1930 Act to introduce domestic securities into the Legal Tender Note Fund. In passing, a reader of the Banking Commission report may find it strange that in all its ample survey, no allusion whatever was made to the possibility of a European war.

38. No. 22 of 1942.

39. Senator Joseph Johnston. *PDSE*, 26, 2126.

40. Sect. 51, first used in 1958 for domestic clearings.

41. Since 1955 the Bank has rediscounted, when necessary, Exchequer bills and bills of exchange. So far as is known, there has been no rediscounting of agricultural or local authority bills.

account of 'an international crisis that caused a freezing-up of gilt-edged securities in the London Stock Exchange coinciding with a crisis affecting one or more banks in this country'.[42] A much greater departure from the recommendations of the Banking Commission was contained in Section 50, which empowered the Central Bank, having obtained the concurrence of the Minister for Finance, to require a bank to make deposits with it whenever 'the assets held (by the bank) within the State fell below a specified proportion in relation to its liabilities within the State, and to maintain such deposits so long as such assets are below the said specified proportion'. The introduction of this power, which was designed (it was claimed) to increase the liquidity of the banking system, was specifically considered and rejected as unnecessary by the Banking Commission.[43] It was criticized in the Senate on the ground that the calculation of assets within the State added unnecessary difficulties to the work of a banking system that operated in both parts of Ireland.[44]

The Act followed the recommendation of the Commission in providing for the retiral of the consolidated bank-note issue. Otherwise the 1927 Act was left unaltered in any important feature except that the provisions governing the assets of the legal tender note fund, already amended in 1930, were again amended. The present position, as laid down by the Act, is that: (i) on a unanimous request of the board of the Central Bank the Minister for Finance may make the necessary order, which must be laid before both Houses of the Oireachtas, but does not require ratification by them, (ii) if the request is made by a majority of the board, the order must be specifically ratified by both Houses. It may be annulled by a resolution of either House passed within twenty-one sitting days after the order has been laid.

The debates on the Bill were on a remarkably varied level. The principal point at issue was the degree of power that a Central Bank would enjoy in Irish conditions and how far it could be increased by legislation. Speakers for the Labour party made much play with a comment of the Irish correspondent of *The Economist* that:

the new Central Bank is likely to be little more than the existing Currency Commission under a new name: it would be more accurately described by the old-fashioned title of a Bank of Issue.[45]

This view, which needs some modification in the light of subsequent events, was not seriously contested. Mr. McGilligan argued that a Central Bank should have the functions of controlling credit, influencing interest rates and controlling the exchange rate of the currency but

42. Mr. S. T. O'Kelly (then Minister for Finance) *PDSE*, 26, 2114.
43. 1938 *BCR*, para. 363.
44. In fact the section has not been used up to the time of writing.
45. *The Economist*, 14 March 1942, p. 363.

that the proposed Central Bank would have none of these functions.[46] Mr. de Valera agreed that in Irish conditions 'you cannot by any central banking arrangement effectively control the volume of credit here'.[47] This, and other issues which arise from the legislation of 1927 and of 1942, may be left for discussion in Chapter Fifteen. The sequence of events since the Central Bank Act became operative, on 1 February 1943, will now be considered.

Operations of the Central Bank

When the Central Bank Bill was before the Oireachtas, in mid 1942, the great fall in the value of money, although already perceptible, was still far from attaining its full momentum. A speaker could still remark that:

the maximum sum that the Central Bank is likely to deal with—as soon as we get away from inflation—is £20 million.[48]

Thus, the Bank's external assets would be markedly less than those of the commercial banks, which totalled, net, £90m. in June 1942. The balance has altered greatly since then.

TABLE 7.3

External assets of the banking system and of departmental funds (£ million), 1938–68

31 December	Central Bank	Associated Banks (net)	Departmental Funds[1]	Total
1938	10.6[2]	61.1	14.7	86.4
1948	47.7	131.9	51.5	231.1
1958	87.3	104.9	13.6	205.8
1960	89.2	103.6	17.1	209.9
1962	104.3	115.1	14.6	234.0
1964	147.9	93.4	0.8	242.1
1965	134.0	89.3	0.8	224.1
1966	167.5	85.2	0.8	253.5
1967	163.6	130.7	0.8	295.1
1968	204.3	74.8	0.8	279.9

Source: *Reports of the Central Bank*

1. This includes external assets of the Post Office Savings Bank. In 1964 almost all these Funds were transferred to the Central Bank.
2. Currency Commission.

Table 7.3 should, however, be read with some qualifications. Since 1964 the Associated Banks have maintained interest-bearing deposits with the Central Bank which has the effect of reducing their external assets, as calculated for the purpose of the table, and increasing those

46. *PDDE*, 87, 62.   47. *PDDE*, 86, 1128.
48. W. T. Cosgrave, *PDDE*, 86, 2530.

of the Central Bank. The increase in the demand for currency led to a transfer of sterling from the associated banks to the Central Bank in order to obtain Irish currency. Other factors, as will be seen later, have combined to restrict the resources of the commercial banks.

The title of Table 7.3 is that now used by the Central Bank. Primarily, however, the external assets held by it in the Legal Tender Note Fund are held against the outstanding issue of currency and are not immediately available to assist the Associated Banks. It is not suggested that the Central Bank would not support the Associated Banks if the necessity arose (an example of such support will shortly be cited); but the present nomenclature may mislead commentators into assuming that the free assets of the banking system, as that phrase is generally interpreted, are much greater than they are in fact. It will also be noted later that even the external assets of the Associated Banks are not wholly free.

Another means whereby the Bank has extended its influence was even less foreseen. Section 8 (a) empowered it to 'make provision for the collection and study of data relating to monetary and credit problems and publish informative material in relation thereto'. Section 6 (b) also provided that the Minister for Finance may 'on such occasions as he shall think proper' request the Governor or the Board to 'consult and advise with him in regard to the execution and performance by the Bank' of its general duty of 'safeguarding the integrity of the currency and ensuring that, in what pertains to the control of credit, the constant and predominant aim shall be the welfare of the people as a whole'. These last words are taken from section 6 (1) which defines the general function and duty of the Bank. Since its establishment, the Bank has freely exercised its right to publish. In the years after 1945 it consistently emphasized the dangers of adding domestic fuel to a world-wide inflation by misdirected programmes of capital investment, by unbalanced budgets, and by deficits in the balance of payments. This attitude was unfashionable; it was then shared only by the comparable institutions of Western Germany and Italy and by the Bank for International Settlements. It was also highly unpopular. The clash of economic values culminated in the report of the Bank for the year ending 31 March 1951, which amounted to a ceremonial repudiation of the policies which, with minor variations, were shared by the Government and Opposition of the day. For months afterwards the report and the Governor who was formally responsible for it were under constant and often bitter criticism in parliamentary debates.[49] In more recent years both the report and its reception have been notably milder. That may be due, in some part, to a greater public awareness of the defects of public policy which earlier

49. The curious reader is referred to the Dáil debate of 7 November 1951, PDDE, 127, passim.

reports had criticized. The White Paper of 1958 on Economic Expansion stated that:

productive capital expenditure—productive in the sense of yielding an adequate return to the community in competitive goods and services—must receive a greater priority than at present in the public capital programme.[50]

Thus the contention of the Central Bank in 1951 was made a principle of public policy in 1958. This provides an admirable example of the educative function which the Central Bank has discharged, always thankless and often highly unpopular, but essential to the proper working of democracy. The Bank has received from *Dublin Opinion* the sobriquet of 'Official Banshee to the Republic of Ireland', a description which is at least milder than several that have been employed. It would not be right to leave this subject without reference to the high moral courage which Governors have displayed in the expression of unpalatable views and to the integrity of successive Governments which have acquiesced in their publication.[51]

The composition of the legal tender note fund has been modified, in one case as a result of the developing functions of the Bank. In 1956 the currency and securities of the Federal Government of the United States of America were added as approved forms of investment for the assets of the legal tender note fund. In 1959 the further addition was made of 'Irish Government Security for advances under sub-section 7 of section 3 of the Bretton Woods Agreements Act 1957'. Both these changes were made at the unanimous request of the board of the Bank. Their effect will be seen in Table 7.4.

A further change in the assets of the Legal Tender Note Fund was made in 1961 (again on a unanimous request) by the addition of a balance in the general fund to the form of assets in which the Legal Tender Note Fund may be kept. This was followed by the transfer of British Government securities and cash amounting to £20m. from the legal tender note fund to the general fund. It is understood that this was done in order to strengthen the resources of the Central Bank for the discounting of Exchequer bills. The first exercise of this power was disclosed in the Bank report for 1955–6 which noted the rediscounting of Exchequer bills and bills of exchange which had been discounted by the Associated Banks. It noted also that both types of bill had been taken into the General Fund during the year. Rediscounting has been noted in each subsequent year;

50. Para. 7.
51. Mention should also be made of the *Quarterly Bulletin*, containing statistics on currency, banking, prices, trade, unemployment, etc., which was first published in 1934. Since 1954 it has contained, from time to time, notes on various aspects of the economy. It might fairly be claimed that the Irish public had much fuller information on the main issues of banking and currency than was available in the United Kingdom before the recommendations of the Radcliffe Committee were adopted.

full details being first given in the report for 1960–1. As the amount of Exchequer bills outstanding has grown, the necessity to have resources available for rediscounting has grown also.[52]

In 1958 the Central Bank exercised its power under section 51 of the 1942 Act requiring licensed bankers to settle through it all clearances

TABLE 7.4

Composition of legal tender note fund (£ million), 1938–69

31 March	Total	Gold	Sterling Assets	U.S.A. Assets	Irish Govt. Security	Balance in General Fund
1938	9.7	—	9.7	—	—	—
1948	43.8	2.6	41.2	—	—	—
1958	77.0	2.6	63.9	10.5	—	—
1960	75.3	2.6	60.3	11.5	1.3	—
1962	85.7	2.6	47.0	11.5	4.6	20.0
1964	100.1	2.6	58.1	11.1	5.8	22.4
1965	106.6	2.6	63.3	11.0	5.9	23.7
1966	110.0	2.6	67.9	10.2	9.4	19.9
1967	114.8	2.6	67.5	10.3	9.4	25.0
1968	122.5	3.1	75.1	11.9	9.4	23.0
1969	132.8	3.1	71.1	11.6	23.7	23.1

Source: *Reports of the Central Bank*

arising between members of the Dublin Bankers' Clearing Committee in Dublin and to make and maintain with it such balances as might be necessary for that purpose. This is an extension of the Bank's activities rather than the provision of a new service because the actual clearing continues to be effected by representatives of the Associated Banks in the same manner as heretofore. The difference is that each bank must now maintain a balance with the Central Bank on which clearance cheques will be drawn. The effect is to transfer the management of some sterling held by each bank in London to the Central Bank.

From 1960 onwards the Associated Banks were invited to maintain balances at the Central Bank. The sums involved gradually increased, the total balances held with the Central Bank being £3.7m. at the end of 1959 and £11.5m. at the end of 1963. The Central Bank Act of 1964, *inter alia*, removed the prohibition imposed by the Act of 1942 on the payment of interest on 'deposits from a Minister of State or any public authority or any Associated Bank, or any other bank or credit institution carrying on business wholly or partially within the State'.[53] The amounts held at the Central Bank by the Associated Banks have further increased since the passage of this amending legislation.

The Act of 1964 also extended the power of the Central Bank to buy,

52. The sterling assets were reduced during 1968.
53. The quotation is from section 7 (1) (b) of the 1942 Act. The growth of deposits by the banks is described in 1964–5 *CBR*, 15–16.

hold, or sell securities to cover securities of any international bank or international financial institution formed wholly or partially by governments. It also altered the form of the law precluding the Governor or a Director from being a member of either House of the Oireachtas.

The Central Bank became a shareholding member of the Bank for International Settlements in 1950. Ireland became a member of the International Monetary Fund and of the World Bank in 1957.

It has been entrusted with the issue and management of Tax Reserve Certificates when they were introduced in 1962. Since May 1965 it has been responsible for the day-to-day operation of exchange control.

The associated banks

The experience of the commercial banks may be followed in Tables 7.5 and 7.6 which set out their liabilities and assets within the State and elsewhere. This division is largely concealed by the smoothness with which the banking system functions; but it might become highly important in certain circumstances.[54] In general, the location of the reporting bank branch is the basis for the distinction between 'within the State' and 'elsewhere'. Capital, reserves and undivided profits are attributed wholly to 'within the State' in case of the banks incorporated within the State, and to 'elsewhere' in the case of banks incorporated outside the State. Notes in circulation are segregated according to the jurisdiction to which the note issue appertains.[55] Cash and balances are segregated according to the place where the asset is held; accordingly, till-money is attributed to the area in which the till is located and a balance with another bank to the place in which such bank is situated. The location of the person or body liable to meet the obligation concerned governs the attribution of money at call and short notice and of investments.

The profits earned by the banks deserve comment. In 1910 their profits, net, totalled just under £1m. There was an expansion in the subsequent period and the comparable figure for 1925 was a little under £2m. (In each of these years, the total includes the profits of the Belfast Bank which no longer operates in the Republic). After 1925 there was a prolonged decline in profits for nearly thirty years and it was not until 1959 that the level of £2m. was reached. Net profits in 1964 were £3,398,000).

It will be seen from Table 7.6 that the assets held in liquid form are

54. e.g. if the parity between the Irish and British currencies were changed or if the present freedom of exchange between the two countries were modified.

55. On 31 March 1969 the amount of outstanding consolidated bank-notes was £125,550. The outstanding notes of the five former banks of issue under the 1845 Act deemed to belong to the Republic amounted to £629,875. Each year some of these notes are presented, to an average value of two or three thousand pounds; but it seems safe to assume that a high proportion of the notes described as outstanding have been destroyed.

TABLE 7.5

Liabilities of the Associated Banks (£ thousand),[1] 1931–68

December quarter	1931[2]	1938	1947	1953	1963	1965	1966	1967	1968
Paid-up capital									
Within the State	4,522	4,522	4,522	4,522	5,622	9,279	18,799	18,979	19,538
Elsewhere	3,540	3,740	3,740	3,740	6,897	7,480	4,480	4,480	5,280
Reserves and undivided profits									
Within the State	5,513	5,782	6,510	6,390	7,961	8,195	12,184	13,001	16,011
Elsewhere	3,335	3,463	4,336	4,342	8,068	9,531	6,480	6,933	7,181
Notes in circulation									
Within the State	5,035	5,142	2,080	929	295	293	160	160	159
Elsewhere	2,912	3,896	10,833	6,717	5,569	5,318	5,472	6,435	8,892
Current, deposit, and other accounts									
Within the State	121,512	113,963	237,620	282,696	418,370	477,820	530,838	587,285	684,191
Elsewhere	39,675	43,045	99,550	110,301	168,254	192,285	159,251	177,457	193,299
Acceptances									
Within the State	—	32	2,739	5,443	1,651	1,466	1,633	2,491	3,244
Elsewhere	30	495	194	185	2,057	2,052	623	1,017	950
Other liabilities									
Within the State	3,192	3,060	7,688	7,063	12,665	13,785	18,813	19,309	22,456
Elsewhere	1,900	2,278	3,432	5,540	12,955	14,256	17,142	16,406	18,624
Total									
Within the State	139,774	132,501	261,159	307,042	446,564	510,838	582,437	641,225	745,650
Elsewhere	51,392	56,916	122,084	130,826	203,800	230,922	193,448	212,728	234,225
	191,166	189,417	383,243	437,868	650,364	741,760	775,885	853,953	979,875

Source: *Reports of the Central Bank*

1. i.e. the eight Associated Banks and the National City bank.
2. Figures in this column are for January 1932 when they were first compiled

Assets of the Associated Banks (£ thousand), 1931–68

December quarter	1931	1938	1947	1953	1963	1965	1966	1967	1968
Cash and London balances									
Within the State	4,143	5,606	14,324	18,938	37,513	53,285	74,160	73,187	80,603
Elsewhere	8,943	9,109	33,892	32,513	36,964	42,904	38,982	45,770	46,917
Money at call and short notice									
Within the State	4	2	—	—	—				
Elsewhere	9,535	8,904	24,765	28,451	33,272	39,334	21,080	47,042	51,259
Government bills									
Within the State	1,000	2,500	483	6,167	12,979	37,199	42,163	53,771	45,824
Elsewhere	2,810	17	33	1,000	6,701	6,702	3,850	—	333
Other bills									
Within the State	6,091	4,650	3,840	3,491	6,782	6,955	6,262	6,615	7,323
Elsewhere	2,290	967	312	444	650	921	625	546	489
Loans and advances									
Within the State	44,664	46,647	81,996	117,898	235,605	275,608	290,882	303,243	360,844
Elsewhere	27,726	25,555	28,703	38,858	88,004	96,434	80,031	78,680	92,251
Government investments									
Within the State	2,078	3,998	8,295	13,539	27,357	23,490	43,462	39,243	81,487
Elsewhere	69,333	63,557	164,513	148,029	122,541	113,970	112,467	144,877	146,184
Other investments									
Within the State	1,581	4,039	3,852	8,726	10,436	9,404	8,293	8,299	7,585
Elsewhere	3,489	5,321	4,614	2,803	5,066	5,849	4,951	3,999	4,168
Premises									
Within the State	2,000	2,005	1,840	2,287	4,899	6,392	6,614	7,248	10,857
Elsewhere	1,071	870	737	1,055	2,833	3,888	4,318	5,122	5,684
Acceptances									
Within the State	—	32	2,739	5,443	1,651	1,466	1,633	2,491	3,244
Elsewhere	30	495	194	185	2,057	2,052	623	1,017	950
Other assets									
Within the State	1,062	1,635	4,104	2,918	6,153	6,985	24,570	22,445	23,372
Elsewhere	3,316	3,510	4,007	5,124	8,901	8,922	10,889	10,358	10,500
Total									
Within the State	62,623	71,114	121,473	179,406	343,375	420,784	498,069	516,542	621,140
Elsewhere	128,543	118,304	261,771	258,462	306,989	320,976	277,816	337,411	358,736
	191,166	189,417	383,244	437,868	650,364	741,760	775,885	853,953	979,876

Source: Reports of the Central Bank

still placed mainly outside the State but the overall position has changed in the last thirty years more than is generally realized. In 1931 assets within the State represented 33 per cent of total bank assets. They were 38 per cent in 1938. In 1946, after years in which the war had restricted domestic activity, they had fallen to 24 per cent. Since 1959 they have risen well above 50 per cent. This is a very considerable change of circumstances. It is due primarily to the great increase in bills, loans, and advances. Today, the London balances, money at call and short notice represent the one form of asset that is still predominantly placed outside the State. This reflects the almost complete absence of a money market. As yet, there are few concerns that are interested in borrowing short. It is possible that in the long run, the development of Exchequer bills will lead to some such market in Dublin: but it is obvious that the need for liquidity demands that money should be placed where it is easily realizable, which at present means the London money market. It is significant that in the case where some short-term funds of the banking system have been deflected into the Central Bank,[56] it has, so far as is known, placed these funds in London just as the banks would have done.

The total net external assets of the commercial banking system in the Republic at various dates are set out in Table 7.3. It will be useful to recall some of the sudden variations in the post-war years. At the end of 1946, when imports of capital and consumer goods were still restricted, they stood at £159.5m. By the end of 1948 they had fallen to £131.9m. In the next two years they were maintained at around that level, partly on account of the operation of Marshall Aid which financed imports that otherwise would have inflicted losses on the banking system. The balance of payments crisis of 1950–1 reduced them from £126.9m. at the end of 1950 to £109.6m. at the end of 1951. Thereafter they rose again to £127.3m. at the end of 1953. The second crisis of the decade brought them from £116.4m. in March 1955 to £75.2m. in June 1956. Thereafter there was a sustained recovery to £119m. in October 1962. This has been succeeded in turn by a prolonged fall to £85.2m. in December 1966. These fluctuations show the alarming rapidity with which assets can disappear. More happily, they also suggest that a period of favourable foreign earnings can restore losses within a relatively short time.[57]

56. Under sect. 41 of the 1942 Act; see p. 30. The formation of a money-market is now under discussion by a committee appointed by the Governor of the Central Bank in 1967. Its report was published in 1969. See also Hein, op. cit.

57. It should be remembered that the proportion of net external assets that is available at any time to meet deficits will be appreciably less than a total may suggest. Assets such as premises are included in the total, while substantial sums are committed at any given moment as working balances.

The volatility of external assets is illustrated by their recovery to £130.7m. in December 1967.

The liquidity ratio of the Associated Banks is now defined as the ratio of their 'net external assets together with deposits in the Central Bank to their liabilities in respect of current and deposit accounts within the State'. For the purpose of computing the ratio, rediscounted Exchequer bills are deducted from the banks' net external assets and deposits in the Central Bank. Developments in 1964–5 have conferred an importance on this ratio which did not exist in the past. In the depressed year of 1933, it was as high as 64.4 per cent. In 1938 it was 51.5 per cent and the interruption of normal trading during the war brought it to a peak of 70.9 per cent in 1945. It was 55.5 per cent in 1948, 45.8 per cent in 1953, and 33.0 per cent in 1958. In that year it was discussed in *Economic Development* which suggested that 'a net external assets ratio of 30 per cent represents no more than a "minimum safe ratio" for the commercial banks as a whole'.[58] In the event, the ratio fell to 27.0 at the end of 1963 and to 23.4 at the end of 1964 without causing undue anxiety. The downward trend, however, persisted during the earlier months of 1965 and in July, which is seasonally a month of a low ratio, reached 17.3 per cent. Directives regarding bank credit, which will shortly be noted, had already been issued in anticipation by the Central Bank, and the ratio had recovered to 25.8 at the end of 1967.

This trend partly reflects the substantial increase in bills, loans, and advances to customers within the state during the post-war period. In each year there are seasonal variations; advances rise between April and October and fall away from October to January. These movements seem to be influenced considerably by the harvest: whether it is early or late, abundant or poor. The Irish banks must guard against the vagaries of the weather: thus advances were perceptibly swollen by the disastrous harvest of 1958 and they remained high because of the drought of 1959. Viewing advances over a longer period, three major periods of expansion may be discerned. In the first period, of restocking after the war, advances increased from £55.4m. in December 1946 to £93.6m. in April 1948. The impact of the Korean war and the rush to stockpile sent advances from £104.3m. in December 1950 to £126m. in June 1952. A slight contraction then reduced them to £120.3m. in April 1953. This was followed by a slow expansion which gained force in the second half of 1954 and grew rapidly thereafter. Advances were £132.7m. in July 1954 and £165.1m. in October 1955. A new contraction brought a slight reduction which (on the quarterly figures) was most apparent in April 1957 at £157.4m. Since then there has been an almost continuous increase to £303.2m. within the State at the end of 1967.

58. Ibid., para. 15. A note on the ratio will be found in *CBQSB* for January 1966, from which the definition contained in this paragraph has been taken. Unless otherwise stated, the ratios cited are for December in each year.

Credit policy

This long-continued expansion led to the emergence of guiding-lines of credit policy. This was first adverted to by the Central Bank in its Report for the year 1964–5. Having noted that it relied 'on the voluntary co-operation, which is readily forthcoming, of the Associated Banks', it went on to remark that an examination of monetary trends and of future prospects suggested that:

a more moderate rate of expansion in total bank credit than during 1964 was desirable. It was evident that the Associated Banks had become very fully lent. In these circumstances the Central Bank considered it appropriate to give advice to the Associated Banks regarding their lending policy.

The terms of this advice, which were summarized in the annual Report, were set out fully in the Central Bank's *Quarterly Bulletin* for January 1966. They were to the effect that during the nine months

TABLE 7.7

Classification of bank advances, January 1939, 1954, 1967

	£ thousand			per cent		
	1939	1954	1967	1939	1954	1967
Farmers, agriculture	11,894	13,164	46,684	21.92	10.40	13.62
Co-operatives	835	2,606	7,151	1.54	2.06	2.09
Mining, manufacturing	3,200	19,202	48,857	5.90	15.17	14.26
Financial	857	3,070	9,873	1.58	2.43	2.88
Wholesalers	2,488	18,849	27,977	4.58	14.90	8.17
Retailers	8,563	16,964	29,744	15.78	13.41	8.68
Gas, electricity, shipping, transport	880	514	2,532	1.62	.41	.74
Builders	1,485	3,694	9,144	2.74	2.92	2.67
All other business, industry, trade	4,509	9,796	31,588	8.31	7.74	9.22
Public bodies	2,789	9,430	16,027	5.14	7.45	4.68
Personal, professional	11,184	18,629	41,980	20.61	14.72	12.26
Schools, hospitals, etc.	1,846	5,953	25,219	3.40	4.70	7.36
Government[1]	1,234	2,500	40,835	2.27	1.98	11.92
	54,264	126,532[2]	342,562[3]	100.00	100.00[2]	100.00[3]

Source: *Reports of the Central Bank*

1. This table does not include Exchequer bills.
2. Including £2,161,000 (1.71 per cent) 'Unclassified'.
3. Including £4,951,000 (1.45 per cent) 'Unclassified'.
4. The basis of classification was changed in 1967.

ending 31 December 1965 the aggregate credit extended by the banks should not expand, in relation to the resources within the State, as rapidly as during the year ended 31 March 1965; that the banks' specific aim should be to reach an average ratio of not lower than 22 per cent over the year 1965 as a whole; that each bank should consult with the Central Bank with a view to determining its own appropriate ratio; and that priority should be given in the granting of advances to projects of a productive nature, particularly those related to exports.[59]

The first published analysis of bank advances relates to the period 1935–7.[60] In January 1935 percentage advances to farmers, co-operative societies, and creameries were 29; the wholesale and retail trade 22; trusts, stockbrokers, agents, professional and private customers 19; manufacturing, building, and transport 8.5; and public bodies 7, the residue being unclassified.

More detailed analyses have been published in the Bulletin of the Central Bank since 1953. The general trend is apparent from Table 7.7.

Few tables reveal more clearly the shift of activity in the economy since 1939. Over-all, advances have increased over sixfold but the rate of increase has been very unequal. By far the greatest expansion has been in the groups covering finance, schools, etc., mining and manufacturing, and transport and communications. On the other hand, agriculture and the private sector have a lower proportion of advances than in 1939. These contrasts owe nothing to any special circumstances in the months or years taken as examples, with the exception of government and local authority borrowing which, at one period in 1954, was as high as 12 per cent of total advances.[61]

This is now an old story in Irish agriculture. It has been frequently noted that farmers place their money on deposit in the banks and that they are slow to borrow from the banks. The Banking Commission reported[62] that in 1937, when agricultural prices were depressed by the economic war, farmers had £35.6m. on deposit and owed the banks £12.6m.[63] No breakdown of deposits has been published since then; but it is understood that this unusual ratio has not been greatly changed. In very recent times there has been some modification of the reluctance of farmers to borrow from the banks; advances in January 1958 to farmers, co-operative societies, and creameries totalled only £20m. or 12 per cent of the total advances. Nevertheless, the contrast between the direction of advances in 1939 and 1966 reflects how the currents of economic activity have shifted in the last generation. The general impression is of a society

59. *CBR*, 1964–5, p. 17; *CBQSB*, January 1966, p. 12. It would appear from the speech of the Governor of the Bank of Ireland at its annual meeting on 23 February 1966 that the Associated Banks invited the Central Bank to give its advice.

60. *BCR*, para. 310.

61. At that time short-term state borrowing was made either by advances from the Bank of Ireland and/or by bills taken up by the banks and eventually repaid out of the proceeds of the next National Loan. The issue of Exchequer bills to the public which of course do not appear in the preceding table, commenced in 1957.

62. Para. 92. At that time total deposits (excluding current and other accounts) from the entire economy were £92m. while advances were £49m. See *BCR*, addendum ii, by Lord Glenavy, p. 386.

63. It should be said that there are difficulties in classifying both advances and deposits; e.g. the common case of a person who keeps a shop or is in professional practice and also owns a farm.

in which the banking system is progressively less concerned with farmers or private individuals and more concerned with manufacturing and commerce. It is a society in which the rentier counts for less and the industrial producer and trader for more; an economy which is much more greatly monetized than it was even twenty years ago.[64]

Interest rates

Since 1920 the rate structure has been determined by the Standing Committee of the Irish Banks.[65] The practice followed up to the early 1930s was fully set out by the 1938 Banking Commission.[66] The principles on which it was based are still relevant, though they have been modified in recent years: they may be illustrated by a short extract from the passage cited.

Banks, as commercial institutions, have to operate on a margin set by competition.[67] They cannot afford to pay a rate of interest upon deposits entrusted to them so low that they would lose deposits to outside institutions. They cannot afford to charge rates on interest upon advances made by them so high that any substantial proportion of their potential borrowing customers should be driven to borrow elsewhere . . . It is obvious also that a commercial banking system must be in a position to earn profits if it is to survive.

Taking first the rates paid on time deposits, the principle was that rates paid in Ireland should move in sympathy with rates in Great Britain. It has always been, and still is, a simple matter to transfer a deposit from the Republic into Great Britain; it is simpler still to make a transfer across the border. The passage just quoted from the report of the Banking Commission ends by stating that:

taking historical experience into account, the Irish Banks' Rate moves at 1 per cent above Bank of England Rate when the latter is below $5\frac{1}{2}$ per cent, and at one-half of one per cent above Bank Rate when that rate is at $5\frac{1}{2}$ per cent and over.

It also refers to the tendency for Irish Banks' Rate 'to fall less fast than Bank Rate for low levels of this rate, and to rise less fast as this rate moves up'.

This represented the position obtaining in the late 1930s. The outbreak of war brought changes in detail which are clearly set out by Mr. Colbert in the book cited in a preceding paragraph. Thereafter, rates in Ireland as in Great Britain remained unchanged for a long period until the incoming Conservative government reactivated Bank Rate in the

64. The annual rate of turnover of Government current accounts increased from 52 in 1947 to 270 in 1964, and of private current accounts from 21 to 23.

65. *BCR*, para. 302.

66. *BCR*, paras. 299–314. See also J. P. Colbert, *Commentary on Misconceptions regarding Money and Bank Credit*, Cahill, Dublin: 1942, pp. 125–8.

67. The growth of Post Office Savings Bank deposits, the expansion of hire-purchase and the issue of Exchequer Bills and Prize Bonds have made competition much stronger than when the Commission reported in 1938.

autumn of 1951. No change in rates was made in Ireland until Bank Rate was raised from $2\frac{1}{2}$ to 4 per cent in March 1952. In Ireland the rates paid on deposits and charged on advances were increased, though not by the same proportion, and they were reduced, though again not by the same margin, when Bank Rate was reduced in 1953 and in 1954.[68]

In January 1955 Bank Rate was raised from 3 to $3\frac{1}{2}$ per cent, and thence to $4\frac{1}{2}$ per cent in the following month. On this occasion the Irish large deposit rate was increased by one-quarter of one per cent in January, and left untouched in February. The small deposit rate and the rate charged on advances were left unaltered on both occasions. The Irish banks, however, felt obliged to follow the London changes in their branches in Northern Ireland so that there were now three deposit rates within the country and even within each bank operating in the two areas of Ireland.

It was officially stated in Dublin that 'the banks had accepted that the different circumstances obtaining in the Republic made it unnecessary to follow the British changes'. There is no reason to believe that the banks held this opinion with conviction, or indeed that they held it at all. However tenable it may have been in early 1955 it became less and less so as the year went on with its gloomy sequence of increasing trade deficits, loss of external assets and, most alarming of all, the conjunction of falling deposits and rising advances. The collapse of the experiment was admitted in January 1956 when the banks became free to increase their charges for advances and their payments on small deposits.

In September 1957 Bank Rate was raised from 4 per cent to the crisis level of 7 per cent. On this occasion, there was clearly no financial emergency in the Republic where the balance of payments was rapidly improving. The Irish changes were therefore much smaller than the British; and the same pattern was maintained when Bank Rate was reduced from time to time during 1958. It was also maintained when Bank Rate went again to 7 per cent in 1961 and 1964 and on its subsequent reductions. It has been repeated in 1967 and 1968.

It will be noted that the preceding discussion of interest rates has made no reference to the rediscount rate of the Central Bank. In practice, from 1943 to 1960 the Central Bank varied its rediscount rate in general, though by no means precise, sympathy with the movements of Bank Rate.[69] As has been seen, these movements lost some degree of

68. The payment of a slightly higher rate on larger deposits, which had been customary before the war, was reintroduced here in March 1952.

69. There were a number of occasions on which a change in Bank Rate was not followed by any movement in the rediscount rate of the Central Bank: e.g. in November 1951, September 1953, February 1957, and June 1958. The changes in London of January and February 1955 and of February 1956 were not followed in Dublin for a considerable period.

relevance to conditions in Ireland as the 1950s progressed. On the other hand, changes in the rate structure in Great Britain could not be wholly disregarded. In these circumstances changes in the rediscount rate of the Central Bank could not always be taken as indications of the monetary and economic policies which the Bank might consider appropriate. At the same time, the level of the rediscount rate was of growing importance on account of the growth in the amount of Exchequer bills outstanding which were rediscountable with the commercial banks at rates not exceeding the rediscount rate fixed by the Central Bank for such transactions. In October 1960, therefore, the Central Bank announced that:

its rediscount rate for exchequer bills should henceforward be fixed and published monthly. The rediscount rate will thus reflect more closely than before the actual short-term conditions in the State. Periodic changes in it will not necessarily have any implication in relation to monetary or economic policy. Any views which the Central Bank may have to offer on economic conditions will be expressed in other ways.[70]

Returns of bank debits have been compiled since the beginning of 1932.

TABLE 7.8

Bank debits (£ thousand), 1932–67

Year	Ordinary accounts	Government accounts	Total
1932	444.1	151.5	596.2
1938	527.6	230.8	758.4
1948	1,318.6	410.5	1,729.1
1958	2,319.8	1,344.4	3,664.2
1963	3,661.1	1,744.3	5,405.5
1964	4,153.9	2,034.4	6,188.3
1965	4,403.0	2,628.6	7,031.6
1967	5,284.0	2,928.5	8,212.5

Source: *Reports of the Central Bank*

Varia

The ratio of the money supply to domestic expenditure has been remarkably stable.[71]

It may be said with much justice that the deposits of the commercial banks were swollen by the First World War and the deposits of the Post Office Savings Bank by the second; which suggests that the distribution of earnings was very different in the 1940s from what it had been thirty years before. Roughly speaking, Post Office Savings Bank deposits quadrupled during the seven years 1939–46 while the annual

70. *CBQSB*, October 1960, pp. 7–8 in which the point is discussed generally.
71. See J. S. Oslizlok, 'Survey of Sources of Monetary Supply in Ireland', *JSSISI*, 1962–3, p. 109.

rate of increase since then has usually been between £4m. and £5m., though it was much lower in 1956 and 1957. It is notable that Savings Certificates have never enjoyed as much popularity as the Post Office Savings Bank.

TABLE 7.9

Money supply and gross domestic expenditure, 1948–68

Year	GDE at current market prices	Currency and current accounts	Percentage
	£ million		
1948	385.2	120.5	3.21
1958	602.1	181.6	3.32
1963	858.7	245.3	3.50
1964	977.9	278.2	3.52
1965	1052.2	292.9	3.59
1966	1079.1	315.7	3.42
1967	1127.0	329.7	3.42
1968	1280.0	356.4	3.59

Source: *Reports of the Central Bank*

Another development remains to be noted. In recent years the banking system has lost a great part of its monopoly of receiving savings. The Post Office Savings Bank was established in 1861. Deposits (for all Ireland) totalled £745,000 in 1871, £3,723,000 in 1890, and £11,931,000 in 1910. The following table shows the subsequent development. Savings Certificates were instituted in 1916.

TABLE 7.10

Post Office Savings Bank deposits and Savings Certificates (£ thousand), 1923–68

	Post Office Savings Bank (including interest) As at 31 Dec.	Savings Certificates (principal and outstanding interest) As at 31 Mar.
1923	1,597	923
1933	4,838	7,818
1939	10,651	7,843
1949	50,463	17,090
1959	96,266	28,243
1962	114,615	34,144
1963	120,061	36,335
1964	126,353	39,405
1965	129,275	43,725
1966	130,469	46,662
1967	137,650	52,648
1968	140,900	56,592

Source: *POSB Accounts*

Bank amalgamations

Some changes in the organization of the banking system remain to be noted. In 1917 the Ulster Bank passed under the control of the Westminster Bank Ltd. of London. In the same year the Midland Bank Ltd. of London acquired control of the Belfast Banking Company which in 1923 withdrew from business in the new State by ceding its branches therein to the Royal Bank of Ireland. The shares of the National Land Bank, which had been established by Dáil Éireann in 1920 were vested in the Minister for Finance in 1924. A majority of the 1926 Banking Commission recommended that its existence should be terminated, and it was sold to the Bank of Ireland in 1926. The title of the Bank, which continues to operate with a head office in Dublin and a branch in Limerick, was subsequently changed to the National City Bank.[72]

There have been further developments in more recent years. In 1958 the capital of the Hibernian Bank was acquired by the Bank of Ireland. In 1965 the Midland Bank, which as has been seen already owned the Belfast Bank, purchased the Northern Bank. Later in the same year it was announced that the business in (all) Ireland of the National Bank Ltd. would be transferred to a new company, National Bank of Ireland. The share capital of the new National Bank of Ireland would be owned by the Bank of Ireland. This agreement was brought into effect in 1966.

Also in 1966, the Munster and Leinster, Provincial, and Royal Banks announced the formation of a new banking group. A new company, Allied Irish Banks Ltd., was formed and offered its shares in exchange for the capital of the three banks.

Merchant banking was for long represented by Messrs. Guinness Mahon which was established in 1836. Very recently Hill Samuel, Hambros, Julian Hodge, Lombard Bank, and Ansbachers have opened offices while other concerns have established links in Dublin.

In 1966 two further merchant banks were established: the Investment Bank of Ireland by the Bank of Ireland with Messrs. Morgan Grenfell and Schroder Wagg, and the Allied Irish Investment Corporation by Allied Irish Banks and Messrs. Hambros.

In 1965 the First National City Bank opened a branch in Dublin. It was followed in 1966 by the Bank of Nova Scotia. Early in 1968 it was announced that the Toronto-Dominion Bank would acquire an interest in the Allied Irish Investment Bank, as the investment Corporation was now re-named. Shortly afterwards it was announced that the Chase Manhattan Bank and the Bank of Ireland Group had agreed in principle, subject to the consent of the relevant authorities, to develop

72. *BC*, 4th report, 1926, part 3. For the National City Bank, see F. G. Hall, op. cit., pp. 340–52.

an International Bank in Ireland. The Chase Manhattan would acquire a 50 per cent share in the National City Bank, a wholly-owned subsidiary of the Bank of Ireland.

In its report for the year 1964–5 the Central Bank referred to the fact that foreign banks and financial institutions had extended their activities to Ireland or were understood to contemplate doing so. It commented that:

While Irish law at present allows considerably greater freedom of entry into the business of banking than is customary in other countries, the position in this regard is under review and the question of recommending legislation to designate a licensing authority with discretionary powers is being considered. Meanwhile, it appears to be generally recognized that consultation with the Central Bank is a proper preliminary step in connection with any proposal for the entry of an external institution into banking business in Ireland.

The number of full-time bank offices in the State grew from 581 in 1925 to 604 in 1934 and 757 in 1961. The number of all bank offices grew in the same years from 960, 1,018 to 1,250.

Participation of Ireland in the Basle arrangements for the support of sterling, 1968

On 23rd September 1968 the Government Information Bureau issued a statement under this heading the relevant parts of which are as follows:

The British authorities will guarantee during the currency of the agreement (three to five years) the maintenance of the U.S. dollar value of the sterling assets of the Central Bank and Government in excess of 10 per cent of total official reserves. This means that sterling so guaranteed together with non-sterling reserves (e.g. gold, dollars and creditor position in the International Monetary Fund) will amount to 90 per cent of total official holdings.

The agreement applies to official reserves. Provision has been made, however, to bring within the scope of the guarantee any sterling transferred from the Associated Banks to the Central Bank for inclusion in the official reserves and the Associated Banks expect to avail themselves of this provision in due course to the extent of about £40m.

In return for this guarantee, the Government have agreed to maintain throughout the period of the agreement a specified proportion of total official reserves in the form of sterling. This proportion will be known as the Minimum Sterling Proportion. Because of the diversification of official reserves during 1968, this proportion will be considerably less than it would have been a year ago. It will initially be 55 per cent but will be raised some percentage points by the transfers of sterling from the Associated Banks to the Central Bank already referred to.

The guarantee, for which there will be no charge, will ensure that a large part of the assets of the Central Bank will be protected against any devaluation of sterling in relation to the U.S. dollar while at the same time earning the substantially higher interest obtainable in London than in New York.

CHAPTER EIGHT

Revenue, Expenditure, and National Debt

TWO FISCAL ISSUES COMMANDED ATTENTION IN THE EARLY years of the present century. First, in chronological order, was the financial relations of Great Britain and Ireland under the Act of Union; second, the problem of how a Home Rule government could be financed.

The first issue was exhaustively discussed in the reports of the Royal Commission on the Financial Relations of Great Britain and Ireland which were published in 1896. Fortunately it is not necessary for our present purposes to enter into what was a detailed and subtle discussion of the incidence of taxation. It will be sufficient to recall that the Act of Union, which came into force in 1801, provided for the immediate union of the parliaments of Great Britain and Ireland. Though it did not provide for the immediate union of the exchequers of the two countries, it set out the conditions in which that union would become effective. These conditions were fulfilled, largely as a result of the expenses of the Napoleonic wars, and the exchequers were united in 1817.[1] In 1894 the Royal Commission was appointed to determine the justice of a growing claim that, as a result, Ireland had been over-taxed. For a variety of reasons, it did not complete this task, but a number of reports were presented and five conclusions were made unanimously, two of which are relevant here. The first was that:

the Act of Union imposed upon Ireland a burden which she was unable to bear.

The second was that:

whilst the actual tax revenue is about one-eleventh of that of Great Britain, the relative taxable capacity of Ireland is very much smaller, and is not estimated by any of us as exceeding one-twentieth.

1. See G. O'Brien, *Economic History of Ireland from the Union to the Famine*, Longmans Green, London, 1921.

In 1896 and for ten years later it was clear that the revenue raised in Ireland exceeded current expenditure in Ireland. Over-taxation was an issue on which Nationalists and Unionists in Ireland could and did join in an unusual harmony, though no practical result followed. These findings, nevertheless, provided a basis for a succession of claims that Ireland was entitled to restitution for the monies raised in Ireland by the United Kingdom for imperial purposes.[2]

The position was altered after 1905 when the social policies of the Liberal government, especially the introduction of Old Age Pensions in 1908, produced a situation in which the traditional position was reversed by 1909–10. This change influenced the controversies over the third Home Rule bill which was introduced in 1912.

This Bill led to the appointment of a new committee of inquiry,[3] which investigated the situation in the light of these developments. The financial clauses of the Home Rule Bill were not such as to induce optimism. All the Irish revenue was to be collected by the Imperial government who would return a 'transferred sum' to the Irish government which, with minor exceptions, would constitute the revenue of the Irish government. It was perhaps no wonder that a review of these provisions should have concluded with the reflection that:

it is a Bill, as far as its financial part is concerned, which England should pass and Ireland should reject.[4]

Opponents of the Bill made much play with the calculation that in the existing situation, even if Ireland had control over customs and excise and non-tax revenue, and made no contribution to the army, the navy, the Civil List or the national debt, she would still face an annual deficit of £3¼m. The best that could be hoped for, it seemed, was that the Imperial Parliament would grant the government in Dublin some kind of 'dole' or, as it was less harshly but surely inappropriately termed by T. M. Kettle, 'a marriage gift'.[5]

In the event no Irish government was obliged to make this perilous experiment. The Home Rule Bill was passed into law in September 1914, but its operation was suspended for a year or the duration of the war, whichever period would be the shorter. By 1918, enough had happened in Ireland to make a new approach necessary. In the meantime,

2. The magnitude of these claims was very great, e.g. an article by C. H. Oldham, 'The Public Finances of Ireland', *JIBI*, 1911, p. 280, suggested a sum of £330m. to be the measure of past over-taxation. It will be remembered that these were gold pounds; the sum quoted represented twice the annual budget for the United Kingdom and rather less than one-half its National Debt.

3. The (Primrose) Committee on Irish Finance, Cd 6799 and 6153 HMSO, London: 1913.

4. 'The Finance of the Home Rule Bill', *JIBI*, 1912, p. 177.

5. See an interesting discussion of the Bill in *JIBI*, 1912, p. 19. The issues were discussed by Erskine Childers in *The Framework of Home Rule*, Arnold, London: 1911.

however, wartime taxation had more than restored the financial relations of Great Britain and Ireland to the position of the nineteenth century.

The extent of the fiscal powers which might be given to an Irish parliament was one of the issues on which the Irish Convention broke down in 1918. The attitude of the interests which were represented in that body was fairly summarized in a Note signed by a number of its nationalist members:

The principal point of difference arose on finance. We asked for full powers of taxation. The Ulster representatives wished to reserve all powers of taxation to the Imperial Parliament and only modified this demand to the extent of allowing to the Irish Parliament some undefined taxing-power of its own. The Southern Unionists were prepared to concede direct taxation and Excise to the Irish Parliament.[6]

By the Government of Ireland Act, 1920, the Imperial Parliament retained the right to levy taxes in the two areas it established, Northern Ireland and Southern Ireland. All taxes, whether levied by the Imperial parliament or by either of the Irish parliaments, were to be collected by the Imperial authority. An Irish contribution to Imperial expenditure was fixed at £18m. for each of the two years after the passage of the Act. It was to be levied in the proportions of 56 per cent on Southern Ireland and 44 per cent on Northern Ireland. Thereafter it was subject to a revision by a Joint Exchequer Board composed of one representative of the Crown, two of the British Treasury and one each from Northern and Southern Ireland. The revision might adjust both the total of the imperial contribution and its appointment between the two areas, according to their relative tax capacities. This Act did not come into force in Southern Ireland, but it is still effective in Northern Ireland.

The Anglo-Irish Treaty of 1921 conferred sovereign powers of taxation on the government and parliament of the Irish Free State. It also provided for a review of the Irish share in the national debt of the United Kingdom.[7] This was a contingent liability which might become highly onerous, but it was later cancelled in circumstances which are described later.[8]

The fiscal separation of the Irish Free State was effected on 1 April

6. Proceedings of the Irish Convention, Cd 9019, HMSO, London: 1918, p. 38.

7. Article 5 of the Treaty provided that 'The Irish Free State shall assume liability for the service of the Public Debt of the United Kingdom as existing at the date hereof and towards the payment of War Pensions as existing at that date in such proportion as may be fair and equitable, having regard to any just claim on the part of Ireland by way of set-off or counter-claim, the amount of such sums being determined in default of agreement by the arbitration of one or more independent persons being citizens of the British Empire'. The counter-claim obviously referred to the Irish claims in respect of over-taxation during the period of the Union.

8. See below, p. 252.

1923. The new State inherited the constitutional practice of the United Kingdom in relation to the raising of taxation. The trend in the main components of revenue since 1923 may be studied in Table 8.1.

TABLE 8.1

Exchequer revenue receipts (£ million), 1922–69

Year ended 31 March	Customs, Excise, Stamp and Motor Vehicles, etc., Duties	Estate Duties	Income Tax, Surtax, Corporation Profits Tax	Post Office and miscellaneous	Total
1923	19.6	1.0	5.3	2.0	27.9
1928	14.4	1.3	4.7	3.7	24.1
1933	16.7	1.1	5.8	6.3	29.9
1938	17.7	1.3	6.3	5.9	31.2
1943	19.2	1.4	12.9	6.3	39.8
1948	36.5	2.3	17.7	8.5	65.2
1953	55.6	2.6	25.9	12.8	95.9
1958	71.9	2.7	28.0	20.2	122.9
1963	91.9	3.5	40.7	27.3	163.4
1964	99.8	3.6	47.9	29.4	184.4
1965	111.3	4.4	56.2	33.6	219.0
1966	120.6	4.6	64.2	37.0	240.7
1967	136.5	4.6	73.3	40.8	272.8
1968	158.2	6.0	82.0	45.8	305.0
1969	166.4	7.6	93.5	50.5	345.5

Source: *Finance Accounts*

Note: Included in the total are items such as the Turn-over Tax and the Wholesale Tax, net receipts from which in 1968–9 were £17.8m. and £9.5m. respectively.

The collection of revenue in the earlier years of the Irish Free State was exceptionally difficult. In the last years of British rule, many persons had abstained from the payment of income tax, for either patriotic or less worthy motives.[9] There followed a year (1922), under a provisional government which had to live almost from hand to mouth and to organize its civil service at the same time as it fought a civil war. It is remarkable that the machinery of government was so soon assembled and put into working order.[10]

The fiscal policy of the new government, after meeting the expenses of the civil war, was directed towards economy in expenditure and the reduction of taxation. Governments and peoples in Europe were concerned to eliminate the heavy public expenditure of the war years and to return to the older habits of light taxation. Prices and incomes had fallen heavily since 1920 and in 1925 Great Britain led other European

9. So much so that later in the decade much resentment was caused by an energetic and meticulous campaign by the Revenue Commissioners to recover the arrears of tax unpaid during the troubled times.

10. The administrative system is described by J. B. O'Connell, *The Financial Administration of Ireland*, Mount Salus, Dublin: 1960.

countries towards the restoration of the Gold Standard. Thus the Irish Free State was born into a period of deflation, which conditioned the subsequent Irish reaction to taxation. The Irish government, however, had a special reason for its policy. It had long been an article of faith that Ireland had been over-taxed under British rule and that the country could be administered much more cheaply under native rule. An Irish government now had the chance to prove the truth of that claim, and little attention was paid by public opinion either to altered values of money or changed standards of public services.[11]

Taxes on income were the principal source of revenue,[12] tariffs representing only a small proportion of the total, but some of those who had paid large amounts in income tax were out of sympathy with the new regime and transferred their domicile to Great Britain. It was therefore a matter of importance that the standard rate of income tax should compare favourably with the British rate, but this was not easy to secure in years when abnormal expenses had to be met and, on its side, the British government was bent on reducing its own standard rate. By 1928 the Irish rate had been brought lower than the British (and it has remained lower under all subsequent governments) but the achievement clearly carried implications for the scope of public expenditure because reductions in taxation could clearly not be confined to the small numbers who paid taxes on income.

In any case, the government was committed to a policy of balancing the budget (then regarded as an indispensable mark of sound public finance) at a low level.[13] Public policy aimed at the reduction of all costs of production in order to enable exporters to compete successfully abroad: this entailed low taxation and therefore low expenditure. Accordingly, as will be seen from Table 8.2, the standard rate of income

11. Thus the political situation in 1927 was affected by a sustained press campaign for greater economy in the public service. The Irish correspondent of the *Round Table* calculated that the cost of governing the Twenty-six Counties, in 1926 values, had been £16m. in 1912–13 against £28m. in 1926. He added that 'this taxation constitutes a crushing burden on the taxpayer', *Round Table*, 1926, p. 596. The standard rate of income tax was then 4s. in £1.

12. Income tax was first imposed in Ireland in 1853. The basic statute is the Income Tax Act of 1918, now replaced by the Consolidating Act of 1967. Super-tax was first imposed in 1909 and was changed to surtax in 1928.

The operation of the system of income taxation was very fully reviewed by the Commission on Income Taxation which was appointed in February 1957 and published seven reports. The last (Pr. 6581), which was signed in March 1962, contains a general summary of its recommendations. Perhaps the most important of these was the recommendation of PAYE, which was adopted by the Minister for Finance in his budget speech in April 1960.

The chairman of the Commission was Mr. Justice O'Dalaigh (later Chief Justice); its membership was as follows—Messrs. Owen Binchy; P. A. Bolger; Professor John Busteed; Patrick Cogan; Alan Dempsey; R. C. Flanagan; Fr. James Kavanagh; F. N. Kelly; James Meenan; Donal Nevin; and J. A. Ryan. Mr. L. de Barra was secretary to the Commission.

13. See above, p. 35.

tax was reduced from the 5s. inherited from British rule to 3s. in the years before the depression.

In sympathy with what was happening elsewhere (particularly in Great Britain), the supplementary budget in the autumn of 1931 brought increases of taxation. The new government which took office in

TABLE 8.2

Changes in standard rates of income tax, 1923–4 to 1966–7

Year ended 31 March	Standard rate s. d.		Year ended 31 March	Standard rate s. d.	
1924	5	0	1942	7	6
1926	4	0	1947	6	6
1928	3	0	1949	7	0
1932	3	6	1950	6	6
1933	5	0	1953	7	6
1935	4	6	1960	7	0
1940	5	6	1962	6	4
1941	6	6	1967	7	0

Source: *Reports of the Revenue Commissioners*

March 1932 was pledged (as Mr. Roosevelt pledged himself later in the year) to the reduction of expenditure, but was committed to a programme of improved social services which it planned to finance by an increase in direct taxation. (At this time the British rate was 6s., the Irish rate was 3s. 6d.) In addition it would soon be obliged to provide bounties to Irish exports in order to alleviate the effect of the penal duties imposed by Great Britain in the economic war.

The first budget of the new government therefore brought a series of protective measures and a sharp increase in the standard rate to 5s. These measures aroused criticism. One commentator declared:

If a Glasgow Communist and a die-hard tariff reformer were merged into a single personality and, having somehow managed to escape certification, became Minister for Finance in the Irish Free State, the result would probably be something similar to the budget introduced in the Dáil on 11 May by Mr Sean MacEntee. It reaches the high-water mark of predatory taxation and tariff imposition.[14]

Within a comparatively short time, however, income tax was reduced again, though the higher rates imposed in the United Kingdom dispensed with the need for the Irish government to make further reductions.

The financing of the State in war time imposed the necessity of increasing income tax rapidly to 7s. 6d. It is to be noted that the end of the

14. *R T*, 1932, 762. The recipient of this diatribe was Mr. Sean MacEntee, who was Minister for Finance from 1932 to 1939 and again from 1951 to 1954. The two terms of office constitute the longest tenure of the Department, the second longest being that of Mr. Ernest Blythe.

TABLE 8.3

Principal sources of net receipts from excise duties (£ thousand), 1924–5 to 1968–9

	1924–5	1927–8	1937–8	1947–8	1957–8	1966–7	1967–8	1968–9
Total net receipts	7,418	6,641	5,932	11,037	17,376	54.9	62.2	25.5
Beer	4,222	3,574	2,839	5,120	8,441	17.6	19.8	23.5
Spirits	2,691	2,398	1,762	3,660	4,898	9.8	—	—
Entertainments	179	156	307	888	1,527	—	—	—
Oil, mineral hydrocarbon	—	—	—	—	—	14.4	24.1	28.3

Source: *Finance Accounts*

war brought no great reduction from this level. A period in which the rate was 6s. 6d., which was well above pre-war rates although also below contemporary levels in the United Kingdom, was followed by a return to a 7s. 6d. rate in 1953, which remained unaltered until 1959. Thus the country remained at a wartime rate over a decade after the war had ended. Comparisons with the United Kingdom became increasingly unfavourable as the Conservative governments reduced the rates of income tax during the 1950s. Writing in 1958, Mr. Whitaker noted that although the standard rate was higher in Great Britain than in Ireland, the position of many British income-tax payers was relatively more favourable. He added:

The positive objective of financial policy must be to arrive as quickly as possible at the point at which it will be possible to give the economy the tonic of a significant reduction, above all, in direct taxes on incomes, profits and savings. This should take precedence over any reduction in indirect taxes (particularly those which bear on less essential imports) and over any increase in expenditure which does not directly promote increased national output at competitive prices.[15]

The standard rate of income tax has been twice reduced since then, in 1959 and 1961 though the Budget of 1966 brought the first increase in fourteen years. Moreover, the policy of the government was set out in a White Paper on Direct Taxation, published in 1961, which stated that:

it is a good principle in the circumstances of this country to place the emphasis of taxation on expenditure rather than on income.[16]

The introduction of the turn-over tax in 1963 and of the wholesale tax in 1966 was in accordance with this principle.

A general tariff has been in operation since 1932, aimed at affording protection for Irish producers; but at all times the revenue from customs duties has come predominantly from tobacco. The receipts from excise duties come overwhelmingly from the duties on beer and spirits and, in more recent years following a switch of duty, from oil.

The incidence of taxation in Ireland was briefly considered by Professor Nevin in his study of the public debt. He quotes total central government tax revenue as being 23.4 per cent of the national income in Ireland in 1960 against 29.5 per cent in Austria, 27.4 per cent in the Netherlands, 23.3 per cent in Belgium, 21.9 per cent in Denmark, and 21.7 per cent in Sweden.[17]

15. *Economic Development*, pp. 23–25.
16. Pr. 5952, Stationery Office, Dublin: p. 15.
17. E. T. Nevin, *Public Debt and Economic Development*, Economic Research Institute, Dublin: Paper No. 11, p. 4. The limitations on the validity of such comparisons are noted there. See also J. B. Broderick, 'An Analysis of Government Revenue and Expenditure in relation to National Accounts', *JSSISI*, 1959–60, p. 132.

Irish taxation depends very greatly on taxes on consumption. Revenue from income tax is limited by low income levels particularly in agriculture and the difficulty of assessing total income of the many individuals who follow several vocations.[18] Professor Nevin points out that in 1960 taxes on income and wealth in Ireland represented 7.8 per cent of national income, compared with 8.9 per cent in Denmark, 9.3 per cent in Belgium, 10.4 per cent in Austria, 11.3 per cent in Sweden, and 16.6 per cent in the Netherlands.[19]

State expenditure

The first decade of self-government witnessed a change from the abnormal expenditure of the early years to a budget designed to balance at a low figure and to serve as an example of thrift. This process was well summarized by Dr. Kiernan:

From 1923 to 1930 the outstanding features of Irish Free State Finance were heavy expenditure in the early years on Army, Compensation and Pensions; a rapid reduction in Army and Compensation expenditure; more than fifty-eight per cent of the abnormal post-revolution expenses paid from taxation: and, apart from these dynamic movements, a consistently heavy charge for Education, Old Age Pensions and Public Works.[20]

The process of change in the following two decades has been surveyed by Mr. J. C. M. Eason in a series of papers read to the Statistical and Social Inquiry Society of Ireland.[21] Their message was summarized by Mr. Whitaker during the discussion on the final paper; and the quotation will give a good picture of the position in 1950.

Mr Eason's surveys throw into relief two significant changes in Irish finance over the past twenty years and more especially during the past decade—the great increase in the proportion of State revenue devoted to social services of all kinds and the enormous expansion in State capital outlay. The current Budget is predominantly concerned with redistribution of incomes and seeing that we have comparatively few big incomes in Ireland, we must now be one of the most egalitarian countries in the world not excluding Soviet Russia. This redistribution of incomes has been almost entirely at the expense of the middle classes on whom taxation has fallen with particular severity. Since 1939 expenditure on subsidies and social services has trebled, the cost of living has doubled, taxation of all kinds has more than doubled, but, if I may use a homely illustration, the average salary of officials in the Department of Finance has risen by only 50 per cent.

18. See L. Reason, 'Estimates of the Distribution of Non-Agricultural Incomes and Incidence of Certain Taxes', *JSSISI*, 1960–1, p. 42. The third report of the Commission on Income Taxation (Pr. 5567, Stationery Office, Dublin) pointed out that the number of persons liable to income tax in 1960–1 was estimated at about 175,000 out of a total of about 1,112,000 persons at work. The number of persons assessed for surtax in 1964–5 was 4,897.

19. Op. cit.

20. In *Saorstát Éireann, Official Handbook*, Talbot Press, Dublin: 1932, p. 85.

21. *JSSISI*, 1930–1, p. 1; *JSSISI*, 1933–4, p. 15; *JSSISI*, 1940–1, p. 123; *JSSISI*, 1946–7, p. 691; *JSSISI*, 1950–1, p. 403.

The paper referred to by Whitaker showed that social health and welfare, etc. accounted for 38.2 per cent of State expenditure in 1949–50 against 16 per cent in 1929–30. On the other hand the proportion represented by expenditure on education had fallen from 20 per cent to

TABLE 8.4

Main heads of current government expenditure (£ thousand), 1958–9 to 1968–9

	1958/9	1960/1	1962/3	1965/6	1968/69 Provisional
Service of public debt	24,639	28,374	34,374	49,035	76,580
Social services	46,889	50,444	57,515	84,163	119,462
Social welfare	25,354	26,129	27,889	38,683	49,139
Education	13,489	15,557	18,908	29,584	44,639
Health	8,046	8,758	10,718	15,896	25,684
Economic services	22,628	24,930	35,039	55,164	85,974
Agriculture	13,284	14,058	22,320	35,795	60,603
Industry	1,580	1,537	1,927	4,693	8,210
Transport	6,965	8,289	9,422	12,518	14,354
Forestry and fisheries	799	1,046	1,370	2,158	2,807
General services	23,409	26,235	30,612	42,784	51,451
Post Office	7,387	7,846	9,694	13,671	17,164
Defence	6,119	7,102	8,065	11,666	12,832
Justice, including Gardaí	4,976	5,591	6,149	8,374	10,327
Public service pensions	4,927	5,696	6,704	9,073	11,128
Other expenditure	8,346	9,718	11,108	16,841	20,382
TOTAL	125,911	139,701	168,648	247,987	353,849
Remuneration included in above figures	39,448	43,845	51,164	75,502	95,631
	1958 £m.	1960 £m.	1962 £m.	1965 £m.	1968 £m.
Gross National Product	599	671	774	1,018	1,260
Current Government Expenditure as % of GNP	21.0%	20.8%	21.8%	24.4%	28.1%

Source: *Current Budget Tables*

The estimated expenditure for 1968–9 should be read subject to the adjustments noted in the source.

10.4 per cent over the same period. Equally remarkable, as it now seems, was the proportion taken by the service of debt, which had been 9.2 per cent in 1929–30 and fell to 7.8 per cent in 1949–50.

Writing in *Economic Development* some seven years later, Whitaker pointed out that State non-capital expenditure had increased from £77m. in 1950–1 to £126m. in 1957–8 (the figure for the later year was described as provisional). The net increase was accounted for principally by an increase of £15.7m. for the service of debt; £12.8m. for social services; £10.3m. for remuneration; £4.7m. for health; and £4.1m. for agricultural price supports. The increase during that period in expenditure on education was £1m.[22] There was a reduction of £11m. under the heading of Consumer Food Subsidies.

The position in more recent years will be seen from Table 8.4, in which it will be noted that over the period 1958 to 1965 there have been heavy increases in the service of debt and in the provision for social welfare and health, education, and agriculture. These figures, however, should be considered in conjunction with the provisions made for capital expenditure.[23]

THE PUBLIC DEBT

The liability of the Irish Free State for a share in the national debt of the United Kingdom was removed by the Boundary Agreement of December 1925. This was an unascertained commitment and might well have led to arguments as refined as those used thirty years before by the members of the Financial Relations Commission.[24] Other liabilities were settled, as it was then hoped, by the Ultimate Financial Settlement reached between the British and Irish governments in March 1926 though not published until the following November.[25] *Inter alia*, this instrument contained one provision of supreme importance for Irish public finance: the conclusion of a double income tax agreement.

The Irish Free State began its existence without any public debt. Soon after the end of the civil war, in 1923, the first National Loan was floated, for £10m., bearing interest at 5 per cent and repayable in 1935–45. It was fully subscribed at 93 in spite of a number of difficulties.[26] In September 1924 the stock was still quoted at 93 though 5 per cent War Loan then stood at 101¾; but by December 1926 both stocks stood at 100. The second National Loan was issued in 1927, $15m. of which

22. *Economic Development*, Appendix iii. See also Farley, *Social Insurance and Social Assistance in Ireland*, Institute of Public Administration, 1964.

23. The budget was divided into current and capital sections in 1950.

24. In a subsequent Dáil debate Mr. Cosgrave (*PDDE*, 13, 1308 et seq.) and Mr. Blythe (ibid. 1586 et seq.) suggested that the British claim might have involved, if upheld by an arbitrator, an annual payment of up to £19m. a year. Much would have depended on the view taken of the Irish counter-claim. These matters are discussed in a useful article in *The Irish Statesman*, 22 January 1927. See also *JIBI*, 1925, p. 193, and *JIBI*, 1926, p. 104, on the double taxation agreement.

25. In the course of a debate on this settlement, Mr. Johnson raised the point, later to be developed by Mr. Eamon de Valera, that the provisions of the 1920 Act entitled the government of the Free State to retain the annuities. See *PDDE*, 17, 658. The point turned on whether the Act of 1920 had ever been in operation in the Twenty-six Counties, a contention which the then Free State government felt itself estopped from advancing.

26. A number of opponents of the Anglo-Irish Treaty stated that the Loan would be repudiated if they came to power.

was raised in the United States and repaid at the first available date, in 1950.

It is to be noted that these issues, with the exception referred to in 1927, were both made in Dublin. The State was slow to exercise the facilities which presumably were available to it, as a member of the Commonwealth under the Free State and as a member of the sterling area under the Republic, of borrowing in London.[27] As a creditor country it was normally able to finance itself from domestic sources;[28] a fact which has been of considerable political importance at various times in the past.

The growth in the National Debt was one of the principal pre-occupations of the Banking Commission which reported in 1938. It stated that:

The large and continuous expansion of the burden of dead-weight debt is one of the most serious matters which we are called on to review. . . . It has come to our notice that there is a widespread impression that the burden of State debt in this country is moderate, or even trivial, as compared with that in most other countries. While it is important that attention should be concentrated rather on the absolute facts of the domestic debt situation and on their implications in the light of the general economy of the Free State, it is nevertheless of some interest to examine the impression in question owing to the danger that it may tend to produce a too ready acquiescence in further expansion of borrowing.[29]

The Commission rejected the validity of comparisons of the debt of the Free State with that of wealthy countries such as the United Kingdom, or of countries such as Australia which possessed undeveloped natural resources. It pointed out that the national debt of the Free State stood at over £24 per head of population against a debt of £16 per head in Denmark, £27 in Norway, £20 in Sweden, and £21 in Austria. It proceeded:

These references, which it would be easy to extend, should suffice to negative the idea that the Free State has a relatively favourable position in this matter. Moreover, the Free State is singular in the rate of increase of its debt, and some of the countries mentioned have effected net decreases even in the past five years.[30]

Its recommendation reads as follows:

In these circumstances the Commission seems called on to consider the making of a recommendation in broad terms as to the policy to be observed about the future course of the dead-weight debt. There are two considerations of special importance in this connection. In the first place, heavy loan expenditure of an unproductive character has a tendency, while it is being incurred, to weaken

27. A loan (£5m.) was floated in London for the first time in August 1966.
28. On 31 March 1968 the external debt totalled £51,902,000 of which £32,480,000 was incurred under the European Recovery Programme.
29. *BCR*, 1938, para. 488.   30. Ibid.

TABLE 8.5

Outstanding public debt (£ thousand), 1926–69

On 31 March	Total	National Loans	Savings Certificates (Principal)	Exchequer Bills	Prize Bonds	Ways and Means advances	Other borrowing
1926	14,102	9,505	1,774	—	—	1,113	1,710
1931	29,313	20,875	6,364	—	—	—	2,074
1936	48,403	24,816	7,770	—	—	—	15,817
1941	65,120	39,991	7,673	—	—	500	16,955
1946	81,347	45,587	11,332	—	—	3,250	21,178
1951	142,284	81,493	13,090	—	—	4,000	43,701
1956	250,365	145,485	18,726	4,500	—	37,110	44,544
1961	377,375	197,583	25,705	19,110	16,592	65,301	53,084
1964	549,872	250,902	31,013	35,000	23,344	128,873	59,235
1965	605,560	290,903	34,616	49,000	26,654	140,559	63,828
1966	680,726	340,239	36,881	59,300	28,539	128,410	87,358
1967	731,075	397,804	42,818	59,000	29,202	134,137	77,114
1968	775,556	424,554	45,945	75,000	30,016	131,419	68,622
1969	861,404	481,963	47,620	82,000	30,500	118,597	100,724

Source: *Finance Accounts*

the economic and financial stability of the country, and especially to place a strain on the balance of payments. From comments made elsewhere in this Report it is evident that the Free State is not in a position to take any increased risk in this matter.

Secondly, increase of the annual net debt charge consequent upon an increase in the volume of dead-weight debt threatens to create a serious position for the budget of the future. The task of balancing the budget must be more difficult according as the proportion of fixed charges in it rises. Expenditure on services that can expand or contract according to varying views of needs of Government policy will always be reasonably susceptible of control, but expenditure to cover debt charges or other contractual obligations of the State, such as pensions, affords no scope for ministerial discretion. This rigid element in the budget has already reached a high level in the Free State and so far as pensions are concerned appears to be still advancing.

The matter could, of course, be viewed with less apprehension if it were possible to entertain a confident opinion about the future prospects of the national income and taxable capacity and the trend of the balance of payments. While we do not want to give expression to any unwarranted pessimism, we think that on the facts and information at present available it would be rash to look lightly upon courses tending to increase the dead-weight debt. Our considered view is that no increase whatever beyond the existing volume of net dead-weight debt should be permitted, and that that volume should be reduced from year to year at such rate as general financial circumstances permit.[31]

The fate of this recommendation was sealed by the outbreak of war a little over twelve months after its publication. In fact, however, the increase of debt during the war years was comparatively limited. It has been in the post-war period that it has grown to spectacular proportions.

In fact there have been only two years since the foundation of the State in which a net reduction in the public debt has been effected.[32] Furthermore the public debt has strikingly increased in relation to the national income. To take one of the tests suggested by the Banking Commission: a comparison of the gross public debt in various countries as a percentage of national income in 1960 shows that the Irish figure of 80.5 per cent was exceeded only in the United Kingdom (136.9 per cent) and in Belgium (88.6 per cent). Taking the other countries mentioned above, the percentage in Australia was 32.5; Denmark 24.7; Norway 38.9; Sweden 36.4; and Austria 18.9.[33] The relevance, and the implications, of these comparisons are discussed elsewhere.[34]

To turn to an examination of the components of the public debt as set out in Table 8.5, the initiation of the series of National Loans has

31. Ibid., para. 489.
32. In 1924–5 Mr. Blythe reduced the public debt by £307,600 and in 1932–3 Mr. MacEntee reduced it by £336,550. These achievements appear still more remarkable when one notices the years in which they occurred, *PDDE*, 146, 1174.
33. Edward Nevin, *Public Debt and Economic Development*, Economic Research Institute, Dublin: Paper No. 11, p. 3.
34. See below, pp. 370–1.

already been noted. These are now issued every year; usually in the autumn when the outcome of the harvest is expected to leave an amount of money available for investment.[35] Irish savings certificates were first issued in 1923 and prize bonds in 1957. Exchequer bills were issued between 1927 and 1930 and again in 1932. They have been issued regularly in recent years: to the banks since 1953 and to the public since 1957. Ways and Means advances originate largely from moneys in the Post Office and Trustee Savings Banks. 'Other' borrowing is principally composed of dollar borrowings under the European Recovery Programme, discussed below, and borrowings from the Central Bank arising out of the obligations accepted by the State as a member of the World Bank and International Monetary Fund and also borrowings from some semi-State companies.

The State debt is very largely held within the State. Reference has already been made to foreign borrowing in the Second National Loan in 1927 and to applications for later National Loan stock from outside the State. The one occasion on which foreign borrowing on a significant scale took place arose out of the European Recovery Programme. The Irish government was associated with the Programme from its inception in 1947. It received financial assistance from the United States, partly by way of a grant ($18m.) and by a loan ($128.2m. or £40.7m. at the rates of exchange obtaining since 1949). The principal is being repaid by half-yearly instalments from 30 June 1956. The interest is calculated at 2½ per cent on the unpaid principal balance and is being repaid by half-yearly instalments from 30 June 1952. The last of these instalments will be due on 31 December 1983; it is calculated that by that time the State will have paid £71.66m. on foot of the original debt.[36]

Several analyses of the public debt have been made, the first by Dr. Joseph Brennan in 1935.[37] whose approach was followed in the report of the Banking Commission.[38] They drew up a balance sheet showing on one side the debt outstanding and the moneys provided for debt redemption. At that time, the total was £81.3m., of which £73m. was composed of the debt outstanding. The components of the other side were liquid assets (£4.8m.); productive assets (£31m.), consisting of telephone capital, the Shannon Scheme and the Electricity Supply Board, the Local Loans Fund and Land Bonds; and gross dead-weight debt (£45.5m.), consisting of budget deficits, property compensation, discounts on National Loans, Dáil Loans, Land Bonds, annuity to the

35. Calculations can be upset by coincidence with changes in the prevailing rates of interest. Foreign borrowing was resorted to on a number of occasions in 1966.
36. Cf. *PDDE*, 146, 1613. This calculation was made on the basis of the pre-November 1967 parity.
37. 'The Public Debt of the Irish Free State', *JSSISI*, 1934–5, p. 37.
38. Ibid., paras. 480–7 and Appendix 23.

British government, Road Fund, Unemployment Fund, housing, and miscellaneous items.

It will be seen that the Commission was concerned with the productive value of the components of the public debt. A more recent examination followed a different line of approach.

The figures have been prepared solely from a book-keeping point of view, and no effort has been made to divide the assets into the categories of productive or non-productive. Besides being outside the scope of this paper, such segregation is likely to give rise to great difficulties, not the least of which is to arrive at an agreed definition of what is to be regarded as productive in terms of national economics.[39]

In this case the balance sheet (at 31 March 1958) showed a total of £431.6m. The liabilities were: (a) money raised by the issue of securities, £316m.; (b) capitalized liabilities (land bonds, housing and health subsidies, compensation for damage to property), £54.8m.; sinking funds and interest thereon, £46.9m.; pre-1922 advances to local loans fund, £6.3m.; and capital fund, £7.6m. The assets consisted of liquid assets, £7.3m.; repayable advances (mainly to State companies and for transport services), £182.7m.; shares in sundry undertakings (State companies and shares in the World Bank and International Monetary Fund), £12.2m.; voted capital services (principally agriculture, forestry, housing, public works and aviation), £81.2m.; and other assets (land bonds, housing subsidies; compensation for damage to property; Dáil loans; Development Funds; budget deficits, etc.), £148.3m.

State investment policies

Long before self-government had been attained it was an article of nationalist faith that public policy should be directed to the development of economic resources. The post-1920 deflation was as unfavourable in Ireland as elsewhere to ambitious programmes; nevertheless the Shannon hydro-electric scheme was initiated by the first (Cumann na nGaedheal) government in 1925. After 1932 the succeeding Fianna Fáil government continued to develop water-power and added projects of its own such as the exploitation of the turf bogs.

Detailed policies for economic expansion were in harmony with the circumstances of the world after 1945. They were encouraged by the European Recovery Programme; and the Irish statement of long-term plans was the first occasion on which specific programmes were laid down to cover a period of years.[40] This development was brought a

39. M. O'Reilly, 'State Debt Balance Sheets', *JSSISI*, 1958–9, p. 30.
40. *The European Recovery Programme; Ireland's Long-term Programme, 1949–1953*, p. 9198, Stationery Office, Dublin: 1948.

stage further in 1949 when the head of the inter-party government which had taken office in the previous year made an important speech to the Institute of Bankers in Ireland.[41] Mr. Costello said that:

Only by large-scale investment can we increase the national wealth of the country or absorb the resources of land and labour which are at present idle. Some of our capital investment will be capable directly of earning revenue. Other kinds, such as housing, will bring social and economic benefits which cannot be measured directly in terms of money, but which are, at present, just as indispensable to the national well-being as directly revenue earning assets... It would scarcely be possible to finance such capital expenditure entirely from the current resources of the community. The Government are satisfied, however, that the need for this investment is so great and the social and economic advantages it will bring so obvious that they are fully justified in drawing, in part, on past national savings to finance it.'

Mr. Costello also announced that the 1950 budget speech would expressly distinguish capital from current expenditure.

This departure was assisted greatly by the availability of Marshall Aid and by the great increase in external assets caused by the contraction of imports during the war. The first source of assistance, however, dried up only a year later;[42] the second was obviously a wasting asset. Nevertheless these policies were pressed by Mr. Costello's government, by the Fianna Fáil government which was in office between 1951 and 1954, and again by Mr. Costello's second inter-party government between 1954 and 1957. They came under increasing criticism, notably in the reports of the Central Bank between 1950 and 1952, as being slanted towards projects that yielded little or no return and being unduly dependent on the liquidation of past savings, so producing continual deficits in the balance of payments and an erosion of external assets.[43]

It is reasonable to conjecture that the acute balance of payments difficulties in 1955–6 hastened a reconsideration of public investment policy. In November 1956 a Capital Advisory Committee was appointed to 'consider and advise, with full regard to the needs and interests of the national economy, on the volume of public investment from time to time desirable, the general order of priority appropriate for the various investment projects, and the manner in which each project shall be financed'.[44] The Committee published a first report in January

41. On 19 November 1949. A not notably sympathetic summary will be found in the *Journal of the Institute of Bankers in Ireland*, January 1950, pp. 6–7.

42. In December 1950, Ireland enjoyed the distinction, which might or might not have been welcome, of being one of the first countries from which Marshall Aid was withdrawn as being no longer necessary.

43. These issues are also discussed by D. Walker, *The Allocation of Public Funds for Social Development*, Economic Research Institute, Dublin, Paper No. 8.

44. Mr. John Leydon was chairman; the other members were William Bland; Professor Charles Carter; General M. J. Costello; P. K. Lynch; K. McCourt; C. K. Mill; R. Roberts; W. J. L. Ryan.

1957 on the capital budget for 1957–8; a second, with minority reports, on the provision of capital for housing, in November 1957; and a final report on the general effect of investment in January 1958. These reports should be read in conjunction with a most valuable paper read to the Statistical Society by Mr. T. K. Whitaker (then newly appointed as Secretary of the Department of Finance) in June 1956.[45]

Mr. Whitaker then proceeded to a full-scale examination of the functions of investment policy in Ireland. His study, *Economic Development*, was published at the end of 1958.[46] It is a major work on national economics and covers all the branches of production. Its aim was defined, in the author's own words, as

(*a*) to highlight the main deficiencies and potentialities of the economy and
(*b*) to suggest the principles to be followed to correct the deficiencies and realize the opportunities, indicating a number of specific forms of productive development which appear to offer good long-term prospects.[47]

This immensely important survey formed the basis for the official *Programme for Economic Expansion* which was issued by the Government as a White Paper and laid before both Houses of the Oireachtas in November 1958.[48] A general introduction stressing the need to redefine the objectives of economic policy was followed by sections dealing with the needs of agriculture, fisheries, forestry and forestry problems, and industry. A concluding section considered the cost of the proposals made—£220m. in the five-year period from 1959–60 to 1963–4.[49]

The programme of public capital investment outlined in the White Paper covered the period from the beginning of the financial year 1959–60 to the end of the financial year 1963–4. It contemplated a capital expenditure of £220.5m. The principal objects of outlay may be set out in round figures as—building and construction, £70m.; agriculture, forestry, and fisheries, £56m.; industry, £36m.; fuel and power, £32m.; communications, £23m.; and tourism, £3m.[50]

This proposed allocation of expenditure may be compared with the constituents of the State capital programmes in the years 1947–8 to

45. 'Capital Formation, Saving and Economic Progress', *JSSISI*, 1955–6, p. 184.
46. Pr. 4803, Stationery Office, Dublin.
47. *Economic Development*. Introduction.
48. Pr. 4796, Stationery Office, Dublin.
49. Useful comments on the White Paper and *Economic Development* will be found in 'Symposium on Economic Development', *JSSISI*, 1958–9, p. 112; in *IBR*, March 1959, and in *JIBI*, January 1959. See also David O'Mahony, 'Economic Expansion in Ireland', *Studies*, 1959, 129.
50. Proposed expenditure on agricultural and industrial credit is included under agriculture, etc., and industry. Communications comprise telephones, transport, ports, harbours and airports.

TABLE 8.6

Projected and actual public investment (£ million) during first economic programme, 1959-64

	1958-9	1959-60		1960-1		1961-2		1962-3		1963-4		5-year period	
	Actual	Projected	Actual	Projected	Actual	Projected	Actual	Projected	Actual	Projected	Actual	Projected	Actual
Building and construction													
Housing	6.53	9.87	7.79	9.67	9.03	8.67	9.20	8.17	10.74	n.a.	12.52	n.a.	49.28
Sanitary and miscellaneous services	1.78	2.30	1.39	2.30	1.84	2.25	2.10	2.00	2.32	n.a.	3.36	n.a.	11.01
National and vocational schools	1.42	1.50	1.70	1.50	1.32	1.50	1.69	1.50	2.27	n.a.	2.60	n.a.	9.58
Other building and construction	0.49	1.55	0.68	1.55	1.03	1.55	0.84	1.40	1.69	n.a.	2.96	n.a.	7.20
Total	10.22	15.22	11.56	15.02	13.22	13.97	13.83	13.07	17.02	12.50	21.44	69.78	77.07
Ports, harbours, and airports	0.91	1.65	1.55	1.55	2.24	1.60	2.65	1.65	2.44	1.40	2.99	7.85	11.87
Tourism	0.02	0.30	0.07	0.35	0.09	0.45	0.18	0.60	0.35	0.85	0.52	2.55	1.21
Agriculture	5.48	7.46	10.98	7.90	10.56	8.60	14.71	7.20	13.50	6.50	13.09	37.66	62.84
Agricultural credit	0.65	0.90	0.84	1.45	0.80	2.10	1.12	2.85	1.55	3.70	1.60	11.00	5.91
Forestry	1.14	1.00	1.31	1.00	1.49	1.00	1.52	1.00	1.63	1.00	1.94	5.00	7.89
Fisheries	0.17	0.40	0.30	0.50	0.20	0.50	0.13	0.55	0.17	0.60	0.29	2.55	1.09
Fuel and power	7.60	6.74	7.45	6.88	7.40	7.16	7.68	5.74	11.25	5.30	13.40	31.82	47.18
Telephones	1.45	1.65	1.35	1.95	2.10	1.95	2.40	1.95	3.68	1.95	4.50	9.45	14.03
Transport	6.27	1.57	4.80	0.83	8.34	1.08	4.05	1.02	3.97	1.02	6.32	5.52	27.48
Industry	0.54	0.80	1.14	3.10	1.71	3.40	3.19	4.35	5.31	4.65	8.37	16.30	19.72
Industrial credit	2.81	3.50	2.08	3.50	2.52	4.00	4.09	4.00	3.55	5.00	3.47	20.00	15.71
Radio Eireann	—	—	—	—	0.10	—	1.35	—	0.30	—	0.25	—	2.00
Miscellaneous (inc. National Development Fund)	0.63	0.50	0.66	0.46	0.50	—	0.34	—	0.38	—	1.48	0.96	3.36
Grand Total	37.89	41.69	44.09	44.49	51.27	45.81	57.24	43.98	65.10	44.47	79.66	220.44	297.36

Source: *Current Budget Statistics*

1955–6 inclusive. In that period the sum of £227.5m. was expended, much the same as that proposed for the First Programme.[51] Its composition was notably different—building and construction, £103.5m.; fuel and power, £55.5m.; agriculture, forestry, and fisheries, £31.9m.; industry, £12m.; and communications, £34.4m. Even allowing for the fact that in this synopsis of the two periods of capital investment building and construction includes the provision of schools and hospitals, it is apparent that building was given a high priority over the direct forms of production.

The White Paper of 1958 ended by suggesting that the fulfilment of the programme would result in an increase in real national income at a rate of about 2 per cent per annum. Such a rate would have been, however modest it may now appear, twice that achieved over the period 1949–56 as a whole. In the event, the achievement has been much better—4.3 per cent a year over the period 1959 to 1963 and somewhere between 4.0 and 4.5 per cent in 1964. Both the amount of public capital investment and its effect on real national income were heavily underestimated.

Table 8.6 shows that the programme went far beyond its anticipated expenditure. This was most apparent in the case of transport, where expenditure was five times greater than the estimate. It was also true in the cases of agriculture, fuel and power, and telephones. On the other hand fisheries and tourism fell below the estimate.[52]

The Second Programme for Economic Expansion was published in two parts. The first[53] appeared in August 1963 and provided a preliminary approach. The second[54] appeared in July 1964 and was very much more detailed. It contemplated investment programmes covering the period up to 1970. The annual growth rate of gross national product in real terms was put at 4.3 between 1964 and 1970. The agricultural programme contemplated an annual average growth rate in gross agricultural product of 3.8 per cent over the same period. The target for industrial growth was put at 7 per cent, a rate of growth which, it was hoped, would vary greatly between various industrial groups. All the assumptions, especially those relating to agriculture, rested on the proposi-

51. Based on Table 10 of Mr. Whitaker's paper to the Statistical Society already cited and, for 1955–6, on the *Irish Statistical Survey*, 1955, Pr. 3630, Stationery Office, Dublin, p. 42.
52. Cf. G. Fitzgerald, 'The First Programme for Economic Expansion', *IBR*, September 1963.
53. *Second Programme for Economic Expansion*, Part i, Pr. 7239, Stationery Office, Dublin: 1963.
54. *Second Programme for Economic Expansion*, Part ii, Pr. 7670, Stationery Office, Dublin: 1964. There is a more detailed discussion of agricultural expansion in *Agriculture in the Second Programme for Economic Expansion*, Pr. 7697, Stationery Office, Dublin: 1964. An article on the Second Programme will be found in the *Irish Banking Review*, September 1964.

tion that Ireland will have become a member of the European Economic Community by 1970.

The amount of public capital expenditure contemplated has been very greatly increased over the levels of the First Programme. It is put at an annual average of £94.9m. in the six years 1964–5 to 1969–70, representing a total of £569m. The constituents appear in Table 8.7. It will be seen that the largest sums involved are in building and construction (which is expected to be increasingly concerned with schools, hospitals, etc.), agriculture, transport and telephones, and fuel and power.

TABLE 8.7

Estimate of public capital programme (£ million), 1963–4 to 1969–70

	1963/4 (actual)	1964/5	1965/6	1966/7	1967/8	1968/9	1969/70 (estimate)
1. Building and Construction:							
(i) Housing	12.12	15.33	20.07	22.62	25.57	28.13	29.56
(ii) Sanitary and miscellaneous services	4.13	4.06	4.02	3.47	3.54	4.50	5.75
(iii) Education	2.69	4.81	6.07	4.88	7.32	10.78	11.12
(iv) Hospitals	1.04	1.81	2.42	3.14	3.63	3.30	3.60
(v) Other building and construction	1.96	1.31	1.38	0.93	1.09	1.13	1.62
TOTAL	21.94	27.32	33.96	35.04	41.15	47.84	51.65
2. Ports, harbours, and airports	2.65	1.49	1.50	1.78	2.53	3.53	5.06
3. Tourism	0.50	0.69	0.87	0.93	1.29	2.15	2.20
4. Agriculture (including arterial drainage)	12.42	14.63	13.10	12.97	13.93	15.46	14.14
5. Agricultural credit	2.40	5.02	5.80	3.76	4.28	5.19	5.25
6. Forestry	1.81	1.85	1.54	1.82	1.93	2.03	2.58
7. Fisheries	0.30	0.21	0.53	0.42	0.62	0.70	0.93
8. Fuel and power	15.26	15.26	13.53	14.51	14.58	18.95	19.82
9. Telephones	4.61	6.10	6.75	5.90	6.10	6.40	7.50
10. Transport	6.29	13.37	9.37	9.14	10.68	19.99	31.94
11. Industry	7.19	8.25	7.41	7.64	9.80	14.13	18.65
12. Industrial credit	2.58	2.87	4.03	3.07	2.77	4.53	5.86
13. Radio Telefís Eireann	0.07	0.33	0.61	0.40	0.50	0.53	0.70
14. Miscellaneous	0.48	0.42	0.29	0.26	0.25	0.13	0.53
TOTAL	78.50	97.81	99.29	97.64	110.41	141.56	166.81

The Third Programme for Economic and Social Development (the change in title is interesting) was published in March 1969. It contemplates an annual growth rate of four per cent over the four years 1969–72 compared with an annual rate of three per cent achieved under the Second Programme in 1964–7. It aims at an increase of 16,000 in total employment over the period. It is assumed that the number leaving agriculture each year will be about 9,000. Against this, it is expected that industrial employment will grow by 31,000 over the next four years. In 1964–7 it grew by 19,000.

The Programme leans very heavily on industrial production and the export trade. The growth target set for gross agricultural production is

1.75 per cent each year. (The target set by the Second Programme was 2.9 per cent per annum: the achievement, in 1964–7, was 0.9 per cent.) Reliance is placed on cattle, milk, milk products, and pigs. On the other hand the principal industrial groups are expected to show an annual average output growth of 6.7 per cent, ranging from 4.5 per cent in food, drink, and tobacco to 9.0 per cent in structural clay, cement, and mining, and 9.4 per cent in chemicals, metals and engineering.

Total exports of goods and services are set to increase each year by 9 per cent. If this were to be achieved, and it is much more than was done in the very good exporting years of the middle 1960s, it would mean that exports would rise from 35 per cent of gross national product in 1968 to 43 per cent in 1972. It seems that the greater part of this increase is to come from new industries entering production.[55]

55. Cf article on the Third Programme in *IBR*, March, 1969.

Part Two

CHAPTER NINE

Political Theories and Economic Facts

AN IRISH PARLIAMENT HAS SAT IN DUBLIN FOR MORE THAN forty years. It exercises functions that are immeasurably greater than were claimed during the struggle for Home Rule. If the possession of legislative power could by itself regenerate a country, the process of national development would be far advanced by now. But the population is smaller now than it was forty years ago; and the rate of economic growth has been much slower than was hoped. Fortunately, the achievement has been more encouraging in recent years. Nevertheless, it would be salutary to consider why the hopes of previous generations are only now beginning to move towards fulfilment. It might be more useful still to consider how far those hopes were practicable.

The most obvious weaknesses of the economy are not new. The Irish people have been accustomed to poverty and depopulation. At the end of the nineteenth century, not yet a lifetime away, a young German economist decided to visit Ireland so that he might 'study backward economic life in the one western country where it had been preserved'.[1]

In the past, however, it was possible to believe that these evils were the result of alien government and that they could and would be removed by native government. It was only a short step further to the belief that native government would remove them almost at once, at the worst within a generation. These are propositions that should be analysed. We must examine the causes of apparent failure and consider how far hopes of rapid improvement have a solid basis. If the expectations are pitched too high, disillusionment is inevitable.

There were, and still are, many instances of confused thought. Their origin and nature continue to vary. A few examples must suffice. In the circumstances of 1922 there was an immediate conflict between political

1. Moritz Bonn, *Wandering Scholar*, Cohen & West, London: 1949, p. 82.

and economic considerations. Its soil and climate had disposed Ireland to the production of livestock and livestock products; its geographical position and political history combined to ensure that this output would be sent to Great Britain. That market was not only the nearest to the Irish producer, it was also the richest and the most attractive. To strengthen the connection with the British market was therefore the most obvious common-sense if matters were viewed in terms of economics. But economic common-sense seemed incompatible with true independence if viewed in the nationalistic terms which were dominant in the 1920s. To foster trade with Great Britain was to strengthen the imperial ties which the nation had lately attempted to break: to foster that trade by increasing exports of livestock was worse again because it perpetuated a type of production which demanded little labour. These objections did not prevent the British market being cultivated with success: but they illustrated a conflict between commercial policy and political feeling which was to appear more clearly in the 1930s, to be repeated then in other fields of economic policy.

Other causes of confusion touched deeper issues. An Irish state had been established with great sacrifice to ensure that Irish people should henceforward be able to live their lives in their own way, ruled by their own values. What did that imply? Was the purpose of public policy to make the economy more efficient in its production and marketing or (what was not at all the same thing, in a short run at least) to provide more employment and check emigration? Was the national aim to strengthen trading links with the rest of the world or to retire into self-sufficiency so as to restore in seclusion an impaired national identity?

These were not abstract issues. Their impact on policy is most obvious in the controversies which raged in the 1920s and 1930s over agricultural policy. If greater trade was desired, then it was clearly necessary to concentrate on producing those things that could be produced most easily in Irish conditions. If self-sufficiency was the aim, then farmers should be induced to adopt a different pattern of production in which livestock and livestock products would count for less and wheat for more. This at once raised the issue whether the farmer should regard his occupation as one from which he might obtain the greatest possible profit or as a means of providing food for the immediate needs of the community. Was agriculture, to put it another way, a business or a way of life?

Forty years later, it is perhaps possible to reach an answer to this question which will receive more general agreement than was possible in the 1920s. But, as long as controversy raged, it was not to be expected that public policy would obtain the fullest return. There were other issues of the same nature. For example, it was (and is) taken for granted that the justification of self-government was to provide a better life for the Irish people and it was (and is) assumed that a better life meant a better life in Ireland. But suppose it did not? Suppose that many of the Irish people decided that life abroad was preferable to anything that could be provided in Ireland? Suppose, in other words, that there was a clash between the interests of the Irish individual and those of the Irish state. We are not, perhaps, much nearer to a solution of this dilemma today. But it is now possible to see that it exists: no such suspicion vexed the hopes of 1916.

The issues which have confused thought since then may be traced to a number of assumptions which had acted as a source of inspiration in the national struggle. The origin and purpose of these assumptions must be remembered. Very often, they were first formulated by political writers in the eighteenth and nineteenth centuries. The circumstances in which those writers lived differed as widely as their definitions of legislative independence would have varied. But popular tradition has blended the centuries as fully as it has obliterated divisions of political, social, and religious belief. In this manner, claims that originally might have been reasonable enough were reiterated decades after they had lost any relevance to contemporary conditions. In the first half of the eighteenth century it may have been all very well to assert that only the commercial restraints held Ireland back from equality with Great Britain. To make the same claim at the beginning of the present century, with the Union substituted for the commercial restraints, was another matter altogether. But it was made; and it has been made many times since, often with some tag from an eighteenth-century writer tacked on as a warranty of its truth. Years ago, Æ remarked that Irish history was a shadow cast by the thoughts of Molyneux, Swift, and Tone. Much the same might have been said about Irish economics.

Some of these propositions can be seen to be ridiculous in the light of what we now know to have been the course of events. But the true absurdity lies not with their authors, who wrote for their time and the encouragement of their generation, but with those in later years who repeated them long after they had lost whatever truth they originally possessed. A peculiarly arid form of traditionalism may be discerned in this repetition of past claims. It is no wonder that another Irish writer, whose name stands in the succession to Swift, should have remarked that 'Ireland is at this moment a regular rag and bottle shop of superseded ideas'.[2]

Traditional assumptions

Some of these ideas have not yet gone out of circulation. It will be useful to examine them in greater detail if only because, in the vicissitudes of economic prosperity, they may sometime regain their strength.

2. George Bernard Shaw in *The Irish Statesman*, 15 September 1923. The views of another Irish writer will be found in the Barney Kiernan chapter of *Ulysses*.

The first is *that the economic development of Ireland was retarded by British misgovernment*. This proposition formed part of the classic case for the repeal of the Legislative Union; but it can be traced back to the eighteenth-century struggle to establish the rights of the old Irish parliament. It is deeply embedded in Irish thought; and it contains a great measure of truth. Here, as so often, the task is to separate the exaggeration from the fact.

Irish readers may not now be as disposed as once they were to ascribe every misfortune to alien government. But the statement of claim against British rule will be long and supported by high authority. It may begin with Swift, who noted that:

Ireland is the only kingdom I ever heard or read of, either in ancient or modern history, which was denied the liberty of exporting their native commodities and manufactures whenever they pleased.[3]

Half a century later his words were echoed by Adam Smith, who referred to the 'invidious restraints which at present oppress the trade of Ireland'.[4] A century later, there were other grounds for complaint. Although he opposed Home Rule, Lecky argued that, if the Irish parliament had survived into the 1840s, it would have averted the worst consequences of the Famine by forbidding the export of cattle and grain.[5] At the very end of the nineteenth century, the contention that Ireland was over-taxed relatively to the rest of the United Kingdom received some support from a Royal Commission.[6]

All this is true enough; but it ignores the other side of the account. There was a great deal of ameliorative legislation in the closing decades of the Union. The code of Land Purchase Acts began effectively in 1885. In the 1890s, the establishment of the Congested Districts Board gave the west the most successful State board that had ever operated in Ireland. A little later, the Department of Agriculture and Technical Instruction was established. In the years before 1914, the social legislation of the Liberal government was highly beneficial to many sections of the community. It is not to be argued that the later good outweighed the earlier evil; nevertheless it should be remembered that the later stages of British rule brought several measures of advancement.

But 'advancement' could have as sinister a sound to Irish ears as had 'amelioration' to John Mitchel. The good intentions of the nineteenth century could be as pernicious as the undisguised hostility of the eighteenth. One example provides an instance of British benevolence and a

3. In *A Short View of the State of Ireland*.
4. *The Wealth of Nations*, Book v, chapter iii.
5. *Leaders of Public Opinion in Ireland*, vol. ii Longmans, Green, London: 1903, p. 303.
6. *Final Report of the Commission on the Financial Relations between Great Britain and Ireland*, C. 8262, HMSO, London: 1896.

hostile Irish reaction. In 1862 the then Lord Lieutenant, the Earl of Carlisle, visited the Spring Show of the Royal Dublin Society. In a speech he remarked that:

... coupling the physical condition of the country with the close proximity of those large English and Scotch markets, where there is such a vast consumption of meat, I believe that Providence has mainly appointed Ireland to be the mother of flocks and herds, and I consequently believe that she will fare all the better the more truly that she keeps to her natural vocation.[7]

In other speeches the Viceroy emphasized the need to accompany cattle-raising by home-grown feeding, which would of course have maintained the tillage area. His remarks on this subject would have fitted perfectly into the Programmes for Economic Expansion which have emphasized the value of cattle and the need for domestic production of feed. But in the 1860s the conjunction of increasing herds of cattle and a falling population affronted national sentiment in which repugnance to Ireland becoming 'a kitchen-garden to England' was deeply rooted.[8] That repugnance was to be expressed in government policy just seventy years after Lord Carlisle had given his well-intentioned advice.

We now turn to a second proposition, *that the economic development of Ireland depends on the policies adopted by the State.* History provides only too many instances which appear to prove the truth of this proposition. The nineteenth century was dominated by political issues and the influence of purely economic forces was easily overlooked. Lecky wrote of this century:

Very few countries in an equal space of time have been torn by so much political agitation, agrarian crime and seditious conspiracy; have experienced so many great economical and social revolutions, or have been made the subject of so many violent and often contradictory experiments in legislation.[9]

His judgement would have been approved by many who did not share his support of the Union. To nationalists, control of the State and power to frame its policies appeared to be the first and essential step

7. *Viceregal Speeches, etc., of the late Earl of Carlisle*, McGlashan & Gill, Dublin: 1866, p. 188.
8. The point was even better put by a contemporary writer, probably unknown both to the Viceroy and his critics, who described Ireland as 'nothing more than an agricultural district of England, separated by a wide arm of the sea from the country to which it yields grain, wool, horses and cattle, and industrial and military recruits'. *Capital* (1928 edition), p. 778. This quotation from Marx will be found in Strauss, *Irish Nationalism and British Democracy*, Methuen, London: 1951, p. 173.
   This issue is very old. Two centuries earlier still, in his *Treatise on Ireland*, Petty had suggested that a million people should be exported to England and the country turned into a cattle factory.
9. *History of Ireland in the Eighteenth Century*, Longmans, Green, London: 1898, vol. v, p. 480.

towards economic development. To them, the loss of independence had brought about restraints on trade in the seventeenth and eighteenth centuries and equally harmful policies of non-intervention and free trading in the nineteenth. Both by its earlier intervention and its subsequent *laissez-faire*, State policy had inflicted deep and enduring damage on the Irish economy. It appeared to be self-evident that, once the framing of policy was regained by Irishmen, progress would be quickly made.

This opinion was by no means wholly mistaken. It was certainly reasonable to hope that a native government would be more solicitous for Irish prosperity than the most well-intentioned Parliament at Westminster.[10] But it eventually aggravated misjudgements. It concentrated attention on politics so that the influence of economics was ignored or under-estimated. This tendency was strengthened by the fact that both sides in the Home Rule struggle drew freely on Irish economic history as an armoury of arguments. In that controversy, economic growth and decay were attributed to causes that had little to do with economic forces. The prosperity of the north-east was credited, by defenders of the Union, to the race or religion (or both) of its inhabitants or to their loyalty to the Crown, which preserved them from wasting energy in unsuccessful sedition. The poverty of the south and west were equally attributed by assailants of the Union to the manner in which Ireland was subjected to whatever policies best suited the interests of the predominant partner. The benefit to north-eastern industry of a long period in which it was possible to accumulate capital and of the enterprise of a few individuals was ignored. Similarly, the decline of manufactures in the south and west after 1800 was blamed on the commercial clauses of the Act of Union rather than on the progress of the industrial revolution which, Union or no Union, would have destroyed manufacturing in an area where capital was even more scarce than coal.

It must be admitted that to separate politics from economics was as difficult as to distinguish cause from effect. Not even the more ardent nationalists could reasonably blame the British government for the absence of coal: they could and did, with some justice, blame it for the absence of capital. In the pre-occupation with politics, other factors such as thrift, self-reliance, and enterprise were disregarded. The feeling grew that everything depended on what was done, or not done, by the

10. It might also govern according to Irish ideas, which was repugnant to many Members of Parliament. Cf. Henry Fawcett in 1874: 'Governing Ireland according to Irish ideas led straight to Home Rule, and Home Rule simply meant the disruption of the Empire.' Quoted by J. L. Hammond, *Gladstone and the Irish Nation*, Longmans, Green, London: 1938, republished by Cass, 1964, p. 157. But, as Mill had remarked some years earlier, it was then a point of honour with British Cabinets to legislate for Ireland out of their heads.

State. Over a century and a half ago Sir Robert Peel, then Chief Secretary for Ireland, wrote in exasperation:

... everybody in Ireland instead of setting about improvement as people elsewhere do, pester Government about boards and public aid. Why cannot people in Ireland fish without a board if fishing ... be so profitable?[11]

His successors in the government of Ireland since 1922 must harbour similar thoughts at times.[12]

A third proposition followed easily from the first and second, *that self-government would almost at once bring economic recovery and prosperity.* A wealth of quotations may be found in the speeches and writings of the nineteenth century, during O'Connell's campaign for Repeal of the Union or later during Parnell's fight for Home Rule. The claims of the 1840s and of the 1880s again echo the earlier struggle for legislative independence in the preceding century. Swift has already been quoted: Molyneux wrote in the same vein before him and Berkeley after him. O'Connell, even in his most expansive moments, could not have pitched his expectations higher than a friend of Wolfe Tone who said in 1791 that:

... if Ireland were free and well-governed ... she would in arts, commerce and manufactures, spring up like an air balloon and leave England behind her at an immense distance. There is no computing the rapidity with which she would rise'.[13]

Twenty-five years earlier, a pamphleteer looked forward to 'a rich and happy people, abounding in plenty, wealth and population', once the commercial restraints had been removed. In the nineteenth century as in the eighteenth, the one thing taken for granted was that Ireland would flourish and prosper the moment self-government was obtained. In the twentieth century Pearse and Griffith shared the same hopes and aspirations, though they may have expressed them in a different idiom.

Few nationalists argued otherwise. Any reservations on the immediate adequacy of self-government might have been interpreted as cloaking opposition to the patriotic claim. Even after fifty years it is still difficult to eradicate the feeling that self-government has failed because it has not brought immediate prosperity and the solution of all economic problems.

Two points have been disregarded. The first is that it has always

11. Quoted by R. B. McDowell, *Public Opinion and Government Policy in Ireland, 1801–1846,* Faber & Faber, London: 1952, p. 211.

12. They should also ask themselves if their policies have not aggravated rather than cured the evil.

13. Dr. McDowell's *Irish Public Opinion, 1750–1800,* Faber & Faber, London: 1944, is most suggestive on this point. The quotation is taken from this book and will be found in *The Life of Theobald Wolfe Tone,* edited by his son, William Theobald, and published in Washington by Gales & Seaton, 1826, vol. i, p. 143.

been much more easy to destroy than to build. The loss of commercial freedom may have quickly brought a decline in trade and manufactures. It did not follow that the restoration of that freedom would reverse the decline immediately. The second is that a self-governing country might, by the very achievement of freedom, be less rather than more able to solve its problems. Separation from the United Kingdom, for example, has meant that Irish farmers do not enjoy the far-reaching advantages of their colleagues across the Irish Sea. Their capacity to sell in the British market has been drastically reduced. The British government is free to support British farmers against Irish producers in a manner which would have been quite impossible if both were still joined in one state. Many people have become so used to regarding political sovereignty as the ultimate prize that they have forgotten that it does not necessarily bring every other gift in its train.

A further proposition is implicit in what has gone before, *that the future of the economy will be determined by what happens in Ireland.* From the belief that economic decline had been caused by the loss of legislative independence, it was a short step to the belief that economic recovery would lie wholly within Irish control when the machinery of government had been recaptured. Here again, high authority can be cited. It is now over two centuries since Berkeley posed the query whether the Irish could not live and prosper if their island were surrounded by a brazen wall. The concept has been agreeable to those in later generations who wished to sever all links with Great Britain, including those of trade, and Berkeley may be regarded almost as a contemporary writer, so great has been his influence over economic thought in recent decades.

But while the Irish state is a political unit, it is not necessarily an economic unit. Few countries are so open to external influences, economic, political and cultural. The fact that so many people have settled abroad and retain contact with their relatives at home means that the ties between Ireland and Great Britain (and North America and the Antipodes) are exceptionally close. The Irish people at home thus possess an acute awareness of what is happening elsewhere. Appearances may suggest an isolated agrarian community; in reality changes in the prospects of employment across the Atlantic or the Irish Sea are known and assessed in the Irish countryside with remarkable rapidity. When the long-established emigration to the United States declined in 1930, some observers hoped for the end of emigration as an institution. Within six or seven years, recovery and rearmament in Britain had attracted a new movement of migrants which, ever since, has progressed as easily as the old.

Prosperity in the United States or full employment in the United Kingdom may therefore cause emigration irrespective of conditions in Ireland itself. The volume of trade carried on by the Irish economy is comparatively large for its size. But the composition and the volume of the export trade may be largely determined, as has happened in recent years, by the policies adopted in the United Kingdom to support British agriculture. On the import side, a sharp change in world prices such as occurred in 1950–1 may turn the balance of payments topsy-turvy. At any time the economy may be affected by influences which are wholly outside the power of an Irish government to control. This is rarely understood. It was, for example, disappointing to see that comment on the First and Second Programmes for Economic Expansion almost completely ignored the possibility that large parts of the policies proposed might be made impossible or unnecessary by changes in markets, prices, or interest rates.

In discussing the bedevilment of policy by assumptions inherited from the past, it is only fair to remember that the Irish experience has not been exceptional. The traditions of other subject peoples have been equally chiliastic. It is, after all, natural that discontented peoples should console themselves with dreams of the future. It is not accounted unworthy if their leaders encourage them by infusing such dreams with the most unbounded hopes of prosperity and power in the future. Every subject people has seen its visions. Most of them have been disappointed by the reality.

What is remarkable about modern Ireland is that these dreams continued long after the attainment of freedom should have brought an awakening. The Irish state has had a more fortunate history than other nation-states which emerged after the First World War; but good fortune does not provoke clear thinking and reassessment. Other peoples have had harsher fates and have been forced to bring their concept of themselves and of their prospects into line with reality. Even when the Irish state was established many of the then accepted postulates of economic policy were already out of touch with the facts. The sequence of political, economic, and commercial changes in the world since the 1920s has made confusion worse confounded.

Distrust of change

A refusal to recognize change is, no doubt, closely linked with a feeling that few changes are necessary. This feeling is perhaps less generally held than it was in the years after 1922: as Bagehot remarked, 'nothing changes the mind of a community more than a change of generation'. But for a long time achievement of self-government appeared to induce a sense of completion. Several forces combined to produce this result. The Irish revolution was political. The causes and interests typified by men such as Connolly, Æ, or Douglas Hyde became subsidiary to the main struggle. After 1922 they never regained the impetus they had possessed before 1916 because the revolution ended, for that time at least, in division and disillusionment. But there were deeper causes at work. The Irish community has been profoundly conservative; and the forces which influence it have been preservative rather than innovatory. Socially, it is difficult to introduce dynamism into a way of life in which the family rather than the individual is still the characteristic unit. In political terms therefore the Irish revolution was essentially conservative. The new state was not inclined towards sweeping changes. The changes that it did introduce, in educational policy and in the encouragement of wheat-growing, to give two widely differing examples, were presented as a return to the past rather than as a step towards the future. When public policy is directed towards restoration of what has been, it is likely to ignore what may be expected in the future.

In an economy so open as the Irish, changes cannot be avoided by ignoring them. But an attitude of distrust, of suspicion that every change must be for the worse, may mean that every beneficial turn of events may be ignored. Two examples may be given. Until the closing decades of the last century the Irish farmer possessed the great advantage of proximity to the British market. That advantage has been steadily reduced by improvements in transport and in the preservation and packaging of foodstuffs. That is fully realized and often lamented. It is not equally appreciated that these developments give an equal opportunity to Irish agriculture to process its livestock products and vegetables so that they can be sold in markets which even twenty years ago were inaccessible but today are comparatively easily reached.

In a quite different sphere, the last generation has seen a profound change in the social structure of rural Ireland. When wants were comparatively few and many of the things then most appreciated in country life were cheap, it was possible for a farmer's brothers and sisters to remain on the family holding and lead a secure if narrow life. The transition to a cash economy has almost destroyed that contentment. Today these brothers and sisters (the 'relatives assisting' as they are described by the census) leave the farm to earn money. The consequent fall in the numbers returned as engaged in agriculture is widely deplored. But it is not all loss. A decade or two ago, the presence of brothers and sisters on the farm was one of the reasons for the low rural marriage rate. The fact that they now leave, which in any other society would be taken as a matter of course, now gives the farmer a better opportunity to marry. This is a change which is not all loss. But the Irish society is suspicious of change.

Possibly this attitude reflects something that lies deep in the national character. It is over fifty years since T. M. Kettle criticized 'this illusion of finality because one sees it everywhere producing a dogmatic conservatism, a feeling of things done and done with, than which there is no greater obstacle to progress'.[14]

Its effect has been to deprive the economy of one of its greatest incentives to development. Few things are more impressive in the modern world than the zeal with which the new States that have emerged since 1945 are reshaping their institutions. In Ireland, however, for many years after independence, the underlying desire was to return to the past rather than to face the future. This may be an honourable sentiment but it is not one that inspires improvement. In particular it lacks appeal to younger people who wish to live in a contemporary world. It may well be one of the contributory causes of emigration in so far as it limits the activities of those who remain. In any case it must weaken that sense of common aim and effort which can inspire the improvement of a society. There is an emigration of the spirit which is as disastrous as its physical form.

This attitude reflects a feeling of frustration, expressed too often in the phrase that *there is no future in the country*. Such an attitude would be a formidable obstacle to progress if it persisted in spite of recent changes. It is possibly explicable when one considers the country's unhappy past and its comparatively narrow present, not to mention the impossible future which has been proposed by excessive optimism. It expresses, however inadequately, the absence of any sense of growth or change, of new things and new ideas, above all of new opportunities or the chance of rising out of the environment into which one is born.

But the phrase can be gravely misleading. It would be instructive to draw up a list of those countries in which, during the last generation, there has been no experience of foreign or civil war, no loss of democratic forms of government, where the Courts have remained open and unfettered, where the plans of parents for their children have not been frustrated by the devaluation of their savings. The list would be short indeed but it would include the Irish state. Other peoples regained their liberties at the same time as the Irish but the Poles, the Czechs, and the Baltic peoples have not enjoyed the same good fortune. More happily, the Irish people have maintained stable government and the rule of law. They have their political problems; and far-reaching emergency measures remain on the statute book; but there is nothing that remotely resembles the tension of political conflict in countries where the past has left a legacy of class war and covert allegiance to a foreign power. It is not only that the Irish state has survived (that might be attributed as much to the exertions of others as to its own), but it has also remained solvent, which was not envisaged fifty years ago. The limited powers which the Home Rule Act of 1914, had it come into operation, would have conferred on a Dublin government have already been indicated.

14. T. M. Kettle, *The Day's Burden*, Maunsel, Dublin: 1910, p. 12.

It was not then thought that the financial resources available would have been sufficient even for such limited responsibilities. But the Irish government today discharges functions which were unthought of then; and its credit is still secure. Its currency is still sound, thus belying prophecies that the public would refuse to exchange British sterling for Irish pounds. Like every other currency in the world, the Irish pound has been devalued in recent decades: it has suffered the erosion of purchasing power which has been almost equally general; but at no time has there been the distrust of it which has made a great country like France so difficult to govern, still less a collapse of its value which has happened twice in Germany during the short lifetime of the Irish state.

There are other advantages which are too easily overlooked: the equable climate and fertile soil of the island, its advantageous geographical position and proximity to the market of the United Kingdom. Despite political changes Irish trade continues to enjoy (admittedly diminishing) advantages in Britain and its principal components, cattle and foodstuffs, although gravely affected by British domestic policies, have not suffered the losses which, as with the Lancashire cotton industry, came from changes of fashion or, as with the coalfields, from technical progress. These matters do not appear clearly in any account of the economy because they have not yet been adequately exploited. Here also may be added the other great natural resource of the nation; the intelligence of its people and their ability to adapt themselves to circumstances. It might well be that if the Irish people thought more about the natural resources with which they and their country have been endowed, and less about the material losses which they have suffered in the past or the difficulties which face them now, the result would be an access of confidence which would increase the one and minimize the other.

To generalize perhaps wildly, our difficulties are not simply that optimism and pessimism lie close together in our temperament. Our ways of thought have been shaped through generations of an apparently hopeless struggle in which the only inspiration to give encouragement was the vision of an Ireland who had shaken off her poverty and, like a princess in a fairy tale, had been restored to her inheritance. Now that the fairy tale has been brought to a penultimate chapter in which the dragon has been slain, we anticipate the ending. We look for a very great deal from our country and we are too easily downcast by every failure of the facts to equal the expectations. An Irish essayist has written of those 'who love Ireland so much that they can forgive her nothing'. The root of our difficulties may lie not only in what the epigram expresses, a proud but unreasonable rejection of imperfection, but also in what it implies, that Ireland is regarded as different from the

Irish people. To idealize our country may have given a sorely needed consolation in the past. In the future the national being can grow and ripen only if we remember that Ireland can never be more than its people and that only their labour, their thought and their spirit can make it better. And if in the future, as must happen at times in life, the performance brings disappointment and discouragement, we should blame ourselves or our mistaken hopes but never our country.

CHAPTER TEN

The Emergent Economy

THE PRECEDING CHAPTER WAS CONCERNED WITH WAYS OF thought which influenced economic policies during the last forty years. They are not yet wholly irrelevant to present circumstances. They are still fashionable in some sectors of policy, and they might regain their strength if anything went wrong with economic policies. Nevertheless, it is to be hoped that they may now be disregarded, except as an explanation of what happened in the past. Signs of change have been multiplied in recent years. The first half of the last decade may prove to be a watershed in the affairs of the country. There is no mistaking the altered tone of public life as one generation gives way to another.

But change has not occurred at an equal pace throughout the economy. There are some sectors where the accustomed land-marks have disappeared; others where the outlook is all too familiar. This chapter will attempt to note some of the principal changes and to set them against other aspects of the economy that by default or misfortune have not experienced an equal rejuvenation.

When the Free State came into existence in 1922 just over one-half of the occupied population was engaged in agriculture and just over two-thirds of the total population lived in the rural areas. The tie with the land was still as close in 1922 as it had been a hundred, or two hundred if it comes to that, years before. In the 1970s a shade less than one-third of the occupied population is still engaged in agriculture and the total population is divided almost equally between the towns and the rural areas. This is a spectacular change, all the more profound because both the working and the total population are smaller now than they were forty-five years ago.

This process is often loosely described as industrialization and it is important to remember what that term means in the Irish context. The Census of Industrial Production returned 264,000 persons as being engaged in industry in 1967. Of these, about one-third was engaged in building and service-type industries and in mining and turf. It is the remaining two-thirds (about 177,000) who may properly be described as being engaged in manufacturing.

These changes have led to alterations in the pattern of economic society which, on account of revised classifications, can only be roughly indicated here. Almost all the 'relatives assisting', who work without regular pay, were and are to be found in agricultural occupations. In 1926 they formed one-fifth of the total of gainfully occupied persons, in 1961 they formed one-tenth. On the other hand, there has been a substantial increase in the proportion of wage and salary earners.

The industries which have grown up under tariff protection since 1924 have been largely based on the processing or assembly of imported raw materials. In general, they have been established around the principal sea-ports, which are also the larger centres of population. This trend has produced quite exceptional results in the case of the capital city and its environs. In 1841 one person in every seventeen lived in the conurbation of Dublin, in 1966, one in every four. Just before the Famine, the rural population out-numbered the urban in the ratio of over five to one. Today the ratio is four to three; and not quite that. Every visible trend still favours the growth of the larger towns, and of Dublin and Cork in particular. In these circumstances, the claim that Irish society is still rural in its way of life, however true that may have been in the 1920s, cannot be admitted today. To sum up the contrast between 1922 and 1970, a great and growing part of the population works in a different way, is paid in a different way and lives in a different way. The change may be welcomed or deplored (sometimes it is welcomed and deplored in the same breath) but it cannot be ignored.

This is in fact a double change; in the type of work done and in the form of its remuneration. There has been a movement of the occupied population out of agriculture into industry and services. Many of those formerly engaged in agriculture did not receive regular wages because they were part of the family labour force. They are now paid wages on a contractual basis. The fall in the numbers working on their own account and in the numbers of relatives assisting while the numbers of wage and salary earners increase is a social as well as an economic change.

This carries some far-reaching implications. The family farm, as it was known forty years ago, provided some form of security for its members. The problems of dependency in youth as well as in old age were tackled within each family to the extent that its resources permitted. Moreover, the farm constituted a constant occupation for the members of the family who remained on it. This system almost certainly led to under-employment of the labour force. It also averted unemployment or redundancy. As long as the family was an economic unit it could cope with many of the personal problems which always arise in life. Social services, such as the old-age pension, supplemented but could not wholly replace the manner in which this social organization discharged its obligations to its members.

Matters are very different when an increasing part of the labour force works for direct monetary reward, outside the social structure of the family. In a cash economy, much greater attention must be paid to problems such as provision for old age and sickness, assistance to widows, the health and education of the young; not to mention the need for compensation for redundancy and for schemes of retraining which a changing economy makes necessary. It is essential to understand that an economic revolution entails a social revolution; and that its fruits will be lost unless provision is made in good time against the human problems that are inseparable from change.

There is one other change to be noted. The mobility of the population (that is to say, the ability to emigrate) is even greater now than it was forty years ago. Emigration was easy enough then but it involved a crossing of the Atlantic and a complete severance of family ties. Today, the emigration is to Great Britain which involves an easier journey than travelling from Derry to Cork. Nowadays, a worker can make his home and a career across the Irish sea while he maintains the closest contact with his relatives in Ireland. The time may come when he may have his home in one country and find work in one or the other country according to circumstances. Our emigrants in Great Britain may remain part of our national life in a sense that was never possible for the emigrants to the United States. If that becomes so, we may have to revise our concept of what effect emigration can have on our economy and society.

To return to those who remain at home, any comparison that can be made suggests a great improvement in their standards of living, and way of life. The marriage rate is still abysmally low; but the age of marriage has fallen in the last forty years, from 35 to 30 for men and 29 to 26 for women; and it continues to fall. Families today have a far better prospect than they had in the 1920s of better housing conditions.[1] By every test, they are much better fed than before: the consumption of calories per head of population in Ireland is one of the highest in the

1. See the Census of Population, 1961, vol. vi. It appears that between 1926 and 1961, the percentage of persons in private households having more than two persons per room fell from 27.2 to 11.5 in the State and, in spite of heavy immigration, from 45.3 to 14.0 in Dublin county borough. Over one-third of the houses in the State and just over one-half of the houses in Dublin county borough have been built since 1919. But the demand still tends to out-run the supply.

world. In the 1920s six in every hundred children aged one year might be expected to die before the age of 15; today the figure is one in every hundred. On the statistics of 1925–27, the expectation of life at birth was 57.4 years for boys and 57.9 for girls. On the figures for 1960–2 it is now 68.1 and 71.9. This represents a notable improvement in public health, housing and the standard of living. Parents now provide more fully for the education of their children than used to be the case.[2] An acknowledgement that much remains to be done should not obscure the very real improvement in the quality of life, so far as it can be measured by statistics such as these.

It is very probable that the country stands on the verge of even greater and more rapid change. A recent study has illustrated demographic trends of the first importance.[3] In the last five years, there has been a considerable increase in the incidence of marriage relatively to the number of people of marriageable age. At the same time, the fertility of marriage remains constant, although at a lower level than ten or twenty years ago. It is suggested that, on the basis of these figures, the population in 1971 will be greater by 100,000 than it was in 1961. That would be an important change in itself, but the composition of the new population can be described as exciting. There would be an increase of 150,000 or more in the number of men and women between 15 and 30 years of age. There would also be an increase in the age-groups under 15 of about 10,000.

It must be remembered that forecasts of population have had an unhappy history in this country. It is never possible to reckon with variations in the force of emigration. It is possible that a high proportion of those who will be under 30 in 1971 may have left the country by then. Nevertheless, if the experience of the 1960s is even reasonably favourable, the population will have been rejuvenated within an amazingly short space of time. To have so many people in the younger age-groups would be not only a change of the first magnitude in itself, it would assuredly be the cause of further social and economic changes. Here again, we may perceive the loom of new problems—in housing, health services, and the provision of schools—against which a prudent society should make timely provision.

There are other things that have hardly changed at all or only in a very small degree. Many towns and districts have achieved a higher level of activity and prosperity by the establishment of factories. Nevertheless the dependence on agriculture of large areas such as Connacht

2. Students in secondary schools numbered 22,900 in 1924–5 and 104,000 in 1966–7; in technical schools (full-time) 2,500 in 1929–30 and 39,800 in 1966–7; in universities 3,200 in 1924–5 and 15,600 in 1966–7.
3. C. E. V. Leser, 'Recent Demographic Developments in Ireland', *JSSISI*, 1964–5, p. 179.

has not been modified in any appreciable degree. This is the more important on account of the rapid changes in the balance between agriculture and industry. In 1926 agriculture contributed twice as much to the national income as industry. As lately as 1957 it still contributed more. Since that year, the contribution from industry has been greater, and the difference between the two sources continues to grow greater each year. The urbanized areas of the country are increasingly more prosperous than those containing a higher proportion of rural dwellers. This is a familiar result of industrial growth and in itself presents no cause for alarm. There is no reason to regret the prosperity of the cities. But it is highly unfortunate that the widening of the gap between industrial and agricultural incomes should be so greatly attributable to the comparative depression of agriculture in recent years.

This affects the pattern of personal expenditure. It goes without saying that the city dweller spends his money in a different fashion from the countryman. He has also more to spend on the semi-luxuries of life which are readily available. On another level, the furnishing and maintenance of new houses demand purchases which are quite different from those that would be made by a rural society. This was well illustrated by a study of trends in personal expenditure between 1960 and 1970.[4] It suggested that expenditure on durable goods would almost double in real terms in that period. On the other hand the increase in demand for commodities such as food and clothing would be much smaller. Such changes in the nature and scale of expenditure originate in the cities and will be followed in the countryside.

The implications for the balance of payments are obvious. As the economy is constituted, increasing industrial production and an improving standard of living depend on the availability of imports, which in its turn depends on the capacity to export. Agriculture is still the major exporting industry of the country. Two contradictory trends thus appear—that industry has grown more rapidly than agriculture by any test, such as income, output or numbers engaged, nevertheless (or rather, as a result) the importance of the export capacity of agriculture has increased rather than diminished.

4. Cf. C. E. V. Leser, 'The Pattern of Personal Expenditure in Ireland', *JSSISI*, 1963-4, p. 1.

NATIONAL INCOME, SAVINGS, AND INVESTMENT

It is a characteristic of estimates of national income and expenditure everywhere that they must exclude many transactions which do not receive a monetary reward. In spite of all the changes that have been noted, many sectors of the Irish society do not rely on contractual relationships and are either unpaid or paid less than the market rate. The national income might look a greater deal larger if all the work done by religious communities in schools and hospitals were to be paid at the market rate. To take another and very different example: it would certainly be larger if Ireland were a member of NATO and had benefited from the flow of American monies which sustained the members of that alliance in the last decade. A great part of life in Ireland is not subject to measurement for national income. The statistics for travel and emigrants' remittances, for example, cannot be accepted as much more than statements of trends.[5] One cannot be precise among such uncertainties; but it is difficult to resist a feeling that the true national income (and the true balance of payments) is rather more favourable than the published estimates suggest.

There has been a considerable redistribution of the national income among the various categories of production. The proportion taken by agricultural profits has gone down while that taken by professional earnings seems to have remained unchanged.[6] On the other hand, the proportion taken by company profits and by non-agricultural wages and salaries has increased. Ireland is moving from a farming and professional society to one that is dominated by industrial and commercial companies and by wage and salary earners. This represents an immensely important shift in the balance of social and economic power. Such changes are much more easily accomplished, and with less injustice, if the total national income grows more rapidly than has been the case in Ireland.

It is usual that three-quarters of personal expenditure has been devoted to consumer goods and services. This is exceptionally high by the standards of European experience in recent years. Many factors have operated to produce this high level of expenditure, such as re-

5. It is possibly arguable whether these remittances are properly reckoned in national income at all.

6. Any statement about Irish agricultural incomes arouses violent controversy; and the validity of statistical measurement is freely impugned. The fact seems to be that the standard of farming and the fertility of land vary so widely that individual examples can be found to discredit any generalization. In all remarks about the income of any section of the community, the social organization should be remembered. Often it is the aggregate income of a family that provides the true picture.

housing, the attainment of more regularly paid employment, and the general consequences of urbanization. It would be difficult to claim, however, that any of these factors have been more powerful in Ireland than in post-war Europe. This may be a result of the break with past ways of living. It is possible that personal expenditure was lower in a previous generation when greater attention was paid to increasing the amount on deposit in the bank.[7] Whatever the cause, a continuance of such high standards of consumption flies in the face of development programmes and must be regarded as a major threat to their eventual success. Enthusiasm at the undeniable success of the First Programme for Economic Expansion has occasionally led commentators into implied comparisons of the Irish achievement with the German *wirtschaftwunder*. These inflated claims should be put aside. Irish expansion has been obtained by the liquidation of past savings and the receipt of foreign capital as well as by abstinence from consumption. It would have been much more sound if there had been more saving and less borrowing and realization of past savings.[8] In a country that is so dependent on foreign trade as Ireland is, there is little enough that can be done within the country to ensure growth. One of the few things that can be done is to spend something less than 15s. in every £1 on personal consumption. Savings are still on too low a level; and their total is liable to oscillate disturbingly from year to year. Too often, a falling off in the rate of saving coincides with a crisis in the balance of payments and recovery is obtained only by restrictive measures designed to restore the balance. It is an expensive way to run a country; and not the least part of the cost is the measureless frustration which is imposed on the more enterprising sections of the community.

It is tempting to leave the matter at this point. It would be symmetrical to say that Irish people do not earn enough; that they do not save enough of what they earn; that they do not invest enough of what they save; and that they do not invest wisely. The undeniable content of truth in such statements should not be obscured by exaggeration. One of the most difficult things to find out about the Irish economy is what exactly people do earn. There is much evidence to show that, at least until very lately, a large number of even non-agricultural incomes were very low indeed.[9] But, granted the strength of family ties and the

7. Which was not directly conducive to growth either.

8. Between 1949 and 1956 current savings fell short of net domestic capital formation by 40 per cent. The shortage was financed by foreign borrowing, investment by foreigners, and the realization of past savings. This process should not be described as a capital investment programme. Cf. T. K. Whitaker, 'Capital Formation, Saving and Economic Progress', *JSSISI*, 1955–6, p. 184. Also A. Kuehn, 'Short-term Aspects of Growth in the Irish Economy', *IBR*, December 1962, p. 21.

9. See L. Reason, 'Estimates of the Distribution of Non-agricultural Incomes', *JSSISI*, 1960–1, p. 42, from which it appears that in 1954 nearly 92 per cent of non-agricultural incomes did not exceed £600 p.a.

degree to which the family is still a social and economic unit, statistics of personal income may be most misleading. The economic strength of many families may well be much greater than is suggested by the individual earning power of their members.[10]

It is also something less than the truth to state that the Irish people do not save enough of what they earn. No doubt the claim is true in the sense that most peoples in the world do not save and never have saved as much as economists and bankers would wish. But it has to be examined in the context of Irish society in the last twenty years. It will not be denied that the greatest change in that period has been the emergence of what is most easily, if a trifle loosely, described as a middle class. The pattern of their expenditure is what might be expected: better housing and the furnishing of homes. They have clearly been prepared, which is greatly to their honour, to spend heavily on the better education of their children. These are important and weighty burdens on income. Savings, moreover, have been gravely hampered by State policy, by the standstill orders on wages and income during the war and by very high direct taxation during most of the period since then.

Nevertheless, it is hardly necessary to point out that the inadequacy of savings has implications which range far outside the field of Political Economy. Savings must come from somewhere if there is to be investment and economic progress. If they do not come from the Irish community, either there will be no progress or the impetus will come from investment by foreigners. This has in fact happened on an appreciable scale during recent years. It has been criticized from time to time on the ground that foreign ownership of our resources is undesirable. Emotive phrases such as 'the national sell-out' or 'the country for sale' have been freely used.

This is a reaction which is easily comprehensible, especially in connection with the ownership of land. It is not peculiar to Ireland. It springs from emotions that run too deep to be measured by economic standards.

No answer based on economic principles can therefore be altogether convincing. Economic progress depends largely though by no means exclusively on the level of investment which in its turn depends on the supply of savings. If the savings do not come in adequate measure from the Irish community, then there will be either no investment and the economy will relapse into its traditional stagnation or the savings will come from abroad and the investment, and its fruits, will be made and enjoyed by foreigners. The community is free to make its own choice in this matter, but if it decides in favour of consumption at

10. See R. C. Geary, 'The Family in Irish Census of Population Statistics', *JSSISI*, 1954–5, p. 1. Further investigations on the lines traced by Dr. Geary and Mr. Reason are badly needed.

the expense of investment there can be no ground for complaint if others step in to profit by the opportunities that it has neglected.

This issue will be with us for decades to come. The changes in the composition of the labour force are not yet ended. It must be expected that urban population will continue to grow, even if the numbers in agriculture became stabilized. The increase in the marriage rate will produce (as it has done already in some degree) an increasing number in the younger age-groups. All this will impose heavy demands in the resources of the community, for housing, for education and to alleviate the burdens of dependency. This must be done while the structure of the educational system, too long neglected, must be overhauled and expanded.

These are only some examples of the manner in which the demand for increased savings will continue for as far ahead as can be foreseen. The community has adopted the aim of an expanding economy. It must now be prepared to pay the price.

CHAPTER ELEVEN

The Balance of Payments

IT IS NOW OVER FORTY YEARS SINCE A QUARTERLY JOURNAL published an article entitled *Are We Living on our Capital?*[1] The purpose of the article was to refute fears of the Irish Free State 'ending its days in the bankruptcy court, if not in a debtor's prison'. Nevertheless, another journal of informed opinion commented shortly afterwards that:

Irish banking statistics for the full year will show that we are beginning to draw on national savings to pay our bills, and if the process continues for long we may have to look for capital abroad if national loans are to be floated.[2]

It will be observed that some aspects of the economy at least have not been greatly changed in the last generation. The balance of payments has provided a problem as persistent as emigration; and arguments will be advanced shortly to suggest that it is a more important obstacle to development.

The most cursory glance at the trade returns of the Republic shows the importance of foreign trade to its economy. Whether total trade be related to the population of the State or to its national income, the ratio is surprisingly high. Ireland is one of the heavier trading countries of Europe.

A complicated situation appears when trade is broken down into imports and exports. The volume of imports fell away during the later 1930s (though not to the degree then expected) and fell to very low levels during the war. It has increased with only minor set-backs (usually reactions from years of abnormally high imports) ever since 1945.

The course of exports has been very different. They fell away in volume (much more heavily than imports) during the 1930s and con-

1. By George O'Brien, *Studies*, 1925, p. 353.
2. *The Irish Statesman*, 7 November 1925.

tinued to decline during the war. Their growth since 1959 has been a cause of justified satisfaction. Nevertheless, the record over the last forty years as a whole has been almost disastrous. The volume of exports reached in 1929 was not exceeded until 1960. Even in terms of depreciated pounds the value of exports in 1929 was not surpassed until 1948. The economy still suffers from this deterioration.

Normally, imports have always been greater in value than exports. The disproportion between them increased during the last generation. At the end of the 1920s the value of exports represented a little over three-quarters of the value of imports. There have been years since then when exports covered only half, sometimes as little as one-third. In recent years, the best achievement has been about two-thirds. Only in the war years, when imports were almost unobtainable, was there an approach to balance.[3]

The volume and value of imports have increased but the content has greatly changed. Today, the imports of finished goods form a smaller part of the total: there is a much higher proportion of raw materials and semi-finished goods. There is also a much higher proportion of capital goods. This is only to be expected from a process of industrialization which was originally based on replacing imports of finished goods rather than on processing raw materials produced at home. On the export side there has been a notable and welcome change from the export of livestock to the export of processed foodstuffs, although the cattle trade is still of paramount importance. Equally there has been, in very recent years, a growth in the export of manufactures which is as promising as, only a few years ago, it seemed unlikely. But the importance of a continued growth in the earning power of the economy in foreign trade can hardly be exaggerated. The ultimate strength of the economy is that even in the worst circumstances it can keep going in some form. It is more than self-sufficient (if a severe limitation of choice be accepted) in the essentials of life. This was seen very clearly during the second war. Ireland in those years never faced the danger of starvation in any sense comparable to the actual experience of large areas of continental Europe or the impending threat in Great Britain; although its people had to accept severe reductions in the standards of comfort to which they had become accustomed. On the other hand, the weakness of the economy is that it cannot provide directly for its peace-time needs out of its own resources. Apart from agriculture and some minerals now in process of development, the natural resources of the country are (so far as is known) exceedingly limited. Many basic raw materials and many forms of consumer goods must be imported. Therefore the standard of living and the maintenance of employment depend on an inward flow of goods. There have been two occasions when that flow was inter-

3. In 1941, and again in 1943 and 1944, there was an export surplus.

rupted; both of them point a moral. In the war years raw materials could be brought in only in very limited quantities. The result was that the volume of production in industries as varied as timber, metalworking, printing and publishing, soap and candle manufacturing fell to less than half the volume of production in 1938. In 1956–7 the necessity to restore the balance of payments led to the imposition of levies on imports. Again, the result was a fall in the volume of production and in the average number engaged in the production of transportable goods. It is tedious to repeat the warning that so much depends on the power to import: but the economy will be in real peril if it is forgotten again.

Our society is much more exposed to reverses, outside or within our control, than it was a generation ago. The early years of the State saw a fall in agricultural prices which directly affected the prosperity of the majority of the population. It was a severe test but it was borne without irremediable political or social strain. Farmers and their families reduced their expenditure and their standard of living. Some years later, after an interlude of comparative recovery at the end of the 1920s, the even more severe test of the depression and the economic war was imposed. Nevertheless the country survived it without economic collapse or, except in a very minor and transient degree, the breakdown of confidence which led so many other peoples at that time to surrender their lives and their fortunes to a dictator. Then, as earlier, a high proportion of the working population was self-employed or working on a non-contractual basis. Many of them, by no means all, had resources to draw upon—the savings made in the good years before 1920.

It has been said very often that a country that could stand the economic war can stand anything. This may be true if it is understood in the ultimate sense already noted. But it should not be assumed that what was possible in the past will be equally possible in the future. People who live in towns are more exposed than rural dwellers to any breakdown in the machinery of exchange. Wages and salaries cannot be adjusted as flexibly as economies can be made by independent producers. Past savings (that is, the external assets) are much lower in proportion to national expenditure than they were. We are much more exposed than we were to the risk of things going wrong. To live prosperously is to live dangerously. It is all the more necessary to realize that mistaken policies can do much greater damage as the economy develops. Even the relatively brief period during which unfavourable trends were allowed to go unchecked in 1954–6 had disproportionately grave effects on employment and earnings. The effects would be much more harmful today.

The choice for Ireland, as Dr. Henry Kennedy said in his minority report in the Smiddy commission on agricultural policy is between exporting goods and exporting people. The choice may not be as clear-cut as the epigram suggests; but it seems certain that there is little hope of maintaining a larger population at its present standard of living, still less of maintaining a growing population at improving standards of living, unless the external earning power of the economy is increased.

It is often taken for granted that the central problem of Irish economics is the fall in population. This simplification obscures the underlying reality. It is not possible to stabilize or increase the population unless the standard of living is acceptable. That cannot be secured without a constant flow of imports which depends in its turn on a healthy balance of payments. It is hardly an exaggeration to state that the balance of payments is the true problem of the Irish economy and that the first step towards reversing the decline of population is to achieve and maintain a payments balance.[4]

MONETARY POLICY AND THE BALANCE OF PAYMENTS

The dependence on imports has deep implications. There is a natural instinct to assume that energetic policies of capital expenditure should be pursued when natural resources are not fully utilized and the labour force is not fully employed. Such circumstances may appear to call for Keynesian policies and for trust in the beneficial results of the multiplier. Unfortunately, the Irish economy is not as simple as that—it is a highly open economy which cannot conduct experiments behind closed doors. The possible results may be judged from what happened in 1956 when credit was freely expanded, regardless of a deficit in the balance of payments, a fall in the value of the external assets at the same time as they were being drawn down and clear signs of a loss of confidence in the future of the economy.[5] The comments of the Central Bank seem as apposite now as they did then, and they will bear repeating lest the same situation should be allowed to develop again. 'Reliance on monetary stimulants', it stated,

postulates that the level of spending determines the level of production and employment. From this oversimplification it is mistakenly concluded that so

---

4. This, of course, is not to be interpreted as meaning a surplus in every year; but in our present circumstances, deficits can be justified only if they are designed to lead to a balance in the future.

5. Of these three conditions, either of the first two can be borne for a while: but to press on with the expansion of credit when all three are present cannot be dignified with the title of a policy.

The limitations of so-called Keynesian policies in the context of the extremely open Irish economy were outlined by T. K. Whitaker in 'Capital Formation, Saving and Economic Progress', *JSSISI*, 1955–6, p. 184. A different approach is made by Marsh, *Full Employment in Ireland*, Browne & Nolan, Dublin: 1945, and by Hooper, *Money and Employment in Ireland*, Fallon, Dublin: 1952.

long as there are unemployed resources within our economy there must be no check to spending. Any effort to restrain credit expansion, for whatever reason, is denounced as harmful to national economic development. It is therefore vitally important to realise fully that domestic credit utilized for external purchases has its counter-part in drafts on external resources and that these should be viewed in the light of the need at all times to preserve the integrity of our currency and our external solvency. Our economic development depends fundamentally on our continued ability to finance the large and growing volume of external trade. Clearly therefore the pursuit of social objectives and greater employment by means of unrestrained domestic credit, to the disregard of monetary stability and of external solvency, would be little short of economic suicide. An expansion of credit is desirable when its purpose is to allow for increased production. It may be inevitable as a consequence of a rise in prices of essential imports. But, unless discretion is thrown to the winds, domestic claims for increased credit cannot be considered without due regard to our external financial position. It is not as widely realized as it should be that the possession of adequate external monetary reserves is a guarantee of political and financial independence. In particular, it must be appreciated that there are circumstances in which external solvency can be maintained only by means of credit restraint.

The connection between domestic credit and external payments is, of course, a feature common to all monetary systems. Inasmuch as it enforces the inescapable dependence of external spending on external income, it is apt to be regarded as a disadvantage limiting the field of independent monetary action. In economies such as ours, characterized by an exceptionally high propensity to import, which is further intensified by large-scale social investment programmes, this limiting influence is felt more acutely. It is important to emphasize that all monetary systems suffer from this 'disadvantage' and seek to reduce its impact by building up and maintaining adequate external monetary reserves which permit an excess of external spending over external income in periods of difficulty.[6]

The reasons for these conclusions can be simply stated. Granted the propensity to import, a rise in expenditure will cause a rise in purchases abroad of raw materials and finished goods. It can therefore be sustained only if foreign earnings are increased at the same time and in the same degree or if external holdings are realized in order to meet the deficit. But if these holdings are reduced incessantly, a stage must be reached where bank liquidity becomes so reduced as to force a limitation of credit. In other words, at that stage it would become impossible to provide employment and higher incomes by means of credit expansion and at the same time to sustain deficits in the balance of payments.[7]

This may appear to be a highly conservative and unimaginative estimate of what monetary policy can do to assist development. The reasons are threefold. First, that the immediate necessity of the economy is to increase exports. That depends ultimately not on monetary

6. *CBR*, 1955–6, p. 37.
7. Unless a depreciation of the Irish pound in terms of sterling is accepted. That possibility is not usually set out as one of the attractions of credit policy.

policies but on acquiring the power to produce better quality goods and to market them properly at competitive prices. Second, that too often monetary policies have been held up as nostrums that will absolve everybody from facing the work and initiative that are required to tackle these problems of production and sale. Third, that the political and economic independence which this State and its governments have enjoyed since 1922 has been based on the possession of external assets. Certainly, an external reserve must not be made a sacred cow. Reserves are built up so that they may be used, and circumstances can easily be imagined in which external assets should be realized.[8] But it would be an unmitigated disaster for the State and for the economy if they were to be squandered incontinently and unprofitably.

These issues have acquired a new importance on account of the manner in which the Second Programme contemplated a series of payments deficits during the remainder of the present decade.[9] The comments of the Central Bank may again be usefully quoted:

From the monetary standpoint it is necessary to express a reservation about proposals which envisage the continuance for a long—and indeed undefined—period of external disinvestment and borrowing. The Central Bank considers it important that persistent deficits in current external payments should not be incurred. Experience shows that when the aim of external equilibrium is accepted it is often difficult to achieve. When that aim is modified there is a danger that the actual outcome may be more unfavourable than has been contemplated, and that in some years it may be so unfavourable that corrective measures—causing both interruption of economic growth and impairment of confidence—may be unavoidable. . . . Eventually of course there is no escape from the discipline of the balance of payments. The effects of deficits can be averted or cushioned for a time by various means, but it is no more possible for a country to have a permanent deficit in its external payments than it is for a business firm to incur permanently an annual loss.[10]

This is a matter on which there is little choice. It is an inescapable obligation of political independence to keep the country externally solvent. A people that has decided to start up on its own must keep its housekeeping accounts and, in the long run, keep them balanced. The alternative, in the long run, is to be obliged to borrow; and in the modern world, to borrow is to incur more than financial obligation.

The balance of payments, then, constitutes a latent threat to the

8. In the last resort this is a matter of common-sense and correct appreciation of circumstances rather than of adherence to theory. To suggest that Keynes may not be applicable to the Irish economy at present is not to insist on obedience to Nassau Senior.

9. Chapter xiv, para. 9: 'The Second Programme, while relying primarily on current savings to finance development, envisages a balance of payments deficit of £16m. in 1970 (at 1960 prices) and deficits in the intervening years of amounts which should not on average exceed that figure. It is considered appropriate to finance these deficits either by reasonable recourse to external reserves or by external borrowing, a general term which includes direct foreign investment in Ireland.'

10. *CBR*, 1963-4, pp. 23-4.

economy. But, if that be agreed, it follows that the degree of the threat should be more accurately measured than has been the case in the past. The payments deficits of 1964 and 1965, for example, disturbed confidence and even provoked loose talk in some quarters of an impending devaluation of the Irish pound. These deficits would certainly have been serious if they had continued; but they were capable of being redressed by comparatively small reductions in consumption and, if necessary, in investment. Their importance was gravely exaggerated. There is need for research into the precise relationship between investment policy and the balance of payments; and for the better education of the public on the relation between payments deficits and the total of the external assets. Dr. Leser has very truly written that:

The truth of the matter is that we do not yet know how to achieve a substantial rate of economic expansion while keeping the rise of prices and the balance of payments under control within desired limits.[11]

It is no consolation that other countries appear to have similar complexities. We will have to live with the problem for many a year to come; and the sooner we learn to understand it the better.

TRADE RELATIONS

For many years after the establishment of the Irish Free State there was no formal agreement governing trade with the United Kingdom. Both countries adopted an all-round tariff within months of each other in 1931 and 1932. When normal trade between them was resumed after the conclusion of the economic war in 1938 it was based on the Trade Agreement of that year. This instrument, amended by subsequent agreements in 1948 and 1960, governed Anglo-Irish trade until the Trade Agreement of 1965. Under its provisions Irish agricultural and industrial exports, with a few exceptions of which the most important was the British duty on Irish man-made fibres, had the right of entry duty free into the United Kingdom. In return, British goods entering Ireland had preferential treatment.

Essentially, this represented a continuation of the concept of Imperial Preference which had been brought to its highest pitch at the Ottawa conference of 1932. It was, however, changed by the developments of the 1950s. The energetic encouragement of British agriculture closed the export market in commodities such as eggs, which had been taken for granted in 1938. Further, the British need to maintain good relations with the other members of EFTA led to regulation of imports by quota, as in the case of butter and bacon in the early 1960s. At the

11. In *The Irish Economy in 1964 and 1965*, ERI Paper No. 27.

same time, the gradual reduction of industrial tariffs in favour of the other members of EFTA reduced the Irish advantage on that side of trade also. Thus the special relationship between the two countries was gradually disappearing. The Irish exporter, farmer or industrialist, was being squeezed between the members of EFTA and the farmers of the United Kingdom.

The agreement of 1965 ensures that Irish cattle exports will not suffer the same regulation by quota as occurred to butter and bacon. It gives some, limited, promise of greater sales of both of these commodities. It contains an undertaking, for what that may be worth, that the British government will in future take Irish export objectives into account. It also removes the British duties on Irish man-made fibres. This is very far indeed from being a triumphant negotiation. These terms would have been regarded as an unmitigated defeat in 1938; and imagination boggles at the thought of the language that Hogan would have used to describe them had they been proposed in his time.

On the other hand, negotiators cannot escape their inheritance from the past. In 1938 both sides were willing and indeed anxious to return to the free trading days of the 1920s, subject to a still relatively light amount of protection and market regulation on both sides. That was not at all the situation in 1965. The British government had incurred heavy obligations to its own farmers, which were politically binding whatever may be thought of their ultimate value to the British economy as a whole.

On their side the Irish negotiators were in peculiar difficulties. Concessions for commodities such as poultry, eggs, and milk were ruled out by British domestic policies. The position in regard to butter and bacon was not promising, on account of the record in preceding years. It is worth recalling that when quotas for butter were first proposed by the British in the late 1950s New Zealand protested against any provision being made for Irish exports to the United Kingdom on the grounds that this country was not a 'traditional' supplier of that market. It could readily have been retorted that Irish butter was sold in Great Britain before the existence of New Zealand had been ascertained. Such a retort would not have been convincing. The record showed that for twenty-five years Irish supplies of butter to Great Britain had been intermittent. The Irish negotiators were handicapped by the past.[12] In such circumstances they could not have been expected to obtain significant concessions. Their most convincing reply to their critics

12. This is not intended as a reference to the policies of the 1930s, though it is obviously true that the Irish bargaining position would have been much stronger if Hogan's insistence on exports had been continued, even in an amended form. In retrospect it seems as if the rot set in during the first half of the 1950s when the present British policies were being formulated and might have been modified by more energetic attention to exports in Dublin.

would have been that the Agreement at least stopped the gradual erosion of the Irish position in the British market and that, with all its imperfections, it was better to have it than to continue to rely on past agreements which were being rapidly emptied of their content.

Little time need be wasted on the spurious emotionalism that criticized the Agreement as a new Act of Union. It is, of course, reversible; and the limitations which it places on economic sovereignty (if such a thing exists) are light compared to those that will be imposed if Ireland becomes a member of the European Economic Community, to say nothing of the implications for political sovereignty. From other quarters it has been objected that the Agreement is not nearly as valuable as even an association agreement with the Community might be, or as full membership, as it is hoped, will be. In this view the Irish government would have been better employed seeking some form of agreement with the Community than in negotiating in London.

Quite clearly, the most clean-cut development would be, as was hoped in 1962, that Ireland and Great Britain should enter the Community together. But one must talk in terms of what is practicable. There does not appear to be any reason to believe that an Irish application for full membership of the Community, without Britain, would be successful. It has been argued, on the analogy of Austria, that an application for association might be entertained by the Community. On the other hand, even the admission of Austria to association (which has not yet happened) would not necessarily prove anything. There are the most obvious differences between the geographical, historical, and social links between Austria and the member countries of the Community compared with the exiguous connections of this country. Moreover, association appears to be regarded as a preparation for full membership. In the last resort, therefore, the question must be asked: would any Irish government sacrifice even the present trading position in the British market for a closer link with the European Community? The advantages of such a course would be very doubtful. The dilemma was forcibly put by Mr. Lemass in July 1964:

All available information, however, points to the conclusion that an essential element in the negotiation of an association agreement with the Community would be the willingness of both of us to join in trading agreements designed to lead to the formation of a customs union between us. . . . There are no grounds for supposing that the Community would contemplate an association agreement with us leading to a customs union while allowing us to retain our preferential arrangements with Britain.[13]

Nevertheless, it must be admitted that the present situation is not satisfactory. A Free Trade Area composed of countries so disparate in their development as Ireland and Great Britain must always be an

13. *PDDE*, 211, 1345–6.

unequal and uneasy association. The two countries have much in common, but it can rarely be to the interest of Ireland to enter into a bilateral relationship with Great Britain. An analogy may be drawn from our political history since the Treaty. In Anglo-Irish relations, Ireland was in a stronger position when it was a member of the Commonwealth and could rely on support from Canada and South Africa than it has been since it left the Commonwealth. In a wider field it has benefited greatly from its participation in the League of Nations and the United Nations. Wide associations suit the interest of this country in commerce as in politics. Membership of the European Free Trade Association has hitherto not been favoured by the Irish government on the ground that the Association is concerned with trade in industrial, not agricultural, products so that Ireland would be obliged to dismantle its tariffs protecting industry without obtaining any compensating advantage. Nevertheless, membership of the Association might be worth consideration on the ground that it would bring us into closer relations with other countries, most (if not all) of whom contemplate membership of the Community when circumstances permit. One of the paradoxes of Irish life has been the coupling of insistence on political separation from Great Britain with the greatest reluctance to develop contacts outside these islands. This paradox should disappear. The moral of our present position must be that a country so dependent on trade as Ireland must have markets somewhere, that it cannot pick and choose between markets, and that it can never afford to take any market for granted.[14]

14. The suggestion of some form of association between the United States, the United Kingdom, and Canada, in which Ireland might well be interested has not been discussed here as it does not appear to be practical politics at present.

CHAPTER TWELVE

Agriculture: Issues of Policy

SEVENTY YEARS AGO THE REPORT OF THE RECESS COM-
mittee began its survey of the economic resources then available with a
sentence which many would argue is equally applicable to Irish agriculture today:

Ours is by common consent one of the simplest and least developed systems
of agriculture in Western Europe, both as regards the want of variety of the
crops and (having regard to the fertility of the soil) the scantiness of the
produce.[1]

It was possible to hope, when the Recess Committee drafted its report
in 1896, that the major problems were in a fair way towards solution.
The backwardness of agriculture was often then attributed to the prolonged struggle over land tenure. Security of tenure was not given to
the occupier until the Land Act of 1881, and the intentions of the legislature could be, and often were, evaded. The first large measure of
land purchase was provided by the Ashbourne Act of 1885, and the
transfer of ownership from landlord to tenant was made general by the
Wyndham Act of 1903. To abolish a pernicious form of land tenure was
only to create the conditions in which progress became possible: it could
not and did not guarantee improvement.

Legacy of the land war
The occupiers of the land, now transformed into tenant-purchasers,
faced economic independence with little capital and less preparation for
its problems. This want of preparation was partly a result of the agrarian
struggle. Initiative and independence were dangerous qualities for a
tenant at will to possess. There were, however, other reasons which

1. *Report of the Recess Committee*, p. 11.

could not be attributed to the system of land tenure. There was a lack, as the Recess Committee stressed,[2] of general and technical education, of higher research, and of a system for communicating its results to the farmer.

Moreover, Irish agriculture was largely composed of holdings which might or might not be economic. Estates were usually divided, as they came under the provisions of the Land Purchase Acts, between the existing occupiers, irrespective of their skill or competence or of the quality of the land. The danger that land purchase would perpetuate uneconomic holdings was recognized at an early stage; and the Congested Districts Board made resettlement one of its principal activities after its institution in 1891. This applied only to the areas under the Board's control, which ultimately consisted of Connacht, the counties of Kerry and Donegal and part of the counties of Cork and Clare. There was no check on what might happen elsewhere in the country. The farms thus created were usually run by family labour. Certainly this meant that Irish agriculture enjoyed the dubious advantage of cheap labour; but cheap labour might also be unskilled labour; or, more exactly, labour that was unaware of the possibilities of improvement. Thus, standards of production varied greatly, not only in accordance with the varying fertility of land but also with the personal qualities of farmers and their families. It was no wonder that Horace Plunkett should talk so often about the economic man on the uneconomic holding and the uneconomic man on the economic holding.

The tenant-purchasers inherited a type of farming in which cattle were supreme. Grazing was encouraged by price movements, by climate and by the properties of the soil. Wheat-growing in Ireland, as in England, had become unprofitable when American supplies flooded the market at the end of the 1870s. Tillage generally formed only a small part of agricultural production. As the century drew to its close, the country was increasingly pastoral.

It was a peculiar type of pastoral economy. An observer writing of the earlier years of the present century remarked that:

Not only is Ireland a pastoral country; it is a pastoral country occupied with the production not of milk, but of meat. It is a cattle-breeding country, which does not even, as yet, fatten the cattle it breeds, but exports them to England or Scotland to be fattened there for the market.[3]

Perhaps little more could be expected in the circumstances of the time. The Irish countryside had recently been, both metaphorically and

2. The report opens with the words '. . . We have in Ireland a poor country, practically without manufactures . . . dependent upon agriculture, with its soil imperfectly tilled, its area under cultivation decreasing, and a diminishing population without industrial habits or technical skill'.

3. Sir Ernest Barker, *Ireland in the Last Fifty Years*, Clarendon Press, Oxford: 1917, p. 42.

literally, a battlefield, and it bore the marks of battle. Oldham declared that:

in the arts of using a most fertile soil in the business of agriculture, it is but a ruined land, wasted and withered by the fifty-years-long struggle to settle the question of land tenure.[4]

In many parts of the country there was no tradition of tillage nor even much knowledge of livestock. As lately as 1945 the Smiddy report noted that:

Farmers have not demonstrated any marked ability to evolve a national agricultural technique particularly suited to the growing and preserving of crops that yield the highest returns in the climatic conditions prevailing, nor, except in the case of horses, have they displayed any particular talent for the production of the highest class of livestock.[5]

Thus the major industry of the country assumed a form, which, if it did not actively promote depopulation, certainly did nothing to create a demand for labour. This led to one of the most puzzling features of Irish life since the Famine, the fact that the pressure of population on the land co-existed with heavy emigration. Speaking of the period after the Famine, Mansergh remarks that:

the number of holdings under 15 acres had therefore materially diminished. But the benefits that might have accrued to the survivors were sensibly lessened by two things: on the one hand the depopulation of the country threw much of the land out of cultivation so that the agricultural output declined, whilst on the other hand the centralization of farms made possible by the disappearance of the smaller farms encouraged the extension of cattle-rearing thereby facilitating the decline of agriculture and lessening the demand for labour. The consequence was that the major advantages were secured by the large farmers and land-owners . . . and were not distributed evenly throughout the population. Because of this revolution in agriculture, which is to be attributed to an economic trend rather than to the grasping character of the landlords, the reproduction of relative over-population more than kept pace with absolute depopulation.[6]

The predominance of grazing had a further consequence. It did not demand, except in a very rough and ready way, any acquaintance with marketing or grading. In these matters, where production and sale intermingled, the Irish farmer of the 1890s had no experience.

The co-operative revival

The period before 1914 saw a great measure of improvement. The co-operative movement, with its insistence on 'better business, better

---

4. 'The Incidence of Emigration', *JSSISI*, 1913–14, p. 218.
5. *Report of the Committee of Inquiry on Post-Emergency Agricultural Policy*, P. No. 7175, Stationery Office, Dublin, para. 132.
6. N. Mansergh, *Ireland in the Age of Reform and Revolution*, Allen & Unwin, London: 1940, pp. 198–9.

farming, better living', brought about a change of approach. Its influence was perhaps especially valuable in its approach to the first goal, of better business. As Adams remarked: 'Without better organization, and better business methods, better farming would not avail, and better living would remain a pious hope.'[7] (That order of priority may well hold good today.) Better organization and marketing were the first requisite of progress. The great achievement of the leaders of the co-operative movement in the last decade of the nineteenth century and the first decade of the twentieth was to instil among farmers a sense of the necessity for better quality, for better marketing and, above all, for dependability. Then and later the success of the co-operative movement lay principally with dairy production, and was not so marked in other forms of farming. Even among the creameries, the co-operative principle was not carried as far as it might have been: there was co-operation between the members of each creamery but very little among the creameries themselves. Plunkett himself, years later, was to describe co-operation as 'an Irish idea, never quite understood in Ireland'.[8] But despite these limitations, there was an unmistakable advance in the arts of agriculture, and in the business of selling its produce, during the early years of this century.

This advance was encouraged by the foundation of the Department of Agriculture and Technical Instruction in 1899. The Department was debarred, both by its constitutional position and by contemporary principles which limited State intervention, from resorting to the measures designed to impose standardization of quality which were freely used in the 1920s. But it provided courses of instruction and sources of information which had been lacking. The quarrel between the Department and the co-operative movement is one of the great tragedies of Irish economic history: much was done by both parties; so much more might have been done.

The ten years that followed 1914 brought much prosperity to farmers, and did a great deal to destroy their chances of maintaining it. By 1914 Ireland was a highly important supplier of the British market, not only of cattle, which had always been the case, but also of butter, bacon, eggs, and poultry. The outbreak of war gave the Irish producer very nearly a monopoly of the market in a period of rapidly rising prices. The opportunity was seized, and abused. A great deal of the advance made towards standardization of quality and regularity of supply was lost: the variability of quality even within a single consignment became a by-word. When the war ended, and continental and overseas producers returned to the British market, the Irish farmers had

7. In the introduction to Margaret Digby's *Horace Plunkett*, Blackwell, Oxford: 1949.
8. In the *Irish Statesman*, 21 November 1925.

made a great deal of money and lost a great deal more of goodwill. In the process, they had also lost a great deal of what they had learned about the principles of co-operation. These principles had been all very well in earlier years when adherence to them would obviously bring better prices: once still better prices were to be got for the asking, they were thrown overboard.

The collapse after the war was intensified by the fall in prices, the Anglo-Irish struggle and the ending of the emergency measures taken to increase production. Years afterwards, when Irish farmers were beginning to recover some of the ground so incontinently lost, the *Irish Statesman* pointed out that comparing 1925 with 1918, tillage had fallen by 34 per cent, cattle by 7 per cent, poultry by 7 per cent, and pigs by 26 per cent.[9] Thus self-government came when prosperity had changed into falling prices, increasing competition and depression. It was not a promising situation in which to set up on one's own.

Aims of public policy

During the ten years that followed 1922, the principles of the majority report of the Commission on Agriculture were followed. Moreover, public policy consciously and deliberately gave priority to the interests of agriculture. This affected not only agriculture but also the policies governing industrial production and the scope and purpose of public expenditure. The issues involved have never been set out better than by George O'Brien in an obituary article on Patrick Hogan.[10] A great deal of that article is quoted directly, still more is paraphrased, in the pages that follow.

Hogan started from the assumption that agriculture was and would remain by far the most important industry in the Free State, and that the touchstone by which every economic measure must be judged was its effect on the prosperity of the farmers. He believed that economic policy should be directed to maximize the farmers' income, because, the farmers being the most important section of the population, everything that raised their income raised the national income of the country. Prosperity amongst farmers would provide the purchasing power necessary to sustain the demand for non-agricultural goods and services, and it was useless to encourage secondary industries unless the primary industry was in a position to purchase their products. The principal aim of agricultural policy in the Free State should therefore be the maximization of the farmers' income, and not, as in certain other countries differently situated, the provision of food for the urban population or the solution of the unemployment problem.

From that postulate it followed that policy should be aimed at the maximization of net rather than gross yields. That in its turn meant that policy should encourage the concentration of public and private

9. 6 March 1926.   10. *Studies*, September 1936, pp. 353–68.

resources on the production and marketing of commodities for which the
country possessed the greatest comparative advantage. In the 1920s,
after eighty years of free trade, it was fairly clear that the forms of production which the Irish farmer had adopted under those conditions
were prima facie those in which he had the greatest superiority.

Farm production formed by far the greatest part of the export trade;
if farmers did not produce for export, the community would find itself
soon unable to finance its normal imports. The export market, therefore,
was vital to the community as well as to the individual farmer. Being an
export market, no Irish government could control the prices which the
farmer would obtain.

Here, therefore, were the *data* of the problem with which Hogan was con-
fronted: (1) agricultural policy must be directed towards the maximization of
the farmers' profit; (2) the farmers' profit is the difference between what they
put into the land and what they take out of it, *i.e.* the difference between costs
of production and selling prices; (3) selling prices were, in most cases, outside
the control of the Free State government. When the problem is stated in this
way, it becomes obvious that the only thing the government could do to help
the farmer was to assist him to reduce his costs of production.

This entailed that products in which a natural advantage was not so
marked were left to find their own level. No encouragement, therefore,
was given, in spite of continuous pressure, to those who argued that the
producers of wheat, or of tobacco, should receive as much encouragement as the dairy farmer. Equally, no tariffs were imposed in order to
encourage a fertilizer factory, nor did the State intervene to secure that
some proportion of the feeding stuffs used should be home-grown. The
farmer, in this view, was to be left free to buy as freely and as cheaply
as he could; he was not, for example, prevented from buying American
bacon for his own consumption while selling his own more highly
priced product abroad.

This refusal to deflect production had much wider results which
should be noted here. The agricultural community formed the principal market for Irish industrial products, whose expansion depended on
its prosperity. It followed that protection by tariff for industry should
be sparingly applied and confined to those cases where there was
reasonable cause to believe that there would not be a permanent increase in costs. Thus, a thorough-going tariff policy was ruled out.
Equally, central and local taxation should be kept as low as possible;
which meant that State expenditure should be restricted, thereby ruling
out not only subsidies but also large-scale expenditure on social services.

This policy therefore entailed a series of choices in which certain
forms of production and objects of expenditure were deliberately set
aside in favour of specific goals. Some aims that were so set aside, for
example the encouragement of wheat-growing, were quite practicable;

others that were pursued only on a limited scale, such as the extension of the social services, were not only practicable but desirable. But the calculation was that if land, labour capital and skill were applied in the first place to the further development of those forms of production which had proved to be most suitable wealth would be increased all the more quickly. Then, but not until then, would circumstances allow a diversion of resources to other objectives. Irish industries, which would presumably depend heavily on the domestic market, would best prosper when that market was prosperous. The money for social services must come out of revenue: the country had to increase its wealth before revenue was available.

For these objectives, the creation of wealth was the first condition. It was also argued that this offered the best hope of conserving the population. It had been shown that the greatest densities of rural population were to be found in the mixed farming areas, and it was this form of production which Hogan especially encouraged with the slogan of 'one more cow, one more sow, one more acre under the plough'. There was no necessary conflict between greater wealth and greater rural population nor, in this view, between tillage and any other form of agricultural production. These points may be summed up by a quotation from Dr. O'Brien.

Every policy must be judged in relation to the circumstances of the place and the time of its application, and, when such circumstances change, changes in policy may become necessary. If Hogan's policy be regarded in relation to the situation in the Free State for the first ten years after the treaty, it can be defended on the following grounds. In the first place, it utilized to the maximum the physical and geographical resources of the country; secondly, it developed those branches of production which are particularly suitable for the average Irish farm; thirdly, it did not involve any breach of continuity in the tradition of Irish farming or in the constructive programme of the Department of Agriculture; fourthly, it promised to provide abundant rural employment, as the agricultural statistics prove that mixed farming with dairying as its principal feature gives more employment per acre than almost any other type of agricultural activity; fifthly, food production would be stimulated and the population of the Free State could never be reduced to famine in war-time. The alternative objectives of agricultural policy, namely employment and food production, would thus be incidentally secured. The final justification of the policy is that it ensured that any public money spent on agriculture would be employed productively by being devoted to the building up of the efficiency of the industry rather than to deflecting production from one line to another.

These principles were discarded after the change of government in 1932. It should be remembered that in the circumstances of the time some change of policy was almost inevitable. The adoption of an all-round protection for agriculture which verged on self-sufficiency followed the example set by many other countries. Even in the British market itself, government intervention was now promised. Had the election of 1932 gone otherwise and given Hogan a further term of office he would have been obliged to revise the assumptions on which his policy was based and to change it accordingly.

But the issues involved went very deep. Even Hogan might have gone unwillingly some distance down the distrusted road of protection for the home market. For him, however, any such measures would have been temporary, to be used only as long as was necessary and discarded as soon as the world had emerged from the depression into better times. In Ireland in 1932, however, the supporters of self-sufficiency did not regard it as simply one type of economic policy, it was rather a matter of principle involving what might have been called national morale, if not indeed national morality.[11] When the issues were couched, if not always defined, in such terms it was useless for Hogan to ridicule the possibility of self-sufficiency for an economy so open as the Irish or to point out that the price of wheat (the crop symbolizing the new policy) was at the lowest level recorded since the reign of the first Elizabeth. He and his opponents were not arguing about the same things.

These issues of agricultural policy have not been fully debated for many years. Protection for the agricultural home market has been maintained; here and there it has been extended. Encouragement is still given, though less energetically, to the growing of wheat. At the same time the importance of the export market has been more clearly realized, although realization has come too late to prevent its almost total loss for several products. This underlines one great change between the circumstances of the pre-war controversies and the present day. In the 1920s and 1930s the availability of the British market could be taken for granted. One government might decide to supply it; another to ignore it. Whatever the decision might be, it was an Irish decision. That is not the case to-day. In many respects the British market is being supplied increasingly by British farmers. Irish agricultural policies must now be suited to those of the United Kingdom.

At the same time, the underlying issue of these controversies has been evaded or ignored rather than settled. It cannot be said with complete justice that Irish agriculture is being treated as an exporting industry. The amount of public money provided for it increases from year to year; but it is still hampered by high costs derived from protectionist policies. On the other hand, it cannot justly be said that agriculture is treated as a way of life. Too many farms, especially small farms, have been abandoned since the war for such a statement to carry conviction. A succession of Ministers have made speeches that might be

11. The reader of the minority report of 1923, which had much in common with the policies of 1932, will note references to 'an illimitable variety of expensive, tasty (and often unwholesome) food products', imported from America, Australia or Europe (ibid., para. 31).

quoted in favour of one view or the other but their policies have not been clear-cut. This cannot continue without risking grave damage to the economy.

Hogan's policy makes a strong appeal to the economist because it is based on choices and priorities. For that reason it is not a policy that will be equally attractive to governments. It is possible that such a policy, stated and executed as uncompromisingly as it was,[12] could have been followed only by a government that was in the exceptionally strong position of the first administration. But if the Irish state ever finds itself obliged to put first things first and to get full value for the money it spends, it will find an admirable model in the manner in which Hogan's policy was framed.

This is not to argue that the policy itself would be applicable today. The postulates that were acceptable forty years ago are no longer valid. It is no longer true to claim that the great majority of the population lives on the land. There are now more people engaged in other occupations than there are in agriculture. An observer in the 1960s would remark rather that it is possible for urban dwellers to enjoy relative prosperity while farm incomes are almost static. The Irish economy is much more complex and varied than it was in the 1920s.

Claims to priority

These changes do not, however, reduce the need to give a very high, perhaps an over-riding, priority to the needs of agriculture. They increase it. Industrialization and urbanization have increased the demand for imports and therefore increase the need for exports to pay for them. The increase in the production of manufactured goods has been a notable achievement and the growth in the volume and value of the export trade in them has been still more gratifying. Nevertheless, total exports continue to lag far behind total imports and the balance of payments is a constant threat to the continued expansion of the economy. Agricultural exports, however, have a high proportion of domestic produce: the off-setting proportion of imported raw materials is much less than is the case with many manufactures. They are based on the natural advantages of soil and climate; and it is generally agreed that the inherent fertility of the soil has been barely developed as yet. One can only wonder how much greater the prosperity of this country would be

12. It must not be thought that Dr. O'Brien's article drew out the implications of Hogan's policy for the first time. They were stated often, and in much blunter language, by Hogan himself. His critics were equally outspoken as will be seen from a study of the Dáil debates, the files of *The Nation* (the Opposition organ until 1931), and lastly *The Catholic Bulletin*, a journal that was rich in political and economic *curiosa*.

The policy followed after 1932 has been described in Chapter Four.

today if one half of the energy, money and devotion that have been engaged in developing less accessible sources of wealth had been directed to the improvement of the land.

The reasons for that deflection of interest are plain enough. To generalize very greatly, there are two principal obstacles to the execution of an energetic agricultural policy. The first is psychological. Irish agriculture has had a long, unhappy, and complicated history. There is often violent dissension among its spokesmen, as much on the very nature of its problems as on the remedies which should be applied to them. Those who decide public policy must be strongly tempted to concentrate on the development of industry which has all the impetus of novelty, where progress is apparent to the eye, whose future performance is comparatively predictable and where (above all) there are few sociological or technical controversies. The second is that agriculture needs a triple revolution, one in the quantity of production, a second in the quality of production, and a third in the efficiency of marketing. Of these, the first and second are dependent on the success of the third, and efforts in marketing have been held up because outlets depend greatly (though not entirely) on trade agreements with other countries. A real breakthrough in agriculture, which is essential to sustain the stability of the economy, depends on the achievement of this triple revolution, which is as much psychological as technical.

These deficiencies spring from the fact that the problems of agriculture are as much social as economic. The normal processes of economic activity are allowed to work only within restricted limits. In land itself, the market is by no means free: it is subject to the operations of the Land Commission, to the special duties levied on foreign purchasers and, very often, to local agitation. Farm sizes cannot be easily adjusted to changing conditions. Too many holders of large farms allow them to run down, through force of circumstances or through lassitude, with impunity. This is a growing weakness when greater capitalization and skill are so urgently needed. It happens too often that a farm is properly run only during the short time the farmer's children still live on the holding and are of an age to help with the work. Before that time, when they are too young, as after it when many have left, the farm is worked below its capacity. At a later stage in the cycle, it is common to see holdings going back because the farmer is elderly but will not make way for the young. These are essentially social issues, but they carry grave economic implications.

The small farms

They are particularly important in the Irish economy because of the sharp fall in the number of small farms. (Small farms today may be defined as those under thirty acres, instead of, as not so long ago, farms of under fifteen acres.) A movement out of agriculture in general and out of small farms in particular has happened everywhere else in the world. It is only to be expected that it should happen in Ireland also. Indeed, the proportion of the occupied population that is engaged in agriculture is still comparatively high in Ireland and the proportion of farms under thirty acres is still significant. A continued fall in the farming population was accepted by the Second Programme which envisaged a fall of 66,000 in agricultural employment in the decade 1960–70, an average annual loss of 6,000. In fact the rate of loss has been much greater. In the period 1961–5 the agricultural labour force fell by an estimated 40,700, an annual rate of loss of over 10,000.

The traditional economy of the small farm was based on the sale of pigs, poultry, and eggs. These could be produced with fair prospect of a satisfactory return as long as feeding-stuffs could be cheaply obtained. The first check to this process came with the protectionist policies of the 1930s which raised the price of feed. The next major blow came in post-war years when the extension of the British domestic farm subsidy programme virtually eliminated the Irish export market for poultry and eggs and severely affected exports of pig-meat.

Small farms are to be found throughout the country but they are especially numerous in the western counties. In these areas, there is difficulty in distinguishing between the genuine small farmer and the farmer who combines ownership of a small holding with work elsewhere. It is clear that the western areas of the country, and Connacht in particular, present a special regional problem. Attwood notes[13] that in 1960 the output per male worker in farm work in eight western counties (the province of Connacht and counties Donegal, Clare, and Kerry) was £350 compared with £570 in the rest of the country. Between 1955 and 1960, however, the number of farms of under thirty acres in Connacht had fallen by 16 per cent.

Small farms throughout the country are caught between two trends: their capacity to make money has decreased while the desired standards of living have risen. It is little wonder, therefore, if the small farm has almost certainly been the greatest single source of emigration in recent years and almost certainly, as things stand, will continue to be so. The assistance that public policy may provide cannot be expected to yield any complete or rapid remedy. Special assistance for the small farm regions is limited by the disconcerting fact that much assistance is already committed to farmers whose economic position is, or should be, a great deal more secure than the western small-holder; in the last resort special assistance should not be expected to underpin a society indefinitely. No one remedy will be sufficient to solve a problem that is

13. 'Agriculture and Economic Growth in Western Ireland', *JSSISI*, 1961–2, p. 172.

due to a combination of mistaken policies in the past and changing circumstances in the present. No doubt, the average size of farm will be increased, if as an unpalatable result of emigration and consolidation of holdings. That will not be an enduring solution unless it is accompanied by research into the soil resources of the area (which is now fortunately in progress), increased technical advice to small-holders and, almost certainly, a greatly increased degree of co-operation between them. All this is a great deal to ask both from the State and from individual farmers. It will encounter serious difficulties from the social structure of the area and its traditional way of life. The problem of the small farm will be with us for many years to come.

This contains a moral which is as true for the larger farms on more favoured land as it is for the west. The pattern of land use, and the density of rural population, largely depend on the efficiency of agriculture. The greater the neglect of research and instruction, of the skills of husbandry and of efficiency in marketing, the greater will be the dependence simply on the natural properties of the soil and climate. The greater that dependence grows, the larger will be the size of the economic farm and the smaller will be the number of families on the land. In our own time, we have seen the accepted unit for a viable small farm increase from twenty-five to forty acres. The same process may yet affect the rest of the country unless the reliance on natural advantages and neglect of technical skills cease to be as great as they have been. If not, the difficulties of the west may be expected to spread to the south and east of the country.

Lines of advance

It is facile enough to indicate the general lines of advance. The clear intention of the Second Programme is that for the remainder of the decade, livestock numbers are to be expanded while tillage output remains virtually unchanged.[14] If so, increased fertility of the soil and the improvement of livestock appear to be the two ways in which a new and enduring impetus may be given to the economy, even if the effects on the non-agricultural sectors are indirect. The well-known dictum on Irish grass-lands, that much of them yields as little as would be possible under an Irish sky, has been quoted elsewhere. It is an example of the waste of resources which has persisted for many years. The land has been taken for granted: its produce is, therefore, far below its capacity. The growing realization that soil fertility must be cared for is one of the most encouraging developments for many years.

14. This closely resembles the policy which Hogan was so abused for adopting forty years ago; although he laid greater emphasis on more tillage being needed if livestock numbers increased.

If soil fertility is improved, it will become possible to carry more stock and ultimately to make agriculture more intensive. Here again the schemes for the expansion of livestock numbers provide an example of progress. But there is a great deal more involved than a simple increase in the number of livestock. Few things are more remarkable than the comparative dearth of research in the past into the type of beast best suited to our conditions or that is needed in the export markets. Other countries that are much less dependent on livestock production than Ireland, have devoted large sums to these matters. The veterinary services fall naturally into this context. Diseases and parasites inflict severe losses on farmers and depress their selling prices. The extension of veterinary, laboratory and diagnostic services, with particular reference to livestock expansion policy, is a welcome feature.

There has been sustained and successful research into the type of wheat best suited to our conditions. The development of another type of feeding-barley has already influenced the system of agriculture. The growing possibilities of vegetable production raise further opportunities for fruitful research.

In particular it must be hoped that there will be sustained enquiry into the means by which agricultural produce can be processed. Few things show the backwardness of agriculture more clearly than the fact that farmers still sell much of their output to middlemen in a manner that cannot have changed significantly in a hundred years.[15] As a country we still sell primary products in their most elementary form. The evolution of processing, packaging, and marketing is still, apart from some obvious and significantly successful exceptions, in its most rudimentary stage.[16] These issues are not solely agricultural. They also affect industry in so far as the processing of foodstuffs appears to be the most promising field that is left for industrial growth.

Many of the matters mentioned in the preceding paragraphs now fall within the province of the Agricultural Institute. But research will be economically unprofitable unless its results are communicated to producers who are capable of applying them. In 1967–8 the State spent £69m. on various forms of provision for agricultural production. Of that sum only £3m. went on research and instruction. In this respect Ireland lags far behind countries such as Denmark and the Netherlands. At present, nine agricultural colleges cater for five hundred students. There is a crying need for expansion, as well as for the development of winter farm schools and agricultural classes. These should not be concerned only with technical instruction: much greater attention should

15. This has been changed to some extent by the introduction of the cattle marts, but it is still broadly true.

16. It will be salutary to consider how many branded Irish foodstuffs can be found in supermarkets in Great Britain, or indeed in Ireland itself.

be paid to the principles of farm management. A start is now being made, very late in the day indeed. It is provocative to turn back to the *Journal of the Department of Agriculture and Technical Instruction* for the years before 1914. The reader will find in its pages all too many suggestions which are being put into effect with energy only now.

It will be a very great advance indeed to tackle the technical problems of production and to ensure that the solutions are made known and put into practice. The full benefit will not be obtained if agriculture continues to be unorganized. It is a very open question whether agricultural production can be expanded on the basis of thousands of farmers producing and selling their produce on their own. It is very easy to see how farmers might be reduced, under the pressure of modern conditions, to the status of producers selling to large combines or middlemen, and getting much the worst of every bargain in the process. In a sense, this effect has always been true of Irish agriculture: its removal is an essential priority. Co-operation has had a limited success in agriculture but farmers will be obliged to consider its very real advantages which would enable them to stand on a basis of greater strength with the organizations which constitute their market. It seems highly probable that if they neglect to do so they will be forced by the pressure of events into a highly disadvantageous position. The achievement of security and independence for farmers was justly regarded as being one of the great triumphs of the nineteenth century: it would be a catastrophe if both were to be lost in the twentieth because farmers failed to adjust themselves to changing conditions.

Ultimately, this is a matter of self-reliance. That quality, however, has been seriously weakened by increasing emphasis on policies which involve subsidies and guaranteed prices. These are instruments of policy for agriculture as for any other form of activity. There is no reason why they should not be used—though if they have to be used throughout decades there must be something wrong with the policy, especially when an exporting industry is concerned—but there should be no doubt about why they are used and what their object is. The primary aim of all price supports is not only to help the efficient producer but to make things uncomfortable for the inefficient. This is difficult in all forms of production, and especially in agriculture. But if subsidies, in one form or another, are to be paid, they should be paid with a specific object in view, not simply as an annual subvention from the rest of the community. Equally, if prices are guaranteed in any form, their level should be related to what will remunerate the reasonably efficient producer, not every possible producer at any standard of efficiency and on every type of land, in every constituency.

Thus we return to emphasizing the importance of costs of production. The great virtue of Hogan's policy was that it concentrated attention on reducing the real and money costs of production, and thus enabled agriculture to engage successfully in a fiercely competitive market. It was natural enough, when the depression brought selling prices well below costs of production everywhere, that such concentration should have been relaxed. It was inevitable that the conditions of wartime should have encouraged a more easy-going attitude. The world today, however, is nearer to the conditions of the 1920s than at any time since the depression, and it is painfully clear that Irish agriculture is not as ready for competition now as it was then. It was comprehensible, but depressing, to notice how the attitude of the farming community to the EEC negotiations was coloured by estimates of the higher prices that would be obtained for farm products if Ireland joined the Community. That attitude was natural, but there was little sign of any realization that profits depend as much on the efficiency of production as on selling price.[17]

In the last resort the success of energetic agricultural policies will depend on the co-operation of farmers. That is not to be taken for granted. The initial effect of such policies may very well be to make things less rather than more comfortable for many farmers. Many spokesmen of the agricultural interest refer with regret to the days when Hogan gave priority to their needs. But their predecessors were not so appreciative of Hogan's policies at the time, even if Senator Oliver Gogarty exaggerated when he said that 'the only function of the Farmers' Party appears to be to oppose everything'.[18] It is highly possible that revised agricultural policies will run initially into storms of protests from farmers.

In a parliamentary democracy, existing policies must be revised comparatively slowly. The success of revision must depend on the co-operation of farmers; farmers must therefore be carried with it. This emphasizes the need for better relations between farmers, their organizations, and the Department of Agriculture. It is difficult to believe that progress will be achieved on anything like the scale that is needed unless there is a greater degree of sympathy and trust. This is a national problem, not a departmental problem and it should be dealt with as such. It will be the more urgent because increased production and more efficient marketing will certainly create fresh problems. The position of the individual farmer may well become less secure than it has been. In the last resort, this is a matter of psychology and attitudes of mind, like so many of what we call our economic problems. Things will not automatically be made better, on the contrary they may be made much more complicated, when Irish agriculture begins to progress.

17. And, it must regretfully be admitted, on the ability of governments to negotiate good trade agreements.
18. *PDDE*, 14, 186.

To return to the central argument, the productive capacity of agriculture is far greater than is required for the immediate needs of the population. If increased production is not directed into exports (which admittedly depend on trade agreements) and must instead be absorbed by a sheltered home market in which prices are maintained by transfer payments, the productive potential of agriculture will not be fully used and there will be no incentive to do so. Its natural resources will remain under-employed, so also will be the people who live by agriculture. In such circumstances, agriculture and those who work in it will certainly be less efficient than they might be and the energies that could be applied to improvement will be diverted to pressing for higher prices. This is a recipe for a stagnant state and a second-rate people.

CHAPTER THIRTEEN

Industry: Problems
of Growth

'A SOCIETY OF DISTILLERS AND BREWERS. DOES ANY OTHER trade prosper in Ireland?' So George Moore asked at the beginning of this century. Many of his contemporaries asked themselves the same question; and were resolved to provide an affirmative answer when a native government had been established. In fact, the degree of industrialization then achieved was highly important. Some forms of production, among which linen and shipbuilding are the most obvious examples, could face competition from anywhere in the world with confidence. They were to be found, however, almost exclusively in the north-east. In Dublin, and generally throughout the south and west, the most firmly established forms of industrial production were the twin industries of brewing and distilling; useful products indeed but not such as would satisfy either the ardent patriot or the author of *Salve*. No discussion of the place of industrial development in modern Ireland can be of value if it does not insist on the strength of the conviction that the absence of industries impoverished the national life, economically, socially, and spiritually.

In this matter writers have been much more influential than economists. The quotation from George Moore may be capped by another from George Russell. Writing years later in *The Irish Statesman*, Æ noted that the argument for protection was

not so much an economic case as an intellectual and cultural case. If the country lives almost altogether by a few industries its intellectual life will lack richness and variety, and our cultural life has lacked richness and depth because agriculture . . . did not find employment for large numbers of engineers, electricians, chemists and bacteriologists.[1]

This discontent with things as they were possessed a peculiarly explosive power because it was based on beliefs that had been held

1. 14 February 1925.

passionately for generations. Any Irish nationalist at the beginning of this century firmly believed in three propositions. The first was that industrial development presented the only hope of arresting emigration and the decline in population. The second was that both the capacity for and the opportunity of industrial development had been weakened by the connection with England. The third was that neither the capacity nor the opportunity could be revived until the legislative union had been dissolved and Ireland had regained the power to encourage its industries.

Thus the encouragement of industry became as much a political as an economic or social issue. It was absorbed into the central controversy about power; the more readily because, through it, new authorities could be found for the separatist tradition. By stressing the industrial grievance, the centuries could be bridged. Perhaps as few people read Swift today as read his contemporary, Bolingbroke. But the one thing that everybody knows about the Dean is that he suggested that Ireland should burn everything that comes from England except their people and their coals.[2] That advice has been quoted from election platforms in our own time.

In this manner, the usual tests by which manufacturers or traders assess business prospects became irrelevant. A project such as the Shannon Scheme was not simply a matter of engineering or the sale of power and light—though in fact these points were very carefully considered by its sponsors. It was also a sign of what people could do to justify their new independence. It was a much more potent symbol of nationhood regained than pillar-boxes painted green. There will be no understanding of industrial policies and problems until it is recognized that both are set deeply into the nationalist tradition and that they have been judged by far other than merely economic standards.

Thus the voluntary movements which flourished around the end of the nineteenth century—the co-operative movement in particular— concerned themselves with industrial growth even if their principal interests were agricultural. The first part of the report of the Recess Committee examined the effects of the eighteenth-century restraints on Irish trade and industry. It was, again, fully characteristic of the prevailing mood that the Irish Industrial Development Association[3] should have been formed on the initiative of the Cork Literary Society.[4]

2. Which he did not. He quoted the phrase as 'a pleasant observation of somebody's'. The passage will be found in *A Proposition for the Universal Use of Irish Manufactures*.

3. Later the National Agricultural and Industrial Development Association which joined in 1967 with the National Buy-Irish Council to form the National Development Association.

4. It was equally characteristic that the Cork Literary Society should have been 'more revolutionary than literary in its aims'. Cf. J. J. Horgan, *Parnell to Pearse*, Browne & Nolan, Dublin: 1948, pp. 120–4, and Riordan, *Modern Irish Trade and Industry*, Methuen, London: 1920.

In 1906 the Association registered a trade-mark which might be placed on goods of Irish manufacture. This trade-mark, which retained its appeal to manufacturers for several decades, represented an appeal to national sentiment as much as an attempt to set a standard of quality, and the fact that it was first used by a prudent manufacturer in Belfast was felt to be vaguely symbolic.

From then onwards, the appeal to 'Buy Irish' was vigorously pressed.[5] On the one side it was taken up by nationalist groups and organizations, on another it enjoyed the favour of the Viceregal Court. Its effects may not have been far-reaching if measured in terms of pounds, shillings, and pence. Economists, such as C. H. Oldham, were at pains to demonstrate that the purchase of Irish goods irrespective of their price or quality did less than nothing to improve the economy and might do much to hinder its growth. True or false, such arguments were felt to be beside the point.

This largely unorganized support of Irish-made goods was soon to be put on firmer foundations. During 1904, Arthur Griffith published a series of articles in *The United Irishman* on the constitutional relationship of Austria and Hungary.[6] His purpose was to make the case for a dual monarchy of Ireland and Great Britain.[7] In November 1904 these articles were reprinted as a pamphlet entitled *The Resurrection of Hungary*, in which Griffith argued the case for a policy of industrialization, aided by tariff protection, in order to restore a balance to the Irish society and economy. His views are best illustrated by quotation from a speech made by him a year later, on 28 November 1905:

A nation cannot promote and further its civilization, its prosperity and its social progress equally as well by exchanging agricultural products for manufactured goods as by establishing a manufacturing power of its own. A merely agricultural nation cannot ever develop to any extent a home or a foreign commerce, with inland means of transport and foreign navigation, increase its population in due proportion to their well-being, or make notable progress in its moral, intellectual, social and political development; it will never acquire important political power or be placed in a position to influence the cultivation and progress of less advanced nations and to form colonies of its own. A mere agricultural state is infinitely less powerful than an agricultural-manufacturing state . . . An agricultural nation is a man with one arm who makes use of an arm belonging to another person but cannot, of course, be sure of having it always available. An agricultural-manufacturing nation is a man who has two arms of his own at his own disposal . . . Let the Irish people get out of their

---

5. The important part played by *The Leader*, a weekly magazine founded in 1900 by D. P. Moran, should not be overlooked.

6. It may be noted that the first reference to the Austro-Hungarian parallel appears to have been a speech made by Griffith on a motion sponsored by the Cork Literary Society, calling on the Irish in America to withdraw all support from the parliamentarian policy. Cf. P. S. O'Hegarty, *A History of Ireland under the Union*, Methuen, London: 1952, p. 641.

7. See above, pp. 19–21.

heads the insane idea that the agricultural and manufacturing industries are opposed. They are necessary to each other, and one cannot be injured without the other suffering hurt. We must further clear their minds of the pernicious idea that they are not entitled or called upon to give preferential aid to the manufacturing industries of their own countries. Sir, if that idea were not met and combated there would be an end to all hope of the development of an Irish manufacturing arm . . . It is also the duty of the individual to pay where necessary a higher price for Irish-made goods; but it is contrary to the principle of Protection and the interests of the country that a manufacturer in Ireland who can produce as cheaply as his foreign competitor should receive an enhanced price. The movement is one to give Ireland back her manufacturing arm, not to make fortunes for dishonest manufacturers.

This speech was published in 1906 as a pamphlet entitled *The Sinn Féin Policy*. Fifteen years later Griffith led the delegation which signed the Anglo-Irish treaty. Full powers over customs and excise were secured in the closing stages of the negotiations; and it is probable that this achievement reconciled him to the less agreeable articles of the settlement.[8]

Growth of protection

There was now no obstacle to putting the Sinn Féin policy into operation. Indeed, the difficulties were fewer than Griffith could have foreseen. If the new State had comprised all Ireland the Belfast industries would certainly have opposed a policy of protection. But, for good or ill, the Six Counties opted out in 1922; and as a result the case for protection looked all the stronger.

In fact, protective measures were imposed from a very early date. Some of the industries that are now most flourishing can date their growth from the encouragement given in the 1920s. But the industrial policy of the first government was not protectionist in principle. Priority was given to the development of agriculture; this did not imply any neglect of industrial production. It rested on the assumption, which could hardly be controverted at that time, that the prosperity of Irish manufacturers depended on the prosperity of Irish farmers, and that

8. His biographer remarks that 'Full fiscal powers meant more to Arthur Griffith than the presence or absence of the Crown in an Irish Constitution', P. Colum, *Arthur Griffith*, Browne & Nolan, Dublin: 1959, p. 302. This does not fully represent Griffith's position. In his view, the Crown would be the Crown of Ireland acting on the advice of Irish ministers, not the Crown of Great Britain.

It is an odd coincidence that in the Treaty negotiations he met another commentator on Irish fiscal affairs. On 25 January 1904, Mr. Winston Churchill M.P., lectured to the Institute of Bankers in Ireland on 'Ireland and the Fiscal Question'. His approach to that issue can be illustrated by quotation of a phrase: 'You will find the pedigree in the stud-book—Rule Britannia by Free Trade out of An Island.' In the concluding part of the lecture he argued that Ireland had nothing to gain from adoption of protection by the United Kingdom. See *JIBI*, 1904, p. 99.

any measure, such as an all-round tariff, which damaged agriculture would inevitably delay the development of industry.[9] Therefore the case for tariff protection was carefully examined and judged by the circumstances of each case.

Griffith died in August 1922, before the new Irish government could settle down to the framing of policy. His followers reproached the new ministers with abandoning his teaching. They were answered by Kevin O'Higgins in a remarkable speech:

the propagandist political writings of any man cannot be accepted simply as revealed truth, requiring no further investigation, something that must be accepted for ever as beyond question, beyond doubt, beyond the need of examination.[10]

Typically uncompromising, this attitude did less than nothing to reconcile the protectionists to government policy. This perhaps did not matter very greatly in the middle twenties when, as has been noted, the mood of business still favoured free trade and the public had bitter memories of exploitation during the First World War.[11] It did mean, however, that the Fianna Fáil party, which was founded in 1926, was free to combine opposition to Griffith's politics with support of his economics. As early as February 1928, six months after the party had entered the Dáil, Mr. Lemass moved a resolution declaring that the Tariff Commission was not sufficiently expeditious in its examination of applications for tariff protection.[12]

A short extract from his speech on that occasion should be quoted because it represents the economic philosophy which inspired public policy after the change of government four years later.

We believe that Ireland can be made a self-contained unit, providing all the necessities of living in adequate quantities for the people residing in the Island at the moment and probably for a much larger number.[13]

This philosophy rested securely (as will be apparent) on the accepted beliefs of generations of Irish nationalists. In the second place, it was increasingly fashionable everywhere after 1929. Its adherents argued with growing conviction that as all-round protection had been adopted by the United States, the countries of continental Europe and even by Great Britain, an extension to Ireland could not be impossible. A little later, they could claim that their views had been expressly approved by the most influential of contemporary economists. In April 1933 J. M. Keynes delivered the first of the lectures which are given in University College, Dublin, to commemorate Father T. A. Finlay S.J.,

9. See above, pp. 301–3.   10. *PDDE*, 16, 1884.
  11. Not only during the war years but also during the subsequent boycotts of British and Belfast products between 1920 and 1922.
  12. See *PDDE*, 22, 206 f.   13. *PDDE*, 22, 213.

who was Professor of Political Economy from 1909 to 1930. The following passage in his lecture made a deep impression on his audience:

I sympathize, therefore, with those who would minimize, rather than with those who would maximize, economic entanglement between nations. Ideas, knowledge, science, hospitality, travel—these are the things which should of their nature be international. But let goods be homespun whenever it is reasonably and conveniently possible, and, above all, let finance be primarily national.

And again:

... if I were an Irishman, I should find much to attract me in the economic outlook of your present government towards self-sufficiency.[14]

It is possible that the protectionist policy was not interpreted by all its supporters in quite the same way. Some of them were already actively engaged in business, had pleaded for full-scale protection from the first government and, in a fateful moment for that government and the country, had been rebuffed. Others had no immediate interest to consider but believed that a manufacturing system, with all that it seemed to promise for increased employment and reduced emigration, could be built up behind high tariff walls. Others again may have regarded high protection as a step towards self-sufficiency, not simply for its own sake but for the immaterial benefits which might accrue from isolation. It may not be wholly fanciful to suggest that behind this feeling lay a longing for older and simpler ways of life. No more appropriate illustration can be given than a statement of Mr. de Valera which was made over forty years ago but does not seem belied by his philosophy in government. In an interview given to the *Manchester Guardian* in September 1927 he was reported as saying that it was not the business of a statesman

to cater for the appetites of Ireland's lower self. I think it quite possible that a less costly standard of living is desirable and that it would prove, in fact, a higher standard of living. I am not satisfied that the standard of living and the mode of life in western Europe is a right or proper one. The industrialized countries have got themselves into a rut and Ireland is asked to hurry along it after them.

There was all the difference in the world between this view of what policy should achieve and the much more pragmatic concept of protection as a means by which Irish people might be enabled to make money for themselves and for their country and to give other Irish people a better chance to live at home. But these diverse currents mingled and flowed with irresistible force in the same direction. Thus an experiment in high protection was almost certainly inevitable.

The advent of Fianna Fáil to power in 1932, therefore, brought a thorough-going policy of protection by tariff and quota which was

14. See the text of the lecture in *Studies*, 1933, 177.

pursued without check until the Anglo-Irish Trade Agreement of 1938. The Agreement would certainly have involved some modification of policy, had its terms been implemented. That did not occur on account of the war. In very recent years emphasis has been placed on the reduction rather than the maintenance of tariffs. Initial reductions were made early in 1963 and again in 1964.[15] For exactly thirty years therefore the economy experienced a policy of all-round protection.

It should not be inferred that the bias of policy now runs altogether in favour of free trade. Nevertheless, there has been a change of atmosphere which may be illustrated not unfairly by quotation from the speeches of Mr. Lemass. As early as June 1958 he said: 'We can no longer rely for industrial development, to the extent we require it, on the policy of protection.'[16] Seven years later he declared that:

we see no permanent remedy of our economic situation in an intensification of protection, on the contrary, and not withstanding the rise in imports, we can see advantages in resuming soon our movement in the opposite direction.[17]

Since then the reversal of policy has been symbolized by the Anglo-Irish Trade Agreement.

It may be that the pressures of a busy life have prevented Mr. Lemass from reading the works of Friedrich List, from whom Griffith drew inspiration. If he ever does so, he will realize that he has fulfilled List's cycle of development by protection from industrial infancy to free-trading maturity.

Results of protection

The results of thirty years of all-round protection should now be reviewed. The most advertised objective of that policy was to end emigration by absorbing the drift from agriculture. The most recent statistics show that the total number of persons at work fell from 1,224,000 in 1936 to 1,063,000 in 1967. The numbers employed in agriculture, forestry, and fishing fell in that period from 600,000 to 322,000. The numbers engaged in manufacturing industry rose from 113,000 to 187,000.[18]

It is fair to add that these figures do not necessarily tell all the story. It can be argued with much justice that emigration and the loss of population would have been far greater had there been no industrialization. Especially in the years after 1945 the normal drift from the

15. No reduction was made in January 1965, presumably on account of the special duties imposed on industrial imports by the British government during the balance of payments crisis in autumn 1964.
   16. *PDDE*, 168, 1519.   17. *PDDE*, 175, 943.
   18. *ISB*, 1969.

land was magnified by the exodus of 'relatives assisting'. It is not necessarily a failure of protective policy that it could not cope with a social revolution. It might be added that those at work, both in agriculture and in manufacturing, in 1967 were a great deal more fully employed than the larger numbers at work in 1936. It is also notable that industrial employment has increased sharply in recent years. The Second Programme suggested that the numbers employed in all industries covered by the Census of Industrial Production would increase by 69,700 between 1960 and 1970. By the end of 1967 an increase of 42,200 had already been made. That is a considerable achievement. But the hopes of thirty years ago, when it seemed so simple to channel the drift out of agriculture into industry, have been disappointed.

In the circumstances of 1932 the most obvious, and most facile, means of industrialization was to impose tariffs on imported consumer goods so that it would be profitable to manufacture them in Ireland. A number of consequences flowed from that approach. Because they depended on imported raw materials, which replaced the finished goods in the import list, the new industries clustered around the major ports, which were also the major cities. This strengthened the forces making for urbanization.

The new industries, again, did not use agricultural produce as a raw material to any great extent. Had they done so, they might have been more widely spread throughout the country; and their growth would have conferred important benefits on the farmers. There was an increased consumption of farm produce as a result of the increased earning power created by industrial employment. On the other hand, the tariffs affected the prices of very many materials and goods that were necessary for agricultural production. The result was to inflate costs. That did not matter very greatly during the depression. It has mattered increasingly since 1945. High costs are by no means the only competitive weakness of Irish farmers; but they are undoubtedly a handicap.

The comparative, if inevitable, artificiality of industrial development thirty years ago had further results. In a number of cases the imposition of a tariff induced British firms, which had been traditional suppliers of the market, to open branch factories. The earnings of these concerns were often remitted to the parent company in Great Britain; thus employment increased but little else was achieved. There was not the ploughing-back of profits which is so necessary for a business in its early years. Again, because attention was directed towards the replacing of imported finished goods, the corresponding Irish industries were stimulated; but these industries were not necessarily related in a way that would form a basis for common growth. Often indeed, tariff protection worked in the other direction: industries were founded on the tariffs imposed on goods or materials which were raw materials essential for other, and sometimes much more important, industries; a system of licensing of imports did little to alleviate these difficulties. The Tariff Commission of the 1920s may have worked slowly but it prevented such clashes of interest.[19]

There were other handicaps which had nothing to do with tariff policy. Many concerns applied themselves to supplying the home market. This may have been unadventurous; but it was natural enough in the early stages of growth. The difficulty was that they had to supply a wide range of goods to a comparatively small market. The result was over-diversification which caused short production runs and higher costs of production.[20]

The policy of high protection has yielded one very important gain. Opportunities for development have been seized even where no industrial tradition had existed. A pool of skilled labour and of managerial experience has been created and can be extended. This development is not uniform throughout the country nor throughout the economy: there is still an astonishing variation between the efficiency of firms engaged in the same industry.[21] The CIO reports constantly refer to the shortage of managerial skill and the lack of technicians. Nevertheless, the situation is very much better than it was even ten years ago.

Present-day problems

Now that a nucleus of industry and industrial manpower has been formed, new factors affect development. The emphasis that was placed on the amount of employment that would be created by a new venture has not been diminished. This is comprehensible in a country of high emigration. Nevertheless the adoption of new techniques is gradually shifting the emphasis from labour to capital and from employment to productivity. Accordingly, the labour content of new industries may be much lower than would have been the case a generation ago and it now costs a great deal more to put people into employment.

Paradoxically enough, granted that Ireland is a country of high emigration, the worst problems of future growth may be found in the supply of labour. It must be expected that when Irish people look for factory work many of them will look for it in Great Britain. Paragraphs 283 and 284 of the Report of the Commission on Emigration show that,

19. In March 1965, a Report of the National Industrial Economic Council drew attention to the 'pyramiding' of protection, i.e. that greater protection was given to intermediate goods than to finished products.
20. Cf. W. J. L. Ryan, 'The Need for Structural Change in Irish Industry', *IBR*, March 1961. Also C. Brock, 'The C.I.O. Industrial Survey', *JSSISI*, 1963-4, p. 176, and an unsigned article 'The Committee on Industrial Organisation', *IBR*, June 1963.
21. Cf. the paper, already cited, by T. P. Linehan, *JSSISI*, 1961-2, p. 220.

up to 1946, the only area that attracted immigration from elsewhere in the country was the city and county of Dublin and that, even there, an appreciable amount of the immigration came from the adjoining counties. A social factor aggravates the immobility of labour within Ireland; the curious preference of people to leave the country altogether rather than seek their fortune in a different part of it. This may well have been the result of an American emigration so heavy and so prolonged that emigrants would find more friends in any American city than in Dublin or Belfast or Cork. It is probably already true of the more recent emigration to Great Britain, and it is not wholly offset by the increase of opportunities of employment in Ireland.

There is a total shortage of some forms of skilled labour required by foreign firms engaged in forms of production hitherto unknown in this country. It can be met by bringing back people who have emigrated and learnt such skills abroad or by training programmes. Neither course presents insuperable difficulties but these shortages should be foreseen rather than made good after they have arisen. New industries do not appear overnight, and their needs can be calculated in advance. This is as much the responsibility of the trade unions as of the employer. There are many encouraging instances where such provision has been made, but it ought to be accepted practice. There are also local shortages of some forms of labour, usually of the older skills. It often happens that a shortage and a supply co-exist within a comparatively small area. It is hard to resist the conclusion that the available supply of labour, particularly of skilled labour, is not being fully used through lack of the necessary machinery. This may be partly due to the immobility of labour within the country which has just been noted. More deeply, it is sometimes the result of restrictive practices in the recruitment, demarcation and promotion of labour. These are to be found in 'white-collar' unions and associations as well as in trade unions. They are to be expected in a country which has suffered so long from a shortage of employment. They will not disappear quickly, but as long as they survive, they represent a constant threat to industrial development.[22]

These matters cannot be separated from the wider issue of the return to labour. Here, the open nature of the economy is particularly obvious. Irish wage-rates may be much lower than the British in the case of unskilled or unorganized labour: otherwise there appears to be little difference and it has been suggested that basic rates in Ireland are sometimes considerably higher than in Great Britain.[23] This relation-

22. These issues have been very fully discussed in the Report of the Survey Team, directed by Professor P. K. Lynch on *Investment in Education* (Pr. 8311). See also a note on the Manpower Authority in *IBR*, May 1966.

23. Cf. D. O'Mahony, *Economic Aspects of Industrial Relations*, Economic Research Institute, Dublin, Paper No. 24. See also E. T. Nevin, *Wages in Ireland, 1946–62*, Economic Research Institute, Dublin, Paper No. 12.

ship, caused by the mobility of Irish labour, means that labour costs in relatively undeveloped Ireland match those of Great Britain which has a mature industrial economy. Accordingly, Ireland's economic development is accompanied by the high costs more usual in later stages of growth. This does not preclude efforts to achieve greater industrialization. Nevertheless, if this country wishes to enjoy the benefits of an industrial revolution, without artificially creating favourable conditions by oppressive legislation, the scope or the pace, or both, of the revolution must be limited by the imperative need to keep costs competitive. Industrial development based on depressed wage rates would be genuinely repugnant to public opinion. That makes it all the more necessary to procure some measure of general agreement on the determination of wages.

It is in this field perhaps that there has been the most serious failure to recognize the implications of economic change. The fixing of wages depends on a complex of facts, statistics, and emotions, and the third element is often at least as important as the other two put together. What can be said is that the method employed since the last war is about as unsuitable to Irish conditions as could be imagined. It has taken the form of periodic increases, applying to practically all industries, which are calculated as a percentage of the existing wage. In between the increases, an industry may have made its own adjustments of wages. But once a wage-round starts, employees in every firm in every industry get the general rate of increase, irrespective of the firm's competitive position, stage of growth, productivity, or conditions in the markets which it supplies. Matters are made still worse by the fact that wage-rounds often start in one of the State-owned enterprises which enjoy a monopolistic position.

An incomes policy

The possibility of a national incomes policy has been frequently canvassed, especially by the National Industrial Economic Council in a report issued in November 1965. This report noted that during the period 1960–4 unit wage costs increased by 14 per cent in Ireland compared with 7 per cent in the United Kingdom. It also stated that real net income increases per occupied person during the same period had varied greatly as between agriculture, industry, the public administration, and other services. It proceeded to suggest three guiding principles:

(a) that increases in total money incomes must be related to increases in national production;

(b) that if some groups get a higher increase than the total percentage increase regarded as tolerable, others must accept a lower percentage increase if the rise in total money incomes is not to be excessive;

(c) that a general consensus is needed on what represents a reasonable difference between wages and earnings in different occupations; between wages and salaries; and between wages and salaries on one hand and other kinds of income on the other.

The NIEC report was criticized on the grounds, which might have been anticipated, that regulation of the incomes of farmers, professional workers, and other self-employed workers should not be discussed by a body on which they were not represented, a defect which the NIEC indeed recognized implicitly as regards its discussion of farm incomes in this context. Nevertheless, the publication of such challenging principles performed a considerable public service by provoking debate on the issues involved.

The comparative narrowness of the terms on which the debate must be conducted should, however, be realized. Being highly dependent on exports, the Irish economy must always have special regard to the level of all costs of production. The mobility of all kinds of labour between Ireland and Great Britain means that many levels of remuneration, especially among wage-earners. are deeply influenced by conditions in the British labour market. It can be highly misleading to speak of an incomes policy for Ireland as if it were open to us to influence wage levels within very wide limits. In fact, there may be very little freedom of choice or of action at all.

There are other issues. One approach to an incomes policy is to conceive of it as an instrument for dividing up each year's increase in the national income. Readers of the NIEC report may receive the impression that this was in fact its line of approach. It must be said that the task of establishing wage norms from one year to another between all the factors of production in general and the various types and skills of labour in particular would place an intolerable burden on whatever body (be it the government or some commission to which a prudent government would probably delegate the task) was entrusted with it. It would be an immense task, almost certainly unattainable with justice and very likely to be influenced by political and economic pressures. It is not easy to see, moreover, why the trade unions should accept a method of wage fixation which they might well regard as depriving them of their principal function.

A more fruitful approach would be to regard incomes policy as something that is a great deal more flexible and that can give greater emphasis to increasing productivity while relating wage and salary increases to the size of the gain in productivity. Admittedly, this method may beg some issues and raise new ones. Productivity agreements have sometimes been so described so that managements can save their face after a bad bargain. Obviously also, there are many occupations in which, with the best will in the world, it is not possible to increase productivity. Nevertheless, the line of approach has some attraction. It is one thing to decide how the national income should be shared: it is another to give as many people as possible an interest in seeing that the national income should grow in size. The development of the Prices and Incomes Board in the United Kingdom may provide some useful lessons in this regard.

Lastly it is to be hoped that the approach to incomes will some day approach more nearly to reality. It would richly repay both employers and employees to give more attention to the manner in which the real value of increased incomes has been so quickly eroded by rising prices, increasing taxation, and higher tariffs. An improvement under any one of these heads would do much to alleviate discontent. More than that, the surest way to perpetuate all three is to press ahead with demands for higher incomes irrespective of productivity.

Admittedly, it is much easier to note the danger than to indicate a remedy. To link wages to some concept such as productivity is neither as easy nor as satisfactory as may appear at first sight.[24] Wage claims have been based on whatever ground may appear most convincing at a particular time: the cost of living or status or simply increased profits. In default of such reasons, the claim may be for a reduction of working hours or for an extension of holidays. Any one of these claims might be reasonable enough at a particular time but any consistency is soon lost if they succeed each other. The manner in which the National Wages Agreement of January 1964 was so soon eroded is a case in point.

The search for an incomes policy was stimulated by the prolonged labour unrest which marked 1964 and 1965 and persisted into the following year. The series of labour disputes during that period was deeply discouraging to those who hoped for an untroubled economic advance. To some it threatened the success of the Second Programme: to others, still more pessimistic, it represented a definitive failure.

Certainly these disputes interrupted, even reversed, advancement. But to regard them simply as a continual struggle for higher wages or salaries was to over-simplify the issues. They were not solely straight-forward trials of strength between employers and trade unions. They sprang from other issues as well, and they represented as much the success as the short-comings of the Programmes for Economic Expansion. Industrial development, with the attendant growth of specialized skills, produced social as well as economic changes. There was resentment among the possessors of the traditional crafts at the incomes

24. Cf. a most useful article by David Walker on this subject in *IBR*, March 1963.

commanded by those who had acquired the skills needed in modern production processes. There was the cleavage between technicians of all grades and clerical workers, exacerbated in this country by the fact that the occupations that traditionally enjoyed prestige were all clerical while modern development shattered old-established rankings and put technical knowledge at a premium. There were other divisions, again horizontal rather than vertical, between employees in privately owned enterprise, in the State companies, and in the civil service. It was significant that the disputes of 1965–6 were as much concerned with status claims and the true interpretation of agreements as with straightforward demands for higher pay, and that the Labour Court, in its review of the year 1965, should note that they were pursued with a tenacity which it had seldom experienced. These were as much social as economic issues. Neither employers nor trade unions could be wholly blamed for a failure to cope with forces that lay as much outside their control as outside their experience.

This is not a matter which can be solved by institutional reforms. To reconstitute the Labour Court, as has been suggested, would be of very limited efficacy. In the last resort, these matters spring from bad labour relations. Great efforts have been made in recent years to bring trade unions and employers together in the hope that a sense of partnership will gradually emerge. The obstacles to such a development are not insuperable but should not be under-rated. In 1916, and again in 1922, the trade unions sacrificed their immediate interests and received little tangible benefit in return. It would not be surprising if their members feel themselves to be on the defensive and are suspicious of co-operation with employers. They share the tradition of British rather than of Swedish trade unionism, and perhaps the worst part of the British heritage at that. Any attempt to ignore a clash of interest which is felt to exist can only end in weakening the cohesion of the trade union movement.

The dilemma of the trade unions is not, perhaps, fully recognized. In Ireland, as in Great Britain, their role was plain enough in the days before working conditions were regulated by legislation and wages were still settled by the relative strength of employers and their workers. Today they operate in an economy in which the power of the State in economic affairs has increased immeasurably and the trend of development is subject to at least a degree of planning. In that planning, trade union officials are inevitably concerned, but they must remember their duty to their members, many of whom may be adversely affected by the results of planning for the future. At the same time, they must defend the interests of their members against those employers who, in many cases, came into industry and trade comparatively lately and have little conception of what labour relations ought to be. The unions and their officials are subject to very heavy strains in these circumstances; and it is comprehensible that at times they are not followed when they give a lead and that at other times they shrink from leading. It is possible to supply occasions for co-operation at official level in bodies such as the National Industrial Economic Council but it is only too obvious that the aims and implications of the Second Programme have not yet been put across to the members of the trade unions.

Lines of growth

It is difficult and highly risky to discuss the possible lines of future growth. In the short space of the last few years Irish industry has changed almost out of recognition. At present it presents a varied picture of concerns that have found and are successfully developing export markets that would not have been dreamed of ten years ago, as well as of concerns that are content to shelter under the tariff protection that called them into an unambitious existence thirty years ago.

In no circumstances that are easily foreseeable will Irish industry be a large scale, or a cheap producer. Industrial concerns are not, with a couple of obvious exceptions, organized to be large producers. Even in the cases where they are, they do not hold a commanding share of the markets they serve. For reasons already given, none of them will be cheap producers, in the sense in which that term can be applied to some Asian countries. Irish industry is geared to western European standards of remuneration of labour. It follows that in industry, as in agriculture, Ireland will have to specialize in quality rather than in quantity. This implies attention to design, packaging, and marketing. These are skills that, again with obvious exceptions, were almost unknown a generation ago; and they are rare enough even today. The importance of personal qualities must grow in these circumstances; a feeling for good design and for good workmanship. These, unfortunately, are precisely the qualities which have been repressed by an unhappy history. There is all the more need to provide the conditions in which they can be revived; and here we return, as so often, to the need of education and instruction. The surest hope of future growth is to be found in the change of thought that has marked the last decade. That is only another way of saying that we must trust to change, even if it sometimes comes in unpalatable forms. The industrial pattern of the 1970s may be altogether different from anything that we can foresee today.

It may be said in conclusion that the problems surveyed in this and the preceding chapter are much the same. Irish industry and Irish agriculture have many points in common. Past political history, not to mention the accidents of personality, have tended to separate them; and even today it is possible to feel that the separation is growing rather than decreasing. Both agriculture and industry are very largely composed of small-scale producers with comparatively little capital, little specialized skill, and little acquaintance with modern methods of marketing at home and abroad. Both sectors suffer from poor labour relations. In both there is an impressive gap between the efficient and the typical producer.

These deficiencies are perhaps more easily tackled in industry than in agriculture because in the former they are usually regarded as technical problems which can be approached dispassionately while in the latter they are regarded as major sociological issues. Together, however, they constitute the underlying weakness of the economy; and they will be most easily made good if they are tackled together.

CHAPTER FOURTEEN

The Trend of Population

IN 1948 A COMMISSION OF INQUIRY WAS APPOINTED 'TO investigate the causes and consequences of the present level and trend in population'. It took six years to complete its report, which ran to 400 pages and contained what was then probably the most sustained and detailed statistical analysis that had ever been attempted in this country.[1] An attempt to compress its findings into some thirty or forty pages would be presumptuous indeed. This chapter is therefore concerned only with those forces which, in the writer's judgement, have played a decisive part in determining the level and trend of population. Neither the level nor the trend, however, can be easily isolated from the rest of the economy. They have deeply influenced, and have been influenced by, developments in agriculture and industry. Some matters have therefore been reserved for discussion elsewhere.[2]

Few countries present so many demographic paradoxes, all so attractive to discuss. Ireland is a country whose population once rose so rapidly as to arouse the fears of Malthus; it has for long provided the one example in the world of a people whose numbers are falling.[3] There are fewer marriages in Ireland, relatively to the population, than in any other country for which records are available; but the fertility of marriage is markedly greater than in any country of western Europe or of European settlement overseas. It is a country whose population is less than half its total in the 1840s; but it possesses more people over 65 now than it did then. It is a country where total population has fallen while the natural increase grows. Thus the Irish community has borne at the

1. *Reports of the Commission on Emigration and other Population Problems,* Pr 2541, Stationery Office, Dublin: 1954.
2. See pp. 297–328.
3. This passage refers to the period since 1847 as a whole.

same time all the strains of a growing, and all the expenses of a falling, population. Finally, here is a people who, in the phrase of their own Edmund Burke, love Ireland with a dearness of instinct which is more than can be justified to reason; nevertheless, like Burke, many leave their country at the earliest possible opportunity and do not return.

All this has gone on, with some changes of intensity, for well over a century. Throughout that period, the Irish people have endured an experience which only the aboriginal races of continents overseas have shared. Nevertheless, in that same period, they have not only achieved their political independence and transformed their social structure and standard of living, they have also made a notable contribution to the heritage of the world in poetry, drama, and the novel.[4] Selectivity is impossible in such a web of paradoxes.

In any circumstances, a prolonged decline of population would be a heavy blow to national self-confidence. It is the more grievous in Ireland because it touches national pride at its most sensitive point; and to many people it has symbolized the failure of self-government. In the nineteenth century it was an axiom of nationalism that Ireland could maintain a much larger population. Even before the Famine, Davis endorsed an argument that thirty-five million could be supported if the country were properly developed.[5] Two weeks before the Rising Pearse wrote that:

in a free Ireland . . . gracious and useful rural industries will supplement an improved agriculture. The population will expand in a century to 20,000,000: it may even in time go up to 30,000,000.[6]

Prophecies such as these were not the result of scientific calculations: they expressed and strengthened the belief that the loss of population would be ended with the subversion of foreign government, which was its principal cause. To many, that loss was not a result of misgovernment but of deliberate policy.[7] It is therefore a deep disenchantment to find that emigration and population decline have not only persisted into the age of self-government but that they were as intractable in the 1950s as at any time in the past. It is true that less friendly prophets than Davis or Pearse were equally discredited by the event. In 1872

4. It is interesting to consider what Irish names might have been mentioned in this context a century ago.

5. In 'Udalism and Feudalism', *Essays*, Dun Dealgan Press, Dundalk: 1914, p. 71.

6. *The Spark*, April 1916.

7. John Mitchel, for example, argued that the Devon Commission, which examined the state of land tenure just before the Famine, had as its 'true function and object . . . to devise the best means of getting rid of what Englishmen called "the surplus population" of Ireland'. See his *History of Ireland*, Duffy, Dublin: n.d., vol. ii, 376.

A valuable survey of these issues will be found in R. D. C. Black, *Economic Thought and the Irish Question, 1817–1870*, Cambridge University Press, Cambridge: 1960.

Froude assured his audience that 'the Irish race seems intended to close its eventful history and disappear in the American Republic'.[8] Even in the 1970s, there are still more Celts on the banks of the Shannon than there are Red Indians on the banks of the Manhattan. But, when things have gone wrong, it is little consolation to reflect that they might have been still worse.

To adjust national aims from an increasing population to assuring mere survival is a bitter reassessment. It has not been made more palatable by the reflection that the part of Ireland which remains under British rule has been able to maintain and increase its numbers. Sixty years ago, George Moore suggested that two million is the ideal population for the country so that there should be 'room to dream and think'.[9] It is not a proposition that will command agreement. The instinct of the race was exactly expressed by O'Connell when he heartened his listeners by the Mallow Defiance during the Repeal campaign: 'We were a paltry remnant in Cromwell's time. We are nine millions now!'

The boast falls on our ears with such irony that anxiety for the trend of population is easily understood. A book, which bears the revealing title of *The Vanishing Irish* attracted much attention on its publication some ten years ago.[10] Its approach is patently sincere, if (as this writer believes) mistaken. Its opening sentences run as follows:

Nothing in recent centuries is so puzzling or so challenging as the strange phenomenon being enacted before our eyes, the fading away of the once great and populous nation of Ireland. If the past century's rate of decline continues for another century, the Irish will virtually disappear as a nation and will be found only as an enervated remnant in a land occupied by foreigners.

The subsequent pages elaborate the contrasts between the population of 1841 and the population of modern times.

This writer will certainly not attempt the impossible task of arguing that the present demographic condition of Ireland is normal. But attempts to improve that condition will not be helped if the problems are wrongly stated at the start. It is misleading, to say the least, to assume that the demographic and economic condition of pre-Famine Ireland was normal and that everything that has happened since was abnormal. Any examination of the circumstances of the country then will show that the population lived at a level which was wretched by the standards of contemporary Europe. It is grossly misleading to regard the conditions of 1841 as some kind of Golden Age and to consider the population level of that year as a mark of well-being. A famine was nothing unusual in that generation. The exceptional and decisive factor

8. J. A. Froude, *Short Studies*, Longmans Green, London: 1888, vol. ii, p. 265.
9. In the fourth chapter of *Salve*.
10. Edited by John A. O'Brien, Allen, London: 1954.

in the Great Famine was that the potato crop failed two years running and in three years out of four. That was the reason why many more people starved to death than in any other of the half-dozen famines of the previous twenty-five years.[11] There is no point in discussing the population of 1841 without acknowledging that it lived on the verge of starvation, from which it might or might not be rescued when the potato crop was got in each year. Population must not be regarded as nothing more than a count of heads. In any country, particularly in Ireland, the standard of living must be taken into account also.

Another point which is highly relevant in this context is that the quality of a people is at least as important as its numbers. Present standards in Ireland, in the arts and sciences, in technical skills and crafts as well as in public spirit and self-confidence may fall far below our aspirations. Nevertheless, there can be little doubt that in all these respects (which are the qualities that distinguish a nation from a tribe) the position today is incomparably better than was the case before the Famine. The event soon showed that British ministers had little to fear from O'Connell's nine million. Their successors found a later, and smaller, generation more difficult to handle.

This matter may be left with a final appeal to the facts. Compared with the years before 1939, the birth-rate has risen and the death rate has fallen. Until quite lately, the fertility of marriage was as high as it had been a generation before. It is still one of the highest in western Europe. The death rates at birth and during infancy have been steadily reduced. The average number of births each year is greater than it was in any decade back to 1911–20. All this represents a great and, it seems, a continuing improvement. It can be summed up by noting that the annual natural increase averaged 15,300 as recently as 1931–40. For the five years 1961–5 it averaged 28,900. For a figure larger than that we must go back to the 1880s when the population was greater than it is today by just over one million people.[12]

These figures show why even well-intentioned talk about 'the vanishing Irish' is misleading and, because it creates pessimism, is also dangerous. In no manner is the race in danger of extinction in the sense in which the pre-war vital statistics of many European countries showed a failure of their peoples to reproduce their numbers. By no test can it

11. The primary source is the Report of the Devon Commission, 1845. See also R. D. Edwards and T. D. Williams (eds.), *The Great Famine*, Browne & Nolan, Dublin: 1956; Woodham-Smith, *The Great Hunger*, Hamish Hamilton, London: 1962; T. W. Freeman, *Pre-Famine Ireland*, Manchester University Press, Manchester: 1957.

A statistical illustration may be of interest. The late Lord Stamp noted that the consumption of tea, tobacco, beer, and spirits in the United Kingdom showed no decline between 1845 and 1848, although in that period three million people in Ireland died or emigrated. Cf. *British Incomes and Property*, King, London: 1922, p. 503.

12. Cf. what has been said above, at pp. 280–1, in connection with Dr. C. E. V. Leser's paper, *JSSISI*, 1964–5, p. 179.

be said that the Irish race is failing to reproduce itself. We have quite enough demographic problems—the low marriage rate and emigration particularly—without inventing others.

It would be pleasant to believe that the preceding paragraphs are of no greater usefulness than flogging a dead horse. There is, unfortunately, only too much reason to believe that Irish people are still so mesmerized by the long fall in their numbers that the wisdom of policies is still widely judged by whether they will lead at once to an arrest or a reversal of that fall. Population, to many, has become the central fact to which everything, in social as in economic life, must be referred. The result is disastrous because preoccupation with decline of population leads to neglect of its causes; and public thought and policy is devoted to treating the symptoms instead of the disease. In the resulting confusion, short-term policies are applied to what is (as will be argued) a long-term problem, thereby often making it still more intractable.

The marriage rate

The marriage rate has moved on an exceptionally low level ever since it was first ascertained in 1864. In other countries its fluctuations have been affected by the ebb and flow of prosperity. In Ireland, however, the rate is notable only for its immobility. Comparative peaks in 1914–16 and again in 1918–21 mirrored the prosperity of war years. But even at its highest recorded level (5.91 in 1946, another post-war year) it remained below the lowest levels reached in normal times in other countries.

The Emigration Commission remarked that:

as Ireland's population has been predominantly agricultural, the deterioration in the marriage pattern, which the Famine set in motion with a severe initial impetus, has been largely a rural phenomenon.[13]

A distinction between town and countryside should not be too sharply drawn. Few Irish towns possess a social structure or a way of life which is easily distinguishable from the surrounding countryside. It is only in very recent years that some of them have begun to develop a character of their own. Even in the cities a high proportion of people are engaged in occupations, such as the professions and services, which do not usually permit early marriage.

Nevertheless the Commission had no difficulty in showing the peculiar demographic features of the rural areas in contrast with the cities and towns. The sex ratio was normal in urban areas, abnormal in rural. The average age at marriage was markedly higher in the countryside than in the towns. Above all, the proportion of people unmarried

13. Ibid., para. 164. A higher rate was recorded in 1967.

in the adult age-groups was far greater in the countryside than in cities or towns. This came from the large numbers returned as 'assisting relatives' in agricultural occupations. In 1951, to take a figure that was not available to the Commission, there were 171,000 people so returned. Their prospect of marriage was to be gauged from the following figures. Among 'farmers' brothers assisting', less than one in every hundred was married in the age-group 25–29 and three in every hundred were married in the age-group 55–64. Among 'farmers' other relatives assisting' the percentages were 5 and 27.

'Relatives assisting' constituted one-third of all persons engaged in agriculture in 1951. They were spread all over the countryside, on all types of land and on all sizes of holding. This suggests that the low marriage rate has been a result of social organization rather than of economic weakness.[14]

In rural areas during the last eighty years the opportunity of marriage depended not so much on the possession of money as on the possession of land. The Land Purchase Acts, however, prevented the subdivision of holdings and therefore tended to stereotype their number. There were few forms of employment in rural areas other than on the land. The opportunities of marriage therefore became restricted; and the pattern of late marriages and celibacy emerged. This was not due, though it may have been assisted here and there, to psychological quirks: it was directly attributable to the fact that those who lived on family farms were part of a social structure based on the possession and inheritance of land. Other causes, such as the survival of either parent into extreme old age or the presence of younger brothers and sisters would present further obstacles to marriage. Given the strength of family ties and the extension of rural ways of life into the towns, the same pattern became discernible even in urban life. Thus the society that emerged from the later decades of the nineteenth century was largely based on the refusal to many of its members of the opportunity to found a home and family. In demographic terms, this was an evil quite as harmful as emigration: in human terms it was more monstrous by far.[15]

It may well be true that some race-memory of the disaster which early marriages and subdivision brought on pre-Famine Ireland may still delay or even prevent marriage where it is economically possible.[16] But many of the peculiarities of rural life which are noted by some con-

14. The proportions unmarried among 'relatives assisting' in cities and towns are also high. But the numbers involved are fewer.

15. Cf. C. M. Arensberg and S. Kimball, *Family and Community in Ireland*, Harvard University Press: 1940, pp. 227–30. Also C. M. Arensberg, *The Irish Countryman*, Macmillan, London: 1937.

16. Cf. K. H. Connell, 'Marriage in Ireland after the Famine', and discussion in *JSSISI*, 1955–6, p. 82.

tributors to *The Vanishing Irish* lose much of their eccentricity if they are regarded as the manner in which people adjust themselves to an environment in which marriage is almost impossible. The low marriage-rate should be recognized for what it is, the form of birth control adopted by a practising Catholic people. As is the case with other methods of birth control, it is a response to a particular set of economic and social circumstances. The point has been well made by Sir Alexander Carr-Saunders:

Ireland would seem to be the only country of which we can predict with certainty that opportunities for further expansion would be followed by a growth of population. For in Ireland alone does the method of keeping the birth-rate down demand self-control: elsewhere the method is agreeable in that it permits the enjoyment of pleasures without adding to the burdens. If another Ireland were raised up from the Atlantic, we might expect to see the Irish birth-rate rise and the vacant land peopled.[17]

EMIGRATION

Emigration has been a feature of Irish life for many generations. Long before the Famine, which is often and mistakenly regarded as its source, Irish youth had acquired the habit of settling abroad. Throughout the eighteenth century there were two streams of emigrants, both of which were attributable to the settlement of Ireland after the Williamite victory and the Treaty of Limerick in 1691. The emigration of the Wild Geese to the service of the Catholic monarchies persisted until the French Revolution. In the same period many Ulster Presbyterians, against whom the Penal Laws were as vigorously enforced as against the Catholics, settled in north America. They were followed in the later decades of the century by a growing number of Catholic immigrants. At the same time, there was a continual emigration to England.

The mobility of the Irish people has been, and still is, quite exceptional. For generations they have been able to move without substantial let or hindrance to Great Britain, the United States, Canada, Australia, and New Zealand.[18] These countries have been, and still are, the great markets for labour: the Irish emigrant has had, and still has, freedom of entry into them. The facility of movement has not been affected by political or administrative changes. Secession from the Commonwealth did not affect freedom of entry into Great Britain or the older domin-

17. *World Population*, Clarendon Press, Oxford: 1936, p. 116.
18. This statement must now be subject to the very sweeping change made by the new immigration regulations of the United States.

ions.[19] When quotas were imposed on immigration into the United States, the provision made for the then Irish Free State was so generous that it has not been filled for nearly forty years. It is ironical that such unbounded freedom to emigrate, which would be received as a priceless boon by so many peoples of Europe, Asia, and Africa, should be regarded by its beneficiaries as something to be deplored.

This mobility goes even further. The Irish emigrant could not only travel freely: he had no reason to fear his reception. In the countries to which he went, he found no change of language or of political institutions. In the last century he fitted into the growing democracy of the United States with the same ease and zest as does his successor in Great Britain today. The institutions might be slightly unfamiliar: their practice presented few difficulties. To go from Ireland to the United States, as now to Great Britain, might certainly be described as changing one's home: there is also a sense in which it might as truly be described as going from one room to another in the same house. In that sense, it might be said without great exaggeration that Ireland is a western extension of Great Britain, an extra state of the United States or Australia, an extra province of Canada. Emigration from Ireland is perhaps easier, cheaper, and quicker than from perhaps any other country in the world. Certainly there can be few countries from which it may be accomplished with no greater preparation than buying a railway ticket.

These matters should be borne in mind by those who are disappointed by the failure of a self-governing Ireland to end emigration. Self-government increased the power of the Irish people to develop their economy: it did not reduce their freedom to leave their country. The establishment of a political boundary might, and did, affect the flow of goods but not the passage of people.

A further point was well made by Dr. M. D. McCarthy and Dr. R. C. Geary in an addendum to the report of the Emigration Commission. They remarked that:

the great majority of the people disapprove of emigration, though this disapproval certainly does not attach to the individual who decides to emigrate even when he could find employment at home.[20]

The ultimate aim of public policy is accepted as being to end emigration. But the standards of public and private conduct differ widely: a parent will boast of a child who has obtained a good job abroad and will expect to be congratulated by his friends. Here the clash of public and private interest is apparent. Unhindered emigration

19. This may be allowed to stand in spite of the legislation concerning immigration into the United Kingdom.
20. Op. cit., p. 203. Cf. also the remarks of Peadar O'Donnell, op. cit., p. 238.

provides opportunities of employment with greater remuneration and far wider ranges of choice than are usually present in Ireland. On the other hand the development of the natural resources of Ireland must demand in its initial stages lower remuneration and a greater degree of abstinence from consumption. It is apparent that in the past the prospects abroad have been more attractive to many than those at home. There can be a conflict between the interests of the State and those of the individual; and each person must decide the issue of that conflict according to his views of the ultimate importance of one and the other.

Nevertheless, the accepted or communal view is that emigration must be deplored. It is regarded as a grave national weakness which has already halved the population and may well, if suitable remedies are not applied, lead eventually to its extinction. It is rarely mentioned without the addition of a pejorative phrase. It is a 'drain' or a 'tragedy'; a 'disease' or, more specifically, an 'haemorrhage'. Above all it is something that must be quickly cured or ended.

To put things in this way is, of course, to compress together a variety of shades of thought, to include in one generalization the belief that suitable policies will eventually end emigration and the advocacy of such measures as making emigration illegal. But it is fair to summarize the prevailing attitude by saying that it regards emigration as something that should be ended by public policy as quickly as possible.

This attitude is only natural; but it has deeply confused public thought. Causes and effects are jumbled together, because neither, until very lately, have been fully analysed. The report of the Emigration Commission marked a great advance but there are many signs that its implications have not yet been fully appreciated. Underlying the public attitude is an unspoken assumption that emigration is something which flows from the weaknesses of the Irish economy and society. In fact, it is both an effect and a cause; it is at least as much the symptom of a disease as the disease itself. In several respects, it cannot be described as a disease at all because it is the ultimate result of quite healthy social developments and personal aspirations. Its volume depends only in part on what is done or not done by governments: it depends equally on the actions and choices of individual men and women in Ireland and on the policies of other countries. If public policy is to be framed so as to secure the greatest advantage, it is essential to distinguish the various forces that work to produce emigration.

One must begin by noting that there are some stimulants to emigration which are not in themselves undesirable. First, the natural increase is growing and is higher than in any of the countries to which our emigrants go for employment. Secondly, the Irish people, if perhaps more slowly than others in north-western Europe, are anxious to improve their material standard of living.

The expansion of the natural increase, which has already been noted, is surely a change for the better. It must be admitted that it has been accompanied by an increase in emigration. Nevertheless, it must be agreed that the balance of advantage tilts in the right direction. No doubt, emigration would be ended if the birth-rate fell so far that the number of new entrants into employment each year was no greater than what was needed for replacement. Is this a likely development; and, even if it should happen, would it be regarded as desirable? In other words, do we not postulate that the birth-rate should remain at a high level relative to western Europe? The issue should be faced—is it better to have a comparatively high natural increase accompanied by emigration or to have a lower natural increase with a smaller emigration? We must take our choice, until we can maintain a high natural increase with a falling emigration.

The second factor, the desire for a higher material standard of living is one which should be welcomed on balance. Prima facie it should act as a spur to improvement. Having few wants may be the mark of a highly contented and happy society which holds the Grecian view that money is needed only to make the good life possible. It may also be the mark of an undeveloped community whose ambitions, and material and immaterial needs, are few.

There is certainly a time-lag in the spread of higher living standards from Great Britain or the United States to Ireland. Within Ireland, there is a further lag between the urban and the rural areas. But this interval has been reduced through the influence of films, radio, and television. In one form or another these influences are at work all over the world, but they are particularly strong in Ireland, where they are reinforced by personal knowledge. In the nineteenth century, descriptions of life abroad came from letters written by emigrants, few of whom returned to visit their relatives. Today the prevailing way of life contains a much greater amount of material comfort than was the case before 1914 and it is vividly described, during Christmas and summer holidays, by those who work in Great Britain. The impact of the contrast between conditions in Ireland and across the Irish sea is far more immediate and therefore more powerful. Further, the Irish people feel themselves to be part of the Anglo-American society and are therefore influenced by its standards. It is a society to which they have access; it is therefore one which they may attempt to imitate in their own lives. It is not a society which, however desirable, belongs to a world into which there is no entry. That is the difference between those who live in rural Ireland and those who live in Sicily or the Peloponnese.

By the light of the official view, that emigration is to be deplored, this may appear to be regrettable. But it is the result of forces which cannot be considered to be in themselves against either an individual or a communal standard of values. By those standards it is not unsatisfactory that the birth-rate should increase; it is not improper that people should wish to better themselves.

Here, however, we meet the factor of mobility again. In a society that, by choice or circumstance, was more dependent on its own resources than is ours, a desire for a higher standard of living would eventually lead to increasing efficiency. But if Irish people wish to make money, it is usually more easy to travel to Great Britain or the United States than to try to make it at home. The economies of these countries are much less static than, until very recent years, the Irish has been. It has often been said that Irish people work harder abroad than they do at home. If there is any truth in that generalization, it is probably because it is much easier to make money by hard work abroad than it has been at home: the difference is not in the person but in the kind of society in which he lives.

Causes of emigration

It has long been customary to group the causes of emigration under the headings of 'push' and 'pull'. The first heading covered the forces that drove people out of the country. Famines and evictions (when the occupation of land afforded almost the only means of subsistence or employment) fell into this category. The second comprised the influences which attracted people abroad such as hopes of greater opportunities or (more specifically) the custom whereby relatives who had already emigrated sent back the price of the passage money to other members of the family so that they might follow. The forces of 'push' were almost always internal, operating within the country; those of 'pull' almost always external, operating outside it. The forces of 'push' could be, and indeed were, substantially reduced by political and social reform. By the end of the nineteenth century the threat of famine had disappeared, security of tenure was becoming general and schemes of land purchase were already in operation. Nevertheless, emigration continued although it was declining both absolutely and relatively. An acute observer remarked, in the first decade of the present century, that

there has come into being a current of voluntary emigration. This I believe to be a very grave sign as regards the future of the country. It is an indication of the power of this movement which, in spite of decreased numbers, retains a singularly strong hold on the people. As yet it shows no sign of being near its end, although it must inevitably bring Ireland to ruin and annihilation.[21]

The course of emigration during the next twenty years seemed to belie this gloomy prophecy. A temporary increase in the early 1920s was

21. L. Paul-Dubois, *L'Irlande contemporaire*, Paris, 1907, translated by T. M. Kettle and published by Maunsel, Dublin, in 1908 as *Contemporary Ireland*, p. 360.

explicable as a result of the suspension of migration during the later years of the first war and the political events that followed in Ireland. It is notable that this increase died away in the later years of the decade when American prosperity was still at its peak. But Great Britain replaced the United States as the goal of emigration in the years just before the second war and the numbers leaving Ireland increased during the war and post-war years. In the 1950s, they were much greater, relatively to total population, than they had been since the 1880s.

The Commission on Emigration set out new definitions of the causes of emigration:

by 'pull' is commonly meant the force of attraction, whether economic or social, which other countries exert, while 'push' describes the forces arising from the failure of conditions at home to provide an adequate basis for livelihood.[22]

The explanation provided by 'push' and 'pull' is unsatisfactory because 'push', in any real sense, disappeared decades ago and can be accepted as a factor now only if it is qualified as in the quotation. It is also a discomforting explanation because 'pull', which writers agree to have been the more powerful factor in modern times, is independent of any action that can be taken in Ireland, by the State or by private enterprise. If 'pull', in the sense in which the term is used above, is outside our control, the inference follows that emigration is also outside our control. That may be true: it is probably at least partially true. But a resolve to deal with emigration will not be strengthened if the first premise is that we can do nothing about it, and if the second premise is that it can be ended only by the desperate remedies of major wars or the decision of foreign governments to restrict the entry of our people. We must try to do better than that.

Another analysis will now be advanced, if only as a basis for argument. It divides the causes of emigration into cyclical and structural causes. Cyclical causes are taken to cover periods of emigration which are influenced by poor employment prospects here or good prospects abroad, resulting from fluctuations of trade or other essentially transitory causes. The peak of emigration in 1956–7, after the imposition of the special levies on imports, may be taken as an example. The wartime emigration to Great Britain may provide another. These cyclical causes are always liable to occur; but they will not necessarily continue for very long.

Structural causes, in this analysis, are those causes which operate in good and adverse times because they are, as it were, built into the economic and social structure of the country. Some of them may be listed. The first, returning to a feature already noted in connection with

22. Ibid., para. 300.

the marriage rate, is the family farm. Traditionally, families were large and few of their members were able to remain on the land through marriage to members of other farming families. Most of them therefore left the farm (which is to say that they left the country), leaving a brother to carry on the family by raising another generation of children, most of whom would emigrate when their time came. This pattern might be repeated indefinitely. In this sense, Irish emigration was self-perpetuating and persisted independently of, although it might be accentuated by, economic forces. It created the conditions by which emigration in the next generation was made possible: it fed on itself and maintained the parent stock. If it had been an emigration of complete families, it would soon have been over and done with.

A second cause, which is closely connected with the first, is the poor prospects of marriage for women. The Emigration Commission noted that in 1951 over half of the women in the age-group 15–44 who lived in rural areas were unmarried.[23] The proportion did not vary greatly from one province to another or from one county to another. It is obvious that the strength of this factor also will not be influenced by variations in economic conditions.

The distribution of population provides a third factor. The Emigration Commission pointed out that:

it is clear from the statistical data presented that emigration tends to be heavy from densely populated areas, from areas where the land is poor (as indicated by its valuation), from areas where there is relatively little urbanization, and from small-farm areas.[24]

This judgement is supported by the fact that in all inter-censal periods for forty years the heaviest rates of net emigration have occurred (with few variations) in the counties of Connacht and the three Ulster counties. These are counties with high proportions of small farms, they comprise a great deal of poor land and (apart from Galway and Sligo, where the figures for rates of net emigration are markedly better than the others) they include no large towns. It is also in these areas, it will be remembered, that demographic eccentricities were found to be most pronounced.[25]

These are some of the causes of emigration which, it is suggested, may be described as 'structural'. But it will be seen that, at least in the countryside, the causes of the low marriage rate are almost indistinguishable from the causes of emigration that have just been men-

23. Fifty-four per cent in 1951 and 52 per cent in 1961.
24. Ibid., para. 282.
25. The counties in this area also occupy a low place in a comparative study of county incomes. Cf. E. A. Attwood and R. C. Geary, *Irish County Incomes in 1960*, E R I, Paper No. 16. It appears, as Mr. Garret FitzGerald has suggested, that much the same pattern is to be found across the border in the contiguous counties of Tyrone and Fermanagh.

tioned. We have seen that the family farm system, when coupled with the shortage of other occupations in the countryside, means that the number of marriages must be comparatively small. But there would be even fewer marriages if the members of each family, other than the son who is selected to carry on the holding and the daughters who marry into other farms, did not leave. To leave the farm, in practice, has meant emigration. Thus a state of affairs was created in which the marriage of some children was conditional on the emigration of others.

If this assessment is even broadly correct, then emigration and the low marriage rate spring very largely (though not exclusively) from the form of Irish rural society and from the fact that, apart from the family farm, no rural pattern of employment emerged from the Land Purchase Acts. If so, emigration (and the low marriage rate) should be regarded as a rational response to a particular economic and social situation. It should not be described in value terms as something that is 'good' or 'bad'. Strictly speaking, emigration can be described as a loss only if productive work can be found for the emigrant. The availability of such work has been limited by factors such as those already noted, the extensive nature of the agricultural economy, the expulsive force of the family farm, and the faulty distribution of population. In such a context, emigration was almost inevitable, and emotive images or adjectives only obscure the truth.

It should be less difficult to accept this proposition because it holds out rich promises of improvement. In the foregoing analysis, it was taken for granted that leaving the farm was equivalent to emigration. That was true eighty years ago: it was largely true forty years ago. It is true enough even today but the increase in the number of opportunities of employment in the cities and towns has changed and is changing the situation for the better. The system of farming is still extensive; indeed the economy is more dependent on cattle to-day than ever before; but it is now possible to see how the rural demand for labour can be increased by improved husbandry on the farms and the development of the processing of agricultural and especially horticultural products. It must be admitted that the social pattern in the counties of the west and north offers less immediate promise of improvement; equally, few areas could be more quickly changed for the better by policies more adapted to their needs. None of these developments, even if achieved, nor all of them if achieved together, will necessarily end emigration. But our economy may well move into a new and hitherto unexperienced situation in which emigration persists but no longer reduces total population nor weakens the confidence of the Irish people in themselves and in their country.

It will be noticed that the forces that have been suggested as causes of emigration, whether they be classified as 'pull and push' or as 'cyclical and structural' are all economic or social in nature. But there is much force in a suggestion which Dr. N. G. Nolan made to the Statistical Society years ago that such theories are inadequate and that the causes lie deeper still.[26] One of the most puzzling things about Irish life is that an acceptance of emigration as inevitable is to be found in some places where it appears to be totally unjustifiable and is not found in others where it would seem pardonable. It is easy to think of townlands and parishes, to all appearances economically similar to each other, where the intensity of the determination to remain in Ireland is utterly different. Much must still depend on the human element, on whether the population is still vital or is exhausted or on whether leadership has been provided at the moment when it can be decisive. It may prove that the future of the small farm areas will ultimately depend on such matters.

It is easily comprehensible why commentaries on emigration should have been concerned with the forces that drove or attracted people out of Ireland. An equal attention has not been given to the forces, latent or active, that persuade people to stay even at the cost of their economic advancement. There are a number of them, all powerful and all capable of being strengthened still further. Many men and women have accepted the hardships of life on a small farm so that the name of the family should survive on the land. Others have remained through attachment to their town or countryside. Others again have sacrificed attractive prospects because they have accepted as their duty the task of helping to rebuild their country. No economic scales can weigh these forces. They may be all the more decisive because they are intangible. We have perhaps done ourselves great hurt by judging emigration as if it were the result of an economic equation between money in Ireland and money abroad. That may well have been true in times of hunger; but it must become decreasingly important as the Irish people leave poverty and immediate want behind them. If the attraction of life in Ireland depended only on its economics, then indeed most Irish people would long ago have abandoned their country and their hopes. It depends rather on the quality of life in Ireland.

Consequences of emigration

The first and most obvious consequence of emigration is that it has provided a working model of the economics of a declining population. Its persistence has diminished the market for all forms of goods and services and for professional activities. In particular it has restricted the opportunities for Irish manufacturers who cannot use the advantages of large-scale production unless they engage in the export trade. In some

26. In a discussion on a paper, 'The Problem of Population', by Professor John Busteed, *JSSISI*, 1936–7, p. 67.

occupations a scarcity of labour has been caused. Mr. Freeman has remarked that the nineteenth century saw an over-populated countryside but that the later twentieth century might see the same countryside suffering from under-population.[27] It is possible that here and there this prophecy has been fulfilled already. A falling population means also a contraction of the field from which revenue is drawn: the imposition of taxation becomes more difficult when the number of taxpayers declines. Above all, Ireland shows the effect of a falling population on the return from durable investment. In the last century, the railway system was constructed for a population which was double its present size. We still struggle with the consequences.

It has been often said that emigration takes the best and most enterprising of each generation. The point was made with perhaps excessive emphasis by Oldham fifty years ago:

What is serious is the quality, not the quantity of the drain. An emigration by individuals is very much more injurious to a country than an emigration of families . . . The economic units are unchanged, but each is depleted and its efficiency reduced. Thus there has been, in Ireland, a perpetuated survival of the unfittest, a steady debasement of the human currency—very similar to Gresham's Law, by which bad money continually tends to displace good money in circulation.[28]

To claim that it was always the most enterprising members in each generation who emigrated seems to assume a great deal. If ever a decision entailed little enterprise and involved few risks it was the Irish emigration to the United States. The emigrant travelled, as has been well said, 'from the known to the known': the contrast with the emigration from southern or eastern Europe is obvious. The passage money was sent back by relatives who had gone before: the ticket was bought in a local shop:[29] the emigrant was met on arrival. This made the least possible demand on the quality of enterprise: a great deal more courage would have been needed to face the hazards of employment among strangers in Cork or Dublin.[30] In more recent years, emigration to the United Kingdom calls for even less initiative.

This much, however, must be allowed. Emigration has always fallen most heavily on the younger age-groups; and it is possible to calculate at each census what amounts to a survivorship-ratio: that is, a calcula-

27. *JSSISI*, 1944–5, p. 404.

28. 'The Incidence of Emigration', *JSSISI*, 1913–14, pp. 213–14.

29. Well into the 1920s one of the few splashes of colour in country towns was provided by placards showing many-funnelled liners of the Cunard or White Star, set outside the shops where the tickets were bought.

30. Cf. in the late 1920s—'Would I tell him that it would be more to my liking to go among my companions beyond than to set out for the capital city of Ireland along with him?' M. O'Sullivan, *Twenty Years A-growing*, Chatto & Windus, London: 1933, p. 255.

tion may be made of the number of children at each census who might be expected to be still in Ireland ten years later. It has been shown, for example, that of the boys and girls who were aged between 10 and 14 in 1936, no less than a quarter of the boys and more than one-third of the girls might be presumed to have emigrated by 1946. In an area of heavy emigration, such as the county Mayo, the proportions would be still greater.[31] These calculations cannot be precise; but in recent decades any error has been on the side of under-statement. It must make some difference to a community's way of life if the proportion of its members who are growing into maturity is permanently reduced. In other countries one may speak of a 'lost generation', caused by the casualties of war and one may point to the loss of continuity and energy which was the result. In Ireland, there is always a lost generation; and the erosion of those qualities with which youth can enrich a society is continuous.

It should be added, if only because it is too often forgotten, that some results of emigration are acceptable in the short run. Granted the fact that the economy did not develop at any rate remotely capable of absorbing the natural increase (and still lags behind even in the later 1960s), emigration has prevented the emergence of an immense surplus of labour and an inevitable driving down of all salaries and wages. It has allowed those who remain at home to enjoy a standard of living which is not justified by the volume of their production. In the short run at least, emigration has done a great deal to make life in Ireland more leisurely and less disturbed by class warfare. If it ended suddenly, that life would become much more competitive and much less remunerative.

But when all that has been said, it remains true that emigration blunts the edge of initiative. Economic growth demands hard work and the acceptance of low standards of consumption, at least in its early stages. Other peoples, such as those of the Mediterranean, must conform to this situation. They have little freedom of emigration; they must therefore make the best of what they have, which is the first step towards making it better. The Irish people need not do so.[32]

A distinction must again be drawn between the interests of the community and the interests of the individual. For the individual it may well be that emigration involves a great deal of personal unhappiness which may or may not be temporary, but usually leads to wider economic

31. Cf. the following extract from vol. ii of the 1961 Census, Table 12. It shows the numbers in certain age-groups in county Mayo.

0–4 years	11,883	25–9 years	4,797
5–9 ,,	12,585	30–4 ,,	5,385
10–14 ,,	13,631	35–9 ,,	6,307
15–19 ,,	10,450	40–4 ,,	7,482
20–4 ,,	5,027	45–9 ,,	8,367

32. Cf. pp. 335–6.

prospects. The economic balance must be weighed down, in the majority of cases, on the side of gain. For the community, it has been pointed out, that under present circumstances, emigration is the condition of the continuance of the present pattern of land-use and that the emigration of people who cannot obtain or will not accept productive work cannot be described as an economic loss. Nevertheless the rearing and education of children who emigrate incurs, directly and indirectly, expenses which are capable of assessment in money terms, though the propriety of using such measurements in matters which touch so closely on parental and family feelings may be disputed.[33] The true cost of emigration to the community is perhaps more correctly assessed in terms of its effect on blunting initiative and weakening determination to make the best of what opportunities lie to hand.

A national population policy

The Commission on Emigration was required by its terms of reference 'generally to consider the desirability of formulating a national population policy'. The ninth chapter of its report deals with this instruction. The reader of that chapter will observe that no such policy was formulated; and he will see the reason. A respect for the liberty of the individual deterred the Commission from recommending the control of emigration in any manner.[34]

As to emigration, the individual exercising his free will is in normal circumstances free to live where he wishes. Consequently, we believe that those who wish to and can emigrate have the right to do so, and that the State should not consider interfering with the exercise of this right, except in the case of a national emergency or where the survival of the nation is in jeopardy. We do not consider that our present demographic circumstances would justify such interference.[35]

For these reasons it declined to recommend

in present circumstances, direct Government action in the demographic field, such as the banning or limitation of emigration, the imposition of a tax on bachelors or the provision of marriage loans and grants.[36]

The Commission's attitude, therefore, was that the remedy for a falling population could not be found in conferring privileges, inflicting disabilities or imposing controls, but rather in general social and economic improvement.

Almost all the influences which determine population growth are matters which properly depend upon personal decisions, and with regard to them, the

33. The 'cost' of an emigrant was discussed by the then Registrar-General, Dr. Grimshaw, as long ago as 1895. Cf. the minutes of evidence of the Financial Relations Commission, vol. i, p. 144.

34. It did not refer to the practical difficulties of enforcing any system of control.

35. Ibid., par. 459.   36. Ibid., par. 470.

role of the Government should be to encourage and, where necessary, to initiate economic and social activities which produce conditions favourable to increased population, leaving people free to take their decisions in the light of these conditions.[37]

It follows that public policy must work, as it were, at secondhand. It is therefore all the more important that, within this restricted sphere, the proper purposes of public policy should be understood. It is not to create employment as such but to increase productive and commercial efficiency. A temporary alleviation of population loss may be obtained by making work, in protected or subsidized industries or services, or again in intermediate ways such as building and construction schemes. A less temporary improvement might be secured by a ruthless division of larger holdings and their replacement by a greater number of smaller farms. In a greater or lesser degree these panaceas have been applied in the last generation. But they can provide no permanent solution unless they rest on a sound economic foundation, unless the industries can survive on a competitive basis or the newly created small farms can provide an acceptable livelihood for the families that work them. If the industries are not competitive nor the farms efficient they can be sustained only for so long as there is sufficient production in the economy that earns enough wealth (rather, foreign exchange) to carry them and those who are employed in them. Always one comes back to the need for greater efficiency. That may make eventually for a larger population: it is quite certain that a greater population at an acceptable standard of living cannot be maintained without it for long. It is the more necessary to insist on this point because what appear to be shortcut approaches to providing employment may in fact weaken the capacity to produce wealth and therefore reduce the power of the economy to retain even its present population. Slogans such as 'twenty-five thousand jobs a year' do less than nothing to solve the problem. It is easy to understand why the establishment of any form of industry should have been accompanied by calculations of how many people would obtain employment as a result; but our population problems would have been ended long ago if they were as simple as that approach assumes.

In the last resort the level of population depends on how much people produce, how much they consume and how much they sell abroad. In the case of Ireland, the population is, largely for historical reasons, economically mal-distributed, on farms that (possibly through the inadequacy of agricultural policy) are inefficient and in industries and services (such as distribution) that are over-manned. It is notorious that agricultural production is less than it might be; both in agriculture and in industry the gap between the efficient and the less efficient producers is startlingly great. On the other hand, the level of consumption

37. Ibid.

is high while standards of remuneration, in many sectors of the economy, approach British levels. In such circumstances, a loss of population has been almost inevitable.

Emigration could be ended, no doubt, by some very drastic solutions. It could be ended if the right to leave the country were to be severely restricted by our government or the power to enter other countries were to be curtailed by governments elsewhere. It could also be ended, or at least severely reduced, if there were a long continued fall in the birth rate. It might be ended, in the long run, if the standard of living were reduced so that an export trade based on cheap labour could offer greater employment. None of these solutions is likely to be acceptable. There are some prices that will not be paid for the ending of emigration.

If that be granted, the conclusion must be that the remedy lies in long-term policies aimed at removing the structural defects of the economy and at making it more efficient. The ultimate aim of such policies is not primarily to end emigration but rather to create conditions in which it may be first reduced to tolerable limits. It should be accepted that the forces which have worked towards emigration in the past will continue to do so for some time to come, even if there is an advance in productive efficiency and prosperity. It is possible that the immediate, as against what may be hoped to be the ultimate, result of such an advance might be to reduce the amount of under-employment and thus, in a short run at least, to encourage rather than to reduce emigration. It is possible that the first steps towards a larger population in the country as a whole may mean that for the time being there will be a smaller population in some parts of it.

This is a gloomy suggestion. One hopes that it will prove to be quite unfounded. But Irish population trends have been highly volatile: the hopes raised by the Census of 1951 were cruelly belied during the following decade. The present favourable circumstances may be changed in their turn. However that may be, two points should be remembered when and if reassurance is needed. The first is that demographic improvement will not necessarily be apparent in all areas of the country nor in all sectors of the economy at the same time. (It has been the point of preceding paragraphs that true improvement may depend on such dissimilarities.) The second is that even if, to imagine the worst, emigration continues to bear away a great part of the natural increase there would still be no reason for despondency, provided the economic trends were in the right direction. A people that feels itself to be reaching out to new activities could easily learn to live with emigration.

It must be admitted that it is difficult to discuss these matters with objectivity. In the history of many countries there have been events that have so impressed the mind of later generations that decades or centuries later they are still alive, still actual, still with power to shape policies and ways of thought; the Thirty Years' War in Germany, the Great Revolution in France and, we may surely add, the Famine in Ireland.

It must be seldom that any people has been so completely drained of hope and self-reliance as was the Irish at the end of the 1840s. Nevertheless, in spite of all appearances, the Famine was not a mortal wound. Its survivors overthrew the system of land tenure: their grandchildren broke the Legislative Union. But it was a wound that has never healed: perhaps because we have never ceased to pluck at it. For over a century, there has been an unending debate on the reasons why people leave Ireland to the neglect of the reasons why people stay. We have been more concerned with past losses than with the possibilities of the present, more conscious of the opportunities that have been missed than with those that are present here and now. This is understandable, in the sense in which it is understandable that the American South still lives in the shadow of its defeat in the War between the States; but it is deeply unhealthy. We need less self-pity and a greater awareness of what can be done now and, above all, of the conditions, of work and self-denial, that must be fulfilled if a lasting solution is to be found.

CHAPTER FIFTEEN

The Monetary and Credit System

THE COMMERCIAL BANKING SYSTEM WAS ALREADY WELL established when the present currency was introduced and the Central Bank set up. It possessed several highly individual features, some of which are now being modified by the march of events. Two characteristics in particular have attracted attention—the high proportion of deposits on which interest must be paid and the large amount of assets which have been invested outside the State.

These characteristics (which are not now as strongly marked as they once were) were two results of the same cause. The high proportion of time deposits in the commercial banking system was the result of a lack of development and enterprise in the national economy in the past. Irish people have saved money, if not nowadays to the extent that is desirable: they have been slow to invest it. Farmers have been tradition- ally slow to invest in their farms. This may have been caused by the prevalence of an extensive system of agriculture which called for little capital or it may have been due to a caution inspired by violent changes in agricultural prices and, more recently, in agricultural policies. In the non-agricultural sector of the community there has been a somewhat greater readiness to use one's own money in one's business; but for a long time this was limited by the restricted amount of manufacturing and commercial activity. To some extent, savers (in cities or in the country- side) bought industrial or gilt-edged shares but opportunities of buying shares in Irish commercial or manufacturing undertakings were few indeed until very recently.[1] For greater security, people preferred to place their money on deposit in the banks.

1. For decades Irish railway shares were regarded as the most secure form of investment. Their collapse in the 1920s and early 1930s must have intensified the cautious instincts of small savers.

The results were shown by the first statistics obtained for banking assets and liabilities within the State. At that time—31 December 1931 —no less than 82 per cent of all deposits were time deposits. Since 1945 things have changed greatly and relatively rapidly. Money is used by its owners to a much greater extent; business and production activity is greater; the levels of consumption are higher. By the end of 1966, 58 per cent of all deposits were time deposits.

In the early 1930s an observer of the Irish banking scene remarked that as bank deposits resembled savings bank deposits it was not unnatural that the investment policy of the banks should resemble the investment policy of a savings bank. Indeed, the banks had little choice in the matter. Nothing remotely approaching a bill market existed anywhere in Ireland. It was inevitable that their idle assets should be placed in London, in the money market or in British Government stock. The habit persisted long after the Treaty had placed a political boundary between Dublin and London.[2] In the earlier decades of the new State the demand for bank credit was held down by the long fall in prices between the wars and the depression itself. Moreover the area of investment even in Irish government securities was exceptionally limited. The first issue of government stock was made in 1923, but as late as 1947 the total outstanding was only £48m. of which a high proportion was held in trustee funds and was therefore withdrawn from the market.

In such circumstances old habits died hard. Money continued to be placed in London although, as a result of the balance of payments deficits of the 1950s, the flow was no longer one-way. After the 1955–6 difficulties had been surmounted, however, there was a long period in which the net external assets of the Associated Banks increased. The increase was not proportionate to the increase in their liabilities; but the disparity gave no cause for alarm.

The sequence of events in 1964 and 1965 changed this position and, as will be seen, precipitated a series of adjustments within the banking system. In that period the borrowing requirements of the private and public sectors increased much more rapidly than resources. The shortfall in the growth of resources was due to a variety of causes. An inadequate supply of savings, a reduction in capital inflow from abroad and increased business activity no doubt all played their part. Whatever the reasons, resources were not sufficient to meet the increased demand upon them. The Report of the Central Bank for 1965–6 noted that:

domestic credit formed 63 per cent of total assets in 1965 as compared with 53 per cent in 1958. External assets fell accordingly from 47 per cent to 37

2. The division of bank liabilities and assets 'within the State' and 'outside the State' dates from 1931: though it is only in the last fifteen years that it has acquired importance. But it should never be forgotten that while the division is of importance to the State and to the Central Bank it is not as meaningful to any individual bank which accepts deposits and makes advances on both sides of the border with Northern Ireland.

per cent over the same period. Among the liabilities, deposit accounts fell by about 6 percentage points while current accounts moved up by some 4 points during the seven years.[3]

A further complication was created by the growing need to finance expenditure by the State. The *Quarterly Bulletin* of the Central Bank for January 1966 pointed out that between December 1964 and December 1965 additional accommodation to the State and public authorities totalled £28m. while the increased accommodation to the private sector was only £0.6m. The banks are obliged to meet the needs of the State at the same time as they must satisfy the growing demand from the private sector which must be expected if development programmes are successful. In such circumstances a failure of resources to grow in any proportion reconcilable with the increased demand for credit creates acute difficulties. If such circumstances were to prevail for any length of time (and it is proper to add that a better balance was reached in 1966) the banking system would come perilously near to being forced out of the functions which it is expected to discharge in a system of private enterprise.

One result has been to direct attention to the liquidity of the banking system which hitherto had always been taken for granted. There has been a consequent search for adequate measurements of liquidity. That which holds the field at present is 'the Central Bank ratio' which is defined in the Annual Report just quoted as 'the ratio between the net external assets of the Associated Banks plus their deposits with the Central Bank less Exchequer Bills rediscounted by the Central Bank, to the total of their current and deposit accounts within the State'.

The difficulty is to define precisely what is meant by liquidity. The ratio refers to the assets of the banking system outside the State in relation to its liabilities within the State. That concept may be relevant to the framing of economic policy within the Republic. It has not the same relevance to any one bank. In the first place, any one bank is concerned with its own liquidity, not with the liquidity of the system as a whole. In the second place, each bank looks at its business, within and outside the State, as a whole; and only two of the Irish banks do not operate on each side of the border. A concept of liquidity which will at the same time serve the purposes of the banking system and of the government is not easy to find; but the need for it is much more urgent now than ever it was in the past.

Moreover, liquidity is not a problem of the banking system only. With the exception of Exchequer bills, government obligations are not fully marketable and cannot therefore be regarded by the banks as liquid. This is a result of an undeveloped domestic financial market.

3. *CBR*, 1965–6, p. 30.

The growth of a domestic market in government paper would greatly ease the problems of the banking system, but it goes without saying that such a market would be useful only if it were a genuine market which commanded the confidence of all concerned.

Thus within a comparatively short space of time, not much more than a decade, both the resources of the commercial banks and the demands made upon them have been changed out of recognition. At the same time they have been obliged to take note of growing pressure for new services: merchant banking activities, foreign exchange and the servicing of exports among them.

The level of interest rates paid and charged by the Irish commercial banks has been the subject of public discussion from time to time. Three general propositions may be set out briefly. The first is that the earnings of the banks, out of which they must pay salaries and wages, provide dividends, and make allocations to reserves come almost entirely out of the difference between what they charge for advances and what they pay on deposits. (In Ireland there is the additional point that the proportion of interest-bearing deposits is still, as we have seen, exceptionally high.) The second is that the rate paid on these interest-bearing deposits must be sufficient to attract deposits into the banking system and to retain existing deposits. The third is that bank deposits are highly mobile. Internally, they may be (and increasingly are) diverted into other repositories for savings—Exchequer or Treasury bills, prize bonds, the Post Office Savings Bank, or into the finance houses. Externally, they can be switched from a bank office within the State to an office of the same bank outside the State with little more formality than a telephone call. In order to protect deposits, therefore, rates in the Republic must be related to rates in the United Kingdom and elsewhere.[4] A wide disparity in rates may not indeed provoke a general shift of existing deposits (though it is especially likely to do so in the case of the larger, and in this context more important, deposits) but it may deter fresh deposits being made. There may not be a run on deposits: there may be erosion.[5]

Interest rates in the United Kingdom vary with changes in Bank rate. Thirty years ago it was taken as axiomatic that Irish rates should change with British rates,[6] but in recent years Irish rates have not ex-

4. A proportion of these moneys must eventually find its way into the commercial banking system but there has been evidence to suggest that some deposits have been channelled into the British banking system.

5. The stability of deposits is by no means a matter for the banks alone. Both the public and the State must be interested, granted the seasonal and quasi-seasonal demands on the banks to take up Exchequer bills, to advance to State agencies, to support State loans, and for ordinary business requirements.

6. Argument about banking rates in Ireland and the United Kingdom should not obscure the fact that there is a considerable gap between them and the rates paid on deposits by finance houses.

perienced changes as severe as those imposed in Great Britain in 1957, 1964, and 1967. It will be observed, however, that a change in Great Britain is usually followed by a change in the Republic. It is hard to imagine that a sharp increase in Great Britain would not be followed by some increase here in order to protect deposits; and any sustained downward movement in Great Britain would certainly lead to a reduction here in the long, and probably in the very short, run.

It is no secret that changes of rates have sometimes been preceded by prolonged discussions between the government and the banks. Successive governments have leaned in favour of low rates. This obviously favours borrowers rather than lenders but it is not out of line with the circumstances of a country in which public and private investment is needed. Nevertheless, these matters must be relative. If it is granted that deposits have to be attracted into the banking system, it follows that rates must be sufficiently high, otherwise deposits will be reduced and advances would have to be reduced in sympathy. Cheap money to borrowers could lead to no money.

Whatever the level may be at any time, there will always be a tug-of-war between the advocates of lower and higher rates. It may not always be possible to discern where the balance could best be struck. Perhaps the one clear sign is provided by a sharp rise or fall in deposits. Thus in retrospect it seems undeniable that the official refusal to allow interest rates to rise in the early part of 1955 was altogether mistaken: the proof being the growing deficit in the balance of payments and the continuing loss of deposits throughout the rest of that year and well into 1956.[7]

Criticisms of the lending policy of the banks have taken sharply opposed lines. A reader of the evidence given to the Banking Commission in the 1930s will note that the banks were then charged with having lent much too freely during and just after the First World War. After the Second World War the criticism was that the banks were lending too little. Some points may be made. Firstly, in an economy which is relatively undeveloped, there is a prima facie case for an easy credit policy. Secondly, for that very reason, the opportunities for immediately productive advances are likely to be limited. Thirdly, banks can hardly be reproached for reluctance to lend when the owners of deposits will not venture them on their own account. Fourthly, banks must guard their external assets, without which they would not be able to lend at all; and therefore they must be alive to any danger that increased credit would be used for consumption rather than production.

7. The payments deficit became so serious that the drastic measure of imposing import levies was used in the spring of 1956. The milder remedy of a small increase in interest rates fifteen months earlier would have saved the country many millions of external assets, allowed industries to hold their normal level of production and maintained some thousands in employment.

Lastly, it must be remembered that Irish banks face special hazards, such as the weather. A bad harvest means that advances remain out indefinitely.

The financial strength of the banks conceals some possible weakness. A high proportion of bank deposits have not been created by the banks: they have been left in the system by their owners, who may recall them at any moment. Some notice of withdrawal is formally imposed: in practice, it can be rarely enforced. On the other hand a considerable proportion of advances cannot easily be called in. It is well-known that advances constitute the working capital of many concerns, particularly of the family businesses which are so common in Ireland. A combination of vanishing deposits and frozen advances, which may be unlikely but is not inconceivable, would create embarrassment and must be borne in mind in the shaping of a credit policy.

The effect that increased advances may have on the external assets of the banking system must also be remembered. This point may best be illustrated by quotation from the report of the Central Bank for the year ended 31 March 1956—a year in which the connection between domestic credit and external assets was all too amply illustrated.

To the extent that domestic finance provided by the banks is used to pay for purchases abroad in excess of current external earnings lodged with the banks, it calls for external funds which are obtained by sales of banks' external assets. This is generally the case when the rise in domestic credit is greater than in current and deposit accounts. In addition, when the note circulation rises, the banks surrender external assets to the Central Bank in exchange for legal tender notes. On the other hand, a reduction in the effective utilization of domestic finance, which occurs when current and deposit accounts rise faster than domestic credit, enables the banks to increase their external holdings . . . The foregoing observations bring into focus the closely related problem of maintaining an adequate degree of liquidity in the banks' resources. It is manifestly the commercial banks' obligation to keep the amount of credit granted at a level consistent with their continued ability to provide the external finance— in the shape of drafts on their external assets—arising out of the use of deposits lodged with them or out of the use of credit granted by them.

Throughout the postwar period, apart from seasonal fluctuations, and a temporary decline during 1952, domestic credit has been growing steadily. The commercial banks did not, however, experience any major difficulty with regard to liquidity in the earlier years due to the large accumulation of external assets during the war and due to the American Loan and other borrowings and net capital inflows, which further extended the domestic credit base. By the end of 1955, however, the net external holdings of the commercial banks had been reduced to a level barely sufficient to support the existing liabilities within the State. In fact, the heavy demands upon the banks' external resources, due to the worsening in external trade and to the large intake of government securities caused by the lack of support for the recent national loan, involved a deficiency in net external holdings of the commercial banks which had to be relieved by the Central Bank.

In the light of these developments the limiting influence of the marked reduction in the commercial banks' net external assets upon further extensions of domestic credit should be abundantly clear . . . The main facts, which are straightforward, can be stated simply. In our economy a sustained rise in domestic incomes and employment involves a sustained rise in imports both of industrial materials and of manufactured goods. A sustained rise in our incomes and employment therefore depends essentially not upon increased availability of domestic credit but upon our capacity to increase our export earnings sufficiently to pay for the necessary imports.[8]

This may be a matter which is in a state of transition. In such circumstances it is useful to summon up a long perspective, to use large maps as military strategists are advised to do. The post-war ratio of advances to deposits is certainly very much greater than was the practice in the 1920s and 1930s. It may be unwise to regard that period as a standard. It was a period in which advances fell on account of a continuing rise in the value of money; it included the depression and the economic war. It may be that bankers have come to regard as immutable a state of affairs which is transitory and that they should be prepared in future to administer a system many degrees less static than has lately been customary. But in that case, other parties must also accept new obligations. There will be a much greater responsibility on the State to ensure that National Loans are used for purposes which will yield a more immediate return than has been the practice. There will be a greatly increased necessity that the public, individuals, or private and public companies, should repay advances in much shorter periods than has been usual. If bankers must accept lower standards of liquidity, neither the State nor the public can expect them to continue to act as though they still possessed abundant assets out of which subscriptions to National Loans or extensions of advances can be made. This, when all is said and done, is only a part of economic growing-up. But in many respects it is not likely to be pleasant either to governments, bankers, or the public; and there is no reason to believe that such changes of habit will be painlessly acquired.

Criticisms of the banking system should not be left without a reference to one which affects their organization. A school of thought has long held that the country is 'over-banked'. In his minority report to the 1926 Banking Commission, the then secretary of the Department of Finance, Mr. McElligott, stated that there seemed to be too many bank branches in the country

with results that are beneficial neither to the public nor to the banks themselves. Banks in most countries are prepared to stand a limited number of unprofitable branches but here the proportion of branches that must show a loss on working seems unduly high. The excessive overhead charges thereby incurred are, of course, ultimately passed on to the customer.[9]

8. Report of the Central Bank for 1956, pp. 40–41.
9. Final Report, p. 63.

These strictures were not adopted by that Banking Commission nor by the later Commission which reported in 1938;[10] but it is probable that they would still be endorsed in the Department of Finance.

For over thirty years, the banks adhered to a self-denying agreement which meant that no new branches were opened. This became increasingly artificial when housing programmes created large new suburbs without banking facilities. The agreement broke down in 1959; and a number of new branches have since been opened. Thus the problem, if there is a problem, has been aggravated. It is easier to state than to solve. It applies not only to the number of branches but also the number of banks. The banks have had very different origins: they have different practices. As Dr. Brennan, a predecessor of Mr. McElligott in the secretaryship of the Department of Finance and in the governorship of the Central Bank, stated:

they differ appreciably in the character of their business and consequently in their respective roles in the monetary activity of the country. They will differ, for example, in their proportions of current to interest-bearing deposits, in the rate of turn-over of current account balances, in the distribution of their business between rural and urban customers, and in many other important respects.[11]

The emergence during 1966 of two major banking groups may eventually alter this situation radically. Nevertheless, a reduction in the number of offices may be hard to make. In theory, banks might agree among themselves on some such plan, but customers will not necessarily fall in with such agreements and transfer their accounts as desired. In banking, as in other economic activities, there is considerable hostility to any suggestion of centralization, and the closing of local offices detracts, in public opinion, from the importance of the area.

THE CURRENCY SYSTEM

The currency system was fashioned by the Currency Act of 1927. It has not been seriously modified since then. The Irish pound is still automatically convertible into sterling; it is still on a parity with sterling: it is largely, though no longer exclusively, backed by sterling assets. These characteristics have survived a major deflation, a world war, a

---

10. The majority report of the earlier Commission referred only to 'an extensive and adequate system of branches and agencies' (ibid., p. 42). The 1938 Banking Commission did no more than note the growth in the number of offices, ibid., p. 9.

11. 'Monetary Functions of Commercial Banks', *JSSISI*, 1942–3, p. 62. One of the 'other respects' is noted by G. A. Duncan who has written of the 'local, political and confessional concentration of clientele'. *Banking in the British Commonwealth*, ed. Sayers, Clarendon Press, Oxford: 1952, p. 310.

major inflation, and four devaluations. It is not surprising that they should have been strongly criticized from time to time, not always for the same reasons. It will be useful at this point to consider some of these criticisms.

To begin with, a currency must be convertible; otherwise foreigners will be unwilling to accept it in payment for their goods. The Irish community can buy tea from India or wool from Australia without difficulty because the exporters of these goods know that they will be paid in an international currency, sterling, which they can use to buy whatever goods they want in whatever countries they choose. Their attitude would be very different if they were to be paid in Irish pounds which could be used only to buy goods and services in Ireland. This consideration governs suggestions such as that the Irish currency should be based on abstract assets; for example, the fertility of the soil. Foreigners will not wish to sell their goods in exchange for an undefined and indefinable share of the land of Ireland. Further, a country that has a frequently unfavourable balance of payments must possess a currency that is freely convertible.[12]

It is hardly necessary to spend much time on the suggestion that the Irish pound should be based on gold. That is not a luxury which a deficit country can easily afford. In any case to place the backing of the currency into gold is to forego the opportunity of investing it in assets (such as Treasury bills) which bring in a return. Between the passage of the Currency Act in 1927 and the British abandonment of the Gold Standard in 1931, the country was on a gold exchange standard, i.e. it possessed a currency which was freely convertible into a currency which was itself freely convertible into gold. This arrangement was generally considered at the time to be most suitable for the smaller countries. Between 1931 and the outbreak of war, it was the most obvious commonsense to follow sterling rather than gold. During the war, as things turned out, the difficulties in obtaining imports sprang from conditions of transport rather than from the comparative absence of gold holdings.[13] It would be impossible to find any occasion since 1945 on which it would have been appropriate to back the Irish pound with gold.

From time to time it has been suggested that the Irish pound should be linked with some currency other than sterling. In 1942, during the debates on the Central Bank bill, the then Minister for Finance stated that the Currency Commission had been asked 'by the last Government and this Government' to consider changing the link to the French franc

12. These points were put by Lord Glenavy in his reservation to the report of the Banking Commission in 1938, ibid., p. 379.

13. The Currency Commission bought some gold in September 1938 but did not add to their holding between that time and the outbreak of war. The reasons for buying in the first place and for not buying in the second excite curiosity, but they do not appear to have been the subject of public discussion at any time.

or the United States dollar.[14] Time has passed its verdict on these official, and on many unofficial, suggestions. Imagination boggles at the proposition that during the post-war years Ireland should have laboured under a self-imposed obligation to pay out dollars for pounds. It is not necessary to elaborate the results of linking the currency to the French franc which went from 123 to the pound in 1927 to 1,380 in 1958 and is now back at twelve, or to the German currency which disappeared altogether in 1945 and today, in its reformed guise, stands at a premium against sterling.

The ultimate reply to such suggestions, however, is not founded on whether other currencies have appreciated or depreciated. It is that the economy does not earn any appreciable amount of currencies other than sterling. A link with a currency other than sterling (e.g. the German mark) could be maintained only by changing our resources in British sterling into marks. It would be a highly artificial arrangement. We are forced back to the fact that the economy earns a lot of sterling and very little of any other currency.[15]

Sterling is the only currency that the Irish economy earns in any significant amount and the foreign investments of the Irish people are mainly placed in sterling securities. Commercial ties and personal habit ensure that Irish currency can be changed into British sterling with a minimum of inconvenience or delay. The objections to the sterling link have usually been made on political rather than on technical grounds. The currency link is simply the result of the trade link. If and when the country earns freely currencies other than sterling (and a widening of its trade is obviously desirable on every ground) it will be in a position to change the present arrangements.

The link with sterling does not necessarily imply that the rate of exchange should be at par. To link the Irish pound with sterling is one decision: to decide that one pound Irish should exchange for one pound sterling is quite another. It might have been decided in 1927 to place the Irish pound at a premium over sterling (for example, exchanging for 25s. sterling) or at a discount (for example, 15s. sterling), or to allow the rate of exchange to fluctuate. In the circumstances of the time it was highly desirable that the new arrangements should cause as little change as possible. But the choices set out can always be looked at from time to time as circumstances alter.

The third choice has obvious disadvantages, from the point of view

14. *PDDE*, 86, 93. It may be suggested, however, that if the modern function of the Legal Tender Note Fund is to provide an ultimate reserve of foreign currency then the case for reducing the proportion of its external assets which is held in sterling deserves examination. This, it may not be necessary to add, raises issues quite different from 'the link with sterling' as such.

15. Cf. a useful booklet by the late M. R. J. Eaton, *Irish Banking, Currency and Credit* (published in 1954 by the Institute of Bankers in Ireland), p. 15.

of importers who might find their capacity to dispose of their goods destroyed by a change in the exchange rate, or from the point of view of farmers and other exporters who could not easily know the appropriate price for their products. The first effect of a fluctuating rate would be to introduce uncertainty throughout the field of foreign trade, which represents an exceptionally large element of the economy. It would also encourage the growth of a particularly pernicious type of middleman who would profit from the difficulties of legitimate traders. It is hard to think of any compensating advantage. As for an exchange premium or discount, the critics of the existing arrangement have shown significant differences. Some of them have stressed the need to encourage exports by depreciating the currency and thus reducing selling prices abroad. Others have denounced a system by which the Irish pound must be exchanged at par for 'worthless scraps of British paper'. Certainly the effect of the Irish pound at a discount could be to reduce the price to foreign purchasers of exports, but it seems highly improbable that this device would in fact boost sales abroad. Irish exports depend rather on the efficiency of production and marketing. Equally a depreciated currency involves an increase in the cost of living in so far as it makes imports dearer and, for that reason, it would handicap all forms of production, particularly in industries which depend on imported raw materials.[16] An appreciated currency would make imports cheaper but it would be a handicap to the export trade. It would also make necessary an austere financial policy which those who speak of the decline in the purchasing power of sterling are notoriously slow to advocate in this country. Circumstances may so alter the position that a departure from the present parity might become justifiable. In the meantime one may echo the words of a speaker on the Currency Bill in 1927 that there were 'only two national calamities that we have been spared from. One was an earthquake and the other a rate of exchange'.[17]

16. On the foregoing points see J. P. Colbert, *Commentary on Misconceptions Regarding Money and Bank Credit*, Cahill, Dublin: 1942, pp. 101–13. Ireland has contracted an amount of foreign indebtedness since Mr. Colbert wrote in 1942. This would, of course, greatly aggravate the consequences of a depreciation of the currency.

17. Major Bryan Cooper T.D., *PDDE*, 19, 1149. The case for putting the Irish pound at a discount against sterling used to be much stronger than the case for putting it at a premium. But, in so far as such decisions are related to the fostering of exports, it is surely incontestable that the problems of the export trade lie not so much in price as in regularity of supply and standardization of quality. It is right to state plainly that the retention of parity has involved four devaluations of the Irish pound, in 1931, 1939, 1949 and again in 1967. This has been unpalatable but inevitable. It cannot be suggested that, for example, in 1949 the Central Bank should have maintained a rate of exchange against the American dollar of 4.04 to the Irish pound.

Speaking in July 1965 Mr. Lynch (then Minister for Finance) stated that if sterling were devalued it would be necessary, having regard to the economic circumstances of the country, to continue to maintain the existing statutory position under which the Irish pound has a parity relationship with sterling. *PDDE*, 217, 1009.

Little time need be spent on the criticisms of Irish association with (rather than membership of) the sterling area. The facts that justify the link with sterling suggest also that the stability of sterling is a major Irish interest. It would be difficult to show that Ireland has suffered by her association with the area. It provided a means of access to dollars in the early post-war period. Since 1955, however, Ireland has enjoyed a favourable balance of payments with the dollar area and it appears to have been a contributor to rather than a dependant on the reserves of the sterling area ever since.[18]

The connection with the sterling area, however, has been remarkably tenuous. Irish ministers have not been present at any of the conferences which have been held from time to time by the Commonwealth members of the area.[19] Thus Ireland has had little or no influence over policies which affect the fortunes of the currency with which it is most intimately associated and the good standing of many investments which its citizens have purchased over the years. At present, it does not appear that Ireland either gains or loses by its association with the sterling area.[20]

It may be as well to refer at this point to the time-worn assertion that, as a result of the Currency Act, the Bank of England controls the Irish banking system and therefore the Irish economy.[21] It should be clear that any form of direct control is out of the question. The Irish banks certainly hold large funds in London. These can always be liquidated and turned into Irish currency, thus escaping control by the Bank of England. The only apparent way in which such direct control could be attempted would be that the Bank of England should freeze the London funds of the Irish banks. This would be an act of discrimination which would be unprecedented and is certainly not obviously practicable. Again, it is not possible that any official or semi-official hint to the commercial banks to restrict or expand their lending could be properly given to the Irish banks. It will be remembered that the restrictions imposed by the British monetary authorities on the lending

In December 1967 the Minister for Finance stated that legislation was being considered which would make the external value of the Irish pound, as declared formally to the International Monetary Fund, the rate at which it would be convertible into all other currencies.

18. It is notable that the Central Bank did not follow the example set by many other members of the sterling area in retaining part of the dollars currently earned by the economy.

19. It is, of course, possible that they would have been embarrassed by a formal invitation. Unofficial contacts are understood to be close and cordial.

20. It should be added that until 1966 Ireland did not exercise one of the most important perquisites of membership; the facility of borrowing in London.

21. See J. P. Colbert, op. cit., p. 96; also B. Menton, 'Theories of Adjustment of the Balance of Payments under Fixed Exchanges', *JSSISI*, 1947-8, pp. 37-9 on it.

by British banks in recent years were not paralleled in Ireland—not even in Northern Ireland.

It is undeniable that changes in interest rates in Great Britain will affect the rates here, though recent adjustments in Ireland have been neither automatic nor of equal degree. This, however, is nothing more than a local instance of what happens all over the world. No country in the capitalist system can remain unaffected by the credit policies pursued in the United Kingdom and in the United States.

POWERS OF THE CENTRAL BANK

The relation between the Central Bank and the commercial banks in Ireland is quite different from that obtaining between the Bank of England and the British banks. The controversies of the 1950s on credit policy were confused by a failure, sometimes a refusal, to appreciate this fact. The Bank of England is the oldest bank in Great Britain: the Central Bank is the latest foundation in Ireland. The Bank of England has played an influential role for generations in the formulation of economic policy and the maintenance of the stability of sterling. Notoriously, and unfortunately, the Central Bank is not always heeded in the shaping of Irish policies.[22] The Bank of England has long determined the cash resources of the British banks. The Central Bank has practically no power to vary the resources of the Irish banks; and it is only lately that its own resources have come to equal those of the commercial banks. Finally, the Central Bank must operate a currency which is statutorily convertible into another currency and which is automatically issuable and redeemable.

These contrasts have not prevented the Central Bank from being of great service to the economy; and they will not prevent a development of its functions which will change its position out of recognition. But it was in a false position for many years after its foundation. The Banking Commission recommended the establishment of 'a monetary authority'. The recommendation (foreshadowed by a strong hint in the terms of reference) was worded, as readers may agree, with much less clarity than was shown in other passages of the Banking Commission's report; for example, those relating to State borrowing or compulsory acquisition of land. The circumstances in which the Central Bank Act was

22. e.g. the Second Programme contemplated a series of deficits in the balance of payments up to 1970, a prospect which certainly falls within the sphere of interest of the Central Bank. It appears from Professor Ryan's paper to the Statistical Society ('The Methodology of the Second Programme', *JSSISI*, 1963-4, p. 120) that the opinion of the Economic Research Institute was obtained on this matter. There is no reference to the Central Bank.

introduced were also unfortunate. The public was told that it now possessed a Central Bank with all the powers of central banks elsewhere to fix interest rates, to rediscount bills, and to engage in open-market operations. It was not told at all so clearly that the new Central Bank indeed enjoyed such powers in law but the resources out of which, and by which, they could be exercised were almost completely lacking.[23] Many who have criticized the Central Bank for its apparent inactivity may be excused for a misunderstanding of what was never made clear.

The principal function which the Central Bank could exercise from its inception, was inherited from the Currency Commission; that is, the issue of legal tender notes in exchange for gold or sterling assets and their redemption under the provisions of the Currency Act of 1927. In effect, the legal tender note was a sterling certificate. The role of the Central Bank was purely automatic: it enjoyed few discretionary powers in regard to issue or redemption. The sterling assets of the Central Bank grew in sympathy with the expansion of the note-issue during the long inflation. The Legal Tender Note Fund could be regarded not only as a cover for the currency but as an ultimate reserve of foreign currency for the economy. This was useful[24] but it did not amount to the practice of central banking. In particular it had nothing to do with the volume and price of credit, and the present power of the Central Bank to vary either will now be discussed.

The Central Bank has certainly operated so as to expand the resources of the commercial banks. It did so first in 1956 when it rediscounted Exchequer bills held by them.[25] It does so nowadays when it rediscounts the much greater number of Exchequer bills that are now running.[26]

The Central Bank has never attempted to contract the resources of the commercial banks. It is very difficult to see how it could do so if it wished. Section 50 of the Central Bank Act provided compulsory powers to compel the banks to make deposits with the Central Bank in certain

23. This point was forcefully stated by Lord Glenavy in his reservation to the majority report at pp. 377–99.

24. Dr. Jacobssen referred to economies, such as the Irish, which were 'subject to considerable strains in the event of a bad harvest or some similar calamity', *BCR*, 1938, Appendix 17, p. 515. The primary function of the Legal Tender Note Fund, in 1927, was to provide reassurance to holders of the new currency notes. Its second purpose was to be an ultimate reserve of foreign currency. It may yet be worth consideration whether the assets in the Fund should maintain some ratio to the total of trade, or the total balance of payments.

25. This was regarded in some quarters at the time as a welcome sign of development. In fact it was the result of the difficulties in which the banks found themselves at the time through a growth in advances, a fall in deposits and a depreciation in the value of their investments. Changes are not invariably a sign of greater strength or self-confidence.

26. Rediscounting of Exchequer bills held by the commercial banks appears to have been automatic but it does not appear that the Central Bank holds itself out as a lender of last resort in all circumstances.

specified circumstances; but it would be a very strained use of the power indeed if it were invoked in order to compel a contraction of the credit base.[27]

It has been argued that the influence of the Central Bank on interest rates cannot be decisive.[28] That is very far from saying that it is not important. The Central Bank (more exactly, the Governor of the Central Bank) has been a highly important participant in discussions between the banks and the government on changes in interest rates. It has used the opportunity to act as interpreter on the occasions when the two other parties are not using the same language. This is a public service of very great importance.[29]

But the question must now be faced—who does control credit in the Republic? The short answer—no one—is misleading. Clearly it is not the Central Bank; equally clearly (and more obviously since interest rates diverged in 1955) it is not the Bank of England. It is not the commercial banks, who cannot simply meet and fix rates as if the country possessed neither a Central Bank nor a government. Control at present lies in the tripartite relationship between the government, the Central Bank, and the commercial banks. To theorists this may appear to be untidy: the answer must be that it has worked. It is useful that the Central Bank should act as a buffer between governments looking for low interest rates to assist capital investment policies to which they are increasingly committed, and a banking system which looks for rates which will safeguard its deposits. This applies in much wider issues of financial policy than interest rates; many of which are not so obvious to the public but are of no less ultimate importance. The balance between the three interests has been maintained in sometimes difficult circumstances. It is an example of empirical skill and tact which should not go unnoticed.[30]

27 . It is quite clear that section 50 was designed to provide a means of forcing the banks to lend more freely, if necessary. Its wording clearly excluded its use to force a reduction of advances. Cf. the view of the Central Bank itself (in its report for 1956–7, p. 38):

> The ratio of the commercial banks' domestic assets to their domestic liabilities has risen from 45 per cent in 1942 to almost 75 per cent at present. This fact gives little support to the view that the Central Bank ought to have exercised the penal power, conferred on it by Section 50 of the Act, to require a licensed banker to make an interest-free deposit with it if the domestic assets held by the licensed banker fall below a specified proportion of his liabilities within the State.

28. The position of the banks in this matter has been discussed on pp. 353–4.

29. In the debates on the Central Bank Bill Mr. McGilligan stated that the Central Bank could 'influence the rate of interest only by co-operation and palavering'; *PDDE*, 86, 1423. It is a very useful form of influence, valuable both to the Central Bank and to the national interest.

30. Credit policy should not be assumed to be solely a matter that is determined by the government, the Central Bank, and the commercial banks. There are other sources of credit, notably the insurance companies and the finance houses that are uncontrolled. In certain circumstances this may demand attention.

The Central Bank's view of its role has developed with the years. A decade ago it stated that:

The influence of the Central Bank as 'a middle term' in Irish financial policy may be expected to increase gradually by natural evolution. Already the Bank is playing a more significant role than formerly in discussions and consultations concerning the responsibility of the banking system in financial and economic policy and in this way it is ready to take a more active part to the extent to which the State authorities desire and encourage such a development. It is by these means that it can make the most useful contribution to the public welfare in matters concerning currency and credit. Over-estimation of the value, in Irish conditions, of technical methods of central banking in use elsewhere tends to distract attention from the basic defects in Irish policy and to encourage the dangerous—and profoundly mistaken—belief that prosperity can be attained by financial devices . . .[31]

Much more recently, the Central Bank restated its position in the following terms:

The Central Bank of Ireland has a statutory responsibility regarding monetary stability, particularly in its external aspect. Within the limits of its specific powers, it is required to take steps 'towards safeguarding the integrity of the currency' and towards ensuring that in matters concerning credit control the welfare of the community will be the 'constant and predominant aim'. The Bank therefore considers it appropriate to keep under review any trends in public policy and in economic relations that are likely to increase costs, to impair the competitiveness of the Irish economy, and to weaken the external monetary reserves. It has repeatedly expressed the opinion that sustained economic growth is the proper object of policy—not expansion so rapid as to entail monetary strain, balance-of-payments difficulties, and consequent recession. In its comments on policies of expansion it has emphasized that it is dangerous to envisage persistent deficits in current external payments; that continuing large external deficits are a sign that the proportion of resources employed in productive investment is inadequate; and that eventually there is no escape from balance-of-payments discipline.

The Central Bank has drawn attention to the over-rapid growth of public expenditure and to the large and increasing proportion of the total which is financed by borrowing. It has raised the question whether these developments are compatible with the stated aims of increasing exports as the key to national prosperity, of improving employment at home, and of progressively reducing emigration. . . .[32]

There is some irony in the reflection that in the past the function of the Central Bank was conceived as being to spur the associated banks into easier credit policies. In the event it emerges as a restraining influence not only on the banks but in much wider fields of public policy. It has therefore become a matter of supreme importance to the economy that the independence of the Central Bank should be maintained. The public would make a bad bargain if the Bank increased its powers

31. *CBR*, 1956-7, pp. 40-1.   32. *CBR*, 1965-6, pp. 7-8

over credit and at the same time fell under the control of the government.[33]

To conclude this chapter as it began; everything in the banking and currency system is in course of evolution, like the economy itself. Development is bound to modify the relationship between the Central Bank and commercial banks, or the backing of the currency. The relationship may be altered in many ways—in one direction if the commercial banks permanently lost a further degree of their external assets, in another if those assets increase. It is not wholly a matter that is determined by conscious policy or by legislation: much in the present situation would alter if the public (for example) came to use cheques rather than notes, so that the funds held by the Central Bank did not increase as rapidly as those held by the commercial banks. The backing of the currency will ultimately be determined by matters, some of which, such as the volume of exports and the stability of the balance of payments, are within our control. Others, such as the strength of sterling in the future, are not. What can be said in conclusion is that it is certainly not obvious that this country has been less well directed than any other in the field of credit policy in recent years—and comparisons of this kind can safely be made with some countries which were once held up as models. And lastly, to repeat what can never be repeated too often, the stability of the currency and the provision of credit ultimately depend on industrial and agricultural production and exports.

33. It is understood that further legislation for the Central Bank will be introduced during the coming (1969–70) session of the Oireachtas.

NOTE

This chapter must be read subject to the transfer of external assets from the Associated Banks to the Central Bank during 1969. A bill dealing with the functions of the Central Bank is now (Spring 1970) before the Oireachtas.

CHAPTER SIXTEEN

Public Finance and Fiscal Policy

THE IRISH STATE BEGAN ITS CAREER WITH A WELL-MARKED pattern of public finance, inherited from British rule. Its sources of revenue were those that had been worked out by the Treasury to suit the conditions of Great Britain. Taxes on income were not obviously suitable to a country such as Ireland where incomes were low in money terms. They became still less applicable when the country was partitioned, thereby cutting off the comparatively well-developed and prosperous area of the north-east. The indirect taxes were more useful in a community where salaries and wages were comparatively few and usually low. They depended, however, very largely on the yields from the taxation of beers, spirits, and tobacco.

The objects of state expenditure were equally a legacy from British rule. The expenses of the civil war provided obligations of expenditure on defence and compensation for property. These, however, were non-recurrent items of expenditure. The new state was faced with one heavy burden which would not be so easily shaken off. The social legislation of the last Liberal government added considerably to the volume of public expenditure. The structure of the Irish population, in which the older age-groups were proportionately far greater than in any other part of the United Kingdom, entailed that old age pensions were exceptionally heavy. That did not matter when they were paid out of the Treasury of the United Kingdom; it mattered a very great deal when they fell to be paid out of the modest resources of the Irish Free State. In the early years, they were one of the largest single items of state expenditure. Moreover, the growth of social services catering for dependency imposed exceptionally heavy burdens on the Irish state where the proportions of young as well as old were particularly large. Thus from the outset, the Irish exchequer found itself faced with burdens which could not be shaken off while the means of raising revenue were limited.

The war years provided a kind of watershed in the development of fiscal policy. Up to that time, taxation had been levied with one eye on what was happening in Great Britain. During most of the 1920s and 1930s the over-riding aim in that country was the reduction of taxation. Irish Ministers for Finance were obliged to follow suit, lest they should lose the comparatively few large payers of direct taxation, whose continued residence in the country could not be taken for granted. With the war, however, British standards of taxation changed completely. It was now possible to increase taxation in Ireland; indeed it was not only possible, it was also necessary granted that neutrality called for greater expenditure in a number of directions. This led to a change in thinking. Higher taxation came to be accepted as a disagreeable necessity; and it was continued in Ireland long after the war had ended. The invisible link with Great Britain was not, however, completely severed. When British tax levels were progressively reduced in the middle and later 1950s, it became necessary to follow suit in Ireland.

Another change, which became apparent after the war had ended, was a much greater readiness to incur heavy capital expenditure. The external assets had been replenished and augmented. Their growth was misleading, in so far as it resulted from the shortage of consumer and capital goods; it represented forced saving rather than a genuine increase of assets. Nevertheless their existence strengthened the argument for vigorous policies of public investment. That argument had received support from the example of the European Recovery Programme. Everywhere schemes of long-term investment were in the air. For the last twenty years, therefore, Irish public finance has not only been obliged to finance a growing volume of current expenditure, it has also had to find the resources for ambitious programmes of capital investment.

In 1958 the position was reviewed in the White Paper on Economic Expansion, in which it was remarked that:

The social capital investment of past years has given us an 'infra-structure' of housing, hospitals, communications, etc., which is equal (in some respects, perhaps, superior) to that of comparable countries. What is now required is a greater emphasis on productive expenditure which by increasing national output—particularly of goods capable of meeting competition in export markets—will enable full advantage to be taken of that 'infra-structure' and in due course make possible and indeed necessitate its further extension. As well as encouraging increased production the government will strive to reduce the effective burden of taxation by moderating the growth in net debt service charges, by achieving the maximum efficiency of administration, by relating further improvements in the social services to increases in real national income, and by reducing subsidies to the minimum necessary to secure a permanent increase in economic production.

Public expenditure has been increasing rapidly since 1958. By itself an increase is not necessarily unjustified, especially where it keeps pace with an increase in national income. In several years, however, public expenditure has increased much more rapidly than national income. This is the prolongation of a tendency which has been noticeable ever since the end of the war. It is comprehensible enough. The period since the war has been one of prolonged inflation which in itself increases the costs of government quite apart from any extension of the field of public expenditure. In the second place, a notable proportion of state expenditure is designed to foster greater production in the economy. That need not be objectionable; but if the greater production is not forthcoming or if it is achieved in ways which do not expand the capacity of the economy to yield higher revenue, the consequence may be unfortunate. One result which is already evident is a greatly increased public debt. Again, that may be tolerable in a period of inflation and of assistance to production. But if the inflation were ever to come to an end or if greater production did not lead to an increase in revenue, the public finances would be gravely embarrassed. What is more, the embarrassment might last for a very long time. It will be right to remember that neither inflation nor deflation lasts for ever; and the state has now incurred debts that will be with the community for at least a generation.

Comment on growing public expenditure has been largely concentrated on current expenditure. It sometimes seems as if it is taken for granted that almost any form of capital expenditure can be justified. This point was well treated in an article in *The Irish Banking Review* which reviewed the budget speech of 1962.

A good deal of the confusion in this matter is caused by the division of expenditure into 'above the line' and 'below the line' categories. Ministers for Finance claim that their budgets are balanced if all 'above the line' expenditure is covered by current revenue. In many other countries budgetary standards are more austere and the budget is not considered as balanced unless expenditure of every kind is covered by revenue. But, even without attempting this standard of extreme budgetary rectitude, a distinction must be drawn between expenditure on capital goods that will yield a revenue and those that will impose debt charges on future budgets. This distinction tends to be slurred in Irish budgetary practice.

Capital expenditure may be roughly divided into three classes: expenditure which provides the means of repayment of debt charges immediately; expenditure which provides the means of payment of debt charges after a shorter or longer delay; and expenditure which is in no way self-liquidating. All these classes of expenditure may be fully justified on political and social grounds, but their effects on the public finances are very different. Expenditure of the second and third classes increases the public debt and debt charges and should be undertaken with caution and circumspection.[1]

1. *IBR*, September 1962.

Granted that it is only in very recent years that national income began to increase appreciably, the difficulties of meeting expenditure from revenue have become acute. It is not simply a matter of whether or not the national income increases. In Irish conditions it would be quite possible for national income to expand very considerably without any proportionate benefit to the revenue. Many of those who live on the land are not assessable to income tax; and would often go free of tax if they were obliged to make returns. Many of them would fall within the exemption limits. In industry it is at present possible for firms to make profits which are wholly or partially free of tax under the existing concessions. In these circumstances the buoyancy of the revenue must be restricted. It is possible to find considerable private prosperity while the public finances are embarrassed. The Irish State may yet resemble what was said of the French, 'a poor state in a rich country'. Indeed, there is much to be said for the view that the public finances are one of the weakest points in the Irish economy.

In a country where the scope of direct taxation is limited and there is a tendency towards high consumption, there is a strong case for taxes on expenditure. A great degree of flexibility has been gained by the introduction of the turn-over tax which presumably will be used in growing measure. The case for a turn-over tax is strongest on the grounds that it catches many who otherwise would pay little tax at all and certainly would pay no direct taxation. There has been some undoing of the very considerable social injustice that came from the levying of income tax at comparatively high rates on a very small section of the community. But, if the turn-over tax has come to stay, consideration will have to be given to its incidence on the necessities of life. Undeniably, it is a regressive tax. In a country in which the economic structure does not give full scope for direct taxation, some degree of use of regressive taxation may be unavoidable. But no one can argue that it is desirable. It is easy to see that there will be a growing need for objective discussion of these issues. The total abolition of the turn-over tax would lead to immense difficulties and to considerable hardships for those who cannot escape direct taxation. It would lead also to considerable social strain because the interests of farmers and of a growing number of wage-earners would be opposed to each other. Some way will have to be worked out by which the turn-over tax and direct taxation are brought into a relationship which satisfies the public sense of justice.

These issues, of course, arise principally when taxation stands at what is thought to be a high level; neither direct nor indirect taxation provokes criticism when it is thought to be bearable. This reinforces the need for prudent policies of both capital and current expenditure. In particular it emphasizes the need to watch any further increase in the deadweight debt.

This is a matter on which misunderstanding appears to be almost ineradicable. The issues involved are very clearly put in the following quotation:

The Banking Commission of 1938 has been misunderstood and misrepresented in its representations with regard to deadweight debt. Deadweight debt is nothing more nor less than debt which is not financially self-liquidating. Any debt which imposes a charge on the Budget is deadweight debt. The distinction between deadweight debt and non-deadweight debt has nothing to say to the desirability of the investment for which the debt is incurred on either political, social, or even economic grounds. If it incurs a charge on the taxpayers it is deadweight debt, however suitable the objective is. If it does not impose a charge on the taxpayers it is not deadweight debt, however unsuitable the objective is . . .

There is another point which I wish to make. The Banking Commission's distinction between deadweight and non-deadweight debt is not the same as the distinction between productive and non-productive debt. There are many objects of investments of a productive character in the long run which impose deadweight debt. An investment that increases the national income of the country, the exports, and the taxable capacity may in the short run not be self-liquidating.[2]

These matters are of even greater importance today than they were in 1951. The public debt has increased substantially since then; and there is every sign, so far as can be judged from the Second Programme, that it will continue to increase in coming years. This is an uninviting prospect; and perhaps the greatest single criticism that can be made of the Second Programme is that the implications of its proposals for the public finances as well as for the balance of payments have not been fully brought out.

It is arguable that today we see only the capital expenditure that has been and is being incurred and that we do not perceive the advantages which it will confer in the future. The fact remains that the service of debt now constitutes so heavy a charge on the budget that it will increasingly limit the freedom of Ministers for Finance during many years to come. Its real burden may be lightened by continued inflation (not the most attractive prospect possible); equally any check to the fall in the value of money will subject State finance to a heavy strain. It can only be hoped that circumstances do not alter for the worse until the benefits of investment policy have matured to strengthen not only the economy but also the balance of the public finances.

2. Speech of Senator George O'Brien on the Supplies and Services Bill in 1951, *PDSE*, 40, 79.

PROGRAMMES FOR ECONOMIC EXPANSION

The First Programme consisted of a general survey of the proposed lines of State action during the period 1959–63: it did not at any time attempt to provide a plan for the economy as a whole. The Second Programme deals primarily with the projected activities of the State between 1964 and 1970. It breaks fresh ground by suggesting targets for increases of production in the private sector, and by associating both management and workers in the private sector with the general plan of development. It is at pains to define what it means by the word 'programme'.[3]

A programme is an attempt to apply to the management of the nation's economic affairs the same foresight, organization, and determination as a competent and prudent person applies to the management of his own household or business. In a democracy the national economic programme cannot be authoritarian. It proceeds on the assumption that there is widespread public agreement on making as much economic progress as possible and on the means by which such progress is to be achieved. Objectives and priorities are outlined but the programme does not in every instance specify how they are to be attained. Rather is it educative and indicative, combining help and guidance from the State for private enterprise with direct State action where this is needed to ensure full use of productive capacity. . . .

Programming involves making the most reasonable estimate of the increase attainable in total production on certain assumptions about major factors such as population, individual output, exports, capacity to finance capital needs. An attempt must be made to foresee the relative contributions of agriculture, industry, and services to overall expansion and to define the economic and financial policies needed to secure maximum output of competitive goods and services. It is only if these policies are effective, and internal and external conditions are favourable, that the desired growth rate can be achieved. A target is an indication of the progress the economy can make if certain assumptions and conditions are fulfilled; it is an aim, not a promise.[4]

These matters have been further elaborated by successive reports of the National Industrial Economic Council. In a report signed on 30 June 1964, it set out the arrangements which should be made to review annually economic performance, prospects, and problems, so that targets and policies could be modified where necessary.[5] Another report, signed on 18 June 1965, contained a survey of the scope of economic planning in the Irish economy.

Changes in the quantity, composition, and use of productive resources do not occur spontaneously, nor are they the result of a few decisions made centrally.

3. All this passage should be read subject to what is said on pp. 380-5.
4. *Second Programme for Economic Expansion*, Pr. 7239, Stationery Office, Dublin: August 1964, paras. 5–6.
5. N I E C, *Report on Procedures for continuous Review of Progress*, Pr. 7794, Stationery Office, Dublin.

In a mixed economy like that of Ireland these changes are the result of a very large number of individual, inter-related decisions, made by public servants, by managers, and by workers and their representatives . . . In the last resort the economic expansion which occurs is the result of the number and quality of the economic decisions which are made in the economy.

Economic planning is a method by which the quantity and quality of economic decisions can be improved and faster economic growth achieved. As a method, it consists essentially in defining future objectives, indicating the means which must be used to achieve them, and providing for the systematic study of economic problems and prospects. These characteristics are exemplified in this country by the second programme for economic expansion. . . .

The publication of a consistent picture of the economy for a future year, giving an estimate of available resources, of the volume of production which these would permit, and of the broad uses to which national production will be put, all shown for the major sectors of economic activity, can by itself make for better economic decisions. Individual firms and industries are given a more coherent view of future developments and to the extent to which this is used, it can influence their own plans for expansion and help to keep them in line with each other . . . The publication of targets can also provide a challenge to economic policy which by compelling the continuous assessment of policy measures ensures that the achievement of the targets is facilitated. The danger in purely *indicative* planning of this kind, however, is that the industrial targets will be neither accepted nor understood, that their relevance to decisions by individual industries or firms will not be appreciated and that the decisions required at all levels to ensure that the targets are achieved will not in fact be made.

If these dangers are to be avoided, economic planning must be *active* as well as being *indicative*. If the targets are to be meaningful to managements and workers, they must be broken down to the individual industry or product level. If the targets are to be accepted as a guide to action, those who make the attempts to achieve them must be involved in fixing the targets . . . If the plan is to maintain a continuing influence on action, managements and workers must be involved in the periodic reviews of performance and in the modification of targets to take account of unforeseeable events, and they must be able to give their views on the changes in policies which these changing circumstances require. . . .

Economic planning, then, is essentially tripartite, and this has been one of its principal characteristics in Ireland. Representatives of managements and workers and the Government have been involved in the articulation of the industrial targets of the Second Programme, and in the evolution of the machinery for continuing review and discussion at industry level. . . .[6]

The report proceeds to discuss, first, the relative roles of managements, workers, and Government departments in the planning process and, second, the problem of ensuring that the plans are implemented.

Thus the Second Programme is a much more elaborate enterprise than the First. It not only sets out targets: it also associates both management and labour in their selection. In this association, it would seem

6. N I E C, *Report on Economic Planning*, Pr. 8367, Stationery Office, Dublin: paras. 5–9.

probable that the initiative will usually rest with the central authority, the State. This may well lead both management and labour very far afield from their present positions. The NIEC Report just quoted is quite explicit on this matter.

As we stated earlier, economic planning is essentially tripartite in character; management organisations and trade unions must also be involved in the planning process. Involvement by itself presents no problems because these bodies have for some time sought greater participation in the making of economic policy, and they are keen to play their full part in the context of economic planning. There is a danger, however, that participation may be desired solely for the opportunities it offers to influence Government decisions and that the responsibilities which go with it may be ignored. When representative bodies participate with Government in reaching an agreed recommendation or decision, they must explicitly accept some responsibility for the implementation of the recommendation or decision. The temptation to seek the best of both worlds—to insist on full participation while at the same time trying to avoid commitment and thus maintain discretion in their subsequent actions—must be resisted.

This temptation may not be apparent in the early stages of economic planning where the main issues under discussion are the technical conditions of expansion and where the main emphasis tends to be laid on future aims rather than on present problems and policies. As planning evolves, however, it will become increasingly important that the responsibilities which go with participation are explicitly accepted. If they are not accepted, some of the problems which are likely to arise may be well-nigh insoluble.[7]

These paragraphs were, let us always remember, drafted by Irish civil servants, and accepted and adopted by the representatives of management and labour after full discussion. But it must be said that potentially they are highly explosive. How they will work out in practice can be learnt from experience. Two points are obvious at once: the position of management and labour *vis-à-vis* the State and their position *vis-à-vis* those whom they represent. It is justly pointed out in paragraph 25 of the same Report that the targets for individual industries were determined in consultation with representatives of the managements of the firms engaged in it. It is also, equally justly, claimed that the exercise of fixing a target helps to raise standards of future performance. A very great deal will depend on how far it proves possible to retain the consultative technique and on whether a situation may ever emerge in which decisions are reached by the over-riding of one party by the other two. What will certainly be of the utmost importance is how far both managers and workers will come to feel themselves bound by the decisions of the NIEC and whether or not their representatives support such decisions. The maintenance of the lines of communication will inevitably be more difficult for labour than for management. A very great deal indeed, for the well-being of the polity and of the

7. Ibid., paras. 17–18.

economy as well as for the success of the Second Programme will depend on whether the non-official members of the NIEC speak with equal clarity and firmness to the State and to those whom they represent.

These observations, it should be said, spring from a personal conviction that economic development is best and most enduringly achieved when it is based on individual enterprise and that in the case of Ireland there is a special necessity to revive and stimulate the commercial virtues of the community. It may be mistaken to fear that a succession of Programmes may inflict grave damage on the paramount liberties and interests of the individual, be he manager or wage-earner. Many will willingly accept a considerable degree of *étatisme* in order to achieve development. It may be that in Ireland, as has happened in other countries at different times, the subordination of private interests to a central authority may be a necessity. It may be that only the emergence of a strong central authority can provide the circumstances in which economic growth can be achieved. But there should be no ignoring the possibility that the political implications may be far-reaching.

If, however, matters are regarded from a different angle, the question must arise whether programming can exercise more than a very limited influence in Irish conditions. The economy is exceptionally open, unusually dependent on foreign trade; and a very high proportion of that trade is conducted with one country. It is therefore exceptionally exposed to changes in world prices and to changes in the policies and the prosperity of the United Kingdom. It is true of every country that its programming must have regard to the balance of payments: in the case of Ireland the need is almost always urgent and impossible to disregard for any length of time. There will be more to say on this point later: but it is clear that Irish programmes must be open to modification in the light of changing circumstances abroad as much as at home.

The Second Programme appears to be unduly forthright in these matters. It is stated at one point that:

The Government will use the means open to it to maintain adequate—while avoiding excessive—demand as a basis for maximum economic advance.[8]

And at another:

The capital expenditure of the Government and other public authorities will be maintained at the level necessary to meet the requirements of economic and social progress.[9]

These declarations are all very well as statements of intent: they can be little more. It is only too easy to imagine circumstances in which the Government may be unable to do one or the other. To say as much is

8. *Second Programme*, Part i, Pr. 7239, Stationery Office, Dublin, para. 12.
9. Ibid., para. 87.

not to criticize the passages quoted but rather to point out the dangers of giving too many hostages to economic fortune. Far too many of the commentaries on the Second Programme that have appeared seem to assume that targets will be achieved and that if by any chance there is a short-fall, the fault will lie with the Irish economy. It is indeed only too apparent that the immediate obstacles to success depend largely on the conduct of producers, both employers and employed. But it is equally possible that any failure to achieve targets may happen through no fault of anybody in the Irish economy. It is wise to insure against unnecessary disappointments which may awaken a latent pessimism and distrust of expansion.

Nevertheless it remains true that targets can be educative and inspiring. They provide a challenge to producers of a sort that has been peculiarly absent from the Irish economy: they have already evoked in many cases a response which has surprised the producers themselves. It would be a great pity if their value was depreciated because they were taken too seriously and regarded as immutable no matter how circumstances might change.

In the long run their success must depend largely on the trading opportunities that are open to the economy and on the extent to which it can adjust itself to their expansion—or contraction. This raises the fundamental assumption of the Programme, that membership of the EEC will be attained by 1970. This is an assumption which is clearly altogether outside the power of any Irish government to fulfill: it depends on so many factors that it is almost a waste of time to discuss the chances of its coming true.

The assumption of EEC membership by 1970 has become a weakness in the Programme in the sense that it has become increasingly difficult to believe in it. But some kind of assumption has to be made, and EEC membership has the advantage that to prepare for it is to prepare producers for competition and thus to strengthen the economy against the future. It is, however, an immense, if unavoidable, difficulty that so much of agricultural policies must depend on the terms on which the Republic conducts its trade with the United Kingdom and with the Community. All that can be done (and it is envisaged by the Programme) is to fit the economy for conditions that are likely to be more competitive than it has known for a generation.

These are the kind of uncertainties which bedevil planning in any country: they are inescapable in a country which is so dependent on foreign trade as Ireland. There remain two issues which have provoked doubt: the proposed level of capital investment and the effect on the balance of payments.

To begin with, it may be agreed at once that investment programmes are especially necessary in an economy that has long been so stagnant as the Irish. The volume of investment in this country has often been compared unfavourably with that of other countries. This may be a salutary exercise in so far as it illustrates what should be done or what should have been done in the past but it may also be thoroughly pernicious. What matters about investment is not its amount but its direction; comparatively modest policies which are rightly aimed will be much more efficacious than more grandiose projects. Again, it is undeniable that the State has been often forced into policies of investment to fill the gaps left by the absence of private enterprise. There is some danger that matters may be pushed to the opposite extreme. A succession of State capital investment programmes is not an inviting prospect. However necessary they may have been (or still are) they should not be necessary when a society has been created which encourages risk-taking and private initiative. The sign of a true development in the economy will be a growth in private investment, in an increasing number of people putting their money, or what money they can raise from the public, into their projects. The time may come when there will be a serious clash between public and private investment. These matters cannot be provided for in advance. It is highly likely that the future Irish economy will be a mixture of public and private enterprise; and it is arguable that public enterprise in this country will capture a great deal of the ability and initiative which elsewhere would have gone into the private sector. In that case, the clash may not be as serious as might be feared: nevertheless, the possibility should be borne in mind.

What is disturbing about the Second Programme's estimate of future capital investment is the difficulty of seeing how it will be financed. It seems that public expenditure financed out of revenue is already as high as it can be pushed: the reliance on borrowing must be expected to become more pronounced as time goes on. A combination of large public expenditure, high taxation, and extensive borrowing cannot be regarded without misgiving. The manner in which the Programme was framed has been explained with complete frankness:[10] the implications for taxation have not been spelled out to the public. There is a great deal in the comment that:

One cannot help asking whether the ends of the Programme are not more clearly defined than the means, whether as much thought has been given to tactics as distinguished from strategy.[11]

These feelings are aggravated by the evident propensity of the investment programmes to widen their scope and increase their cost. The original estimates of public capital investment between 1959 and 1963

10. By Dr. W. J. L. Ryan, 'The Methodology of the Second Programme', *JSSISI*, 1963–4, p. 120.
11. 'The Second Programme', *IBR*, December 1963, p. 15.

proved to be well below the mark: there seems to have been a similar experience between 1963 and 1965.

Under-estimation appears also in the vitally important sphere of the deficit in the balance of payments. In the event, it is well known that both in 1964 and in 1965, the external deficit was very much greater than was suggested in the Second Programme. This has led to remedial action which it is hoped will avert an acute financial stringency in the future.

Once again it is necessary to insist that there is no inevitable conflict between growth and monetary stability. Such a conflict can arise only when policies are not trimmed to meet a change of conditions. Much earlier in these pages the distinction made by the Recess Committee between 'the resources of today' and 'the resources of tomorrow' was recalled. In any programme which extends over a period of years, there will occur occasions when it would be highly dangerous to pledge the as yet undeveloped resources of tomorrow. Ultimately, this is a matter of priorities. Economic activity in any country depends very largely on the solvency of the state and the stability of the currency. If those attributes are lost it would become impossible to assure continued economic growth, unless at the expense of widespread social injustice. Their preservation is immensely more important than the achievement of any pre-announced measure of growth in any year.

Fortunately, programmes can be adjusted when the need arises; and there is nothing in the Second Programme to suggest that it claims immunity from world conditions and trends. One may conclude by quoting the comment of the Central Bank:

The programme has not of course been put forward as an inflexible plan. It is no doubt intended to be open to reconsideration and revision not only at the beginning but also at every subsequent stage. It is to be anticipated that in the process of revision full account will be taken of financial and monetary considerations and that, if necessary, targets in particular sectors of economic and social progress will be reassessed.[12]

PROGRAMMES AND PRIORITIES

In the late summer of 1967 it became apparent that the revision of the Second Programme noted above will be more thorough-going than was at first suggested. Some commentators have assumed that this implies the virtual abandonment of all programming: others have suggested that it clears the way for the emergence of a Third Programme. However these matters may turn out, the interval will be usefully

12. *CBR*, 1963-4, pp. 24-5.

employed in considering some of the lessons that may be learned from the experience of the last nine years.[13]

One lesson is the degree to which the pace of economic development in this country is dependent on world trends. Elsewhere in these pages it is remarked that a disappointing feature of the reception given to the Second Programme was the lack of appreciation that events abroad might make some of its assumptions impossible or unnecessary to fulfill. During its course a great deal of the running commentary on it suffered from the same defect. With the advantage of hindsight it is apparent that its success was gravely handicapped by the sequence of events in the United Kingdom: the balance of payments crisis of 1964, the imposition of import levies which affected Irish trade especially severely, the subsequent restriction of demand which still continues, the virtual embargo on the export of capital from the United Kingdom to Ireland and the devaluation of 1967. These developments reflected the peculiarly delicate state of the British economy, but they also reflected the general increase in interest rates and the slackening almost everywhere of the rapid rate of growth which had marked the late 1950s and earlier 1960s.

By no means all the things that went wrong were outside domestic control. It its original form the Second Programme would have engaged a great part of the resources available, leaving very little in reserve against things going wrong. Whatever room for manoeuvre there may have been was soon filled by the addition of further objects of capital expenditure. On top of these again were (and still are being) piled a series of measures, especially in the sphere of the social services, which may be admirable in themselves but had (and have) the effect of increasing the demands of the State on the resources available. The public finances thus fell into such disorder that during 1965 and 1966 not only was the State forced into foreign borrowing on remarkably unfortunate terms, but it was also obliged to lean so heavily on the banking system that in 1965 nine-tenths of the increased credit available was taken up by it to the exclusion of the needs of the private sector. These developments, moreover, led to a sharp increase in taxation. The effect of all this on the private sector, which already suffered from the difficulties outlined earlier, needs no emphasis. Finally, during all this unhappy period production and trade, especially in the manufacturing and commercial sectors, were convulsed by struggles over wages, salaries, and status claims.

The cumulative effect of all these influences was to reduce sharply the growth of production and exports. The balance of payments, which the Second Programme contemplated as showing an average annual deficit of £17m. over the period 1963–70, in fact showed deficits of £31m.

13. The following pages were written before the appearance of the Third Programme in March 1969.

in 1964 and of £42m. in 1965. In the middle of the latter year there was talk in some quarters, for the first time since 1956, of a devaluation of the Irish pound in terms of sterling. This talk seemed at the time, as it did when viewed in retrospect from the much healthier position of 1967, to have been as alarmist in 1965 as it was in 1956. But the fact that it existed at all was a disturbing sign that confidence in the economy was highly volatile.

Responsibility for the failure to reach the targets of Second Programme (in so far as failure lay in the performance rather than in unreality of targets) can therefore be distributed according to choice or interest over a number of factors. The weakness that seems most apparent, and that was noted at the outset, was that it committed the resources of the economy, both actual and potential, so fully that there was insufficient provision for things going wrong. Indeed, it is fair to add, insufficient provision was made for things going right, for the new claims (that is to say) that might and did arise among wage and salary earners who, for the first time in their experience, found themselves caught up in an expanding economy. It is also fair to add that the Irish record may be found to compare very favourably with the experience of other countries, when the various national plans of the early and middle 1960s come to be examined in perspective. But, just as praise for the Second Programme when it was going well, was often lavished on its inherent merits to the neglect of the favourable world conditions in which it began; so responsibility for the failure to achieve its targets is now thrown on it rather than on changes in world trade. Both praise and blame were and are being exaggerated. Economies such as the Irish which rely heavily on trade cannot advance as quickly as is desired unless international circumstances are favourable. Economic growth is not a form of parthenogenesis.

Let us turn to consider the position that now obtains, in the interregnum between the Second Programme and its successor. What follows may not receive general acceptance but it may serve to provoke a discussion which is urgently needed.

We may begin by noting that two great weapons of economic policy which have been freely used to promote development will not be equally available in future. The Second Programme assumed membership of the EEC (and a consequent reduction of protection by tariff) by 1970. The validity of that assumption is as it may be. In any case, the State is bound to reduce tariffs against the United Kingdom under the trade agreement of 1965. At the same time, there is no firm ground for believing that, if the intended adhesion to the EEC and to GATT is successful, it will be possible to continue the assistance of exports by tax remissions and grants. Further, it is not to be assumed that the inflow of capital which marked the early years of this decade will necessarily continue. In these circumstances, one thing is clear: we must rely to a greater extent than we have known since the last war on our natural advantages of soil, climate, and minerals while the need to use wisely our resources of manpower, skill, and capital will become greater than ever before.

This involves priorities and, to repeat what has been said in an earlier chapter, priorities may mean not doing B now so that A can be done properly. The First Programme represented an advance all along the line in every sector of the economy, and this approach may well have been proper in the depressed circumstances of 1958. The Second Programme adopted the same approach. Today it is necessary to use resources with greater selectivity and to husband them for use where success can be most fruitful.

The importance of expanding export capacity has been insisted upon many times in these pages. No apology will be made for returning to it now nor for arguing that it should receive first priority in the drafting of economic policy. To recapitulate once again. The Irish are a highly mobile people. They look for an acceptable standard of living and if that standard cannot be obtained in Ireland then (saving the loss of that mobility or a change in their ways of thought which reconciles them to lower standards at home than are available abroad) they will emigrate to get it. The standard of living in Ireland depends largely on the capacity to import raw materials and consumer goods, and the capacity to import depends on the capacity to export. This is the ultimate argument for giving priority, in the framing of taxation, in the provision of grants and loans, and in the reduction of vexatious tariffs and quotas to all forms of production, agricultural and manufacturing, and to services such as tourism (and indeed several forms of education) that strengthen our capacity to earn foreign currency.

Agricultural production has just been mentioned. Its claims for high priority are (as again has often been said above) very great. It relies on one of our major natural advantages—the soil and climate of the island. Its production does not depend to the same extent as occurs in many manufactures on imported raw materials which constitute a countervailing item in the balance of payments. It is capable (granted access to markets) of comparatively rapid expansion. Lastly, any such expansion would go with the grain, as it were, of the economy.

But there is more to be added. If agricultural production is to be given high priority, both farmers and farmers' associations must accept the implication that they are engaged in business. Advantages given to them must be accompanied by improvements in standards of production. Moreover, the very nature of agricultural production in this context needs to be defined. What is involved is not only an increase in the numbers of livestock or of the ploughed area, though these may be the first condition of advance. It is much more a matter of rising from elementary production to the processing of foodstuffs, which will command better prices and be a great deal less vulnerable to tariffs elsewhere. This will require powers of organization and co-operation which unfortunately the farming community has had little inducement to develop. General Costello's insistence on the necessity for this form of advanced agricultural production, as it may be called, is a great service to public thought on this matter.

The second priority concerns the other great natural advantage of the country; the intelligence and adaptability of its people. Here again, farmers are concerned because they have long been depressed by standards of education and of technical ability which are far lower than the potential of the majority and the achievement of a number. Better education and technical training are equally important in non-agricultural production and services. The dependence of Irish manufactures on imported raw materials is in no way an unusual nor an irretrievable handicap. Many industries flourish elsewhere that are in the same position. They do so because they can command the enterprise, the technical knowledge, and the feeling for design that in the last resort come from good general education and training.

The implications of this argument range beyond the borders of economic activity. Education is the one great force that may act as a solvent of the passivity and acquiescence in existing conditions which is one of the great barriers to progress. This is a society that is stable, hierarchic and conservative. These are not negligible virtues; but there is a need for the *carrière ouverte aux talents*. It is the more necessary because when our people go abroad many of them are able to adapt themselves and rise to opportunity. This suggests that we have not appreciated that the most important immaterial resource at our disposal is the adaptability, the tenacity, and the intelligence of our people. Perhaps we have been so busy counting the number of people in Ireland that we have given insufficient attention to their quality, as also to the standard at which they live. No doubt numbers are important but the civilization of a community is not judged by its populousness. The fact that educational programmes and their organization have at last been taken under review is one of the most encouraging signs of recent years.

Public current expenditure should be examined with the same sense of relative priorities. In Irish circumstances there is a constant need to watch current expenditure because the sources of revenue are comparatively limited. It is therefore only too easy to raise taxation to levels at which it becomes a true disincentive to enterprise and growth as it might be argued, occurred in the years immediately after 1945 and again between 1953 and 1959. Once this position is reached it may be long continued because it is desperately difficult to reduce taxation in a country where the trend has been for so long towards rising State expenditure on current as well as on capital account. In the circumstances of the later 1960s, when taxation has again been increased severely, it can be argued with great force that a reduction would provide the greatest impetus possible to the economy: if it is accepted, that is, that private enterprise, private savings, and private property have still a part to play in our society.

But taxation depends on the volume of expenditure. There is constant pressure on the State to increase current expenditure for economic reasons. A less easily soluble problem is presented by the social services. It cannot be argued that they are adequate to meet the need. Equally it has to be realized that there are social problems that are peculiar to our society, such as the disproportionately large numbers of children and elderly people. Perhaps the greatest weakness in the social services is that they have been almost wholly derivative, inherited from or modelled on British legislation which was drafted for a community which, both economically and demographically, was as different from our own as could be imagined. Desirous as we are to join the EEC, we might prepare the way for eventual admission and at the same time redistribute existing burdens more justly if we studied more closely both the manner in which the bulk of taxation has been raised, and many social services are financed, in the Community.

The foregoing paragraphs have been depressing to write. The ultimate source of encouragement, however, must lie in appreciating that the economy is still highly resilient. It recovered quickly from the stagnation of the middle 1950s. There is no reason why it should not do so again when trading conditions again favour expansion. Not all the conditions for recovery and progress lie within our power to control: there is therefore all the more reason why we should do what we can in matters, such as the use and development of material and immaterial resources, that are susceptible to public policy.

NOTE

The Second Programme was in operation when this chapter was first drafted. It seems best to leave the present text unaltered until the relationship between the Third Programme and public policy can be more clearly seen.

CHAPTER SEVENTEEN

Problems and Perspectives

PRECEDING PAGES HAVE DISCUSSED LINES OF PUBLIC POLICY: they have been concerned only incidentally with the actions of individuals. The emphasis has fallen on what the State has attempted to do rather than on what entrepreneurs have done. The account of events since 1922 has been dominated by the description of what policies were pursued by successive governments and why those policies were adopted. A reader might be pardoned for wondering if he were reading the economic history of a highly centralized and socialist state rather than of an unintegrated society which has chosen parliamentary democracy for its form of government and the maintenance of private property for its social inspiration. But we are indeed dealing with the affairs of the parliamentary Republic of Ireland, not with those of a People's Republic.

State intervention in this country does not date from 1945 nor from 1922. For good or ill, it influenced the course of development in the nineteenth century as in the eighteenth. It has, however, grown greatly in the last forty years, and the pace of its growth has been accelerated in the last ten. This is a situation which deserves attention.

Admittedly the State cannot be a cipher in economic affairs. It exercises an influence by the very fact of its existence. It may confine itself to preserving conditions in which private enterprise may flourish. In fact, from the very first years of the State, governments have not hesitated to intervene (as Hogan did in agricultural production and marketing) and also to initiate (as his colleagues did when they sanctioned the Shannon Scheme). The scale on which the State now regulates production and marketing, finances its enterprises and borrows money for them would have appeared incredible to the ministers of the first government; but it is little more than a logical result of their policies.

If that be so, it becomes necessary to face some consequential problems. There should be a much deeper and wider discussion of capital investment policies than has been the case so far. It is remarkable, to take one example, that the Dáil did not find time to debate either the First Programme in 1958 or its successor in 1963. If memory serves, Mr. Lemass actually deprecated a suggestion that the Second Programme should be reviewed by the Oireachtas. It is still more remarkable that neither of the Opposition parties pressed for a debate. In such circumstances, there is no reason for surprise if there is still a lack of appreciation of what economic programmes are intended to achieve and of what they may cost, not in terms of money but in terms of saving and the restraint of prices, wages and salaries. If there is no such appreciation, it is difficult to see how any programme can successfully survive the strains that are inevitable in the shape of inflation and payments deficits, and the unpalatable remedies for them.

The absence of parliamentary discussion raises highly important issues which can only be mentioned here. Economic programmes are likely to increase the powers of the executive at the expense of the legislature, with unwelcome results for parliamentary democracy. Planners acquire authority even if unwillingly, and all the more quickly and widely when a void is left to them. Such a development will disturb the checks and balances on which depends the parliamentary system as it is understood in this country. What is possible, what may be desirable, in France or elsewhere is not necessarily either possible or desirable here. Nevertheless, the decline of parliamentary government is likely to continue until the political parties realize that a great deal of politics nowadays is concerned with the aims, methods, and consequences of economic policy. As things are, the really important decisions may soon be taken by the National Industrial Economic Council, not by the Oireachtas. The institution of consultative bodies, such as the N I E C, which include representatives of the employers, the trade unions and the public service, is a healthy development, It may well represent a strengthening rather than a weakening of the democratic process. But there can be a conflict of interest in the short run. If the N I E C truly becomes responsible for the economic policy of the State, it will take much power away from the Oireachtas: if the Oireachtas settles economic policy, the N I E C becomes superfluous. The remedy seems to be that the Oireachtas should bring its practice and procedure into line with the needs of the 1970s. It is a great loss to the public welfare that no parliamentary Standing Committee examines how economic programmes are working out, whether the results conform to expectations and whether their costs bear any relation to the estimates.

State policies might regain a badly needed flexibility from such discussion. Granted the momentum which these policies acquire, and the degree to which administrators become identified with them, there is a very real danger that development may be pursued along paths which lead in the wrong direction or that policy will continue to be based on sets of assumptions which have clearly lost their validity. Indeed this possibility clearly emerged during 1965 and 1966 and has been highly damaging. Among the business and commercial community there has been a perceptible loss of confidence in State programming and intervention. It was not reckoned a fault in the Second Programme that by the middle of 1965 its expectations were not being realized. That was taken as one of the things that happen in an imperfect world and the chance that it might happen was possibly more widely and earlier accepted in the business world than it was among the framers of the Programme. What eroded confidence was that fresh commitments were undertaken by the State when all the evident circumstances seemed to call for prudence.

Likewise the position of many State companies is in need of constant review. So far they have been agents of development and change. Few things in modern Irish life have been more welcome than the zeal and pride with which many of them discharge their functions. They command respect and support because they obviously strive to deserve it. But this happy situation is not to be taken for granted. Standards of service can decline. It is possible to think of a couple of public images in this sphere which have become tarnished in recent years, perhaps through the fault of the State company concerned, perhaps simply because it has come to be taken for granted. This is not the only danger. State companies may often need protection against ministers and administrators who do not accept their judgement on technical matters. There is no lack of examples that might be given.

This can happen for the best of reasons. The constitution of the Electricity Supply Board, for example, was drafted on the principle that it should be as autonomous as possible and free from ministerial control. Parliamentary discussion of its activities has therefore been greatly restricted, and the Board has been thereby enabled to get on with its work. A much less happy result has been that controversies have raged behind the scenes (for example, on rural electrification or on the turf-fired power stations) on which the public was not informed, although heavy public expenditure was involved. Another example is the widely varying fashion in which the State companies present their accounts. A greater uniformity would help to instruct the public; and it is increasingly important that the public should consider itself to be, what indeed it is, a partner in these activities and as such entitled to understand what is being done.

Moreover, these State companies are likely to remain in existence for a long time. This is easily explicable in the case of the provision of services such as electricity; but many of the companies have been established to fill the gaps left by the lack of private enterprise. Their establishment was a sign of under-development: in logic it should follow that their abolition would be a sign of growth. An impressive number of State companies would be clearly superfluous if this were or became a developed country. But one doubts if the State company in Ireland will wither away any more than the State has withered away in Russia. State investment and State companies will be with us for many a year to come.

The activities of the State and the State companies make it all the more necessary to insist on the importance and value of private enterprise. The Irish economy has been curiously dependent on a comparatively few individuals or families who have built up their business in recent decades. They are often the dynamic force in their areas. In another sphere it is noticeable that some townlands in country areas present a picture of unrelieved decay and depopulation while others are able to prosper although they are in no way better endowed with resources. The explanation is often found in the presence or absence of individual initiative. This is the factor that is essential for development. To put it bluntly, economic development will not come from even the most elaborately drafted programme of investment unless it is complemented by private initiative. In the last resort, everything in Ireland, as everywhere else, depends on people doing their jobs and doing them better as time goes on.

The economy needs a class of entrepreneurs, ready to experiment and to use and develop inventions and new ways of marketing. Signs of the emergence of such a class are to be noted: they are possibly the best justification of the policy of tariff protection. But there can never be too many of such people: and the supply still lags behind the need.

Irish economic problems are not simply matters of deciding where and how capital investment should be infused; as if all that were needed were some form of economic engineering. If the matter were no more than that, it would be much simpler. The task is rather to transform a free people into an economically minded society which is quite a different and a far harder thing to do. Being free, they cannot be forced, as other now rapidly evolving societies are being forced. They must be convinced, and that is a slow business. It will be slower still if the mind of those who form opinion is not clear on the vital importance of the qualities of education and instruction, of thrift and enterprise and of all the other virtues which have lost none of their importance because they have become copy-book headlines. There is a saying of Bagehot that 'no policy can get more out of a nation than there is in a nation. A free government is essentially a government by persuasion, and as are the persuaders, so will the government be.' The first business, then, is to be clear on the importance of fostering the economic aptitude of the community, the second is to convince the community. It is a mistake to over-rate the difficulty; but it is difficult to believe that progress will be possible until it is faced. The limited results of capital investment programmes have been largely caused by the fact that they have been carried out in a society that does not possess, or is slow to use, the qualities of thrift and enterprise which will make the most of the opportunities which investment should bring.

Some part of the failure to develop these qualities may be attributed to the bias of State action. Public resources have been freely spent to encourage production. There has been comparatively little insistence on efficiency: the resources have been placed impartially at the disposal of the efficient and the inefficient, particularly in agriculture. The result is that the Irish economy shows contrasts between good and bad producers which are more glaring than are normally found. It would be unjust to call it an inefficient economy: it is easy to think at once of many things which are as well done in Ireland as in any country in the world. But it is an economy in which inefficiency carries very light penalties; indeed it is difficult to imagine any economy in which the feckless use of land or unenterprising management in business has been so immune from disaster. This may make for a leisured and pleasant society; but the inversion of values is surely dangerous for one that aspires to economic development. If inefficiency incurs no punishment, there is little inducement to efficiency. As so often happens, the point can be illustrated by a remark of Hogan. He said once that his policy as Minister for Agriculture was 'helping the farmer who helped himself and letting the other fellow go to the devil'. No minister would talk like that today, and more's the pity.

It is not only a matter of encouraging entrepreneurs who know their business: it is also necessary to foster the kind of society in which they can prosper; that is to say, a society that does not fear change. It has been said elsewhere in these pages that successive programmes of development have had limited success because the public has never accepted the fact that they depend on restraint in consumption. It might be added that even the nature of the fruits of success have not been frankly explained. Development has been presented as a means of making the country richer and more populous. It may do so: but in the process it will have many other results, not all of which will be so attractive. It is all very well to talk in Rostovian terms about a 'take-off'. It will be difficult to achieve one without considerable strain and changes of habit. Most breakthroughs involve abstinence from consumption at the best; at the worst they may mean injustices and inequalities of sacrifice. There will always be a risk of social strain when people start to do new things and follow unaccustomed occupations within the framework of a traditional society. It should be realized that economic growth will present the community with challenges of a nature which are quite novel to its experience. It will not be an easy nor a comfortable business. It will require painful readjustments of social and economic status as well as difficult compositions of opposing interests. It will require determination and self-confidence because many things may seem to be getting worse before they are generally seen to be getting better.

This should be seen in human terms. It is comprehensible that commentaries on economic development should lay so much stress on convenient indexes such as, for example, a percentage growth of so much per cent in the national income and so on. But those who are interested in quantifying economic activities are in greater danger than some of them seem to realize of becoming more interested in the statistics than in the medley of human hopes, fears, and decisions which those statistics, not always perfectly, represent. Many people, on farms and in factories as in shops and offices, may be severely affected by change. There is danger of unnecessary social and political tension being created whenever individuals or whole sections of society feel that they are powerless to influence their environment or to influence the policies which may determine how and where they will live in Ireland. If they feel powerless they will feel frustrated and they will react with instinctive and often wasteful opposition. To a large extent, this is a matter of communication; but any prolonged breakdown could blight hopes of improvement. In any country there is a latent conflict between the interests of those who are governed and of those who govern. That was well understood in Ireland before 1921: there is some danger that it is being forgotten now.

It is high time to look at the social problems that will arise. Redundancy, for example, will be almost inevitable in some parts of the economy: it will be necessary to make provision for retraining and redeployment, with the least possible financial loss to the worker. Provision must be made for those, such as the pensioners or those who are thought too old to be retrained, who would not otherwise share in growing prosperity. In a quite different but no less important sphere, it will be necessary to take steps now to see that development does not lead to unsightly building nor to the destruction of what has been inherited from past generations nor the exclusion of our people from the beaches and beauty of their countryside. These are matters that can be solved if they are faced in time. There must be care that material wealth does not mean social squalor.

But these things will not be done unless there is a realization that economic development will create new problems at least as quickly as it solves the old. Many changes can be provided for in advance; but there is little chance of that happening if it is generally felt that no change is to be expected from growth except change for the better. A great deal of nationalist thought has always assumed that all that is needed is more industries and more people and that then we will continue to lead the same kind of life in the same kind of way. That is precisely what cannot happen. Development, in agriculture, manufacturing or the services, is not a once-for-all change. It is a continuous process which forces a community into new ways of life, of thought and of behaviour. It makes continuing demands on the power of people and of communities to adapt themselves and their political and social institutions to new circumstances.

These issues involve economic decisions but it may well be that their solution transcends economic motives. It has been generally assumed for many decades that our problems (or difficulties or whatever it may please people to call them) are economic in their nature and are therefore soluble by economic policies. But they are not solely economic. It cannot be denied that many aspects of Irish life such as under-investment, emigration, and lack of enterprise are economic in their nature. But other instincts and motives of human action are involved. As for under-investment, there is rarely a true scarcity of savings. What happens is that an unusually large proportion of savings is invested abroad, and the reasons for that are not wholly economic. In emigration and lack of enterprise, it is a commonplace that many now leave the country who are not economically compelled to do so and that when they go abroad they often show considerable enterprise in taking, and making a success of, occupations that they would refuse to consider at home. No-one will dispute the high economic content in these matters but their explanation must lie more deeply than economic policy by itself can touch.

To turn to a different aspect of the same point. One writes 'problems' as a kind of shorthand for the complex of economic difficulties which confront our society such as those just mentioned, the balance of payment, inefficient production and marketing, and so on. Their existence cannot be denied. Their importance must not be under-rated. It would be salutary, however, to consider if the Irish economy in fact suffers from any absolute economic 'problem' in the same sense as, for example, India. There, it may be suggested, a true economic problem can be found, an absolute disproportion between means and ends. In Ireland on the other hand, it has been possible to work a fertile soil less intensively than any other in western Europe, to live at a higher standard than is justified by production and therefore to maintain a comparatively leisured and stable way of life.

These are not achievements on which we should congratulate ourselves. They depend ultimately on the continued freedom of our people to find work abroad and on the maintenance of the purchasing power of the currency in which so much of the community's savings have been invested. A society that is based, whatever its public protestations may be, on the continuation of emigration and the realization of the savings of earlier and more thrifty generations cannot claim that it is firmly founded. It cannot claim the admiration of other peoples nor even the respect of its own. Least of all should it complain of its 'problems'. These arise largely from an almost total lack of relation between the aims for economic development that are publicly accepted and the willingness of everybody to make the sacrifices necessary to attain them. This must not be described as a 'problem': it more closely resembles the more undignified and less tragic difficulties of Mr. Micawber.

A very great deal of the frustration which has marked Irish life for so long comes not so much from low rewards or restricted opportunities, important though these causes may be. It comes rather from a feeling that we have used neither our resources nor our qualities to the fullest possible extent. For very obvious reasons, the concept that a people may have a mission in the world has fallen into discredit during recent decades. Nevertheless there is an abiding sense in which peoples, and the individuals who compose them, must be true to their character and exert their highest qualities on pain of decadence. As a Christian society the Irish people must believe that it has a mission in the sense that it has an obligation to fulfill its potentialities and to contribute their fruit to the common stock of mankind.

In the past, it possessed a sense of possessing qualities and characteristics of its own which could not fructify without independence. That sense was not lost even when the future seemed to hold no hope. Such certitude has been lost now that the immediate goal has been reached. It has not yet been replaced with any aspiration which corresponds to altered circumstances and wider opportunities. As a result the Irish people has no clear idea of its place in the world nor of what contribution it can make to the world. It is near enough still to foreign rule to know that independence is the essential condition of self-realization. It has not yet possessed independence long enough to appreciate that self-government is not an end in itself but must be justified by the manner in which it is used, not only for our own benefit but for the benefit of those with whom we live. There is, therefore, some lack of a sense of purpose which diminishes the economic (and indeed every other) side of life. There is no reason to believe that this uncertainty is more than a transitory phase such as other peoples have had to live through in the course of their history: but it has to be lived through with courage and self-confidence. The Irish people has had such a past that it should never despair in any future: but it must decide what future it wants.

Charts

ILLUSTRATING THE TRENDS
AND THE CHANGING PATTERN OF
THE IRISH ECONOMY

1. POPULATION TRENDS

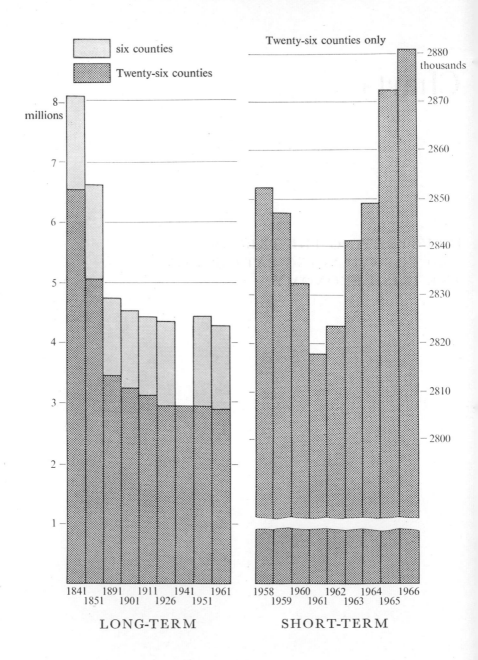

Source: *Census of Population.* See also Table 6.1, page 184.

2. CHANGING DISTRIBUTION OF THE POPULATION OF IRELAND BY AGE-GROUP

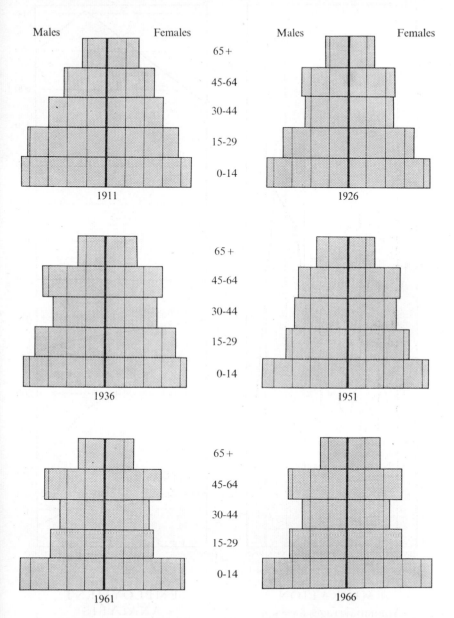

Each age-group is divided into segments representing 100,000 people.

Source: *Census of Population.* See also Table 6.5, page 191.

3. EMIGRATION AND EMPLOYMENT

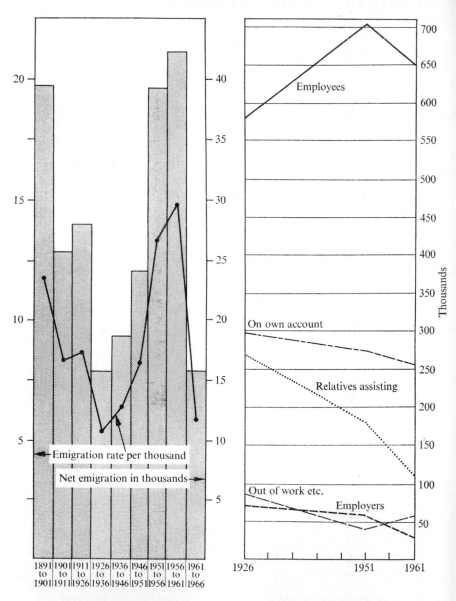

EMIGRATION

Annual averages for each
intercensal period.

See also Table 6.13, page 206.

EMPLOYMENT
ANALYSIS

Persons aged 14 and over

See also Table 2.7, page 49.

Sources: *Census of Population* and *Reports of Registrar General.*

4. CHANGING COMPOSITION OF
TOTAL OUTPUT

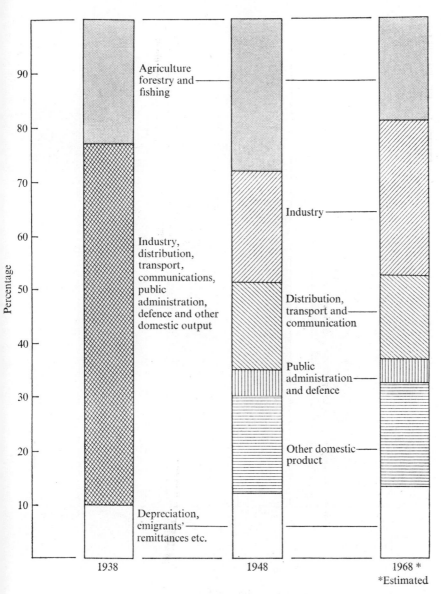

Gross national product at factor cost

Source: *National Income and Expenditure*. See also Table 2.16, page 62.

5. CHANGING COMPOSITION
OF EXPORTS

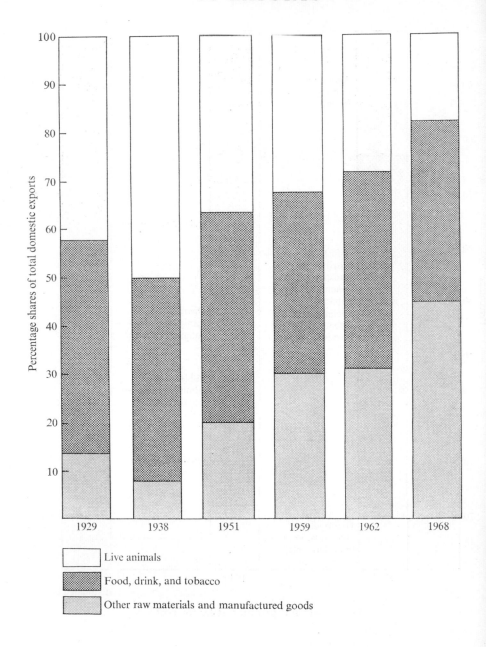

Source: *Trade and Shipping Statistics*. See also Table 3.5, page 75.

6. DISTRIBUTION OF MANPOWER

CHANGES 1926–66 IN IRELAND

INTERNATIONAL COMPARISON 1968

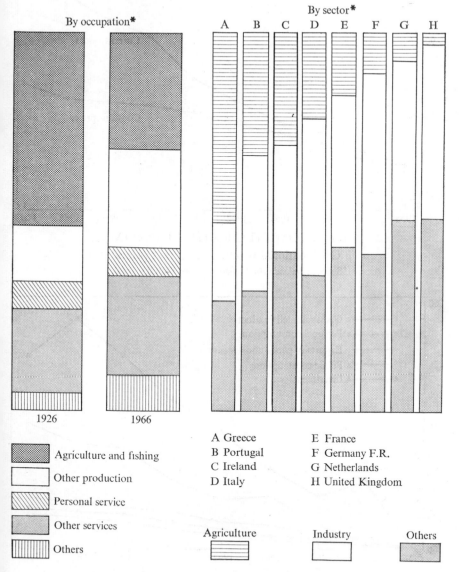

By occupation*

By sector*

A   B   C   D   E   F   G   H

1926   1966

Agriculture and fishing

Other production

Personal service

Other services

Others

A Greece
B Portugal
C Ireland
D Italy

E France
F Germany F.R.
G Netherlands
H United Kingdom

Agriculture

Industry

Others

* For differences between these two classifications see Chapter Two, para. 2.

Sources: *Census of Population*, and *Ireland: An Economic Survey*, OECD 1968.
See also Tables 2.1, 2.5, 2.6, pages 41, 47–8.

7. IRELAND'S ECONOMIC GROWTH

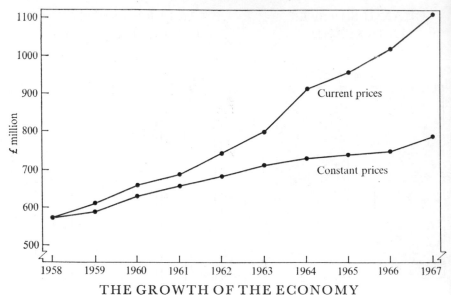

THE GROWTH OF THE ECONOMY
Gross national product at market prices
Source: *Ireland: An Economic Survey*, OECD, 1968.

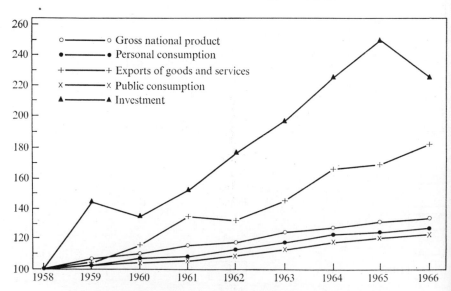

THE RELATIVE GROWTH OF SECTORS OF
DEMAND AND TOTAL OUTPUT
Index: 1958 taken as 100
Source: *National Income and Expenditure*, 1966. See also Table 2.16, page 62.

8. COMPARATIVE GROWTH RATE OF THE IRISH AND UNITED KINGDOM ECONOMIES

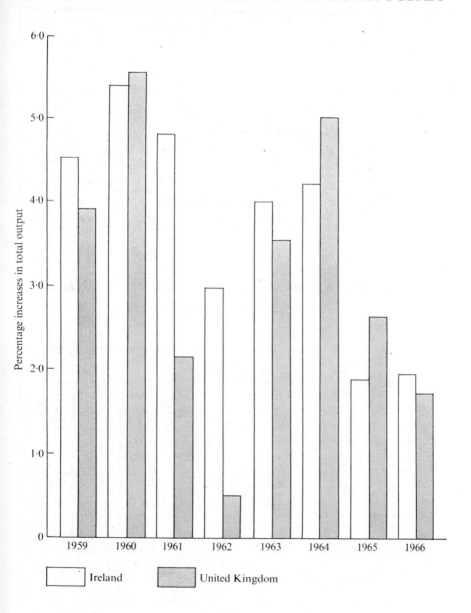

Source: *Economist Intelligence Unit*, Dublin and London.

9. SECTORS OF GROWTH

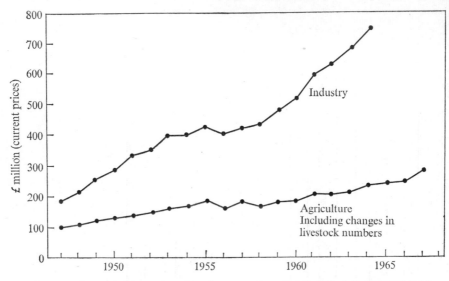

INDUSTRIAL AND AGRICULTURAL PRODUCTION

Source: *Statistical Abstract of Ireland.*

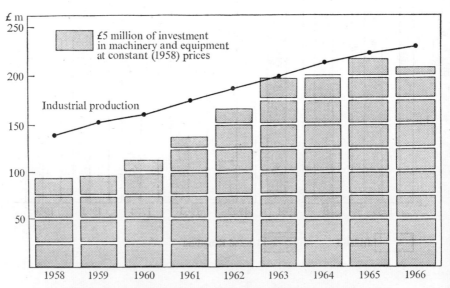

THE CONTRIBUTION TO EXPANSION OF INDUSTRIAL INVESTMENT

Source: *National Income and Expenditure 1966.*

10. SIZE OF THE TRADE GAP

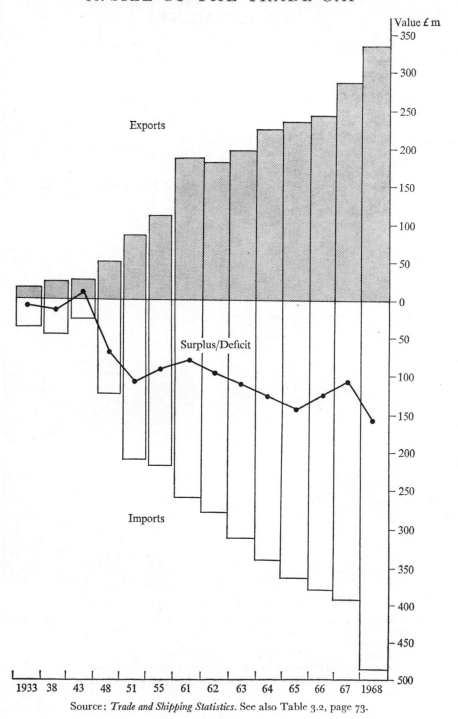

Source: *Trade and Shipping Statistics*. See also Table 3.2, page 73.

11. PATTERN OF THE BALANCE
OF PAYMENTS

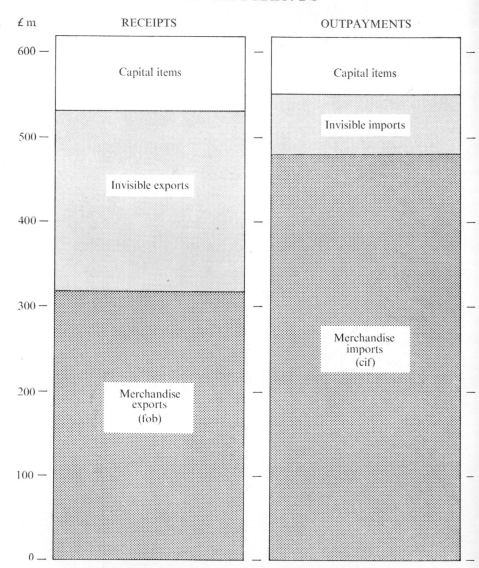

£ m   RECEIPTS   OUTPAYMENTS

600 —

Capital items   Capital items

Invisible imports

500 —

Invisible exports

400 —

300 —

Merchandise
imports
(cif)

200 —

Merchandise
exports
(fob)

100 —

0 —

1968 BALANCE IN SUMMARY FORM

1. In this diagram merchandise imports includes the cost of insurance and freight whereas merchandise exports does not. The cost of insuring and carrying exports is included in invisible exports.
2. The figures for invisibles include emigrants' remittances and legacies.
3. The balancing item, £8,689,000 in 1968, is included in invisible exports.

Source: *Irish Statistical Bulletin*. See also Table 3.9, pages 86–7.

Appendices

GENERAL ELECTIONS SINCE 1922

	Number of seats	Anti-treaty	Pro-treaty	Labour	Farmers	Independents	Others
1922	128	35	58	17	7	11	—
			Cumann na nGaedheal				
1923	153	44	63	14	15	17	—
		Fianna Fáil					
1927	153	44	47	22	11	14	15[1]
1927	153	57	62	13	6	12	3[2]
1932	153	72	57	7	4	11	2[3]
1933	153	77	48	8	—	8	12[4]
			Fine Gael				
1937	138	69	48	13	—	8	—
1938	138	77	45	9	—	7	—
				Clann na Talmhan			
1943	138	67	32	17	14	8	—
1944	138	76	30	8	11	9	4[5]
1948	147	68	31	19	7	12	10[6]
1951	147	69	40	16	6	14	2[7]
1954	147	65	50	19	5	5	3[8]
1957	147	78	40	13	3	8	5[9]
1961	144	70	47	16	2	6	3[10]
1965	144	72	47	22	—	2	1[11]
1969	144	75	50	18	—	1	—

1. 8 National League, 5 Sinn Féin, 2 Independent Republicans.
2. 2 National League, 1 Independent Labour.
3. 2 Independent Labour.
4. 11 National Centre Party, 1 Independent Labour.
5. 4 National Labour.
6. 10 Clann na Poblachta.
7. 2 Clann na Poblachta.
8. 3 Clann na Poblachta.
9. 4 Sinn Féin, 1 Clann na Poblachta.
10. 2 National Progressive Democrats, 1 Clann na Poblachta.
11. 1 Clann na Poblachta.

APPENDIX II

MEMBERS OF GOVERNMENTS 1922–70

	Government	Taoiseach[1]	Finance	Agriculture	Industry and Commerce
1922 Dec.	Cumann na nGaedheal	William Cosgrave	William Cosgrave	Patrick Hogan	Joseph McGrath
1923 Sept.					
1924 Apr.			Ernest Blythe		
1932 Mar.	Fianna Fáil	Eamon de Valera	Seán MacEntee	James Ryan	Patrick McGilligan
1939 Sept.			Seán T. O'Kelly		Seán Lemass
1941 Aug.					Seán MacEntee
1945 June			Frank Aiken		Seán Lemass
1947 Jan.				Patrick Smith	
1948 Feb.	Inter-party	John A. Costello	Patrick McGilligan	James Dillon	Daniel Morrissey
1951 June	Fianna Fáil	Eamon de Valera	Seán MacEntee	Thomas Walsh	Seán Lemass
1954 June	Inter-party	John A. Costello	Gerard Sweetman	James Dillon	William Norton
1957 Mar.	Fianna Fáil	Eamon de Valera	James Ryan	Seán Moylan	Seán Lemass
Nov.				Patrick Smith	
1959 June		Seán Lemass			John Lynch
1964 Oct.				Charles Haughey	
1965 Apr.			John Lynch		
1966 July		John Lynch			Patrick Hillery
1966 Nov.			Charles Haughey	Neal Blaney	George Colley
1970 May			George Colley	James Gibbons	Patrick Lalor

1. Until 1937, President of the Executive Council.

Notes: (i) Mr. Sean Lemass was Minister for Supplies during the existence of the Department from 1939 to 1945.
(ii) Mr. Erskine Childers was Minister for Transport and Power from the establishment of that Department in 1959 until July 1969 when he was succeeded by Mr. Brian Lenihan.

Select Bibliography

PERIODICALS

Official Publications

Agriculture, Journal of the Department of (annually since 1900).
Irish Trade Journal (quarterly until 1963).
Irish Statistical Bulletin (quarterly since 1964).
Statistical Abstract (annually since 1931).

Other

Administration (quarterly from the Institute of Public Administration).
Agricultural Institute (quarterly from the Agricultural Institute).
Banking and Finance (weekly, Dublin).
Economic and Social Research (papers published by the Institute of).
Economist, The (weekly, London).
Institute of Bankers in Ireland, Journal of (quarterly).
Irish Banking Review, The (quarterly, Dublin).
Irish Independent, The (daily, Dublin).
Irish Press, The (daily, Dublin).
Irish Statesman, The (weekly, Dublin. First series, 1919–20. Second series, 1923–30).
Irish Times, The (daily, Dublin).
Management (monthly from the Institute of Management in Ireland).
Round Table, The (quarterly, London).
Statistical and Social Inquiry Society of Ireland, Journal of (annually, Dublin).
Studies (quarterly, Dublin).

GENERAL BACKGROUND

Official Publications

Convention, Proceedings of the Irish, HMSO: 1917, Cd 9019.
Parliamentary Debates, Dáil Éireann.

Parliamentary Debates, Seanad Éireann.
Saorstát Éireann, Official Handbook. Dublin: 1932.

Other

BARKER, E. *Ireland in the Last Fifty Years.* Oxford: 1917.
BECKETT, J. *The Making of Modern Ireland.* London: 1966.
BLACK, R. D. C. *Centenary History of the Statistical and Social Inquiry Society of Ireland.* Dublin: 1947.
BONN, M. *Wandering Scholar.* London: 1949.
BROMAGE, M. *De Valera and the March of a Nation.* London: 1956.
CHILDERS, E. *The Framework of Home Rule.* London: 1913
CLAMPETT, G. J. T. 'The Economic Life of Ireland', *JIBI*, 1928.
COLUM, P. *Arthur Griffith.* Dublin: 1959.
CONNOLLY, J. *Labour in Irish History.* Dublin: 1910.
COOGAN, T. P. *Ireland Since the Rising.* London: 1966.
COYNE, W. P. (ed.). *Ireland: Industrial and Agricultural.* Dublin: 1902.
CURTIS, E. *History of Ireland.* London: 1960.
CURTIS, L. P. *Coercion and Conciliation in Ireland, 1880–1892.* Oxford: 1964.
FREEMAN, T. W. *Ireland: A General and Regional Geography.* London: 1965.
GEARY, R. C. 'Irish Economic Development since the Treaty', *Studies,* 1951.
GRAY, T. *The Irish Answer.* London: 1966.
GREAVES, C. D. *Life and Times of James Connolly.* London: 1961.
GWYNN, D. *The Irish Free State.* London: 1928.
HAMMOND, J. L. *Gladstone and the Irish Nation.* London: 1964.
HANCOCK, W. K. *Survey of British Commonwealth Affairs,* vol. i, 'Problems of Nationality'. London: 1937.
HENRY, R. M. *The Evolution of Sinn Fein.* Dublin: 1920.
HICKEY, T. J. 'Ireland's Economic Problems and Prospects', *JIBI,* 1954.
HOLT, E. *Protest in Arms.* London: 1960.
HORGAN, J. J. *Parnell to Pearse.* Dublin: 1948.
INGLIS, B. *The Story of Ireland.* London: 1965.
KEYNES, J. M. 'National Self-sufficiency', *Studies,* 1933.
KING, F. C. (ed.). *Public Administration in Ireland.* Dublin, vol. i, n.d., vol. ii, 1949, vol. iii, 1954.
LARKIN, E. *James Larkin,* London: 1965.
MACARDLE, D. *The Irish Republic.* Dublin: 1951.
McCRACKEN, J. L. *Representative Government in Ireland.* Oxford: 1958.
MACMANUS, F. (ed.). *The Years of the Great Test.* Cork: 1967.
MANSERGH, N. *The Irish Free State.* London: 1934.
MANSERGH, N. *Ireland in the Age of Reform and Revolution.* London: 1940.
MANSERGH, N. *Survey of British Commonwealth Affairs: Problems of External Policy, 1931–9.* London: 1952.
MANSERGH, N. *The Irish Question, 1840–1921.* London: 1965.
MEENAN, J., and WEBB, D. (eds.). *A View of Ireland.* Dublin: 1957.
MEGHEN, P. J. *Statistics in Ireland.* Dublin: 1964.
O'BRIEN, C. C. (ed.) *The Shaping of Modern Ireland.* London: 1960.
O'BRIEN, G. *The Four Green Fields.* Dublin: 1936.
O'BRIEN, G. 'The Impact of the War on the Irish Economy', *Studies,* 1946.

O'BRIEN, G. 'The Economic Progress of Ireland, 1912–62', *Studies*, 1962.
O'CONNOR, F. *The Big Fellow* (biography of Collins). London: 1937.
O'DONNELL, P. *There Will be Another Day*. Dublin: 1963.
O'FAOLAIN, S. *The Irish*. London: 1969.
O'HEGARTY, P. S. *A History of Ireland under the Union*. London: 1952.
O'MAHONY, D. 'Economic Theory and the Irish Economy', *JIBI*, 1960.
O'MAHONY, D. *The Irish Economy*. Cork: 1967.
O'SULLIVAN, D. *The Irish Free State and its Senate*. London: 1940.
OLDHAM, C. H. 'The Interpretation of Irish Statistics', *JSSISI*, 1924–5.
PAKENHAM, F. *Peace by Ordeal*. London: 1962.
PAUL-DUBOIS, L. *Contemporary Ireland*. Dublin: 1908.
PAUL-DUBOIS, L. *The Irish Struggle and its Results*. London: 1934.
RYAN, A. P. *Mutiny at the Curragh*. London: 1956.
RYAN, D. *The Rising*. Dublin: 1957.
RYAN, W. P. *The Irish Labour Movement*. Dublin: 1919.
TAYLOR, R. *Michael Collins*. London: 1958.
USSHER, A. *The Face and Mind of Ireland*. London: 1949.
WEBB, D. A., and MEENAN, J. (eds.). *A View of Ireland*. Dublin: 1957.
WHITE, T. DE V. *Kevin O'Higgins*. London: 1948.
WILLIAMS, T. D. (ed.). *The Irish Struggle*. London: 1966.

NATIONAL INCOME, ETC

Official Publications

Cost of Living in Ireland, Report on. Dublin: 1922.
Cost of Living Index Figure. Report of Commission on. SO, 1933. P 992.
Household Budget Inquiry, 1951–2. SO, Pr 2520.
Irish Statistical Survey (annually 1949–58). SO.
National Income and Expenditure, 1938–44. SO, P 7356.
National Income and Expenditure, Tables of, 1944–50. SO, Pr 350.
National Income and Expenditure (annually since 1959), SO.
Vocational Organisation, Report of Commission on. SO.
Youth Unemployment, Report of Commission on. SO, Pr, 709.

Other

ATTWOOD, E. A., and GEARY, R. C. *Irish County Incomes in 1960*. ERI, 1963.
BUSTEED, JOHN. 'The National Income', *JIBI*, 1946.
BYRNE, J. J. 'Prices, Wages and the Cost of Living', *JIBI*, 1956.
CARTER, C. F., and ROBSON, M. 'Comparison of National Incomes and Social Accounts of Northern Ireland, the Republic of Ireland and the United Kingdom,' *JSSISI*, 1954–5.
COWLING, K. *Determinants of Wage Inflation in the Republic of Ireland*, ERI, 1966.
DUNCAN, G. A. 'The Social Income of the Irish Free State', *JSSISI*, 1939–40.
DUNCAN, G. A. 'The Social Income of Éire, 1938–40', *JSSISI*, 1940–1.
GEARY, R. C. *The Official Cost of Living Index Figure and its Critics*. Cork: 1951.
GEARY, R. C., 'Towards an Input–Output Decision Model for Ireland', *JSSISI*, 1963–4.

GEARY, R. C. and ATTWOOD, E. A. *Irish County Incomes in 1960.* ERI, 1963.

KIERNAN, T. J. 'The National Expenditure of the Free State in 1926', *JSSISI*, 1932–3.

LESER, C. E. V. *The Pattern of Personal Expenditure in Ireland.* ERI, 1965.

MARSH, A. *Full Employment in Ireland.* Dublin, 1945.

NEVIN, E. *The Irish Price Level. A Comparative Study.* ERI, 1962.

O'HERLIHY, C. ST. J. *Wages, Prices and Employment in the Irish Manufacturing Sector.* ERI, 1966.

QUINLAN, P. F. 'A Dynamic Model of the Irish Economy', *JSSISI*, 1961–2.

REASON, L. 'Estimate of the Distribution of Non-Agricultural Incomes and Incidence of Certain Taxes', *JSSISI*, 1960–1.

ROBSON, M., and CARTER, C. F. 'Comparisons of National Incomes and Social Accounts of Northern Ireland, the Republic of Ireland and the United Kingdom', *JSSISI*, 1954–5.

Symposium on 'National Income and Social Accounts', *JSSISI*, 1951–2.

WHITAKER, T. K. 'Capital Formation, Saving and Economic Progress', *JSSISI*, 1955–6.

TRADE AND PAYMENTS

Official Publications

Bord Fáilte, Annual Reports of (since 1953).

Coras Trachtála, Annual Reports of (since 1952).

European Economic Community, White Paper on. SO, 1961, Pr 6106.

European Economic Community, White Paper on, SO, 1962, Pr 6613.

Free Trade Area Agreement (with the United Kingdom). SO, 1965, Pr 8623.

Trade Returns (annually since 1924). SO.

Other

ADAMS, W. G. S. 'Some Considerations relating to the Statistics of Irish Production and Trade', *JSSISI*, 1909.

DUNCAN, G. A. 'The Trade Statistics of the Irish Free State', *JSSISI*, 1937–8.

LESER, C. E. V. *A Study of Imports,* ERI, 1967.

MEENAN, J. 'The Balance of Payments', *JIBI*, 1952.

RIORDAN, E. J. *Modern Irish Trade and Industry.* London: 1920.

Symposium on 'The Trade Statistics of the Irish Free State in 1924', *JSSISI*, 1924–5.

Symposium on 'The Future of Irish External Trade', *JSSISI*, 1943–4.

Unsigned. 'The Anglo-Irish Trade Agreement', *IBR*, 1966.

AGRICULTURE

Official Publications

Advisory Committee on Marketing of Agricultural Products, Reports of. SO.

Agriculture, Annual Reports of Department of. SO.

Agriculture, Journal of Department of. SO.

Agriculture, Report of Commission on. 1923.

Agriculture in the Second Programme for Economic Expansion. SO, Pr 7697.

Agricultural Statistics, 1847–1926. SO, I, 22.

Agricultural Output of Saorstát Éireann, 1926–7. SO, 1928, P 132.

Agricultural Statistics, 1927–33. SO, 1935, P 1577.

Agricultural Statistics, 1934–56. SO, 1960, Pr 4335.

Agricultural Statistics, 1960. SO, Pr 7540.

Drainage Commission, 1938–40, Report of. SO.

Economic Committee 1928. First and Second Interim Reports on Wheat-growing and the Question of a Tariff on Flour. SO.

Fisheries, Report of Survey Team on. SO, 1964, Pr 7983.

Forestry Mission to Ireland, Report of FAO. SO, 1951, Pr 664.

Irish Agricultural Organisation Society, Annual Reports of.

Post-Emergency Agricultural Policy, Reports of Commission on SO, P 7175.

Present State and Methods for Improvement of Irish Land, Report on the (Holmes report). SO, P 9248.

National Farm Survey 1955/6–1957/8, Final Report of the SO, Pr 6180.

Small Western Farms, Report of the Inter-departmental Committee on. SO, 1962, Pr 6540.

Other

ANDERSON, R. A. 'The Irish Meat Industry', *JSSISI*, 1913.

ATTWOOD, E. A. 'Agriculture and Economic Growth in Western Ireland', *JSSISI*, 1961–2.

ATTWOOD, E. A. 'Agriculture in the Irish Economy', *IBR*, 1962.

ATTWOOD, E. A. 'Some Economic Aspects of Land Use in Ireland', *JSSISI*, 1964–5.

BARRINGTON, T. 'A Review of Irish Agricultural Prices', *JSSISI*, 1925–6.

BONN, M. *Modern Ireland and her Agrarian Problems.* Dublin: 1906.

BYRNE, J. J. 'The Inter-relation of Agriculture and Industry in the Irish Economy,' *Studies*, 1954.

BYRNE, J. J., 'Agriculture in the National Economy', *Studies*, 1955.

BYRNE, J. J. 'Investment and Research in Irish Agriculture', *Studies*, 1955.

BYRNE, J. J. 'The Role of Economic Analysis in Agricultural Policy', *Studies*, 1955.

BYRNE, J. J. 'Some Provincial Variations in Irish Agriculture', *JSSISI*, 1958–9.

COYNE, E. J. 'The Future of Agricultural Productive Co-operation', *Studies*, 1955.

COYNE, E. J. 'The Small Farm in Irish Agriculture', *Studies*, 1958.

CROTTY, R. 'Irish Agriculture: Three Surveys', *Studies*, 1963.

CROTTY, R. 'Agriculture and Economic Expansion', *Studies*, 1964.

CROTTY, R. *Irish Agricultural Production*, Cork: 1966.

DIGBY, M., *Horace Plunkett.* Oxford: 1949.

FENNELL, R. *Industrialization and Agricultural Development in the Congested Districts.* Agricultural Institute, Dublin.

GEARY, R. C., 'Variability in Agricultural Statistics', *JSSISI*, 1956–7.

HARNETT, P. 'The Significance of Veterinary Medicine in the National Economy', *JSSISI*, 1955–6.

JOHNSTON, J. 'The Outlook for Irish Agriculture', *Studies*, 1939.

JOHNSTON, J. 'The Capitalisation of Irish Agriculture', *JSSISI*, 1941–2.

JOHNSTON, J. 'An Economic Basis for Irish Agriculture', *JSSISI*, 1947–8.

JOHNSTON, J. *Irish Agriculture in Transition*. Dublin: 1951.

KENNEDY, H. 'Some Problems of Our Agriculture', *Studies*, 1938.

KENNEDY, M. 'Our Dairying and Cattle Industries', *JSSISI*, 1946–7.

KILROY, J. (with WALSH, T., and RYAN, P. F.). 'A Half-Century of Fertiliser and Lime Use in Ireland', *JSSISI*, 1956–7.

O'BRIEN, G. 'Patrick Hogan', *Studies*, 1936.

O'BRIEN, G. 'Father T. A. Finlay', *Studies*, 1940.

O'CONNOR, R. 'The Economic Utilization of Grassland', *JSSISI*, 1959–60.

O'DONOVAN, J. *The Economic History of Livestock in Ireland*. Cork: 1940.

O'MAHONY, D. 'Irish Agriculture, Prospects and Opportunities', *Studies*, 1959.

O'MAHONY, D. 'The Economics of Irish Agriculture', *JIBI*, 1960.

OLDHAM, C. H. 'Some Perplexities in Regard to the Agricultural Statistics of Ireland', *JSSISI*, 1923–4.

Recess Committee, Report of the, Dublin: 1896.

RYAN, P. F. (with KILROY, J., and WALSH, T.). 'A Half-Century of Fertiliser and Lime Use in Ireland', *JSSISI*, 1956–7.

SCULLY, J. J. 'The Pilot Area Development Programme', *JSSISI*, 1967–8.

SHEEHY, E. J. 'The Future of Agriculture in Ireland', *Studies*, 1938.

STAEHLE, H. 'Statistical Notes on Irish Agriculture', *JSSISI*, 1950–1.

Symposium on 'Agriculture and Employment in the Free State', *Studies*, 1930.

Symposium on 'A Farming Programme for Ireland', *Studies*, 1952.

Symposium on 'Fisheries', *Administration*, 1959.

WALSH, T, (with KILROY, J., and RYAN, P. F.). 'A Half-Century of Fertiliser and Lime Use in Ireland', *JSSISI*, 1956–7.

Unsigned. 'The Agricultural Institute', *IBR*, 1958.

Unsigned. 'Agriculture: Problems of Development', *IBR*, 1959.

INDUSTRIAL PRODUCTION

Official Publications

Bord na Móna, Annual Reports of.

Coras Iompair Éireann, Annual Reports of.

Electricity Supply Board, Annual Reports of.

Fair Trade Commission, Annual Reports of.

Fiscal Inquiry Committee, Report of. SO, 1924.

Industrial Organization, Reports of Committee on. SO.

Industrial Production, Annual Census of. SO.

Irish Airlines, Annual Reports of. SO.

Irish Shipping, Annual Reports of.

Labour Court, Annual Reports of.

National Industrial Economic Council, Reports of.

Shannon Free Airport Development Company, Annual Reports of.

Transport, Report of Tribunal on Public. SO, 1939, P 4866.
Transport, Inquiry into Internal. SO, 1957, Pr 4091.
Vocational Organization, Report of Commission on. SO.

Other

Anon. *Civil Aviation in Ireland.* Dublin: 1956.
AGNEW, J. A. 'Manpower Policy', *JSSISI*, 1967–8.
ANDREWS, C. S. 'Some Precursors of Bord na Móna,' *JSSISI*, 1953–4.
BOOTH, J. C. *Fuel and Power in Ireland*, ERI, 1966–7.
BRENNAN, P. 'The Finance of Air Tranport Services in Ireland', *JSSISI*, 1950–1.
BRISTOW, J. E. 'State Enterprises and Economic Planning in the Irish Republic', *JSSISI*, 1964–5.
BROCK, C. 'The CIO Industrial Survey', *JSSISI*, 1963–4.
BROCK, C. *The Work of NIEC, 1963–6.* SO, 1967.
BROWNE, R. F. 'The Electricity Supply Board', *JSSISI*, 1951–2.
CONNOR, M. M. 'Financing of Industry', *JIBI*, 1964.
CONNOLLY, J. *Labour in Irish History.* Dublin: 1910.
CONROY, J. C. *History of Railways in Ireland.* London: 1928.
COWLING, K. *Determinants of Wage Inflation in the Republic of Ireland.* ERI, 1966.
FITZGERALD, G. *State-sponsored Bodies.* Dublin: 1963.
HENRY, E. W., and HEELAN, L. J. 'Capital in Irish Industry', *JSSISI*, 1962–3.
KANE, R. *The Industrial Resources of Ireland.* Dublin: 1844.
LARKIN, E. *James Larkin.* London: 1965.
LESER, C. E. V. 'Problems of Industrialization in Developing Countries and their Implications for Ireland', *JSSISI*, 1967–8.
LEYDON, J. 'The Remuneration of Capital of Certain State-sponsored Companies', *IBR*, 1963.
LINEHAN, T. P. 'The Structure of Irish Industry', *JSSISI*, 1961–2.
MACCORMAC, M. 'Management Education in the Irish Economy', *IBR*, 1965.
MEENAN, J. 'Irish Industrial Policy, 1921–43' *Studies*, 1943.
MEENAN, J. 'Irish Industry and Post-war problems.' *Studies*, 1943.
MORTISHED, R. J. P. 'Trade Union Organization in Ireland', *JSSISI*, 1925–6.
MORTISHED, R. J. P. 'The Industrial Relations Act', *JSSISI*, 1946–7.
MURRAY, C. H. 'Some Aspects of the Industrial Capital Market', *JSSISI*, 1959–60.
NEVIN, E. T. *The Irish Economy and the EEC.* ERI, 1962.
NEVIN, E. T. *Wages in Ireland.* ERI, 1963.
NEVIN, E. T. *The Capital Stock of Irish Industry.* ERI, 1963.
NEVIN, E. T. *The Cost Structure of Irish Industry, 1950–60.* ERI, 1964.
O'DONOVAN, J. 'State Enterprises', *JSSISI*, 1949–50.
O'MAHONY, D. *Industrial Relations in Ireland*, ERI, 1964.
O'MAHONY, D. *Economic Aspects of Industrial Relations*, ERI, 1965.
O'RAIFEARTAIGH, T. 'Changes and Trends in our Educational System since 1922', *JSSISI*, 1958–9.
REYNOLDS, D. J. *Internal Transport in Ireland*, ERI, 1962.

REYNOLDS, D. J. *Road Transport*. ERI, 1963.
REYNOLDS, D. J. 'Some Aspects of Internal Transport', *JSSISI*, 1962–3.
RYAN, W. J. L. 'Measurements of Tariff Levels in Ireland', *JSSISI*, 1948–9.
RYAN, W. J. L. 'Protection and Efficiency of Irish Industry', *Studies*, 1954.
RYAN, W. J. L. 'Irish Manufacturing Industry; the Future', *Studies*, 1955.
RYAN, W. J. L. 'The Need for Structural Change in Irish Industry', *IBR*, 1961.
ROBERTS, R. 'Trades Union Organization in Ireland', *JSSISI*, 1958–9.
SHIELDS, B. F. 'Analysis of the Legislation, Published Accounts and Operating Statistics of the Great Southern Railway, 1924–37', *JSSISI*, 1937–8.
SHIELDS, B. F. 'Analysis of the Financial and Operating Statistics of the Great Southern Railway and the Great Northern Railway', *JSSISI*, 1945–6.
SHIELDS, B. F. 'An Analysis of Irish Transport Acts', *JSSISI*, 1953–4.
SHIELDS, B. F. 'An Analysis of the Census of Distribution, 1951', *JSSISI*, 1957–8.
Symposium on 'The Electricity Supply Board', *Administration*, 1957.
Symposium on 'Bord na Móna', *Administration*, 1958.
Symposium on 'Irish Shipping', *Administration*, 1954–5.
Unsigned. 'The Irish Airlines', *IBR*, 1959.
Unsigned. 'The Irish Tourist Industry', *IBR*, 1960.
Unsigned. 'The Shannon Industrial Estate', *IBR*, 1961.
WHEELER, T. S. (ed.). *The Natural Resources of Ireland*. Dublin: 1944.

POPULATION AND EMIGRATION

Official Publications

Annual Reports of the Department of Health (since 1945).
Annual Reports of the Registrar-General (from 1864).
Censuses of Population.
Emigration and other Population Problems, Reports of the Commission on. SO. 1954.

Other

ARENSBERG, C. M. *The Irish Countryman*. London: 1937.
ARENSBERG, C. M., and KIMBALL, S. *Family and Community in Ireland*. Harvard: 1940.
BUSTEED, J. 'The Problem of Population', *JSSISI*, 1936–7.
CONNELL, K. H. *The Population of Ireland, 1750–1845*. Oxford: 1950.
CONNELL, K. H. 'Marriage in Ireland after the Famine', *JSSISI*, 1955–6.
COYNE, E. J. 'Irish Population Problems', *Studies*, 1954.
FREEMAN, T. W. 'Migration Movements and the Distribution of Population in Ireland', *JSSISI*, 1938–9.
FREEMAN, T. W. 'Emigration and Rural Ireland. *JSSISI*. 1944–5.
GEARY, R. C. 'The Future Population of Saorstát Éireann', *JSSISI*, 1935–6.
GEARY, R. C. 'Irish Population Prospects', *JSSISI*, 1940–1.
GEARY, R. C. 'Irish Population Problems', *Studies*, 1954.
GEARY, R. C. 'The Family in Irish Census of Population Statistics', *JSSISI*, 1954–5.

KIMBALL, S., and ARENSBERG, C. M. *Family and Community in Ireland.* Harvard: 1940.

LESER, C. E. V. 'Recent Demographic Developments in Ireland', *JSSISI,* 1964–5.

McCARTHY, M. D. 'The 1961 Census of Population', *JSSISI,* 1960–1.

McCARTHY, M. D. 'Some Irish Population Problems', *Studies,* 1967.

MEENAN, J. 'Some Causes and Consequences of the Low Irish Marriage Rate', *JSSISI,* 1932–3.

O'BRIEN, J. (ed.). *The Vanishing Irish.* London: 1954.

OLDHAM, C. H. 'The Incidence of Emigration', *JSSISI,* 1913–14.

OLDHAM, C. H. 'The Reform of the Irish Census of Population', *JSSISI,* 1925–6.

Symposium on 'The Irish Population Problem', *JSSISI,* 1937–8.

Symposium on 'The Report of the Commission on Emigration', *JSSISI,* 1955–6.

THOMPSON, W. J. 'The Development of the Irish Census', *JSSISI,* 1910–11.

THOMPSON, W. J. 'The First Census of the Irish Free State', *JSSISI,* 1925–6.

BANKING AND CURRENCY

Official Publications

Banking Commission, Reports of. SO, 1926.

Banking Commission, Reports and Minutes of Evidence of. SO, 1938.

Central Bank of Ireland, Annual Reports of (since 1944).

Central Bank of Ireland, Quarterly Bulletin of (since 1934).

Other

BRENNAN, J. 'The Currency System of the Irish Free State', *JSSISI,* 1930–1.

BUSTEED, J. 'Banking and Currency in Ireland since the Treaty', *JIBI,* 1932.

COLBERT, J. *Commentary on Misconceptions regarding Money and Bank Credit.* Dublin: 1942.

GIBSON, N. 'An Amended Irish Monetary System', *JSSISI,* 1956–7.

HEIN, J. *Institutional Aspects of Commercial and Central Banking in Ireland.* ERI, 1967.

HOOPER, L. *Money and Employment in Ireland.* Dublin: 1952.

MENTON, B. 'Ireland and International Monetary Institutions', *JSSISI,* 1957–8.

O'BRIEN, G. 'The Central Bank Bill', *Studies,* 1942.

OSLIZLOK, J. S. 'Survey of Sources of Monetary Supply in Ireland', *JSSISI,* 1962–3.

OSLIZLOK, J. S. 'Our Currency and Banking System', *JIBI,* 1963.

SMIDDY, T. A. 'Some Reflections on Commercial Banking', *JSSISI,* 1935–6.

Unsigned. *Irish Banking, Currency and Credit.* Institute of Bankers in Ireland: 1954.

Unsigned. 'The Sterling Area and Ireland', *IBR,* 1958.

WHITAKER, T. K. 'Ireland's External Assets', *JSSISI,* 1948–9.

PUBLIC FINANCE

Official Publications

Capital Advisory Committee, Reports of. SO, 1957–8.
Direct Taxation, White Paper on, SO, 1961, Pr 5952.
Economic Development. SO, 1958, Pr 4803.
Economic Expansion, Programme for, SO, 1958, Pr 4796.
Economic Expansion, Second Programme for, Part I. SO, 1963, Pr 7239; Part II. SO, 1964, Pr 7670.
European Recovery Programme, Long-term Programme for, SO, 1948, P 9198.
Financial Relations of Great Britain and Ireland, Reports of Royal Commission on. Final Report. HMSO: C8262. 1896.
Income Taxation, Reports of Committee on, SO, 1959–62.
Industry, Report of Commission on Taxation on. SO, 1956, Pr 3512.

Other

BRENNAN, J. 'The Public Debt to the Irish Free State', *JSSISI*, 1934–5.
BRODERICK, J. B. 'Analysis of Government Income and Expenditure in Relation to National Accounts', *JSSISI*, 1959–60.
BUSTEED, J. 'The Financial Situation of the Irish Republic', *JIBI*, 1957.
COLLINS, J. 'Irish Social Services', *JSSISI*, 1942–3.
EASON, J. C. M. 'Analysis of the National Finances of the Irish Free State', *JSSISI*, 1930–1.
EASON, J. C. M. 'Comparison of the Objects of Expenditure and Sources of Revenue of the Irish Free State in Certain Years', *JSSISI*, 1933–4.
EASON, J. C. M. 'Analysis of National Expenditure, Sources of Revenue and the Debt in Certain Years', *JSSISI*, 1940–1.
EASON, J. C. M. 'Analysis of National Expenditure, Sources of Revenue and the Debt in Certain Years', *JSSISI*, 1946–7.
EASON, J. C. M. 'Summary of the figures of Expenditure and Revenue presented in the Finance Accounts for the Years 1929–30, 1939–40 and 1949–50; *JSSISI*, 1950–1.
FITZGERALD, G. 'The First Programme for Economic Expansion,' *IBR*, 1963.
NEVIN, E. T. *Public Debt and Economic Development*. ERI, 1962.
O'CONNELL, J. B. *The Financial Administration of Ireland*. Dublin: 1960.
O'LOGHLEN, B. A. 'The Patterns of Public Expenditure in Northern Ireland and the Republic', *JSSISI*, 1967–8.
O'MAHONY, D. 'Economic Expansion in Ireland', *Studies*, 1959.
O'NUALLAIN, L. *Ireland: Finances of Partition*. Dublin: 1952.
O'REILLY, M. 'State Debt Balance Sheets', *JSSISI*, 1958–9.
OLDHAM, C. H. 'The Public Finances of Ireland', *JIBI*, 1911.
OLDHAM, C. H. 'The Public Finances of Ireland', *JSSISI*, 1919–20.
RYAN, W. L. J. 'The Methodology of the Second Programme', *JSSISI*, 1963–4.
Symposium on 'Irish Social Services', *JSSISI*, 1942–3.
Symposium on 'Economic Development', *JSSISI*, 1958–9.
WALKER, D. *The Allocation of Public Funds*. ERI, 1962.
WHITAKER, T. K. 'Financial Aspects of the Second Programme', *JIBI*, 1965.

Index